OXFORD HISTORICAL MONOGRAPHS

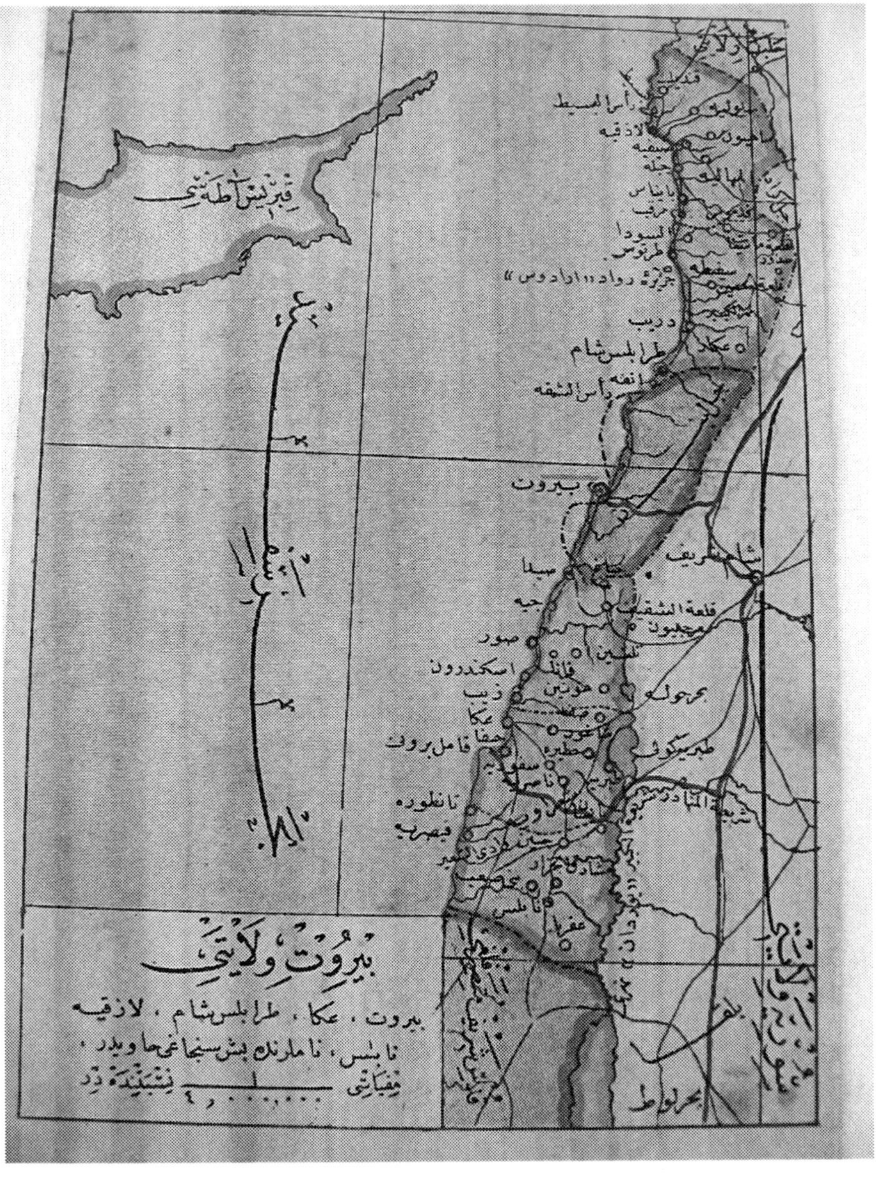

Ottoman postcard of the province of Beirut, *c.*1900

Fin de Siècle Beirut

The Making of an Ottoman Provincial Capital

JENS HANSSEN

CLARENDON PRESS · OXFORD

This book has been printed digitally and produced in a standard specification in order to ensure its continuing availability

OXFORD
UNIVERSITY PRESS

Great Clarendon Street, Oxford OX2 6DP

Oxford University Press is a department of the University of Oxford.
It furthers the University's objective of excellence in research, scholarship, and education by publishing worldwide in

Oxford New York

Auckland Cape Town Dar es Salaam Hong Kong Karachi
Kuala Lumpur Madrid Melbourne Mexico City Nairobi
New Delhi Shanghai Taipei Toronto

With offices in

Argentina Austria Brazil Chile Czech Republic France Greece
Guatemala Hungary Italy Japan South Korea Poland Portugal
Singapore Switzerland Thailand Turkey Ukraine Vietnam

Published in the United States
by Oxford University Press Inc., New York

Oxford is a registered trade mark of Oxford University Press
in the UK and in certain other countries

Published in the United States
by Oxford University Press Inc., New York

Reprinted 2006

ISBN 0-19-928163-7

To
Carol and Eugene

ACKNOWLEDGEMENTS

This book was conceived in May 1994 when my supervisor and I were ruminating through the library of St Antony's College's Middle East Centre in search of a meaningful topic for an M.Phil. thesis. I dismissed a topic on Jordan. We zoomed in on Syria, then Lebanon. As we stood on a ladder each in one of the rows of shelves, Eugene passed me a page of a book with a map of the province of Beirut. I was curious. A new Ottoman province created as late as 1888?

The province of Beirut consisted of three territories separated from each other by the autonomous province of Mount Lebanon. It stretched all along the Eastern Mediterranean coast from Lattakia in the north to Nablus in the south. The fact that this late Ottoman political entity did not metamorphose into a colonial nation state after the dissolution of the Ottoman Empire as did Lebanon, Syria, and Palestine only triggered my archaeological instincts. I was to excavate an extinct geographical, administrative, and political frame within which—unacknowledged by historians—so much of late Ottoman Lebanese, Syrian, and Israeli/Palestinian history operated.

How did it come to this administrative oddity? Who decided on the borders of such a random provincial construct which covered territories in latter-day Lebanon, Syria, and Palestine? Once put in place, how did the creation of the province of Beirut affect society, politics, and trade in the region? How did Beirut relate to its administrative hinterland? Pursuing these and other questions over the past decade gave me the sense of just how important the 1890s and 1900s were for modern Middle East history.

Looking back, this book has always been more about effects and consequences than origins and causes. It became clear to me that the memory of the sectarian violence in 1860 cast a long shadow over the social and political order in late Ottoman Beirut. The municipality of Beirut emerged as a kind of nerve centre for many urban issues in post-war Greater Syria: urban design and planning, public health, education, and intellectual currents. In all of these areas, Ottoman imperialism emerged in competition with European colonial capitalism as a vital force of urban change. Above all, however, it emerged just how much the 'sons and daughters of Beirut' participated in that change and crucially shaped the city as their own.

This book could not have been written without the support of a number of individuals and institutions. It has been guided from beginning to end by my supervisor Eugene Rogan. Without his patience, incision, and occasional putting me 'in my place' this book would not have seen the light of day. To him go my thanks first and foremost. Also in Oxford, Nadim Shehadi, director of the Centre for Lebanese Studies, has helped all along the way with biographical information, books, photographs, coffee, cigarettes, and contacts.

A number of funding bodies have made my research possible. The Oriental Institute, the Middle East Centre, the Beit Fund, the Graduate Studies Committee, and, most generously, the Scatcherd European Foundation, all of Oxford University, have provided travel grants that allowed six months' research in Paris, Nantes, Marseilles, and Aix-en-Provence in 1996. The Skilleter Centre for Ottoman Studies, Cambridge University, has funded three months' of archival work in Istanbul in autumn 1996. In Beirut, the German Academic Exchange Service, DAAD, funded eighteen months of my stay, and a Junior Research Fellowship at the Deutsche Morgenländische Gesellschaft financed another twelve months. Thanks to the Socrates Exchange Programme of the European Union I was able to return to Aix-en-Provence in 2001 to write up. The postdoctoral funding provided by the Fritz Thyssen Foundation has allowed me to explore further the link between city and literature.

A book cannot be written without the help of selfless archivists. In Istanbul, the members of staff at the Yildiz photo archive, the archives of the Ottoman Imperial Bank, and in the Başbakanlik have unearthed catalogues for me. In the Bodleian Library Oxford, the Public Record Office, and the British Library, the Quay d'Orsay, the Bibliothèque Nationale, and the archives of Marseilles and Nantes, I was met with unbridled helpfulness.

Great scholars and academic directors have been supportive and influential. In Beirut, I benefited from a superb working environment. The director of the Center for Behavioral Research (CBR) at the American University of (Ras) Beirut, Samir Khalaf, and the director of the German Orient Institute in Zuqaq al-Blat, Beirut, Angelika Neuwirth have been an inspiration and provided a lively setting to develop ideas. Angelika has opened my eyes to the possibility of integrating the thinkers of the *nahḍa* into urban history. So, too, have Fawaz Trabulsi and Yusuf Mouawad in their different ways. The working groups at the Orient Institute have all left their traces. The participants and particularly my fellow co-organizers, Thomas Philipp and Stefan Weber, of the 1999 conference on *Arab Provincial Capitals* have introduced me to the multiple ways of seeing Ottoman imprints 'elsewhere' in the Arab world. Our Zuqaq al-Blat working group at the Orient Institute, particularly the indefatigable Ralph Bodenstein, has fine-combed Beirut's extant architecture from the Ottoman period with me.

To the 'spatialists' at the CBR this thesis owes its particular theoretical bent. Maha Yahya, Yasmin Arif, and especially Daniel Genberg have done much to sharpen my awareness of space. Dania Sinno and Zeina Misk have become critical colleagues and friends. The benefit and joy of the daily lunches at AUB with Carol Hakim throughout my two-and-a-half year association with the CBR cannot be expressed in the dry setting of an acknowledgement. Further in Beirut Stefan Weber, Jim Quilty, Jihan Sfeir-Khayyat, Yasser Munif, Wolf-Dieter Lemke, Badr al-Hajj, Hashim Sarkis, Elizabeth Picard, have discussed many of my ideas and offered their thoughts and material generously.

In Germany, Thomas Philipp offered generous advice and relentless support. He has been a second 'doctor father' to me. He has charted the road from Acre to Beirut and read the manuscript in its various stages. Klaus Kreisers shared freely his knowledge about late Ottoman monuments. In the US and Canada, I must thank Robert Blecher for his valuable comments and discussion of the medical history of Syria, as well as Engin Akarli, Jim Reilly, Keith Watenpaugh, Ilham Makdisi, Melanie Newton, and Carol Hakim who have read previous drafts of the manuscript. Leila Fawaz has taken time to comment on parts of the thesis and encouraged me to explore the everyday life of Ottoman Beirut. Isa Blumi, John Chalcraft, Ussama Makdisi, and Paul Sedra have provided encouragement and constructive criticism on assorted chapters. Amal Ghazal and Mostafa Minawi have helped with editing and indexing the final version. At OUP, Anne Gelling, Louisa Lapworth and Kay Rogers have been a reliable and understanding team of editors.

In Aix-en-Provence, André Raymond, Robert Ilbert, Randi Deguilhem, and Leyla Dakhli have made me feel welcome and freely given their time, thoughts, and in Leyla's case a place to stay. Particularly discussions with André Raymond have shown some unexpected links between Henri Lefebvre and Middle East scholarship. In Paris, the late Fuad Debbas opened the doors to his immense private historical collection of Beirut. Finally and most importantly, this book owes its existence to my wife Melanie Newton. Her patience, generosity, and 'connaissance' of human struggle in the Middle East have kept me going.

JPH

March 2005
Toronto

CONTENTS

LIST OF ILLUSTRATIONS AND FIGURES

LIST OF MAPS

LIST OF TABLES

NOTE ON TRANSLITERATION

The transliterations in the book are based on the system used by the *International Journal of Middle East Studies*. In late Ottoman Beirut, the boundaries between Ottoman and Arabic languages were naturally blurred and it is generally impossible to impose a rigid diacritical system to represent an accurate linguistic correspondence. Generally, for Ottoman positions I use Ottoman transliteration (*vālī*, not *wālī*) whereas for local positions I use Arabic transliteration (*baladiyya*, not *belediye*).

I have not changed the transliterations of names adopted by authors who write in European languages (e.g. Kemal Ismail, not Kemal Ismāʾīl; Néguib Azoury not Najīb ʿAzoūrī). I have translated place names to conform as closely as possible common usage (e.g. Bilad al-Sham, not Bilād al-Shām, ʿAin al-Mreisse, not ʿAyn al-Muraysa). Place names and Arabic and Ottoman words widely used in English are left in the familiar form (e.g. Sidon, pasha). Terms from Arabic publishing that appear in the text (newspapers, printing presses, books) have title cases whereas Arabic titles of societies or schools are in lower cases.

NOTE ON CURRENCIES

	1880	
1 pound sterling	= 126 piastres (or qirsh)	
1 Ottoman lira	= 115 piastres	
1 Russian imperial	= 102 piastres	
1 golden napoleon	= 100–102 piastres	= 0.9 Ottoman lira
1 ducat	= 60 piastres	
1 French franc	= 5 piastres	
1 silver mecidiye	= 22 piastres	
1 shilling	= 6 piastres	
	1892	
gold		
1 pound sterling	= 136 piastres	= 1.1 lira
1 Ottoman lira	= 124 piastres	= 25 francs
1 napoleon	= 108 piastres	
silver		
1 franc	= 5 piastres	
1 mecidiye	= 23 piastres	
	1907	
100 piastres	= 1 gold Ottoman lira	= 18 shillings
20 piastres	= 1 mecidiye	= 3 shillings 7d.
1 silver franc	= 9.5 shillings	

Source: Karl Baedeker, *Syrie, Liban et Palestine* (Leipzig).

Introduction

> A city, that is to say a geographical concentration of a large population, can only subsist or develop within a system of coherent relations between its society and the space in which it expands.
>
> (André Raymond)

> The city and the urban sphere are thus the setting of struggle; they are also, however, the stakes of that struggle.
>
> (Henri Lefebvre)

Provincializing Beirut

In the early 1880s, one of Beirut's flourishing printing presses published the first six volumes of a monumental Arabic encyclopedia: *Dā'irat al-ma'ārif*, composed by Buṭrus al-Bustānī. In the fifth volume, the city's most prolific nineteenth-century writer and influential public intellectual dedicated ten pages to the long history of Beirut.[1] The encyclopedia entry, which culminates in lists of architectural landmarks and demographic details, not only informs the reader of Beirut's coordinates in the global grid of latitudes and longitudes, in the Arabic alphabetical order 'Bayrut' also ranges between the entries for Peru (*Bayrū*) and Perugia (*Bayrūjā*). In a world of words, the city of Beirut had entered the academic stage of urban representations. In the Beirut entry of *Dā'irat al-ma'ārif* the entire history of the Eastern Mediterranean and Greater Syria—or Bilad al-Sham—is told as the story of the changing fortunes of this city.

Beirut was not only represented as one amongst equals, but by the 1870s had assumed centre stage in the writings of its literati. Pride of place was given not only to antiquity *per se*, but to Beirut's extant architecture and to what it became during the Ottoman centuries: a mixed society enriched by urban diversity. Even after the European powers moved their consuls from Acre to

[1] 'Bayrūt', in Bustānī (1875–81: v. 744–53).

Beirut in the 1830s, the presence of the foreign merchant community never dominated the cityscape and urban affairs as it did in so many other Mediterranean port-cities. The intramural markets, shops, inns, religious buildings, private and collective houses shared features and functions with coastal and inland cities in Bilad al-Sham with which they were connected through commercial, religious, and family networks. Busṭānī, in fact, made it clear that the borders between city and countryside were rather fluid.[2] As more immigrants came to Beirut, orchards turned into suburbs, which emerged concentrically around the nucleus of the old town and along established traffic arteries.[3]

Bustānī's text on Beirut begins with a few columns on Beirut's Phoenician origins. Next, a narrative of an ever-accumulating urban past covers Greek and Roman rule, the ʿAbbasid epoch under Harūn al-Rashīd, Ṣalāḥ al-Dīn's struggle against the Crusaders, and the Ottoman conquest of Ṣyria and Egypt in 1517. This was by no means a natural choice and Bustānī's particular periodization differed from contemporary Ottoman and English histories of Beirut.[4] On the one hand, 'Holy-Land-scaping' and philologico-archaeological discoveries of the time tended to favour an inverted interest in ancient history over a recent past deemed in decay and therefore unworthy of study. On the other hand, military and then capitalist mappings viewed Beirut purely in terms of its strategic location or as a future investment site.[5]

Beirut's population grew steadily as immigrants from the immediate surroundings and far-away Arab towns settled or passed through.[6] Unlike most other coastal towns in the Levant, Beirut had retained its Christian population after the Mamluks took over from the Crusaders. This tolerance of religious diversity was institutionalized by the Ottomans under the millet system. Until the eighteenth century, Druze, Maronites, and Shiites kept away from the towns and Jews were few in number.[7] The Sunni Muslim community constituted a relative majority and its dignitaries operated the legal and commercial institutions of the town. Greek Orthodox Christians were the dominant minority but soon after the Greek Catholic community split from the Eastern

[2] On Beirut's population growth, demographic changes, and the umbilical link between city and mountain, see Fawaz (1983: chs. 3–5). [3] Davie (1996).

[4] See e.g. the illustrated history of Beirut printed in the Ottoman *Salname* of 1908/1326 for Beirut (pp. 224–30). The Ottoman text, taken from Şemseddin Sāmī Fraşeri's *Qāmūs al-aʿlām*, focuses on the pre-Islamic grandeur of Alexander the Great while purposefully accompanying the narrative with photos of the Ottoman clocktower, Grand Serail, Petit Serail, a police station, and two panoramas of Beirut. Compare also with Harvey Porter's undated 'History of Beirut' (partially reprinted in Amīn al-Khūrī, *Dalīl Bayrūt* (Beirut, 1889) and fully in *al-Kulliyya*, Beirut, 1912) who concludes that, since the 18th cent., 'Beirut was evidently in decline'. [5] For a study of three 19-cent. maps of Beirut, see Davie (1984: 37–82).

[6] Bustānī estimated Beirut's population in the 1870s at 75,000 inhabitants, many of whom, he insists, were registered in Mount Lebanon. [7] Fuess (2001: 325–62).

Church in 1734 it, too, began to play a prominent role in Beirut's economic life.[8] Although by the early nineteenth century travellers noted the presence of Maltese and Italians in the port area, non-Muslim minorities were largely Ottoman *ḍimmi*s rather than Europeans as in the cases of Algiers, Tunis, or Alexandria.[9]

Significantly, over half of *Dā'irat al-Ma'ārif*'s Beirut text is dedicated to Ottoman history. Bustānī's narrative did not subordinate Beirut to its natural environment of Mount Lebanon and Bilad al-Sham. Instead, Bustānī presented regional and global events and epochal transformations through the prism of Beirut's own histories of adaptations, changes, and resistances under local potentates such as Imam Uzāʿī (707–74), the Tanūkhīs, and Arslāns during and after the Crusades (twelfth to sixteenth century), and after the Ottoman invasion of 1517. Since the rule of Fakhr al-Dīn al-Maʿnī (1590–1633), Beirut and the surrounding mountains became more and more socio-economically integrated, often, though not always, forming a political entity.[10] In the nineteenth century, Beirut began to expand dramatically beyond its city walls as Christians in the mountains fled from decades of peasant struggle and sectarian violence.[11]

The reinstatement of direct Ottoman rule over Mount Lebanon in 1861 ended two decades of civil strife in Mount Lebanon and Bilad al-Sham. Commerce with Europe began to boom again, especially the silk trade, benefiting particularly Beirut's traders and moneylenders. The harbourfront and markets in the old city continued to be the centre of commercial activity even as the merchants and notables moved their residences to more lofty locations on the terraces overlooking the port. Clusters of mansions soon became urban quarters proper, which were identified over time as the new and modern city.[12] While the port was the economic heartbeat, the new city was the place where social elites of all confessions—foreign, Ottoman, and local—mingled and where schools, hospitals, libraries, clubs, salons, and diplomatic residences mushroomed in the 1860s and 1870s.

City of Letters

Buṭrus al-Bustānī's particular reading of Beirut raises a number of important historiographical and methodological questions that this study intends to address. The central thesis of this study is that modern Beirut is the outcome of

[8] Kaidbey (2002). [9] See e.g. Reimer (1991: 135–57). On colonial Algiers, see Çelik (1997).
[10] Abu-Husayn (1985). See also Kamal Salibi's critique of Lebanese historiography in Salibi (1988).
[11] Leila Fawaz (1983: 21–7). See also Chevallier (1971). [12] See Davie (1996).

persistent social struggles over the production of space. First, the tenacious Beiruti struggle for a provincial capital between 1861 and 1888 provides the historical lens through which I examine the integrated political economy and public sphere of Bilad al-Sham. Rivalling representations of urban consciousness between inhabitants of Beirut, Damascus, Tripoli, Haifa, and other towns in Bilad al-Sham brought about a proliferation of overlapping imagined communities stratified into urban, provincial, and imperial geographies. Second, I will argue that the city of Beirut was at once the product, the object, and the project of imperial and urban politics of difference. Overlapping European, Ottoman, and local civilizing missions competed in the political fields of administration, infrastructure, urban planning, public health, education, public morality, journalism, and architecture.[13]

Discursive practices of social exclusion and inclusion were at the centre of the production of space in late Ottoman Beirut. On the one hand, a distinctly Ottoman version of Orientalism represented distant Arab provinces as stagnant peripheries and backward others.[14] On the other hand and in contradistinction to the Orientalist forms of power which the imperial government employed in Sanʿa, Baghdad, or rural areas such as Mount Lebanon, Ottoman bureaucratic reform pursued a policy of social integration—albeit highly elitist—in the provincial cities of Anatolia and Bilad al-Sham. The provincial, urban elites of the reform period—the holders of economic, social, and cultural capital—were attracted to the Ottoman state-building project through symbolic, ceremonial, and selectively participatory politics.

The late nineteenth-century tensions between Ottoman exclusion and inclusion, participation and Othering, ran right through Beirut's social fabric. The fact that Europeans emerged as powerful contestants in a number of political fields only contributed to Ottoman and local determination to carry out urban transformation. In the various Ottoman, local, and European urban discourses, Beirut's population seemed to straddle the putative divide between provincial simplicity and capital sophistication.

The post-war period from 1860 to the creation of the provincial capital of Beirut in 1888 was a foundational moment of Beirut's history in which local

[13] The term 'political field' is borrowed from Pierre Bourdieu's concept of the constructed nature of social space: 'When I describe a given social space as a *field*, it means a field of power which possesses an obligatory necessity [to exist] for the actors engaged in it. At the same time, it means a field of struggles in which actors compete with each other by different means and purposes that depend on their positions within the field of power, and thereby contribute to the continuation or transformation of its structure.' Bourdieu (1998: 49–50; my tr.).

[14] On colonial knowledge/power relations, see Makdisi on 19th-cent. Mount Lebanon (2002*b*, 2002*c*), Kühn (2002) on Ottoman Sanʿa, and Herzog (2002) on Ottoman Baghdad.

notables, merchants, and public moralists joined forces in an attempt to formulate a modern vision for Beirut. Their claims to represent the city were systematically and insistently articulated in the struggle for the provincial capital, in municipal politics, and in newspaper journalism. The period after 1888 ushered in a second pivotal moment in Beirut's modern history. In the 1890s a series of factors combined to transform fundamentally the city's urban fabric and physical appearance: the Hamidian state, European colonialism, capitalist urbanization and subaltern resistance. Beirut's encounter with Ottoman state reforms, European colonialism, and migration from Mount Lebanon—particularly after the traumatic experience of the civil war of 1860—gave rise to particular social norms and physical forms in ways that are still felt in Lebanon today. A third pivotal moment in Beirut's late Ottoman history was the Young Turk revolution of 1908/9 which ousted Sultan Abdülhamid II and introduced party politics to the empire. In the province of Beirut this event was received enthusiastically. Electoral politics mobilized the provincial hinterlands beyond the urban centres and generated patron–client relationships between notable and constituency that was to dominate Lebanese politics throughout the twentieth century.[15]

During the course of the nineteenth century, urbanization and expanding literary and artistic horizons produced a distinct political field in Beirut very much analogous to other late nineteenth-century cities in provincial European and colonial circuits.[16] Intellectual elites, literary societies, and journalists acted in the field of tension between a centralizing imperial state and an evolving capitalist economy.[17] A critical consciousness in Arab thought had already flourished in intellectual networks between Cairo, Istanbul, and Damascus since at least the eighteenth century.[18] What distinguished the intellectuals in the nineteenth century from their predecessors was their effect on society and their transformative power. If urbanization and education increased rates of Arabic literacy,[19] then the challenge of this study lies in relating the literary networks to municipal politics and to the production of space in *fin de siècle* Beirut. That is to treat Beirutis' intellectual activities not just as reflections of

[15] On Lebanon's political system of patronage, see Johnson (1986).

[16] Schorske (1994) has been an inspiring reference in the ways he blended intellectual, political, and urban developments in Vienna. Cooper and Stoler (1997) has informed my understanding of Beirut's comparative global position in imperial circuits and non-European political fields. Beirut's relation with Istanbul and Damascus, and the political field it produced, was comparable to the urban relationship between 19th-cent. Vienna, Prague, and Budapest; Berlin and Hamburg; Madrid and Havana; or Rome, Florence, and Venice, but none fully explains the Ottoman case of Beirut. On these examples, see Hanák (1998), Jenkins (2003), Schmidt-Nowara (1999), Riall (1998) respectively, and more generally Ross and Telkamp (1985).

[17] See Jürgen Habermas's classic, if Euro-centric and normative, study *Strukturwandel der Öffentlichkeit* (1994).

[18] Gran (1979). See also, more recently, Sajdi (Ph.D. thesis, 2002).

[19] Hafez (1993).

the socio-economic phenomenon of urbanization, but as one that played a formative role in the changing relation between society and the space in which it expanded.

The intellectual production in and of Beirut had a profound impact on self-perception as well as the physical shape of the city—it produced Beirut as a simultaneously real and imagined city. Widely circulated newspapers such as *Ḥadīqat al-Akhbār* (1858), *al-Jinān* (1870), *Thamarāt al-Funūn* (1875), *al-Muqtaṭaf* (1876), *Lisān al-Ḥāl* (1878), and *al-Mufīd* (1909) not only created a new, frugal and utilitarian form of print Arabic—*lughat al-jarā'id*—that would convey and represent the social reform project of its editors. They also provided the 'broad strokes of narrational order' by determining the topics of the day which would be discussed and disseminated amongst the urban population.[20] Municipal elections, construction laws, and urban measures were not only published in official announcements as well as fervently postulated and criticized in front-page, city news sections.

I argue that it was the journalistic institution of *al-akhbār al-baladiyyāt* ('city news') or *al-maḥalliyyāt* ('domestic news')—the local sections on pages 1, 2, and often 4—that structured the imagined public sphere most immediately and fundamentally. However insignificant the particular events covered in the *baladiyyāt* may appear to the historian, Lefebvre reminds us that '[wo/m]an must be everyday, or [s/]he will not be at all'.[21] Every trifling fragment of news mediated the built city in all its versatile urban rituals and diverse human activities.

Their editors-in-chief—men of letters like Khalīl al-Khūrī, Buṭrus and Salīm al-Bustānī, ʿAbd al-Qādir al-Qabbānī, Yaʿqūb Ṣarrūf, Khalīl Sarkīs, and ʿAbd al-Ghanī al-ʿUraysī—also published critical essays and opinion pieces on urban government as well as social and personal reform. Invariably, they shared a positivist belief in the emancipatory powers of education and knowledge acquisition—especially of women—responsible citizenship, the embrace of the modern age, and altruistic love of the homeland. Significantly, many held positions in the Ottoman bureaucracy and stood for municipal elections. By the early twentieth century, a Beirut-based network of intellectuals spanned almost the entire globe with émigrés like Aḥmad Fāris al-Shidyāq, Muḥammad ʿAbduh, Jirjī Zaydān, Amīn al-Rīḥānī, and Khalīl

20 Frietzsche (1998: 4–5). Exact readership numbers are difficult to assess. Suffice it for our purposes to rely on Philippe de Tarrazi's and Ami Ayalon's vague estimates of 400 subscriptions for *Ḥadīqat al-Akhbār* (plus copies sold on the streets) and up to 2,000 copies of issues of *Lisān al-Ḥāl* sold. Tarrazi (1913–33); Ayalon (1995: 45).

21 Lefebvre (1991*b*: 127).

Jibrān projecting their visions of Beirut from Istanbul, Cairo, Paris, and New York.

In the following chapters we encounter Buṭrus al-Bustānī—one of this study's 'tragic' intellectual heroes—and others as tormented, middle-class individuals, rather than cultural icons of Arabism, who were driven to put their world in order after the devastation inflicted on civilians in the war of 1860. In Bustānī's writings, Ibn Khaldūn's (d. 1406) classical antonyms of 'urban civilization' and 'tribal barbarianism' or 'urban society' and 'kinship community' reverberated strongly. Could we go as far as Peter Gran who has argued that the revival of Ibn Khaldūn's work in nineteenth-century Arab thought was a reflection of the emergence of 'a critical consciousness among writers of the middle class'?[22] In the context of a critical bourgeois commentary, the Aristotelian notion of the 'virtuous city'[23] certainly assumed redemptive or emancipatory qualities for Beirut's cultural revival movement which ascribed a distinct civilizing discourse to urbanity.[24]

Al-Bustānī's encyclopedia entry integrated his 'Bayrūt' into four revolving cultural circles of belonging: Eastern, Ottoman, Arab, and Syrian. Significantly, Bustānī never categorically prioritizes any one element over the other and the entry contains minimal reference to European 'influence'.[25] Bustānī and other men of letters persistently discerned a society that was shaped by multiple notions of being in space as much as by being in time. Neither the concept of Westernization nor national fulfilment were the driving forces of Beirut's late Ottoman history. Rather the active relationship between inhabitants and the multiple social spaces they inhabited determined the political economy and urban culture of *fin de siècle* Beirut.

Although colonial pressure was mounting on Beirut, especially in the fields of finance, health, and education, I do not present European colonialism *per se* as the primary lens of historical analysis. Instead, I prioritize from the outset the human agency of Beirutis to make their city a provincial capital. Autonomy of human action implies the capacity to demand and institute change.[26] Their struggle constituted a successful urban positioning within the unfolding imperial state system and the structures of the emerging world-economy. By challenging the status quo of the Ottoman administrative geography—by positively 'provincializing' Beirut—the campaigners upgraded their city's

22 Gran (1979: 68).

23 This is the literal translation of Abū Naṣr al-Farābī's (870–950) foundational treatise on Aristotelian political philosophy, *al-Madīna al-fāḍila*. See Dieterici (1900).

24 The word civilization first entered Ottoman state vocabulary in the 1830s. See Baykara (1992: 24–5).

25 Abu Manneh (1980: 287–304).

26 M. Weber (1980: 419).

political scope within the Ottoman empire, and by 'capitalizing' their city, the petitioners hoped to generate urban investment and lasting prosperity.[27]

The Production of Space and Everyday Life in Beirut

The Moroccan philosopher Muḥammad ʿĀbid al-Jābirī has argued that critical Arab thought since the nineteenth century has been grappling with a fundamental structural tension between authenticity and modernity.[28] According to al-Jābirī, the pursuit of the Arab project of modernity remains unfinished. It rests on an endogenous process in which critical and self-reflexive interpretations of the past can be developed. To acknowledge the multiple paths and contextual nature of modernity—or alternative modernities—allows the Arab-Islamic world to engage in universal history 'not as patients but as agents' of modernity; or put differently, not as passive victims but as claimants of history.[29]

Modernity as I conceive it in this book is primarily an urban phenomenon whose origins are ownerless and not nationally bounded. It is neither ontologically European nor non-Western but appeared at the philosophical and physical encounter between the two.[30] As 'a vital mode of experiences' modernity encapsulates the condition in which the relations between space and time, self and others, were fundamentally reconfigured across the globe. Invariably, these new human relations were framed in a politics of difference in the pursuit of improving the human condition.[31]

The Ottoman administrative reforms of 1864 and 1867 turned the imperial government into a powerful organizer of the historically heterogeneous space of empire. This power was not repressive as the pernicious trope of 'Oriental Despotism' once suggested, but was, instead, highly productive. In the search for a solution to the crises of provincial rule in the first part of the nineteenth century, the Ottoman state referred neither to 'time-honoured' principles nor to outright adoptions of 'Western' models of governance. The imperial reforms were historically conscious, future-oriented, and found inspiration in the empire's own provinces. The provinces were, in fact, laboratories of governance where imperial inspection tours, local petitions, and model provinces offered a plethora of blueprints for reform.[32]

27 By provincializing Beirut I aim to take Beirut out of the historiographical fangs of 'Westernization' and resituate it in much more layered historicity without neglecting the formative influence of European capitalism and colonialism. See also Dipesh Chakrabarty's call for *Provincializing Europe* (2000).

28 See ʿĀbid al-Jābirī (1991).

29 ʿĀbid al-Jābirī (1999: 4).

30 Mitchell (1999: 1–34).

31 Berman (1988); see also Kern (1983) and J. Scott (1998).

32 See Hanssen (2002: 49–74).

Particularly under Sultan Abdülhamid II (1876–1909), many Ottoman cities and towns received 'face-lifts' and public health regulations. Railway, port, and telegraph networks criss-crossed the empire, while the increasingly mobile members of the new Ottoman mass bureaucracy became omnipresent bearers of state power in the provinces. Yet, at the same time, the modern Ottoman state was neither omniscient nor omnipotent, and local power continued to appropriate its own spheres of influence. As Ottoman state power infiltrated and colonized urban everyday life in the provincial peripheries, the scope of locality power, both urban and provincial, also grew.

Thus, although the web of social, administrative, and technological ties tightened in a politically integrated geography and the Ottoman state penetrated provincial societies in unprecedented ways, the government often adopted existing social structures in order to implement imperial policies. Moreover, permanent and elected provincial councils functioned as at times uncomfortable channels of the will of local elites and urban notables. Although the exchange between Istanbul and the provinces was rarely equal, localization—the production of locality—did not occur against, much less outside, the Ottoman state context but was facilitated by the very political and infrastructural centralization which it challenged.

Beirut's ascendancy in the intersecting circuits of the Ottoman empire, the world-economy, and regional urban rivalries was shaped to a far greater degree than has been acknowledged by the tactics of its leading merchants and the constant struggle of its political representatives. Provincial and other 'small-scale societies', Appadurai reminds us, 'do not and cannot take locality as a given. Rather, they seem to assume that locality is ephemeral unless hard and regular work is undertaken to produce and maintain its materiality'.[33]

Nineteenth-century cities experienced tremendous physical transformation because of new dimensions of world trade and international transportation. Within the Eastern Mediterranean subsystem of the world-economy, port-cities like Beirut, Izmir, and Salonika operated as strategic locations of trade.[34] For example, the port of Beirut was estimated to handle 11 per cent of the total trade in the Ottoman empire in 1907—level with Salonika but behind Izmir's 17 per cent and Istanbul's 33 per cent.[35] The world-economy produced these cities as the object and the project of its expansion.

From the 1880s onwards, particularly in Beirut, European capitalism commodified space and 'conquered' distance through infrastructural investment in

[33] Appadurai (1996: 180–1).
[34] Özveren (Ph.D. thesis, 1990).
[35] Faroqhi *et al.* (1997: 831).

transport, communication, and 'public services'. Of an estimated 205 million francs of major European investment in Syria between 1860 and 1914, over 72 million went into the city of Beirut.[36] Considering that the 4.2 million-franc construction of the Beirut–Damascus Road was the only major investment in pre-provincial capital Beirut, the years between 1888 and 1914 clearly brought about the most profound changes to the social and urban space Beirut had experienced up to that point in time.

Urbanization critically sustained capitalism both as a mode of production and as a structure of social relations.[37] The work of the philosopher of space, Henri Lefebvre (1901–91), has been a major influence on the way I have approached Beirut's urban history. In particular, his *The Production of Space* (1974)—in many ways the culmination of his writings on cities—has allowed me to consider Beirut as a history of 'counter-spaces . . . not fragmented but differential in character'. In spite of gargantuan efforts to subdue the city, it always contained times of harmony without homogeneity, and maintained spaces of difference without segregation.[38]

At root, my study sets out to restore the heterogeneous *spatial* dimensions of Beirut's modern history. According to the geographer Edward Soja, for too long now history has treated *time* as the dynamic field of social development. In particular, historians of non-metropolitan places tended to take as axiomatic that Europe dragged human beings along an evolutionary path towards modernity. As Soja has criticized, while 'History was socially produced . . . Geography was naively given', and he invites the urban historian to become sensitive to spatial dimensions of social change.[39]

Soja takes his cue from Michel Foucault to ask why it was that time—and in particular European time—has been treated as 'richness, fecundity, life, dialectic' while in contrast space has been typically seen as 'the dead, the fixed, the undialectical, the immobile'.[40] 'A whole history remains to be written of *spaces*—which would at the same time be the history of *powers*—from the great strategies of geopolitics to the little tactics of the habitat.'[41]

As a 'spectral analysis' of urban life, Lefebvre's exploration of 'why space matters' examines the impact of planning technologies, ideologies of the centralizing state and capitalist intervention (often, but not automatically, working hand in hand) on the spaces and places of everyday life. Translated to the late Ottoman context, I argue that the reform project of the modernizing state

[36] Issawi (1988: 135). The rest of the investments went into other cities in Bilad al-Sham.

[37] Lefebvre (1991*b*) and Harvey (1985).

[38] Lefebvre (1991*b*: 303, 379) wisely cautioned that 'not all hope should be placed, after the fashion of American liberals, in pluralism *per se*, but it is not unreasonable to place some hope in things that pluralism lets by.'

[39] Soja (1996: 169).

[40] Soja (1993: 137).

[41] Foucault (1980: 149).

attempted to give the space of empire the appearance of a formal, rational, homogeneous order, hierarchized into different levels of geography and administration. At the same time, this abstract space of the modern Ottoman state also generated and contained internal conflicts, sectarian prejudice, and sources of social domination that lurked behind the very appearance of order.

Lefebvre differentiates three interconnecting modes of modern spatial production that help us disentangle the complex set of relations between city, state, and society in pre-colonial Beirut: the perceived, the conceived, and the lived.[42] The first space is a product of human geography, urban functions, material and physical manifestations of social relations, forms of spatial organization, the urban sites, residential patterns, and the built environment.[43] In contrast, conceived space contains the abstract, the mental, and the epistemological sphere, as well as the signs and codes of the city. This is the abstract space of visuality, order, and future, dominated by rulers, planners, cartographers, and state institutions. Significantly, these spatial representations are both abstract and concrete: although the concept of 'Bayrūt'-as-text (or as-map) is not the same as Beirut-as-reality, the recurrent literary and cartographic representations of the city ('Bayrūt') produced a particular urban reality (Beirut) as a simultaneously real and imagined city. As Italo Calvino reminds us, 'the city must never be confused with the words that describe it. And yet between the one and the other there is a connection.'[44]

Urban social space cannot be understood either as a mere product or as a figment of the human imagination at the mercy of (modern) technologies of production as this binary opposition would imply, and Lefebvre reinstates the historical and ontological dimensions of space by introducing a third spatial element. This third space denotes the directly lived, representational spaces of the inhabitants, the way they create their city as 'users' through practices, images, and symbols: lived space 'overlays physical space, making symbolic use of its objects [and forms]'.[45] This is at once the space of everyday life dominated by the political stakes of state and capitalist intervention and the space of resistance to that intervention.

The everyday life is where the urban historian's subaltern humanism resides and where the space of human agency and lived experience interacts with the physical and conceptual dimensions of the production of space. Lefebvre's work anticipates many of the subjectivity-restoring strategies that have become the hallmark of postcolonial studies over the last three decades. In the context of urban culture, everyday life is the space of the user, *differential* space, both

[42] Lefebvre (1991*b*: 33). [43] Ibid. 38. [44] Calvino (1974: 61).
[45] Lefebvre (1991*b*: 39).

'real' and 'possible'. As such it contains the sources of collective memory and subaltern mobilization that lay outside the conceptual powers of the state and challenged the logic of capitalist expansion.[46]

Henri Lefebvre provides historians with a path to understand urban culture as subversive activity that defies conventional grand narratives and the triumphalist 'histories-of-becoming': becoming modern, secular, national, civilized, etc. He allows us to look beyond the seemingly boundless scope of the state and capitalism without abandoning the project of critical history for the sake of urban nostalgia. By focusing on particular themes of the politics of space in Beirut, we may bring out vital modes of social change and urban experience that a chronologically arranged city biography would have failed to notice or deemed insignificant details of a distant past. Beirut's spatial past matters because it resonates with the city's post-war present.

Lefebvre's final and unfinished research project was to explore Mediterranean cities and the rhythms and rituals 'which *punctuate* daily life' in them. He asks the pertinent question: 'Does the characteristic ambiguity of Mediterranean cities in relation to the State manifest itself in the rhythms of social life?'[47] For Lefebvre,

> [t]o think about the city is to hold and maintain its conflictual aspects: constraints and possibilities, peacefulness and violence, meetings and solitude, gatherings and separation, the trivial and the poetic, brutal functionalism and surprising improvisation. The dialectic of the urban cannot be limited to the opposition center–periphery, although it contains it . . . Thinking the city moves towards thinking the world (thought as a relationship to the world) . . . the universe, space-time, energies, information, but without valuing one rather than another . . . One can hope that this will turn out well but the urban can become a place of barbarity, domination, dependence and exploitation . . . In thinking about these perspectives, let us leave a place for events, initiatives, decisions.[48]

The Provincial Capital: a Frame and a Scale for an Alternative Approach to Urban History

'[Y]ears ago Beirut was a place of compromises and alliances, which now seem miraculous; the place of a polyrhythmy realized in an (apparent) harmony'.[49]

[46] Lefebvre. 385. [47] Lefebvre (1996: 234).

[48] Henri Lefebvre, *Qu'est ce que penser?* (Paris, 1985), 110. Quoted in Lefebvre (1996: 53).

[49] Lefebvre (1996: 240).

Fernand Braudel's notion that a Mediterranean space-time continuum exerted its own rhythm and, indeed, its structural limits to individual and state agency is valid, too, for nineteenth-century Beirut. However, the traditional cosmopolitanism of the Mediterranean and the relative cultural autonomy of its port-cities were challenged, shattered, and often destroyed by nationalism, sectarianism, and colonial borders by the early twentieth century.[50]

In many ways nineteenth-century Beirut was an archetypal Mediterranean city. It had a confessionally, ethnically, and socially diverse population, which owed its wealth to maritime trade with Europe and cultural exchange with other cities around the Mediterranean. It shared its heritage, habits, rhythms, lifestyles, and developments with other, connected port-cities. However, whereas usually foreigners dominated urban economies in the North African and Ottoman Mediterranean, in Beirut local Muslim, Christian, and, to a lesser extent, Jewish merchant houses shaped the balance of trade.[51]

The unusual historical development of a confessionally mixed, indigenous political economy may well account for the persistence of the city's multicultural and cosmopolitan licence long after it had given way to colonial, national, and ethnic homogenization in other port-cities of the Mediterranean. Yet, the violent eruption of the Lebanese civil war in Beirut in 1975 suggests that we may have been distracted from noticing that Beirut's multicultural cosmopolitanism was fraught with historically rooted, structural inequalities and injustices.

By the end of the nineteenth century 'progressive time' became an important marker of social difference not only for the state but for the local bourgeoisie, too. In Beirut, one of the recurring and underlying themes of the Arabic literary movement was the notion of the new age (*al-ʿaṣr al-jadīd*), which carried a particular *Zeitgeist* (*rūḥ al-ʿaṣr*).[52] On one level, contemporary writers and journalists in Beirut celebrated modern times (new technologies, scientific inventions, and discoveries) as the force of the future that would purge their society from an allegedly ignorant, backward, and violent past. On another level, this kind of 'epochalism' was also a powerful social tool in the hands of public moralists and bourgeois intellectuals who identified the practices of other, non-conforming classes as pre-modern while establishing themselves as the vanguard of provincial modernity.

[50] See the special issue of the Braudel Center's journal *Review*, 16 (1993) on 'Port Cities in the Ottoman Empire'. [51] See Fawaz (1983).

[52] See Khalīl al-Khūrī, *al-ʿAṣr al-jadīd* (Beirut, 1858/9); Salīm al-Bustānī, 'Rūḥ al-ʿaṣr', *al-Jinān*, 1 (1870), 385–8, and 'Rūḥ al-ʿaṣr', *al-Jinān*, 3 (1872), 505–7.

The Ottoman provincial mission shared many of the features of a French *mission civilisatrice* with which it competed over control of the Levant. Conceived as a means to catapult the empire into an age of modernity, 'the *mission civilisatrice* of the *Tanẓīmāt* man was carried forward into the Hamidian era'.[53] I argue that, like in the civilizing mission of French governors general in West Africa whom Alice Conklin has examined recently, Hamidian bureaucrats were generally driven by 'the burden' that their imperial mission placed on them to civilize distant provincial peripheries.[54] In this process, I argue, *fin de siècle* Beirut was an outpost, a platform, even a launching pad for competing civilizing missions while its own urban fabric was constantly valorized and contested. For Ottoman Beirut was similar to but not the same as European provincial towns and port-cities. It was familiar to Europeans—but in unexpected ways. If, as the Jamaican Marxist critic of colonial discourse, C. L. R. James, argued the Caribbean was 'in the West but not of it', then Mediterranean places like *fin de siècle* Beirut found themselves 'of the West but not in it'.

The experience of the *fin de siècle* at the end of the nineteenth century was universally marked by a perceived discrepancy between unprecedented material progress and moral panic.[55] Indeed, the term *fin de siècle* first entered the literary domain in metropolitan France in 1888 and thus conveniently coincided with the creation of the province of Beirut. That year a play entitled 'Fin de Siècle' about shady deals, adultery, and murder hit the theatres in Paris while an editor of the financial weekly magazine *Le Fin de Siècle* proclaimed that the *fin de siècle* character at its most acute was 'struggle for life'.[56]

In the words of Stefan Zweig, the Viennese biographer of the European *fin de siècle*, generally 'this generation was inhibited in free expression by the pressures of the spirit of the age'.[57] As a social and cultural experience, the *fin de siècle* was by no means limited to metropolitan centres like Vienna or Paris. Robert Ilbert's *Alexandrie 1830–1930* (1996) and Eleni Bastéa's recent exploration of nineteenth-century Athens have enriched the historical inquiry into cities by focusing on non-metropolitan, Mediterranean localities.[58] Borrowing from Schorske and Eugen Weber, the term '*fin de siècle* Beirut' is meant here as the project and object of cosmopolitan desire of an Ottoman-Arab intermediary bourgeoisie to belong to a distinctly modern epoch.[59]

[53] Deringil (1998: 168). [54] Conklin (1997). [55] E. Weber (1986: 2). [56] Ibid. 10.
[57] Zweig (1998: 90). [58] Bastéa (2000). See also Jenkins (2003).
[59] The term 'intermediary bourgeoisie' is chosen not to convey a sense of Western acculturation but the universal rise of an urban, propertied middle class that based its emergence on generally utilitarian ideas, non-feudal social relations, and intellectual, commercial, or administrative work. See Sennett (1993: 48).

Ottoman military and political reassertion in Bilad al-Sham came on the heels of Egyptian occupation and subsequent provincial violence between 1840 and 1860. It was sustained by a collective will on the part of imperial bureaucrats, urban notables, and intellectual elites to contain and overcome the assumed destructive instincts of their society and emancipate their provinces from the heavy burden of a violent past. In many instances, I argue, this first generation of public moralists and cultural critics suffered from the trauma of a perceived civilization deficit. Against the experience of communal violence in the mid-nineteenth century, early Arab intellectuals such as Buṭrus al-Bustānī, Aḥmad Fāris al-Shidyāq, and Jirjī Zaydān understood and used the notion of *tamaddun* ('urbaneness/civilization') as 'a generic term behind which disquieting compromise[s] lurked' for the concept of Arab civilization.[60]

The nexus between city and civilization was most clearly expressed at the time in a new discourse on public health. European, Ottoman, Egyptian, and local authorities began to apply workable techniques of containing disease. I argue that, for Beirut in the aftermath of the 1860 civil war, public health concerns gradually became social ones, and social relations were increasingly described in medical terms. Literary elites personalized and gendered Beirut as 'the Bride', 'the Flower', or 'Julia Felix', and began to imagine their city as a bodily structure prone to pathological aberrations.

By the nineteenth century, Ottoman authorities and Arab literary elites used classical Arab and European Renaissance discoveries of blood and air circulation to develop a scientific and medical vocabulary for Beirut's economic processes and urban rhythms. Under these new conditions urban reforms were meant to produce a healthy city, which breathed freely, pulsated with life, and moved towards growth. This new urban discourse was intricately linked to the moralist and confinary practices of the Ottoman state, the production of social (class) distinctions, and ultimately to the physical transformation of *fin de siècle* Beirut.

Class and Community in Beirut

The long-standing intermediary power of urban notables in Ottoman centre–periphery relations continued during the Ottoman reform period and Hamidian imperialism. Indeed, the nominal autonomy of action that Hourani has famously ascribed to this social category effectively dissolved into the integrated administrative structure of empire.[61] In the context of post-1860 Beirut,

[60] Berque (1978: 13).

[61] Hourani (1968: 41–68). See also P. Khoury (1991) and Toledano (1997).

urban order and social hierarchy hinged on Ottoman state institutions and bureaucrats, European consular protection, and a cross-confessional, pacifying collusion of the city's notables.[62] Both Muslim and Christian notables drew their socio-political status from the 'vertical' ties to the religious community they represented, from their 'horizontal' ties of class with members of other communities with whom they shared a general economic, political, and cultural outlook, and from access to employment in the Ottoman administration.[63] As such, late Ottoman 'institutionalism' was as much a representation of class as of community—the legal consecration of the former perpetuating the hierarchy within the latter. Together, these ties constituted the resilient system of reciprocity between the authorities of the Ottoman state and the local notables that sustained the *tanẓīmāt*'s conservative reform project.[64]

The autobiography of Jirjī Zaydān, who—like many of his peers—emigrated from Beirut to Cairo in the 1880s, provides a contemporary definition of Beirut's post-war class structure. Addressing his son when he entered the Syrian Protestant College in 1909, Zaydān divided Beirut's society into 'three distinct classes'. *Al-khāṣṣa*—the distinguished elite—consisted of 'the people of the government and the rich'. This class possessed social and economic capital which the *al-ʿāmma*—the undistinguished general public—lacked. Zaydān considered the latter 'the riff raff, the artisans, all the other people with menial occupations, and the small merchant'. They were 'immoral crooks' and 'idle vagrants' who got drunk and 'were uneducated because of the few schools available'.

But Zaydān insisted there emerged an independent 'third class after the unrest [of 1860]'. Cultural capital allowed Beirut's literary elite—the local *Bildungsbürgertum*—to climb the social ladder while their humble background distinguished them from the people who inherited wealth or status. At the same time, Zaydān realized that this group of educated individuals maintained ideas and dress codes which 'the common people considered a sinful breach with tradition'.[65]

In *fin de siècle* Beirut, perceptions of social norms and conformity to morals structured class relations as much as access to means of (urban) production. In the hindsight of this popular Arab writer, during the course of the nineteenth century intellectuals emerged as a class in and of themselves, distinguished by

[62] Fawaz (1983: 109–20).

[63] While strictly speaking Albert Hourani's notable ideal-type applies exclusively to Muslim notables in inland Ottoman Syria, I extend his definition to Christians who gained access to similar means of power and prestige as Muslim notables after Ottoman legal-, land-, and bureaucratic reforms.

[64] Zubaida (1989). [65] Philipp (1979: 147).

common habits and tastes and by worldviews that distanced them from other social groups around them. However, up until the emergence on the scene of lower middle-class nationalists in the 1930s, intellectuals shared with wealthy merchants and reform-minded notables certain perspectives on urban life, lifestyles, social values, and pedagogies.

Despite their varied sources of social power these groups were members of a self-consciously constituted middle class.[66] Not capitalist penetration and Westernization *per se*, but an urban discourse on what a city should look like, how and by whom it should be governed, and what end it should serve, produced a city where the intermediary bourgeoisie could achieve social entitlement, economic success, and political distinction all the while feeling threatened by lower classes who defied this urban order.

The City between Society and State

André Raymond, the leading urban historian of the Middle East, has argued, 'A city, that is to say a geographical concentration of a large population, can only subsist or develop within a system of coherent relations between its society and the space in which it expands'.[67] Raymond's 1985 landmark study *Grandes Villes arabes à l'époque ottomane* echoes Lefebvre's compassion for everyday life in cities.[68] Significantly, instead of affirming the essentialisms contained in the dominant Islamic or Oriental city paradigms, Raymond chose a relational framework between the Ottoman state and the provincial urban centres.[69]

Economic decline in the seventeenth and eighteenth centuries, he argued, was in fact a figment of latter-day, European colonial imagination. Rather, an unprecedented degree of security, prosperity, and urban expansion as well as 'moral and material unity' developed during the age of the 'Ottoman Commonwealth'. Raymond attributes this to a specific imperial–local interplay of power that varied from place to place.[70] He argues that the transformation of historic Arab capital cities like Damascus, Aleppo, Sayda, Mosul, Baghdad, Tunis, Cairo, and Medina into Ottoman provincial capitals subordinate to Istanbul actually led to urban growth and prosperity in these cities.[71]

66 Dubar and Nasr (1976). 67 Raymond (1994: 17).

68 It is significant to note that his personal life has been closely connected to that of Lefebvre whom his parents sheltered from Nazi raids in the early 1940s. His older brother Henri Raymond (a prominent urban sociologist in Lefebvre's inner circle at the University of Nanterre in the 1960s and 1970s) supervised Nada Sehnaoui's remarkable MA thesis on the Westernization of everyday life in 19th-cent. Beirut (1981). Peronal conversation with André Raymond, Aix-en-Provence, 3 Mar. 2001. See also Nancy Gallagher's interview with André Raymond (1994: 69). 69 See, most recently, Wirth (2000).

70 Raymond (1985: 38). 71 Ibid. 24.

Raymond's analysis of urban culture replaced the dominant epistemology of the religiously regulated city with the methodological framework of historico-geographical materialism where class differentiation was reflected and expressed in inner-city spatial relations, 'radio-concentric residential patterns', as well as in the types of houses and neighbourhoods.[72]

A comparison between the form, function, and structure of Arab provincial capitals that Raymond has described and those of nineteenth-century, coastal Beirut brings out the specificities of late Ottoman urbanism. In comparison to the age of imperialism, state power and '*qāḍī* urbanism' before the nineteenth century were constantly negotiated and exercised on a consensual, *ad hoc* basis. Islamic law was applied to urban society rather than society adapted to the law. In his words, what distinguished the age of the 'Ottoman Commonwealth' from the nineteenth century was that 'the actions of the authorities made them felt more in a corrective than in a normative framework of development'.[73]

The most challenging approaches to nineteenth-century urban history have been inspired by Frantz Fanon's descriptions of colonial Algiers.[74] Colonialism created dual cities on the North African shoreline where new European quarters 'lay siege' to the indigenous city centres which colonial planners kept 'frozen in time'. This duality was nurtured by powerful, deliberate, and constant representations of colonial truths on 'Oriental backwardness' and cultural superiority of Western rationalism, progress, and modernity.[75]

So compelling were these colonial representations that, according to Timothy Mitchell, they convinced the colonized themselves of their own deviation from that constructed truth. But here this anti-colonial approach to urban culture becomes problematic. There exists a paradoxical continuity between certain assumptions about the local internalization of this colonial construct on the one hand, and the inescapable passivity of the inhabitants of both the 'Islamic' and the 'Colonial City' on the other. Powerful European armies, steamships, companies, and banks nipped all nascent local initiative in the bud. By extension, then, there prevails a sense not only that both models share Max Weber's underlying assumption that cities in the Middle East are locales of illegitimate authority, but that there had once been an authentic core that has irretrievably been destroyed by the evil forces of modernity.[76]

The late Ottoman provincial capital certainly prepared Beirut for its later role as national capital of the Republic of Lebanon when the scale of social organization and the measure of urban intervention was drastically expanded. Although the French authorities often completed urban designs already

[72] Raymond (1985), 271–3. [73] Ibid. 129. [74] Fanon (1967: 35–67; and 1990: esp. 29–30).
[75] Mitchell (1988: 165). [76] M. Weber (1958: 87 ff.).

launched in the late Ottoman period, Beirut's authorities did not create a fully fledged bifurcated city that had become so commonplace in the North African Mediterranean until Beirut became the headquarters of the French colonial government in the Levant in 1920. As French officials occupied the higher echelons of government and the foreign population exploded from 5 to 15 per cent of the total, the urban fabric, particularly the old city and the coastline, was radically transformed through a systematic colonial attempt to cast the new French civic order in modern architectural form.[77] In the late Ottoman empire, the imperial capital Istanbul was the first city to undergo a veritable urban revolution in which urban spaces became increasingly differentiated economically and symbolically. The grand plans for Istanbul, the ostentatious architecture of new sultanic palaces, government buildings, huge apartment blocks, and private villas along the shores of the Bosphorus gave the Ottoman capital a powerful appearance of political reinvigoration.[78] Like the capitals of European empires, Istanbul underwent an architectural boom in the nineteenth century that reinforced the imperial government's perceptions of metropolitan superiority *vis-à-vis* the empire's provinces.

Outside the imperial capital, Ottoman modernity and the Hamidian *mission civilisatrice* were systematically staged in the regional centres. While most cities had been provincial capitals throughout much of Ottoman rule (Damascus, Aleppo, Mosul, or Baghdad), Beirut was granted this status only as a consequence of nineteenth-century economic prosperity and local lobbying. As a provincial capital, Beirut became a site of new and enforced manifestations of state presence as well as local and regional consciousness. The introduction of administrative changes brought about new provincial boundaries, state institutions, imperial architecture, and urban planning. It was in these material domains that the Ottoman state inscribed its imperial project most visibly, tangibly, and effectively. Within the provincial context, free-standing administrative buildings, monuments, wide boulevards, and sumptuous squares created an image of a specifically Ottoman symmetry, regularity, and order, which appeared to physically frame everyday life in public places.[79]

In the imperial hierarchy of Ottoman cities, Istanbul stood at the centre. At the height of Sultan Abdülhamid's rule in 1900, the imperial metropole commanded twenty-nine provincial capitals or *vilāyet merkezi*.[80] More or less permanent representatives from these provinces sat on the Council of State (*şurāyı devleti*) where they channelled provincial matters into the central legislative process.[81] Provincial capitals generally ruled over four to six

[77] Thompson (2000: 177–8); Davie (1996: 86–92). [78] Çelik (1986).
[79] Hanssen (2000). [80] Birken (1976). [81] Shaw and Shaw (1977: 90).

subprovinces and their respective urban centres (*sancak merkezi*) but some of the *sancak*s or mutaṣarrifiyyas, like Mount Lebanon or Jerusalem, were regionally autonomous and under direct rule from Istanbul.[82] These subprovincial centres, in turn, administered districts, *ḳāżās*. The smallest unit in the Ottoman provincial administration was the commune (*nāḥiye*) or, in the cities, the neighbourhood (*maḥalle*) run by a quarter leader (*mukhtār*). Towns occasionally climbed up or down this ranking but this nomenclature remained the basic structure of Ottoman provincial rule between the provincial reorganization of the empire in the 1860s and the First World War.

In sum, four qualities of the Ottoman provincial capital emerged out of the reform period. First, it was invested with an administrative function and a political size. Second, it was marked by relational capacities, towards both Istanbul and the province between which it mediated power, dominant meaning, and culture. Third, it was both contextual because of its own historical space and the long-standing relations with its natural environment, and conjectural because of its dependence on the abstract space of the new Ottoman politico-administrative system of which it was part. Finally, it was maintained by a population conscious of its urbanity. In Buṭrus al-Bustānī's words: 'The inclination among the people of Beirut is urban' (*al-hawāya ʿind ahl Bayrūt maddānī*).[83] Through these processes and phenomena, the Ottoman provincial capital became a model space 'in a matrix of imperial regulations' that applied to the entire geography of the empire.[84]

Beirut's provincial capital dimension thus offers an analytical framework that captures both the scale and the scope of its particular and its universal modern history. In the late Ottoman galaxy, Beirut was a bright star, a regional centre of administration, learning, and leisure, but it was part of larger imperial constellations. Although Beirut constantly interacted with the wider world, in particular through trade and migration networks, as a provincial capital, Beirut was first and foremost operating on the scale of a regional subsystem.[85]

82 Invariably, a *sancak* is also referred to as a *mutaṣarrifiyya* or *liwāʾ* in modern Arabo-Ottoman terminology.

83 *Muḥīṭ al-Muḥīṭ*, 949. The word *al-hawāya* was one of many Arabic neologisms invented during the *Nahḍa*. It connoted appeal, tendency, or desire.

84 Foucault (1984: 241). For an application of these four sets of qualities to other cities of the Ottoman Empire, see the contributions to Hanssen *et al.* (2002).

85 The local newspapers disseminated this provincial sense of political scale and imagined community as they organized their news into municipal, then provincial—with dispatches from Nablus or Lattakia—and finally news from places outside the provincial borders such as Damascus and Istanbul. On scale as an analytical unit, see Barth (1979).

At stake in this study of provincial Beirut is to trace not merely the momentum of temporal transitions from one stage to another but, more importantly, to trace the moments of spatial difference. By taking the thirty-year experiment of the Ottoman province of Beirut as the historico-geographical frame, this study aims to step out of the conventional periodization in modern Lebanese historiography which has generally been structured by either Beirut's 'encounter with the West' or the territorial integration and institutional particularity of Mount Lebanon.

I

Capitalizations

I felt [Beirut] is a different city: It is not the city of 'endings', like Damascus, but the city of 'beginnings'. It is not the city of 'certainty', but of 'searching'. Thus, it is not a finished building, which you have to enter just as it is, and live in it as it is. It is, to the contrary, an open project, which is never completed. I felt that Beirut is like love: a constant beginning; and that it is like poetry: it must always be created anew.

(Adonis (1993), tr. in Khairallah (2002: 514))

I

The Struggle for Self-determination

> The important fact of the growth of Beirut in the nineteenth century was not simply the replacement of one major trading port by another—Beirut was not simply the successor of Sidon and Acre—but the growth of a new kind of relationship with the . . . hinterland.
>
> Hourani quoted in Polk and Chambers (1986: 22)

In May 1865, a milestone petition reached the Ottoman government from Beirut.[1] Two hundred signatories from among the urban merchants, notables, and clergy demanded nothing less than that the sultan change the empire's administrative geography and grant Beirut the status of an Ottoman provincial capital. The subsequent struggle over the administrative geography of Bilad al-Sham—or Greater Syria—which was finally decided in Beirut's favour in March 1888, demonstrates two pivotal and overlooked aspects of the social history of the late Ottoman Empire.

First, it shows the local identification with one's city and the extent to which urban consciousness was mobilized by urban elites in order to transform the strategic position of their cities within the evolving Ottoman administrative hierarchies and provincial boundaries. Second, the intensity of the ensuing provincial rivalries between cities suggests that Bilad al-Sham constituted a single integrated political economy in which a host of overlapping imagined macro and micro communities competed with each other. These political rivalries and competing representations of urban consciousness provided a rich cultural and geographical repertoire on which the various Arab nationalist movements that emerged out of the historical conjecture of the First World War could draw.

[1] Başbakanlık Arşivi (hereafter BBA), Istanbul, ID, *37280*.

The first part of this book thus offers an analytical scope that transcends and pre-dates the geographies of latter-day nation states. Historically, urban rivalry evolved around processes of towns and cities vying not only for markets but also to be designated the seat of a court or imperial administration. The term capitalization entered the English journalistic vocabulary in the same year the Beirutis launched their first petition. Commenting on the urban effects of the transfer of Italy's imperial capital from Turin to Florence in 1864, the *Pall Mall Gazette* opined that 'Florence is being summarily subjected to the advantages of capitalization.'[2] Cities began to serve as models of the modern state in the nineteenth century.[3] As in France, and Italy where 'new networks emerged and winning a law court, a tax office, or a prefecture lifted a town's status and provided economic benefit',[4] in Bilad al-Sham, urban rivalry instilled a sense of local, urban patriotism or even a 'chauvinisme des villes' as Antoine Abdel Nour called it.[5] Urban patriotism provided the ideological underpinning for a will to urban government and to public spirit. Rivalry between urban centres intensified in the nineteenth century, as the stakes increased and towns and cities in Bilad al-Sham underwent a dual integration, commercially with the world-economy and politically with the Ottoman Empire.

Beirut first boomed economically in the early nineteenth century less because of an advantageous geographical position within the unfolding world-economy, than because of two diametrically opposed strategies of the city's notables. I argue that Beirut owed its initial ascendancy to its merchants' subversive activities to undercut the monopoly system imposed by the rulers of Acre on the Levant.[6] In contrast to this strategy, the second half of the century was marked by concerted local efforts to invite Ottoman state power to Beirut by upgrading the city to the status of a provincial capital.

From Acre to Beirut

The *échelle* of Acre has for long been regarded only as a fortified town whose governor takes umbrage at any foreigner who settles in it because he wants to be the only monopolist of the products of his territory . . . Beirut has always been a port with great commercial potential; but for a very long time it was held as a fief, by the princes of the

[2] *Pall Mall Gazette*, 9 (10 Oct. 1865), quoted in *Oxford English Dictionary*: ' "Capitalization" 1. a. The action of converting into capital, or of representing an annual income or payment by its capital value; 1. b. The sum or figure resulting from the action of converting into capital. 2. Conversion into a capital city.' I would like to thank John Chalcraft for pointing me to this reference.

[3] Foucault (1984: 241–2). [4] Cohen (1998: 16). [5] Abdel Nour (1982: 265–6).

[6] Here I take my cue from Philipp (2002).

Mountain . . . Before and even after 1814 there was only one European merchant in this port, yet Beirut was already considered to be the most active trading port of the coast; from this one can infer that *it was not precisely the establishment of European trading houses that gave Beirut its importance.*[7]

On the following pages, I shall demonstrate what factors—if 'not precisely the establishment of European trading houses'—led to the rise of Beirut during the long nineteenth century. The turn of the eighteenth century marked the climax of the power of local potentates in the Arab provinces.[8] A series of Ottoman military defeats against European empires and a worsening fiscal crisis allowed ambitious provincial tax farmers (*multazims*), tax collectors (*muḥassils*), and urban notables—against an annual tax payment to the Ottoman sultan—to gain significant political autonomy in the expanding realms of Egypt, Damascus, Northern Palestine, and Mount Lebanon. Within this regional power constellation in which the provincial rulers frequently fought wars against each other, Acre emerged as the unconstested port-city of the Levant serving as the entrepôt of cotton, grain, and olive oil from the valleys of the Galilee, Nablus, and the plains south of Damascus.[9] It became the administrative centre of the Ottoman province of Sidon when Aḥmad Pasha al-Jazzār moved the seat of government from Sidon to Acre in 1788.[10]

Acre's economic boom was largely based on an effective implementation of a system of monopoly over regional exports. So long as al-Jazzār paid his dues to the Sublime Porte in Istanbul, he had a free hand over the political economy of his realm. This system was politically and militarily administered by consecutive pashas of the well-fortified port-city of Acre, who controlled the vast coastal strip from Tripoli to Gaza. Between the 1740s and the 1800s, these rulers were able, often with brutal force, to establish themselves as sole middlemen between the French merchants and peasant production by guaranteeing supply of produce in return for fixed prices.[11] As long as European demand for cotton or grain rose, Acre's rulers profited handsomely. The city was set for a prosperous future.

The Moment of the 'Merchant Republic'

Acre's prosperity was undermined, however, by the growing commercial assertion of a small community of mainly Damascene merchants in Beirut at the

[7] MAE, Paris, CCCTB 1821–1828, vol. 1, Beirut, 15 Jan. 1827. Quoted in Issawi (1988: 160). Italics added.
[8] Hourani (1968: 41–68). [9] Cohen (1973). [10] Havemann (1983: 322).
[11] Philipp (2002: 102–3).

beginning of the nineteenth century. The growing trading activity of this community with British merchants—first clandestinely and then more openly in defiance of Acre's commercial monopoly—broke the city's tight control over the entire region. And it was made possible precisely because at that particular moment in history, Beirut lay outside the military reach of the regional power in Acre.

Although considerable efforts went into reinforcing Beirut's fortifications and water supply after ousting the Russian occupation of 1772, Beirut's trade had generally dwindled under Aḥmad al-Jazzār. There had been efforts of little consequence by Italian and Danish merchants to promote Beirut's harbour in the eighteenth century. Then, in 1808 a French consular representative in Acre recognized that Beirut had replaced Sidon as the port of Damascus.[12] Because of monopoly control in Sidon and Acre, captains of the British merchant fleet soon began to realize that better deals could be struck in Beirut. Sulaymān Pasha al-ʿĀdil, the ruler of Acre between 1804 and 1818, was disturbed by these activities and in 1811 imposed a heavy fine on the merchants of Beirut. When Beirut refused to comply he considered military intervention. Significantly, resistance to the authorities in Acre was led by Muslim clerics (*ʿulamāʾ*) and Damascene merchant houses with branches in Beirut.[13] With the memory of their eviction from Beirut by Aḥmad al-Jazzār in 1773 still fresh, Druze leaders south of Beirut also teamed up with the merchants and *ʿulamāʾ* in Beirut to protect the city against Sulaymān Pasha's punitive strike and the Beiruti merchants continued to undermine the prices set in Acre.

The erosion of Sulaymān Pasha's control over Beirut turned out to be the weak spot in Acre's monopoly system and Thomas Philipp argues that 'if one looks for turning points in history this act of successful open resistance by the merchants of Beirut could be considered the beginning of Beirut's rise'.[14] When the prolific British globe trotter James Buckingham visited Syria and Palestine in the mid-1810s, Beirut was already considered a flourishing commercial city with an estimated 8,000 inhabitants. At this time an impressed French consul of Acre, Pillavoine, visited Beirut and commented: 'the Pasha of Acre is without authority. His customs official, who is one of his slaves, is taunted if he causes the least irritation. The representative of the Pasha is nothing, the Mufti everything.'[15] Consul Pillavoine suggested to the Quay d'Orsay that the consulate be moved from Acre to Beirut and emphatically summed up his assessment with the explanation that Beirut had become 'a

[12] Philipp. 127–8.

[13] 13 Nov. 1812. Quoted in Philipp (2002: 129). Many of these traders dealt privately with a merchant from Mount Lebanon, a certain Yūsuf Karam, in Malta.

[14] Quoted in Philipp (2002: 129).

[15] 15 Oct. 1813. Quoted in Philipp (2002: 129).

Republic of Merchants [a byword that has stuck until today] with their own powers and laws'.[16]

Immigration shaped the first phase of Beirut's regional ascendancy as a mercantile enclave in a region of monopoly rule. As a 'merchant republic', Beirut thrived against the odds of the regional urban hierarchy and, I argue, against the adverse structure of its own urban layout. So far, Beirut's ascendancy was not the outcome of a deliberate government planning effort. On the contrary, the city distinguished itself as an urban asylum for immigrants from embattled regions in Bilad al-Sham. For all these migrants, Beirut's walls provided protection while the town's notables acquired something of a reputation for bravely defying the regional authorities.

Beirut became not only a cherished prize but also an uncomfortably autonomous entity in the struggle for regional hegemony. Since his capture of Beirut in 1777, al-Jazzār Pasha had been required to pay the sultan in Istanbul an annual tithe of 60,000 piastres for this urban tax farm or *iltizām*.[17] By 1809, tenancy of the Beirut *iltizām* had risen considerably and cost Sulaymān Pasha of Acre some 60 *bourses* (or 300,000 piastres) per year.[18] The growing prosperity of Beirut made it an attractive but expensive city to hold as well as a difficult city to control.

The Egyptian Occupation and the Making of a Port-City

Of all the *échelles* of the Levant at the turn of the eighteenth century, Beirut was the maritime town with least imperial authority within its walls. Ottoman governors resided elsewhere and military barracks were still absent.[19] Its commercial assertion notwithstanding, Beirut's formal politico-administrative recognition was still denied by the regional powers residing elsewhere. At the beginning of the nineteenth century, Beirut did not yet have a customs office while Tripoli was promisingly considered 'a small-scale Marseille' as major endpoint of the Mediterranean silk trade.[20] Although the customs authorities in Tripoli already expressed worries about the increasing trade going through the port of Beirut, it was only under Egyptian rule in the 1830s that Beirut was transformed into a port-city (see Figure 1).

The main concern of Ibrāhīm Pasha, the Egyptian general and son of the ruler of Egypt, Meḥmed ʿAlī Pasha, was to reinstate Damascus as the region's

[16] 24 Oct. 1814. Quoted ibid. 130.

[17] Ismail and Chehab (1976: i, 50, 1, Dec. 1788).

[18] Ibid. 223, 2 July 1809.

[19] The first military barracks *intramuros* were built by Maḥmūd Nāmī Bey under the Egyptian rule in the 1830s. Between 1853 and 1861, the first extramural military complex was built on the Qantari hillside. See Ch. 9.

[20] Özveren (Ph.D. thesis, 1990: 117).

FIG. 1. Port of Beirut, 1830s

political centre between Adana in the north and Gaza in the south. With public security (temporarily) restored in Mount Lebanon and coastal trade revived, Beirut matured into the uncontested port of Damascus.[21] Under Egyptian military rule, the power of the emir of Mount Lebanon, Bashīr II al-Shihābī, was circumscribed by Ibrāhīm Pasha. In contrast to the joint jurisdiction of mountain and plain under al-Jazzār, the Egyptians soon placed the coastal cities under loyal administrators (*mutasallims*) who were independent of the Shihābī emirs of the Mountain.[22] Meanwhile, the Egyptian government heeded a recommendation of the Damascus advisory council to furnish Beirut with a local council. It consisted of a president, the French-trained, Egyptian officer-engineer, Maḥmūd Nāmī Bey, and twelve members, six Muslims and six Christians: ʿAbd al-Fattāḥ Agha Ḥamāda, ʿUmar Bayhum, Aḥmad al-ʿArīss, Ḥassan al-Barbīr, Amīn Ramaḍān, Aḥmad Jallūs, Jibrāʾīl Ḥumṣī, Bishāra Naṣrallah, Eliās Manāsa, Naṣīf Maṭar, Yusuf ʿAyrūṭ, and Mūsā Bustrus.[23] With the possible exception of Eliās Manāsa, whose father Yūsuf worked in the district administration of Beirut during Sulaymān's rule in Acre, none of these

[21] Chevallier (1968: 205–22). [22] Bowring (1840: 127).

[23] Rustum (1967*a*: 60). The Ḥamāda family was originally from Egypt before the family settled in Beirut in the early 19th cent. For biographical details on these families, see Hanssen (D.Phil. thesis, 2001: annex).

councillors were affiliated with the previous, burgeoning network of scribes, administrators, and financiers under the rulers of Acre.[24]

Instead, the council was a precursor to the municipal council of the 1860s where many of the sons and nephews of these members grappled with similar issues of urban development.[25] At the same time Ibrāhīm Pasha also paved the way for a rapid increase in European consular, commercial, and missionary presence in Syria.[26] By the 1830s European commercial expansion—especially the silk trade with Mount Lebanon—propelled Beirut into the orbit of the Europe-centred world-economy. The presence of Egyptian and Albanian soldiers and the establishment of a host of European consulates and businesses led to immigration and a hike in real estate value.[27] These changes facilitated unprecedented prosperity—a trend that was only magnified during and after the Crimean War (1853–6) before it came to a temporary halt during the civil war of 1860.[28]

The way in which the Egyptian officers—Ibrāhīm Pasha, his *mutasallim* Sulaymān Pasha, and the president of the Beirut advisory council, Maḥmūd Nāmī Bey—conceived of the city of Beirut differed fundamentally from how Jazzār Pasha had at the end of the eighteenth century. The maritime threat from the Russian fleet in the 1770s and Greek corsairs in the 1820s had forced Acre's rulers to consolidate Beirut's town walls, and fortify the seven gates and eight towers around the town centre. At the same time, the port of Beirut remained deliberately neglected as Acre's rulers discouraged trade from Beirut as a means to sustain their monopoly trade system with Europe. Whereas under the rulers of Acre military considerations had been paramount to urban development schemes of Beirut, the Egyptian rulers of the 1830s focused on facilitating maritime trade.

At the beginning of Maḥmūd Nāmī Bey's term of office, the new advisory council of Beirut was probably still busy clearing up the rubble from the 1821 earthquake. The port basin was exposed to violent storms and clogged up by what a contemporary traveller believed to be Roman columns.[29] Lacking sufficient funding for any large-scale port construction, the council was limited to building a single jetty from the debris in the basin to improve at least landing and loading facilities.[30] Moreover, traffic connections between the city centre and the port were non-existent and urgently needed development if Beirut was to attract the new steam-line trade in the Eastern Mediterranean.

[24] Philipp (2002: appendix C, p. 216). [25] See Ch. 5. [26] Makdisi (2000).
[27] Bowring (1840: 116–17). [28] See table in Chevallier (1968: 214).
[29] Blondel (1840: 57). [30] Seeden and Thorpe (1997–8: 246).

British consular sources complained in the mid-1830s about 'various local inconveniences to which commerce is exposed from the want of a sufficient number of warehouses—the State of the Customs House—the want of a mole'.[31] These and other critical assessments alarmed Nāmī Bey who applied his training as a naval engineer to generate urban development in Beirut. He divided Beirut into eight intramural districts and placed a police station in each. He then ordered street names to be posted on the main throughways, created commercial and health councils, and supervised the construction of the quarantine.[32] Under his leadership, the main intramural khans were renovated and warehouses enlarged near the port in order to improve handling of the growing volume of import and export trade.[33] The traveller Edouard Blondel noted the developments of the port area towards the end of Egyptian rule in Beirut: 'The streets closest to the sea which are inhabited almost exclusively by Europeans, consuls or merchants are of medium size. The houses which line them . . . are extremely irregular but built entirely of stone. It is true that penetrating further [into the city] the streets become narrower and winding.'[34]

Maḥmūd Nāmī Bey effectively transformed Beirut from a well-fortified tax farm into an open port-city servicing Mediterranean trade—a project his son Ibrāhīm Nāmī Bey was to continue as municipal president in the 1870s.[35] Beirut's urban restructuring occurred just in time for the Ottoman–European free trade agreements between 1838 and 1840 to take effect. As a newly shaped port-city, Beirut's merchants benefited from the commercial opportunities from the 1840s onwards.

However, 'opening' Bilad al-Sham to the world economy under Ibrāhīm Pasha came at the expense of the Druze community, especially their notables.[36] The Bowring report of 1840 and consular observers of the Egyptian occupation noted both the impoverishment of Maronite peasants and the alienation of Druze feudal lords. Harsh Egyptian conscription[37]—including some 2,000 men from Beirut, Sidon, and Tyre—and new taxation demands added to Bashīr II's long-standing policy of eviction, expropriation, and assassination of the Druze leadership and led to the anti-Egyptian and anti-Shihābi rebellion of Druze commoners in 1835–8.[38]

[31] British commercial report, 1835, quoted in Issawi (1977: 94).
[32] Rustum (1967*a*: 59, 61).
[33] On the khans in Beirut, see Chevallier (1982: 9–28).
[34] Blondel (1840: 11–12).
[35] See Ch. 5.
[36] See Polk (1963).
[37] Fahmy (1997: esp. 76–112).
[38] Havemann (1983).

Incorporating a Port-City

The administrative geography of Beirut within the Ottoman context had shifted for centuries according to the tides of regional politics. The town's immediate administrative superiors alternated between Damascus, Sidon, and Acre. For Druze emirs in the Shuf Mountains south of Beirut or Ottoman pashas ruling from provincial capitals, Beirut was a lucrative tax farm. In the 1830s, the Egyptians then turned Beirut into a port-city. Their eviction coincided with the proclamation of the Ottoman *Ḥaṭṭ-i Sherif* of 1839, which formally abolished tax-farming and ultimately paved the way for the incorporation of provincial towns into the new geo-administrative hierarchy of centralized Ottoman rule.[39]

In the 1840s, the 'men of the *tanẓīmāt*' devised schemes of crisis management whereby a select group of model provinces were designated as test cases. Based on these provincial experiments the administrative reforms were then applied to the rest of the empire's provinces.[40] The province of Sidon was chosen as such a model province mainly because of a sense of urgency to check European interventions and local unrest in adjacent Mount Lebanon. The province of Tripoli, on the other hand, was abolished altogether and incorporated into the enlarged province of Sidon. Although temporarily under the authority of the governor in Acre, Tripoli had been the capital of its own province for centuries. However, after the redrawing of administrative boundaries in Bilad al-Sham following the Provincial Laws of 1864 and 1867, Tripoli never recovered its former status.

The relationship between Mount Lebanon and Beirut became an issue of international concern by 1840. British consuls in Beirut were keen to see the jurisdiction of the emir of Mount Lebanon extend to the coastal cities, arguing 'that the influence in Syria of a Maritime Power like that of Great Britain would be much increased and fortified'.[41] The Maronite Shihābī factions for their part, too, pressed their French allies to support the incorporation of Beirut's coastal plain into the jurisdiction of their Christian mountain district. This process further weakened the long-standing, hereditary authority of the *muqāṭaʿa* estates of Druze Arslān and Tanūkhī landlords over Beirut.

With the outbreak of sectarian violence in Mount Lebanon in 1841, the Ottoman government shifted the headquarters of the governor general of the province of Sidon from Acre to Beirut (Map 1). This burgeoning port-city was chosen as a model city for local government reforms along with the towns

39 ʿAwwāḍ (1969: 64–5). 40 Hanssen (2002). 41 Consul Moore in Farah (2000: 71).

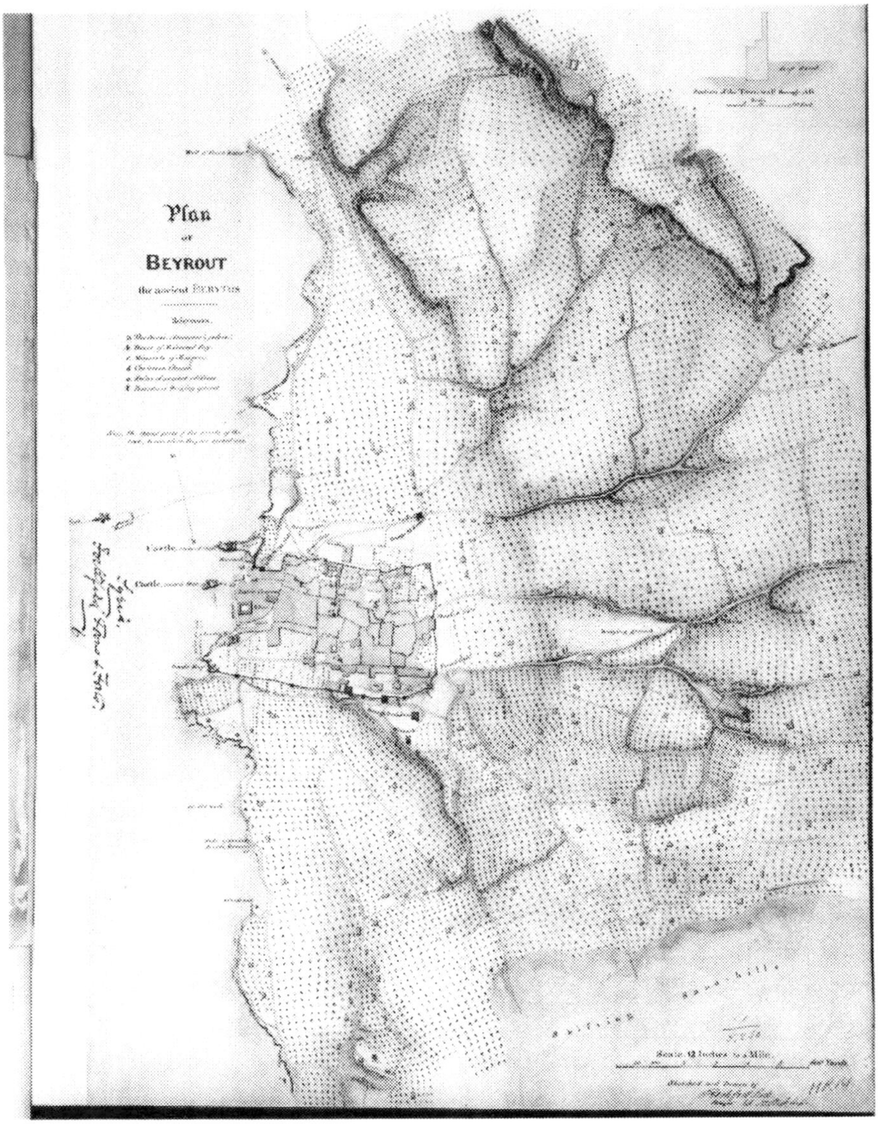

Map 1. Beirut in 1841, after Egyptian rule

Bursa and Adrianople. A provincial council manned by sixteen members consisted of imperial bureaucrats, local *ʿulamā,*ʾ and dignitaries, and convened regular sessions. According to British parliamentarian David Urquhart who visited the region in the mid-1840s, these councillors quite effectively checked the imperial authority of both the governor and the treasurer. 'The Megilis had complete authority over every branch of law, criminal, civil and commercial' and full competence over fiscal and public works planning where 'the Pasha is only one of its members, and its President his rival. . . . Here is a small Parliament, in which every member attends in his place during transaction of business, with a virtue and a patriotism.'[42]

For most years between 1841 and 1860, the position of the president of the urban advisory council in Beirut was held by ʿAbd al-Fattāḥ Agha Ḥamāda, who replaced Maḥmūd Nāmī Bey and whose son Muḥyī al-Dīn was a leading figure in municipal politics and Muslim reform organizations in the 1870s and 1880s:

> [t]he former Divan Effendi of this Ayalet . . . Feti Aga [Ḥamāda] had filled the office under successive Pashas from the times of the Egyptians. He managed them all, and made himself necessary to each, by knowing how to pull strings of the various Marionettes of plain, city and mountain; turning knowledge into power and power into money.[43]

'Emasculating Damascus'? the 'Capitalization' of Beirut

Thus far, I have populated, localized, and fine-tuned the story of the structural formation of a port-city, which Beirut shared with a number of other rival port-cities in the Eastern Mediterranean.[44] However, there was nothing about this process that guaranteed Beirut's lasting economic and political primacy. Why did Beirut maintain and expand its strategic economic position even against the odds of extensive warfare and destruction in its hinterland?

After the civil war of 1860, a passionate battle of petitions between Damascenes and Beirutis erupted which was driven by the general perception that prosperity proved elusive. The lobbyists in Beirut reasoned that their city required political weight through administrative upgrading in order to jump-start economic life and political stability after the sociocide in the mountains.

In an economy increasingly determined by mass export production and monetarization under chronic instability of currencies, the moneylending '*seraff* system' provided the vital link in the supply and commodity chains between peasant production and Mediterranean trade.[45] In 1848, a British consular report listed the 'most respectable' merchant houses of Beirut.[46] A host of

[42] Urquhart (1860: 159, 164, 225). [43] Ibid. 153.

[44] For a good study of this formation see Özveren (Ph.D. thesis, 1990). See also Quataert *et al.* (1993).

[45] Doumani (1996: 135–401).

[46] PRO, FO 78/754, Beirut, 27 Dec. 1848, quoted in Issawi (1977: 98).

newcomer families, mainly Christians who had migrated to Beirut from Aleppo, Damascus, Tripoli, Acre, Sidon, and Mount Lebanon a generation or two earlier, joined the seven leading Damascene merchant families that had resisted Acre's dictate in the 1810s and 1820s. As a group of families with a Midas touch, common goals, and fears, they formed the nucleus of Beirut's political economy in the latter parts of the nineteenth century. Many of these notable families were to champion the struggle for the province of Beirut and were to dominate its political economy.

Some of these notables had already been influential under the Egyptians, such as the *ʿālim*-cum-merchant Barbīr brothers and Aḥmad al-ʿArīs, and the councillor in the Egyptian *diwan*, ʿUmar Bayhum. New representatives included the Greek Orthodox merchants and moneylending houses Dabbās and Fayyāḍ, the Fīʿānī brothers, Bustrus and Nephews, Niqūla Sursuq and brothers, Sursuq and Jammāl, Rizqallah and Ibrāhīm Ṭrād, Naʿmatallah Khūrī, Yūsuf Sayyūr, and Yūsuf Dāghir.[47] Non-Orthodox Christians included the Naqqāsh brothers, Tūbiyya and Aṣfar, the Farajallahs, Thābit and Co., Buṭrus Kabbāba, Niqūla Jāhil and son,[48] Ḥabīb Dahhān, ʿAbdallah Ḥannā and ʿAwda, ʿAbdallah Khūrī and Anṭūn Naṣrallah. The Nawfal brothers had recently arrived from Tripoli. One of them, Naʿmatallah, was to become head of Beirut's customs office after 1860 and official Ottoman–Arab translator, while Niqūla Nawfal became a member of the Ottoman parliament.[49] Francis and Antūn Misk were Roman Catholics originally from Aleppo. Francis had become an influential British protégé in the service of Bashīr II in the powerful position of a *divan efendisi* who was 'to the Pasha what the grand vizier was to the sultan'.[50]

Despite the growing number of very wealthy local merchants and moneylenders, however, one frustrated chief accountant of the Beirut office of the Imperial Ottoman Bank (BIO)—the first branch to open in the Arab provinces in 1856—discerned a distinct lack of capitalist spirit among these wealthy Beirutis:

> There is a large amount of wealth accumulated in the towns; but it must be borne in mind that wealth is not capital, and although we may be, like Midas, surrounded with

[47] On these Greek Orthodox families, see Kamel-Salameh (1998).

[48] Niqūla Jāhil's family arrived in Beirut from Acre. His son was a member of the Syrian Scientific Society of 1868 and a dragoman at the American consulate.

[49] Niqūla Nawfal entered parliament in 1876 as a deputy of Tripoli, Syria, and famously ridiculed the Ottoman capital during a parliament session: 'We are from the provinces, we have been voting since the beginning of the *tanẓīmāt*, Istanbul, however, has encountered elections only this year.' Hanssen (2002: 71).

[50] Farah (2000: 79).

gold, yet if that gold be unproductive, it is valueless. The essence of wealth consists in the capacity of supplying the wants and ministering to the desires of men, and not in the capacity of being accumulated; and it is, therefore, only when wealth is made use of for the purpose of reproduction that it becomes really useful, and takes the name of capital. *In Syria there is a great deal of wealth, but very little capital.*

The insecurity of property, which existed for so many years under the Ottoman rule, and the total absence of any establishments in which money could be safely deposited, compelled the Syrians to invest their gains in the most valuable and, at the same time, the most portable articles [like] jewels, and it is startling, when visiting at the private houses of the native population, to see the quantity of diamonds and other precious stones worn by the females of the family.[51]

This lonely accountant was very much a precursor of a new dimension of the capitalist system that fundamentally restructured existing economic practices and dynamics, urban planning, and state–city relations—processes in which '[c]apital accumulation and the production of urbanization [went] hand in hand'.[52] In late Ottoman Beirut, these processes were driven by political *and* financial capitalization which Beirut's emerging middle class was well-positioned and able to appropriate. By the time the sultan announced the centralized provincial structure, the Ottoman government relied on these intermediaries to operate its policies locally. Beirut's merchants and notables were willing and demanding partners in the application of reform. They actively sought a political path to Istanbul in order to mould financial capitalization at home.

The Provincial Law of 1864

When the Sublime Porte dispatched the pacification mission to Beirut to investigate the atrocities of the 1860 civil wars in Mount Lebanon and Damascus, the special envoy Fuad Pasha successfully averted the imminent threat of French military occupation. He based his policies as much on the recommendations of the International Commission of Inquiry as on the body of previous Ottoman reform experiences in Bilad al-Sham.[53] Between Lord Dufferin's pro-imperial proposal to assimilate Mount Lebanon into the rest of Syria on account of what he considered the previous failure of 'native government',[54] and French consul general Béclard's vision for an independent 'Christian Mountain', Fu'ād Pasha's plan to keep the two provinces of Mount

[51] Farley (1859: 37–8; emphasis added). See Ch. 3. [52] Harvey (1985: ii. 190).
[53] Makdisi (2002*a*: 601–17). [54] Zachs (2000: 160–76).

Lebanon and Damascus distinct and to institute an independent supreme council of district governors (*qaimaqam*) proved more realistic and won the day.[55]

When the *Réglement Organique* was finally ratified in 1861, it constituted a model of shared rights and responsibilities carried by the first inter-confessional, administrative council of a unified Mount Lebanon.[56] Indeed, the new order in Mount Lebanon was to be adopted in other provinces and ultimately served as one of the blueprints for the provincial law of the entire empire in 1864.[57] But the incorporation of Mount Lebanon into the orbit of direct—albeit regionally autonomous—Ottoman rule antagonized powerful clerical and landed Maronite circles in the mountain. Supported by like-minded French diplomats and missionaries, they lobbied against what they considered the imposition of an Ottoman governor. Maronite resistance to Dāwūd Pasha, the first governor of Mount Lebanon, remained strong until the unsuccessful revolt of 1866, which was led by the ambitious young notable of the northern mountain, Yūsuf Karam.[58]

In significant contrast, a veritable 'honeymoon' between Christian and Muslim urban notables and Fu'ād Pasha unfolded in Beirut. The Ottoman special envoy used lavish medal ceremonies to forge allegiance between the city's upper echelons and the reforming Ottoman state.[59] The notables of the city reciprocated in this highly conspicuous political grooming game. In *Ḥadīqat al-Akhbār*, Beirut's first bi-weekly newspaper, the city's literati outdid each other with poetic eulogies to Fu'ād Pasha.[60] The Sursuqs flew Ottoman flags from their family mansion in East Beirut and held a banquet for the special envoy from Istanbul.[61] Jirjī Mudawwar organized a sumptuous party for Dāwūd Pasha after his inaugural speech.[62] In emergency measures, the local authorities repaired and paved roads in the quarter of al-Qīrāt connecting the residence of Fu'ād Pasha and his officers with the Grand Serail across town.[63] In honour of the Ottoman government the main throughway from al-Qīrāt to the city centre was renamed 'Ṭarīq Fu'ād Pasha', and the road to the Grand Serail became 'al-Ṭarīq al-Sulṭānī'.[64] The newspaper praised the re-

[55] Farah (2000: 682, 685, 692). [56] Khalaf (1968: 245), and Akarli (1993: 149–62).

[57] Spagnolo (1971: 25–48). [58] Hakim (D.Phil. thesis, 1997: 64–74).

[59] *Ḥadīqat al-Akhbār* mentioned the award ceremonies of Muḥyī al-Dīn Bahyum, the provincial Arabic scribe Khalīl Ayyūb, Ḥabīb Muṭrān, and Yūsuf Thābit in 1860–1. Fu'ād Pasha's successors in Syria continued this practice.

[60] *Ḥadīqat al-Akhbār*, Naṣīf al-Yāzijī: 20 Dec. 1860; ʿAbd al-Raḥmān Naḥḥās: 3 Jan. 1860; Francis Marrāsh: 7 Feb. 1861. [61] *Ḥadīqat al-Akhbār*, 21 Feb. 1861. [62] *Ḥadīqat al-Akhbār*, 25 July 1861.

[63] *Ḥadīqat al-Akhbār*, 29 Nov. 1860. [64] *Ḥadīqat al-Akhbār*, 31 Jan. 1861.

establishment of order and stability by Fu'ād Pasha and passionately pressed for continued Ottoman presence.

The innovations in telecommunication and transportation that swept the Ottoman Empire at the time nurtured this process of integration. In November 1860, Beirut became the first city in Bilad al-Sham to open a telegraph station, although it was connected to Istanbul only after Aleppo's station was completed.[65] The first telegram was sent from Beirut to Istanbul on 1 February 1863.[66] In the same year, the Beirut–Damascus Road was completed after some five years of construction. The road crossed Mount Lebanon at midpoint and shortened the arduous and often dangerous passage over the mountain from two days to twelve hours.[67] Over half a dozen European steam lines called regularly at the port of Beirut and the trade volume began to exceed pre-war levels. In particular, the rapid extension of the local silk industry after 1860 spearheaded Beirut's economic recovery.[68] The development of Beirut as a transport and communication centre also affected public throughways inside the city. Writing on Beirut's post-war recovery, the American missionary Henry Jessup commented that 'the streets of Beirut were being widened and macadamized to allow the carriages of the French Damascus Road Company to pass'.[69]

The Beirutis had every reason to be optimistic and felt they were in favour with the imperial government in Istanbul. In 1862, the sultan donated to Beirut 'three hairs from the beard of the prophet Mohammed, to be placed in one of the mosques', in recognition of the city's position and function as one of the gateways to the Kaʿba—the official port of the Ottoman pilgrimage to Mecca.[70] Beirut was linked to Istanbul and Damascus not only infrastructurally but symbolically as well.

On 8 November 1864, the sum of twenty years of provincial inspection tours, petitions, rule by councils, and model provinces became codified in a forty-odd-page legal document known as the Provincial Law.[71] The provincial capital was declared the centre of power. The governor general was directly appointed by the sultan and from 1864 onwards given paramount authority over a host of carefully compartmentalized provincial offices whose head bureaucrats were also appointed from Istanbul. Most importantly, governors

[65] On the telegraph network in Syria, see Rogan (1998: 113–28). [66] Jessup (1910: 265).
[67] Tresse (1936: 227–52). See also Fawaz (1998: 19–28).
[68] Labaki (1984: 88–96, 103–4). In 1867, fifty-five out of a total of sixty-seven factories were locally owned.
[69] Jessup (1910: 265). [70] Ibid. 245.
[71] BBA, YEE, 37/302/47/112. The law was fine-tuned in 1867 and 1871, and overhauled in 1913.

general depended on the cooperation of members of half-elected, half-permanent provincial councils which were made up of *ʿulamāʾ* and wealthy local dignitaries. These representatives held considerable popular support and mediating power *vis-à-vis* the representatives of the Ottoman state. Canonized in printed law and applied empire-wide, this appearance of administrative order 'intended to be essentially an extension of the civil bureaucracy at the center'.[72]

The Changing Political Geographies of Bilad al-Sham

> The art of geography is of immense benefit for mankind to the extent that some people give it priority over the art of history because man is concerned with the divisions of his existence, of where he resides and what it constitutes. Therefore he requires first to look at his house [bayt—also family] then to his clan and his people. The reason why I give this speech is [my belief] that the geography of the province of Syria is more important [for us] than world geography.[73]

The growing number of prominent merchants, professionals, and dignitaries in Beirut applauded the reforms but, in an arguably unprecedented move, arrogated the right to determine the administrative geography of Greater Syria by calling for 'provincial self-determination'. Notably, the Beiruti struggle for a provincial capital sought not to oppose but to improve this law and Ottoman rule more generally. When the Provincial Law was applied to Bilad al-Sham in 1865, the news came as a heavy blow to the aspirations of Beirut's notables. Beirut had been a model city of Ottoman provincial reform in the 1840s, but the official announcement of the imperial *firmān* in Damascus on 1 May 1865 decreed that the historical provinces of Sidon and of Damascus be merged into a single new 'super-province' of Syria with Damascus as its capital. As a consequence of this annexation, Beirut lost its privileged status as provincial seat of government of Sidon.

Administrative offices were dismantled, staff were required to move to Damascus, and the city's new secondary administrators were left without initiative and authority. Beirut was downgraded to one of eight *mutaṣarrifiyya*s (subprovinces, or *sancak*s) reporting to the capital Damascus. In his reform proposal to the imperial government dated 21 July 1865, Rushdī Pasha justified his division of Bilad al-Sham at great length. He insisted with no small satisfaction that his reorganization of local councils and tribunals reflected the

[72] Findley (1986: 4).

[73] Yūsuf Shalfūn [1868], 'Fī-taqsīm Sūriyya', in Y. Khūrī (1990: 153–64). Shalfūn had been a student of Khalīl al-Khūrī and later launched his own printing press in Beirut, *al-maṭbaʿa al-ʿumūmiyya*.

region's complex sectarian composition. His proposal, he claimed, was based on statistics, 'on a map of Syria, and on recourse to those with an understanding of true information about geography'.[74]

The merchants and notables of Beirut were devastated and began their campaign as soon as they learnt of the plans for the super-province of Syria. Between 1864 and 1888, joint petitions by Muslim and Christian dignitaries were frequently sent to the Porte begging the sultan to turn Beirut into a provincial capital.[75] On 24 April 1865—a week before the official announcement of the provincial reorganization—the Greek Catholic patriarch of Syria, Gregorius, who resided in Beirut, sent a petition in Arabic to the Sublime Porte in Istanbul.[76] This petition was signed by priests, teachers, and merchants. They effectively invited the imperial government to assume direct rule as a way to facilitate urban growth at a time when ideologues of the mountain were still advocating an 'Ottoman-free zone' in Mount Lebanon.

Some eighty urban notables signed a second petition two days later calling for the establishment of an Ottoman provincial capital in Beirut.[77] The petition first thanked the Sublime Porte for the recent construction work in Beirut, 'as a reinvestment for the tax collections in Beirut'. To nip criticism from Damascus in the bud the petition went on to assure that

> Beirut is not envious of Damascus or other inland cities, since commerce, the annual pilgrimage and the surrounding agriculture of Damascus had made it a successful but different city. Damascus does not need the status of a capital, as the most important factors are its hinterland and the headquarters of the imperial army. By contrast, our city has only flourished at the time it became a seat of government for the province of Sayda. Beirut's progress is dependent on attracting more people to the city. At the moment, imperial coffers do not provide for that, [which] is a pity, after Beirut has progressed so much in the architectural domain.[78]

The signatories left no doubt that they saw themselves and their city as acting in the spirit of Ottoman reform. Indeed, the text effectively criticized the

[74] BBA, ID *Meclis-i Vala no. 24238*, translated into Arabic in ʿAwwāḍ (1969: 347–51). In the Ottoman reform period statistical and cartographical representations of space were beginning to determine provincial boundaries. Prior to the *tanẓīmāt*, a place's demarcations and administrative belonging were ranked in pyramid-shaped lists from the capital down to the smallest hamlet unit, the *nāḥiye*. While Ottoman cartography had a long legacy, *tanẓīmāt* maps of the Ottoman Empire represented a break in technique, application, and dissemination and were part and parcel of Ottoman education and—by extension—of the Ottomanist reform project of the Hamidian regime. See Fortna (2001; 164–201).

[75] Four of these petitions are kept in BBA, ID, 37280. This struggle has previously been discussed with the assumption that the province of Syria was a more natural entity than the split into two provinces in 1888. See Abu Manneh (1992: 9–26).

[76] Gregorius became bishop of Acre in 1856 and later founded the Greek Catholic Patriarchal School in Beirut. He died in Damascus in 1897. See S. al-Khūrī (1992: 363).

[77] Both petitions are enclosed in BBA, ID, *37280*. [78] BBA, ID, *37280*, 26 Apr. 1865.

imperial government for not doing more to promote Beirut as an Ottoman city. The second petition seems to have been drafted by leading Muslim clerics. But seals of denominational institutions (the Maronite and Armenian patriarchs) and Christian families attest to a supra-confessional campaign for the city of Beirut.[79] The list of the two hundred petitioners was a 'who's who' of nineteenth-century Beirut.[80] Many of them will reappear throughout this study as municipal members, journalists, educators, patrons of public construction, or real estate investors and concessionaires. Drawn together in the common cause for 'their' city, these individuals and their families were to constitute the local, formative force behind Beirut's development in the second half of the nineteenth century and beyond.

The Damascene notables for their part sent irate counter-petitions to Istanbul. They employed a narrative of persuasion that was based on the city's customary privileges. The petition accused the Beirutis of destabilizing the empire. Their insolent claims, the Damascenes wrote, were entirely illegitimate because they violated tradition and disregarded history:

> The Beirutis have submitted a petition demanding that their city be the *markaz* of a *wilāya* [arguing that] their city is a commercial place. [In doing so,] they did not take into consideration the fact that Damascus unites different worlds and pillars [commerce and other]. It is the responsibility of the city of Damascus to bring different *millets* to coexist and to take care of their different aspirations. Damascus is the gateway to Mecca and dealing with aspects of the pilgrimage is one of the most noble duties that cannot be regulated without the presence of a [strong] governor general. Nor did they consider that their thoughts are below the ideas of the Sublime State [*al-dawla*] in demanding to change what the Sublime Porte has decreed . . . We submit this petition hoping that you do not consider the demands of the Beirutis.[81]

The difference in self-representation between the two documents is striking. The Beirutis argued in the language of reform, holding the Ottoman government accountable for its reform intentions and demanding they be applied to their own cause. In order to avoid sounding too disrespectful of imperial authority, they phrased the text so as to play down the gravity of their demand by reminiscing about the days when Beirut had been Ottoman provincial capital of Sidon. By contrast, the Damascenes presented themselves as the time-honoured guardians of the sultan's rule and the protectors of the religious minorities in Bilad al-Sham. Were the sultan to grant the demands of the

79 The names on this petition, as far as they could be deciphered, are listed in Hanssen (D.Phil. thesis, 2001: annex).

80 The name of the then *muftī*, Shaykh Muḥammad Fatḥallah, was the only conspicuous absence.

81 BBA, ID, *37280*, undated, but judging from the dates on the seals, it was the same year, 1281/1865.

Beirutis, he would betray his most loyal servants in Damascus while putting his lot in with a disrespectful bunch of merchant upstarts in Beirut.

The popularity of the governor general dwindled fast and when he failed to find ways to contain the 1865 cholera epidemic he was recalled to Istanbul. Rushdi Pasha appeared overwhelmed with the task of applying the Provincial Law in his new 'super-province'—a province that would have been 'too vast even for Plato to administer', to forestall Khalīl Ghānim's later polemic in parliament. After a brief and equally hapless attempt by his successor to manage the vast province, Meḥmet Rashīd Pasha took office in Damascus (August 1866–October 1871).[82]

Upon his arrival in Damascus, the new governor general laid the foundations for a new administrative and infrastructural centre outside the walled city. In the years to come, and particularly during Midḥat Pasha's rule (1878–80), Damascus underwent a resounding building boom. Marja Square was developed as a new government quarter around the Old Serail (built in 1808) where administrative and public buildings mushroomed. As capital of a super-province, Damascus became a model *tanẓīmāt* city and underwent a tremendous architectural and urban expansion *extramuros*. The Damascene countryside of previous centuries was connected through wide boulevards to the city centre, to distant Hawran in the south, Aleppo in the north, and on the Beirut–Damascus road to the Mediterranean coast.[83]

The Beirutis were jealous. They had envisaged these urban developments for their own city and felt stifled. To appease them, Rashīd Pasha granted Beirut the provincial seat of the commercial court and the residence of the foreign relations officer of the province of Syria.[84] He also convinced his government in Istanbul to fund a military school in Beirut which appears to have been in planning since 1861.[85] These measures did little to console the Beirutis. The annexation to Damascus had come at a particularly bad time for Beirut. After two good years of trade, import and export activity of the port dropped sharply when a cholera epidemic hit the Levant in the summer of 1865, costing 3,000 lives and causing the evacuation of tens of thousands of Beirutis.[86] Trade came

[82] Rashīd Pasha was previously stationed in Izmir where he was initiated to a masonic lodge. See Morris (1875: 3).

[83] Weber (1998: 292–343).

[84] *Ḥadīqat al-Akhbār* (16–28 May 1867). This post was occupied by none other than Khalīl al-Khūrī himself for over twenty years until he fell out with the governor general of Syria. His influence and pro-Ottoman convictions were much resented by the French consuls. Ismail and Chehab (1976: xv. 123, 17 Oct. 1884 xv. 145, 12 Oct. 1885 xv, 160–1, 10 May 1886). Khalīl al-Khūrī (1836–1907) was born into a Greek Orthodox family in the mountain town of Shuwayfat. His family moved to Beirut after the withdrawal of the Egyptian army from Bilad al-Sham in 1840.

[85] *Ḥadīqat al-Akhbār* (27 Aug. 1867 and 20 Dec. 1861).

[86] Issawi (1988: 51–4).

to a near standstill in Syria and when it picked up again in 1867 the balance of trade was markedly negative.[87]

Under these worrying circumstances, the Beirutis put much hope in the first general assembly of the new super-province of Syria, held in Beirut in December 1867. In the run-up to the meeting of representatives from every sub-province, the Beirut newspaper *Ḥadīqat al-Akhbār* sent clear messages to the Ottoman government. It expressed frustration at Beirut's administrative downgrading and linked it causally to the recent recession: 'Last year Beirut was afflicted by severe financial setbacks leading to a suspension of its trade. This is clearly a consequence of the abolition of the *eyālet* of Sidon, and of the transfer of the centre of the province to Damascus.'[88]

In October, Khalīl al-Khūrī, the editor of *Ḥadīqat al-Akhbār* and noted hobby archaeologist, stepped up the pressure and publicly floated the idea of power-sharing between Damascus and Beirut:

> The people of Beirut are still severely affected by the economic downturn that has gripped their city and their properties. They complain that this is related to the transfer of the provincial centre from their city [to Damascus] . . . We have already published their grievances that the sultanic government which is obliged to continue the cultivation [*ʿumrān*] of the country and the well-being of its population, does not respect the city of Beirut which is among the principal cities under the shadow of the Caliphate of his Majesty the Sultan . . . We derived from what we have learnt that the imperial government plans to uplift the damaged city. If it has not been made a permanent centre given the importance of internal matters accorded to Damascus it is necessary that Beirut be made to share with its neighbour the centre of the province.[89]

The idea of this article was later formulated as a petition demanding a power-sharing compromise, whereby the governor general was to reside in Damascus in the summer and in Beirut in the winter.[90] When the petition arrived in Istanbul in early 1868, the government studied the proposal carefully, but in a long report on the conditions in the province rejected it on the grounds that it was impracticable.[91] Nevertheless, under the new governor general, relations between Beirutis and the provincial government improved considerably. Rashīd Pasha himself appeared to have been efficient and popular in equal measures. He was able to divert Beiruti demands for an administrative upgrading of their city onto other more feasible issues such as the enlargement of the port and the establishment of a municipal council. Rushdī Pasha's previous claims to cartographic 'accuracy' notwithstanding, provincial borders and hier-

87 Kalla (Ph.D. thesis, 1969: table 32).
88 *Ḥadīqat al-Akhbār* (28 May 1867).
89 *Ḥadīqat al-Akhbār* (21 Oct. 1867).
90 *Ḥadīqat al-Akhbār* (31 Dec. 1867).
91 BBA, AD, vol. 905, 48–50, 6 May 1868.

archies continued to be challenged and negotiated. In June 1872, orders arrived from Istanbul to sever the Palestinian districts from Syria and create a new province in Palestine around Jerusalem.[92] The governor general of Syria, Ṣubḥī Pasha, considered this an attack on his authority and offered to resign. His resignation still pending, the newly appointed governor of Beirut arrived in August with orders from the grand vizier, Midḥat Pasha, to detach Beirut from the province of Syria and establish an autonomous coastal subprovince.[93] Not much else is known about this scheme and before any new directives could be implemented Midḥat Pasha was replaced by a rival at the Sublime Porte after only two months in office.

However, elsewhere in the province of Syria changes occurred. Probably under European diplomatic pressure on the Sublime Porte, Jerusalem was turned into a regionally autonomous province—a *mutaṣarifiyya* similar to Mount Lebanon—directly subordinate to the Ministry of the Interior in Istanbul.[94] The Ottoman decision to make Jerusalem the capital of a regionally autonomous subprovince set the stage for future campaigning in Beirut. Christian notables sensed a new opportunity for the creation of the province of Beirut, and argued a case of precedent at the Porte. However, they were rebuffed 'for such unreasonable and self-interested demands, and threatened with . . . punishment'.[95] The Porte must have suspected that the motive of the prime movers behind the petition, Ḥabīb Bustrus and Niqūla Sursuq, was personal benefit. In 1872 the two families owned about 230,000 *dönüms* (*c.*57,500 hectares), with a peasant population of some 4,000 inhabitants in seventeen northern Palestinian villages.[96] Shifting the jurisdiction of their newly acquired land to the courts of capital Beirut would place their landowning affairs on their own doorstep.

The Phoenician Card and the Parliamentary Debate

In the mid-1870s, the newly established newspaper, *Thamarāt al-Funūn*, joined the struggle for the province of Beirut.[97] An article in the local news section held the Ottoman government responsible for the city's welfare, particularly with regard to recent cases of precedent in the Ottoman coastal provinces:

> It is well-known that the majority of the coastal population—and Beirut in the vanguard—has sent telegrams to the Porte to request to separate it from the administration

92 Abu Manneh (1999: 44–5). 93 Gross (Ph.D. thesis, 1979: 186–90). 94 ʿAwwāḍ (1969: 71).
95 BBA, AD, vol. 902, 12 Oct. 1872. 96 Muslih (1988: 43).
97 On the early spread of newspapers in Beirut see Tarrazi (1913: i).

of the province of Syria. The annexation has proven to be a strain on work and it is no longer feasible. If one's eyes are closed who will know the aspects of injustice. The coastal people are not demanding something outrageous and unprecedented, given what formations have recently occurred. Adana with its dependencies was severed from Aleppo and made an independent province. Likewise the island of Cyprus was severed from the province of Mediterranean Archipelago and made an independent *mutaṣarrifiyya*. In this familiar pattern, the *mutaṣarrifiyya* of Jerusalem was made independent.[98]

By the late 1870s, the campaign drew larger circles and the Beirutis took their cause to the imperial capital itself. The general euphoria around the establishment of the imperial parliament provided a new and wide window of opportunity for provincial grievances to be voiced and heard in Istanbul. The delegates for Beirut managed to raise their cause in three parliamentary hearings on 31 December 1877, and 17–18 January 1878. A series of heated debates pitted the Beirutis Niqūla Naqqāsh, Khalīl Ghānim, ʿAbd al-Raḥīm Badrān, and the forceful reformer Yūsuf Żiya al-Khālidī from Jerusalem, in an alliance against the Damascene and Aleppine delegates.[99]

The Beirutis and al-Khālidī presented a memorandum to the Lower House of Parliament and argued for a separate province of Beirut on two grounds. Not only would a coastal province be nothing more than a return to the previous state of two provinces, but subsuming the districts from Acre to Tripoli under Beirut's auspices would also contain the same geography as ancient Phoenicia and could therefore be called the province of Phoenicia, 'Finikye vilāyeti namiyle'.[100] Ernest Renan's 1864 archaeological study *Mission Phénicienne* clearly reverberated in the regional political imagination.

Invoking the mythical lands of Phoenicia as the basis of a modern administration was more than an obvious polemic against the Syrianist interpretation of Bilad al-Sham's history espoused since the late 1850s by the Protestant missionaries and the ubiquitous Khalīl al-Khūrī.[101] The fact that the idea of Phoenicia as a political entity was used in public discourse by the late 1870s suggests that it predates the invention of latter-day national myths and originated in the battle over the nature of 'benevolent reforms' of the Ottoman provincial administration and the administrative divisions of Bilad al-Sham.

In Parliament the Beirut lobby argued against the Damascenes' charge that an administrative change in favour of Beirut would result in 'a misallocation of

98 *Thamarāt al-Funūn* (21 Feb. 1878).

99 Us (ed.), *Meclis-i Mebusan Zabit Ceridesi* (Istanbul, 1939–54), i/9 (1st term, 19. session), 132–5, i/19. 252–53, i/20. 265–8.

100 Us, *Meclis-i Mebusan*, 132. In the 1890s, the Ottoman discovered and banned the Phoenicia Lodge in Beirut. See BBA, YHUS, 265/96, 9 Oct. 1892 and YHUS, 265/177, 18 Oct. 1892. Asher Kaufmann (2000) has recently discussed the origins of political Phoenicianism.

101 Zachs (2001: 145–73).

resources for the central government'.[102] On the contrary, they retorted, 'the dissolution of the current province will yield results that would be beneficial to the imperial treasury [as] the wages of the governor general will be covered by extra income'.[103] With Beirut's estimated 'annual budget of around 240.000 piastres . . . the division of Syria will raise no complaints or extra costs'. The memorandum concluded by 'proposing to inaugurate the new province around Beirut at the beginning of the next fiscal year [in April 1878]'.[104]

In constant contact with proceedings at Parliament, the journalists in Beirut also stepped up their pressure. At the January session a telegraphed petition with some twenty signatures from Beirut was read out that reminded the House of the inconvenience of distance between the two cities. The first to respond, Tawfīq Efendi al-Majālī from Karak in the province of Syria, retorted that 'the journey from Beirut to Damascus only takes about ten hours. That is not a big deal!'[105] One Saʿīdi Efendi from Aleppo wondered whether the then governor of Beirut, Ra'ūf Efendi, might be behind the latest Beiruti request seeking personal promotion. One ʿAlīsh Pasha from the Danube province defended the status quo because 'at this time we have so many marshals and governors general. We do not have enough subprovinces (*mutaṣarrifliks*)'.[106]

Incensed by these evasions, Khalīl Ghānim took to the floor: 'The people there [in Beirut] wrote for the sake of their own welfare. They do not necessarily want Ra'ūf Efendi as a governor general. If the Porte wishes, it can send another official.'[107] He suggested that more 'research into the matter was needed'. He argued passionately that

> the Beirutis want to be separated from Damascus. Beirut is a commercial place. Moreover, between Beirut and Damascus lies the special province of Mount Lebanon. They are cut off from each other. I also wish general welfare to Damascus, but Beirut and Damascus are different, they are not connected. Tripoli is similar to Beirut, like Hawran is similar to Damascus. Hawran is an arena for cotton production. Tripoli and Beirut are arenas of trade. One province is too vast. There are immense problems in the subprovince of Hawran. That is where, as Badrān Efendi informed you yesterday, the Druze Mountain is located and the situation is fragile. And there is another mountain range near Tripoli, that of the Nusaris [Alawis]. In short, even Plato could not have governed there. So how can the existing administration be made equitable? Naqqāsh

102 Kayali (1992: 29). 103 Us, *Meclis-i Mebusan*, 132. 104 Ibid.
105 Ibid. 252. 106 Ibid.
107 Ibid. 253. Khalīl Ghānim was a Maronite journalist and lawyer from Beirut who became a leading francophile, Arab Young Turk in the 1890s. He died in Paris in 1902. In the 1890s, the Hamidian government suspected him of having been a member of the 'Phoenicia' Lodge. In the 1860s Beirut had a population of around sixty to seventy freemasons who were divided into the Palestine Lodge, founded in 1861 by the Grand Lodge of Scotland, the Lebanon Lodge, founded in 1869 by the Grand Lodge (Orient) of France, and 'the Phoenicians'. See Morris (1875: 215–220, 556).

Efendi presented us with a memorandum. Now we need to form a committee to investigate. The inspectors will inform us by telegram on the basis of which a general reorganization may be proposed to the House.[108]

After the president of the House heard the arguments of both sides, he decided to heed Ghānim's proposal for a parliamentary commission of inquiry. However, back in Beirut the composition and work of the commission attracted sharp criticism from the local press which complained about parliamentary intransigence and lack of sympathy regarding their entirely legitimate cause:

We held great hopes when the Syrian delegates [discussed the issue] in parliament, and we waited patiently until we read in a newspaper from Istanbul what happened in the council. But we wonder with curiosity why the Syrian delegates agreed to charging Saʿīdī Efendi, the delegate for Mar'ash [in the province of Aleppo] who does not have insight into the concerns of the coastal people, with the leadership [of the parliamentary inquiry]. Or for that matter ʿAlīsh Pasha, the delegate for the Danube who has no interest in the conditions of the Arab lands, and he speaks from outside the issue. Both interpreted our demands with misunderstanding and changed what we wanted without knowledge of our situation and the urgency of our needs. For overcoming this separation is akin to the needs of the thirsty for water and is intended for the benefit of the state and the people. Imagine the increase in revenue which would only multiply in the future! It is misunderstood to be saying that this demand is the opinion of Raʿūf Efendi, our current *mutaṣarrif* because he is sincere and these people do not provide evidence for their claims . . . The demand [of a separation from Damascus] comes not only from Beirut but also from Acre and Haifa. Clearly it is not only some misled people of Beirut who desire it [a province] but rather people of education and lovers of the homeland. The knowledge that we have, especially after the abolition of oppression and the free expression of thought, obliges us that we demand the best for the welfare, success and progress of our country.[109]

Istanbul judged that the time was still not ripe for a promotion of Beirut. The success of Syria's governor general in 1878, the exiled former grand vizier Midḥat Pasha, caused more discomfort than pride in Istanbul where, two years prior, palace intrigues placed the young and inexperienced Abdülhamid II on the Ottoman throne. In the eyes of the Ottoman government, the hesitation of the parliamentary inquiry to give Beirut the status of provincial capital was vindicated when a few months later anti-government posters in Beirut and Sidon alleged widespread anti-Ottoman sentiments in the province of Syria.[110]

[108] Us, *Meclis-i Mebusan.* [109] *Thamarāt al-Funūn* (21 Feb. 1878).

[110] Under Midḥat Pasha's term of office in Damascus, there surfaced some anti-Ottoman posters in Beirut, which the Ottoman authorities took very seriously. See Shamir (1974: 251–7), and more recently Abu Manneh (1998: 251–67).

The conservative camp at the Sublime Porte around Maḥmūd Nedīm and Küçük Saʿīd Pasha registered with concern the fading deference towards Ottoman rule in Syria while the popularity of Midḥat Pasha among the population of Beirut appeared to be rising. In Istanbul, Beirut was still considered the gate for European influence in the Arab provinces. Suspicion of the cultural and educational societies in Beirut and Sidon meant that the Sunni *jamʿiyyat al-maqāṣid al-khayriyya al-islāmiyya* of 1878, whose formation had been encouraged by Midḥat Pasha, was quickly dissolved and incorporated into the provincial educational board under his successor in Damascus.

The Grand Vizier Tips the Scales

The times were changing and the tide turned in Beirut's favour after the Ottoman Empire lost its Balkan and Egyptian territories to European powers in the early 1880s. The palace felt, with some sense of urgency, the need to achieve better services and more comprehensive control over the remaining Arab provinces. In 1883, Sultan Abdülhamid II dispatched an imperial commission to Damascus, which ostensibly was to assess French activities in the region. The commission returned with the recommendation that the province of Syria be divided into two provinces: a coastal province, with Beirut as the capital, and an interior province centred around Damascus.[111]

Such proactive proposals remained in government drawers until 1885. Matters seemed to turn in Beirut's favour when Meḥmed Kāmil Pasha (1832–1913), a former provincial official in Damascus, Beirut, and Jerusalem and member of Beirut's Syrian Scientific Society in the 1860s, assumed the grand vizierate. Like Midḥat Pasha before him, Kāmil Pasha had first gained government experience in the provinces.[112] During Kāmil Pasha's term of office in Istanbul, Syria received more attention than under his predecessors. He held close relationships with Arab circles in Istanbul around Joseph Muṭrān and Aḥmad ʿIzzat Bey al-ʿĀbid who at the time were employed in the department of commerce in the Ottoman government.[113]

The long-serving British consul in Beirut, Jackson Eldridge, commented that Kāmil Pasha's appointment 'has had an excellent effect in Syria where he is well known, highly respected and esteemed by all classes'.[114] Although neither his memoirs[115] nor a biography[116] give any indication of his role in the creation of the

[111] Gross (Ph.D. thesis, 1979: 362–3).

[112] It is possible that the very appointment of this stranger to palace politics was due to the Syrian entourage that Abdülhamid II kept since the mid-1880s.

[113] *Lisān al-Ḥāl* (27 Feb. 1890).

[114] Quoted in Gross (Ph.D. thesis, 1979: 375).

[115] Kāmil Pasha (1913).

[116] Bayur (1954).

province of Beirut, it appears to have been the perception of at least one newspaper in Beirut that Kāmil Pasha could have been the person to tip the scales: 'In a letter from Istanbul somebody says the most important thing for every Beiruti, nay, everyone in the new province is to thank the Sultan's wise concern and the grand vizier Kāmil Pasha who has not forgotten his time in Beirut.'[117]

Indeed, two years into Kāmil Pasha's term of office, the palace received a memorandum from an Ottoman resident in Beirut which reiterated the necessity for an administrative upgrading of Beirut. The sultan duly ordered Kāmil Pasha and the Council of Ministers to devise a plan for a provincial reorganization of Syria.[118] The ministerial discussions in Istanbul that ultimately led to the imperial decree for the creation of the new province leaked out to the Arab Arabic press and consular staff in December 1887. The news generated hectic mobilization of lobby groups in Beirut and Damascus akin to that of 1865, the year of the first petitions. Initial jubilation in Beirut was promptly nipped in the bud by reports that the Council of Ministers had rescinded the separation plan whereupon *Lisān al-Ḥāl* warned its readers that 'the province of Beirut is no longer a subject of discussion' in Istanbul.[119]

Sultan Abdülhamid II was hesitant and halted all further developments. He was torn between continuing a policy of procedural blockading *vis-à-vis* European agents in a weak subprovince of Beirut on the one hand, and a policy of imposing Ottoman regulations on the European powers under a strong and more experienced governor general based in Beirut on the other. The impracticality of dealing with the Ottoman authorities in distant Damascus had long been an obstacle for European diplomats.[120] However, an efficient administration in Beirut could also provide a buffer zone against European influence into the heartland of Ottoman Syria and could control and reduce political brinkmanship. Finally, some time in February 1888, the sultan irrevocably backed the creation of the province of Beirut.

Under these conditions of administrative limbo, unrest occurred in the outlying areas of Beirut.[121] South of Beirut, 'in a quarter called Mazraʿat al-ʿArab, Arabs have raised their arms against police officers', and violent clashes between Greek Orthodox and Muslim residents escalated after heavy-handed police retaliation.[122] A month later a Muslim attacker killed two Greek Orthodox Christians near a church.[123] The European consuls were convinced

[117] *Lisān al-Ḥāl* (12 Jan. 1888). [118] Abu Manneh (1992: 24). [119] *Lisān al-Ḥāl* (23 Jan. 1888).

[120] Mr Eyres, the British consul in Beirut, complained about arduous travels across the Lebanese mountains in a number of correspondences to the British ambassador to Istanbul. See e.g. PRO, FO/195/1613, 14 Mar. 1888. [121] MAE, Nantes, CEB 1888, Beirut, 12 Feb. 1888, and 12 Aug. 1888.

[122] BBA, YHUS, 210/65, Beirut, 9 Feb. 1888. [123] BBA, YHUS 211/17, Beirut, 8 June 1888.

that it had to do with the Ottoman government's decision to separate the provinces of Damascus and Beirut.[124] The governor general of Syria for his part complained to the Porte against 'misled', influential Beiruti circles at the palace.[125]

To Rashīd Nāshid Pasha, governor general from 1885 to 1888, the imperial decision to reduce his authority without consulting him was the swan song of his five years of troubled administration. He addressed the Beirutis in *Thamarāt al-Funūn* and criticized them for lack of respect for the benevolence of the sultan. Nāshid Pasha repeated the old arguments that a new coastal province would play into the hands of foreign powers and would lead to a drop by half in revenues. But his was a lost battle by early 1888. Instead of heeding his advice, the Porte recalled him from office even before Beirut was officially separated from Damascus. Apparently he died of a heart attack the day he received notice of his dismissal.[126]

Apart from a brief spell of rumours in 1895, purporting that Beirut was going to be re-annexed to Damascus, and that Jerusalem was to be elevated instead to a full province that comprised Beirut's southern subprovinces, Beirut was once and for all severed administratively from Damascus.[127] Provincial self-determination put Beirut under the direct rule of Istanbul and established it as an equal partner of Damascus—so much so that in 1902 the governor general of Beirut, Rashīd Bey, reacted brusquely to revived attempts by the then governor of Mount Lebanon, Muẓaffar Pasha, to incorporate the coastal cities into the mountain-*mutaṣarrifiyya* and reportedly quipped that 'to Christianize Beirut would [totally] emasculate Damascus, and the Porte would never accept this eventuality'.[128]

The imperial decree for the creation of the province of Beirut was finally proclaimed from the Grand Serail, the Ottoman headquarters in Beirut, upon the arrival of the first governor general, ʿAlī Riḍā Pasha, on 7 March 1888. The event drew a large crowd of people, which included local administrative, military, clerical dignitaries, Naṣṣuḥī Bey, the incumbent governor of Beirut, and Vāṣā Pasha, the governor of Mount Lebanon. Accompanied by the obligatory marching music of an Ottoman military orchestra, the imperial decree was read out first in Turkish by ʿAlī Riḍā Pasha's secretary, and

[124] PRO, FO, 195/1613, Beirut, 20 Jan. 1888. According to Eldridge 'it would be in the highest degree desirable that this question should be settled and that a *Vālī* should be appointed to Beirut. More especially as the *Mutaṣarrif* Naṣṣūhī Bey has displayed a most lamentable weakness' and considers himself not responsible in this case for the restoration of public order.

[125] Abu Manneh (1992: 25).

[126] Gross (Ph.D. thesis, 1979: 401).

[127] MAE, Paris, CPCTB, vol. 39, Beirut, 9 Oct. 1895.

[128] Ismail and Chehab, (1976: xvii. 241).

then in Arabic, by ʿAbd al-Qādir al-Danā, the president of the Commercial Court.[129]

ʿAlī Riḍā Pasha's arrival in Beirut was met with citywide celebrations. Beirut had finally obtained its governor general, and further, this governor general was also the preferred candidate of the Beirutis. For a week the notables of Beirut sent welcome messages to the governor general, and he replied by visiting the notables and the foreign consuls. On ʿAlī Pasha's assumption of office, a Beiruti journalist expressed in *Lisān al-Ḥāl* what the population expected from the new governor general: 'The people trust him; that is to say, that he will spot those bureaucrats who are corrupt and who corrupt their tenure secretly or publicly.'[130] The explicit admonition of corruption was as much a protest against previous practices as a future condition for local cooperation: 'His highness [ʿAlī Pasha] should spread justice and security among the Beirutis, improve education, facilitate trade, revive agriculture, and initiate public work projects and in return it is upon us, the people, to support His Ottoman Highness (*dawlatuhu*).'[131]

When the Beirutis finally got their way, the implementation of the Beirut province surprised both the French and British consuls in Beirut who suspected the other's governments of secretive machinations and speculated what gains the other side could expect to achieve from the new situation.[132] However, as I have demonstrated, the making of the province of Beirut was an entirely Ottoman decision pushed for by the burgeoning intermediary bourgeoisie of Beirut. For them, access to central authorities was essential to cultivate the friendship and goodwill of the Ottoman governor and the senior officials.

Conclusion

Introducing the subject of this book—*fin de siècle* Beirut—as the outcome of a protracted urban struggle for 'provincial self-determination' allows us to reconsider the nineteenth-century history of the Ottoman Empire and the development of the towns and cities in its Arab provinces. This first chapter began by tracing Beirut's development from a minor maritime town subversive to the regional powerhouse in Acre to a port-city during the Egyptian occupation and

129 The speech was printed in most Beiruti newspapers, *Lisān al-Ḥāl* (12 Mar. 1888). An intimate friend of grand vizier Kāmil Pasha, al-Danā had accommodated the new governor general in his mansion between his arrival in Beirut and his taking office. Likewise, when ʿAzīz Pasha arrived, he was first lodged at al-Danā's place.

130 *Lisān al-Ḥāl* (8 Mar. 1888).

131 *Lisān al-Ḥāl* (12 Mar. 1888).

132 MAE, Nantes, CEB 1888, Beirut 5, 1888.

to a provincial capital during Hamidian rule. The provincial rivalry in the late eighteenth and early nineteenth centuries had been fought out by military means between Ottoman governors and local potentates. In significant contrast, the power struggle between urban centres in the second half of the nineteenth century—venomous though it was—was conducted through the decidedly civilian means of petitions, parliament, and newspapers.

The dynamism of the ever-expanding intermediary bourgeoisie brought about a process of constant reworking of commercial, political, and cultural horizons. Thus, late Ottoman Beirut emerged neither as driftwood on the sea of world-economic forces nor as the natural product of Ottoman imperial *fiat*. Rather, it was a city of its own making. While local merchants and urban landowners shaped the city to fit its needs, other groups of notables, such as the Druze emirs, lost their hereditary positions of power. At that, the making of a provincial capital was central to the forging of an urban identity and solidarity that utilized the Ottoman reform discourse and targeted urban rivals in the region. Beirut's campaigners were not only conscious of their own urban milieu, they demanded a capital status for their city.

Some foundational urban trends also seeped into the course of this chapter whose importance will crystallize more clearly in subsequent chapters. The struggle for the capitalization of Beirut became the most enduring theme of the city's newspapers between 1865 and 1888. Continuous coverage of developments not only saw the collusion of journalists and petitioners but also suggests the emergence of a newspaper-based political field similar to the emergence of bourgeois public spheres in provincial Europe and colonial cities.[133] In fact, the passing of certain types of historical actors by the first half of the nineteenth century and the protracted struggle for a provincial capital in the second, has exemplified a more profound transformation of urban power and nothing short of a bourgeois urban revolution. The emergence of a dominant bourgeois class coincided historically with the emergence of the centralized state. Both mutually reinforced each other.[134]

The intelligence and persistence with which Beirut's urban elites argued their case for an upgrading *within* the Ottoman provincial system speaks of self-confidence and self-assertion. That they should appeal to (and even ingratiate themselves with) the Ottoman sultan, adopt the language of reform, and form a pact with the imperial state may surprise liberal and Marxist historians of Lebanon.[135] More importantly, perhaps, this chapter falsifies the teleological claims of Arab nationalist historians who have relied on British and French

[133] Cooper and Stoler (1997). [134] See Marx (1987).

[135] Such as the eminent works of Leila Fawaz and Michael Johnson respectively.

consular judgements that late nineteenth-century disgruntlements in Beirut and Damascus were early manifestations of Arab desires for independence from the Ottoman Empire.[136] Finally, this chapter has introduced a number of layers in the production of space whose workings will be explored further in the following chapters. The tremendous influence of the provincial structure during the Ottoman reform period brought about not only physical and economic change of cities in the Arab East, but also affected the urban consciousness of their inhabitants. Beirut's urban identity and the dynamic interaction between society and the space in which the city expanded has created a modern subjectivity and an evolving political field of tension between Ottoman imperialism and European capitalism.

[136] See, *inter alia*, Antonius (1939: 79–100), and Zeine (1973: 46–72).

2

A Nation of Provincials

The successful Beiruti struggle to persuade the Ottoman government to make Beirut a provincial capital fundamentally altered the urban hierarchy and territorial imagination in Bilad al-Sham in Beirut's favour. During the years of the province's existence, Beirut's scale of social organization expanded in terms of geographic, demographic, and administrative size. The relation between city, state, and society became more complex and diversified but also more formalized and standardized. The clue to understanding these changes is not to jump automatically to inquiries into nationalism or nation-states-in-the-making—essential though the context and effect of the late Ottoman organizational expansion for such analytical concepts are. Rather they need to be historicized in the context of internal politico-administrative units in which cities and inhabitants operated.

This chapter seeks to demonstrate how Beirut extended its political power far beyond the confines of geographical, confessional, or familial ties with Mount Lebanon. From 1888 onwards, merchants and politicians up and down the Eastern Mediterranean coast had to travel to Beirut in order to make their representations and press their cases. On the fiscal level, most of the annual provincial revenues first went to the treasury in Beirut before being redistributed in the new dependencies. The creation of the province consolidated Beirut's economic position through the political functions performed by a late Ottoman provincial capital. In Beirut, the administrative channels of the entire province converged. Here the developments of other cities were determined, and their planning controlled. But as Beirut began to shape its administrative periphery, its privileged position was also frequently challenged by neighbouring provincial authorities and inside the new dependencies.

After the Young Turk revolution of 1908/9, the relationship between imperial centre and provincial periphery was renegotiated. Political groups reformulated and challenged the Hamidian state system. Ottomanist, Turkish, Islamic,

Arabist, Syrianist, and Lebanist ideas began to compete with each other over the ideological gap left by the Hamidian regime, while rivalling European powers carved out spheres of economic influence in the region.[1] For the first time and a brief moment, Beirut became the political centre of the Arab reform movement in 1912 that culminated in the First Arab Congress in Paris of 1913. Not only were the main instigators from Beirut and Beirutis exiled in Cairo and Paris, but the congress also adopted Beirut's decentralist manifesto in their final resolution.[2]

Against the background of the well-documented origins of triumphant nationalisms, this chapter traces the development of a particular counter-community—a 'nation of provincials'—that emerged in defence of an Ottoman empire of provinces. I argue that, although the province of Beirut was a recent creation and a geographical oddity with no apparent bearing on latter-day colonial–national borders, it remained a central reference in the territorial imagination and political struggles of the intellectual mainstream in late Ottoman Beirut. Though popular in France, advocates of a Greater Lebanon who claimed the territorial inclusion of the Biqaʿ, Bilad Bisharri, Marj ʿAyun, and Lake Hula as well as Beirut's coastal districts were fringe at home until the dissolution of the Ottoman Empire.

Lebanist intellectuals like Henri Lammens, Būlus Nujaym, and Yūsuf Sawda may have convinced French colonial officials and subsequent historians that the *mutaṣarrifiyya* of Mount Lebanon was 'just a stepping stone towards real independence, which would one day be gained with the help of Europe'.[3] In the streets of Young Turk Beirut, however, the decentralist formula was on everybody's lips and Istanbul was the point of reference.

Borderlines: A Provincial Capital Shapes its Administrative Periphery

As a provincial capital, Beirut ruled over a geographical oddity of multiple, territorial enclaves that today spans four nation states in the Middle East (see Map 2). The subprovinces that fell under Beirut's jurisdiction—Tripoli and Lattakia in the north and Acre, Haifa, and Nablus in the south—were separated from their provincial capital by the coastal strips of Mount Lebanon. In total,

1 See e.g. Tauber (1993); Kayali (1997).

2 The congress was prepared by *al-Mufīd* editor ʿAlod al-Ghauī al-ʿUraysī, Dr Shiblī Shumayyil and the delegates, Salīm Salām, Aḥmad Mukhtār Bayhum, Aḥmad Ṭabbara, Michel and Yūsuf Sursuq, Ayyūb Tābit, and Khalīl Zayniyya.

3 Jouplain (1908: 589). On Lebanese nationalism, see Hakim-Dowek (D.Phil. thesis, 1997).

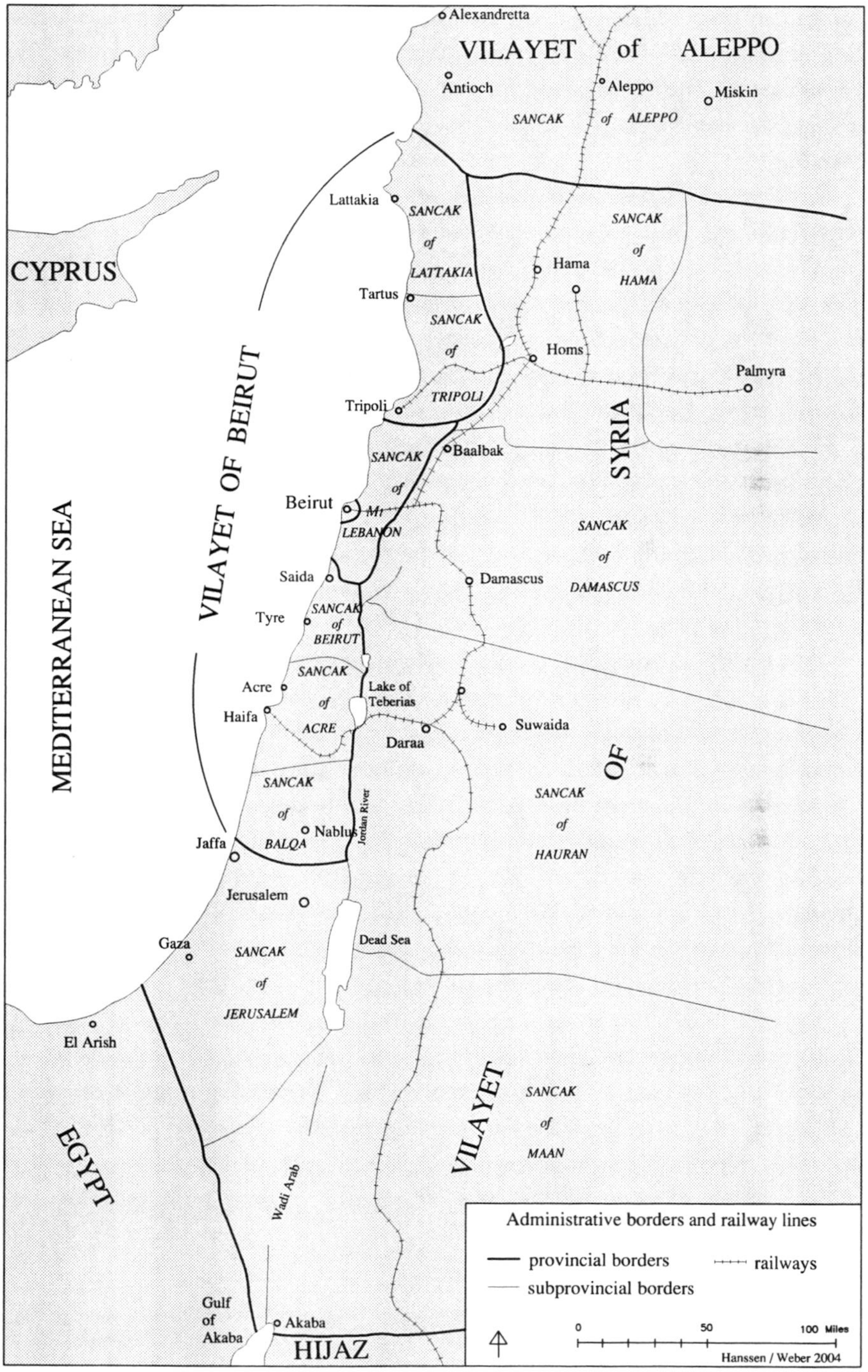

MAP 2. Map of Administrative Divisions and Railway network of Bilad al-Sham, *c.*1910

capital Beirut stretched over a surface area of 30,500 km² containing a population estimated by the French geographer Vital Cuinet in 1895 at 533,000.[4] In Beirut's own subprovince, the governor general ruled directly over a total of 323 villages in the enclaves of Sayda (Sidon), Sur (Tyre), al-Jalil (Galilee), and Marj ʿAyun.

In the northern and southern subprovinces, he delegated his authority to representatives, *mutaṣarrifs*, or governors. The governor of Acre administered the districts of Haifa, Tabariyya, Safad, and Nazareth and a total of 222 villages. The subprovince of the Balqa was administered by the governor of Nablus. It included the districts of Jenin, Tulkarm, and Salfit and 212 villages. In the north, the subprovince of Tripoli incorporated 567 villages in the districts of Tripoli, Safita, Akkar, and Husn al-Akrad.

Finally, in the far north, Lattakia was probably the most surprising inclusion into the new province. The subprovince of Lattakia had the most densely populated hinterland of 150,000 inhabitants in 1,250 villages. The imperial decision to make Lattakia a dependency of Beirut deprived Damascus not only of its vast areas of tobacco cultivation but also of any Mediterranean outlet in its truncated province.

Unsurprisingly, to many people the boundaries with Mount Lebanon were arbitrary and artificial. The first governors general of Beirut realized that it was one thing to have boundaries drawn up but another to have them accepted and acted upon by the population. Provincial boundaries drawn from cartographical representations came to impact realities on the ground as they determined revenue flow, administrative competence, and tax collection, even though the 'truth of the map' sometimes brought consternation to the people living with the new divisions. In the case of the map of the province of Beirut, whoever had sketched out the original boundaries in Istanbul did so with little knowledge and concern for the natural and human conditions of the land divided.[5]

Even the inspecting governor general Ismail Kemal Bey (1891–92) noticed upon familiarizing himself with the geography of his new assignment the peculiar relations between capital and countryside: 'There are houses in the town [of Beirut], the gardens of which are outside the territories of the *Wilāya*.'[6] Like so often with modernization, state-making, and nation-building, social realities on the ground fell victim to the reality of their representations on paper.[7]

[4] Cuinet (1896: 3–4). The province of Beirut was thus three times the size of Mount Lebanon and had half the population in one-third of the territory of the province of Syria. Ibid. 306–7. See also *Salnāme—Bayrūt Vilāyeti*, 1310 (1892/3).

[5] On the provincial map of Beirut, see Hanssen (D.Phil. thesis, 2001: 83).

[6] Kemal Bey (1920: 193).

[7] See Scott (1998).

The particular cartographical location of Maghdusheh, a tiny village above Sidon, almost caused a major diplomatic incident when a property dispute between a local Protestant mission and residents revealed tax irregularities. A full British consular inquiry into the status of Maghdusheh established that the root of the dispute was that the village was under the administration of Beirut and Mount Lebanon 'in unequal halves': while authorities in Mount Lebanon taxed each inhabitant half the dues, the Beirut authorities charged the full dues to a list of *half* the population. As a result, total confusion ruled in which opportunistic Protestant property holders tried to avoid double taxation by 'migrating' between the legal authorities of the two provinces when convenient.[8]

The new political reality of the region was challenged on numerous occasions, particularly from the authorities in Mount Lebanon. In the first of a series of challenges from Mount Lebanon, the governor Dāwūd Pasha had campaigned for the incorporation of the coastal towns into Mount Lebanon soon after he took charge in 1865.[9] While the Maronite clergy and the Mountain as a whole remained silent on the issue of the incorporation of the coastline, bickering over jurisdiction increased tensions between the city and the Mountain after the creation of the province of Beirut. Thus in early 1892, the ageing governor general, ʿAzīz Pasha, was dismissed over 'inappropriate interference' in the jurisdiction of Vāṣā Pasha, the governor of Mount Lebanon.[10]

At the end of the 1890s, the governor general of Beirut and the governor of Mount Lebanon accused each other of trespassing on each other's territorial authority, and they were both removed from office by order of the sultan after the September 1903 riots in Beirut's southern suburbs.[11] The first serious and sustained campaigns to merge Mount Lebanon and the coastal province came during the decentralist negotiations with the Ottoman government in February 1913 when Lebanese activists gathered in Istanbul and Paris and staged a double demonstration in Mount Lebanon and the province of Beirut.[12] During the Damascene struggle against the creation of the province of Beirut, the Balqa region around Nablus had been the most hotly contested subprovince and the last line of defence for the governor general of Damascus. The British occupation of Egypt in 1882 provoked the Ottoman government into a sense of urgency in strengthening the imperial administration of the southern frontier of Bilad al-Sham.[13] Even after the new governor general had arrived in Beirut,

[8] PRO, FO 206/229, 'Report on the Protestants in Mount Lebanon, 1903'.

[9] Ismail and Chehab (1976: xvii. 241).

[10] BBA, YHUS, 253/14, 5 Nov. 1891.

[11] See Ch. 7.

[12] MAE, Nantes, CEB, Beirut, 8 Feb. 1913. See also Haddad (1998).

[13] A number of schemes were proposed, including the creation of a province of southern Syria 'combining the regions of Jerusalem, the Balqa and Maʿn as a buffer against foreign incursions'. Rogan (1999: 52).

his colleague in Damascus still insisted on keeping Nablus for Damascus. Instead, against violent protests in Nablus itself, the Balqa was partitioned, with the eastern districts ceding to the newly created Damascene subprovince of Karak, and the villages around Nablus to Beirut.[14]

Beiruti merchants benefited from this territorial acquisition. It enabled them to enter a locally controlled commodity chain which the Ottoman government had long wanted to break up by auctioning to external merchants the right to collect tax-in-kind.[15] From 1888 onwards, Nabulsi had to travel to Beirut instead of Damascus to plead their cases in court. In the new provincial capital, family connections with court officials tended to favour their Beiruti merchant rivals.

The Beirut courts acquired such an anti-Nablus reputation that many Nabulsi refused even to show up.[16] In an attempt to put an end to this structural disadvantage, in 1906 Nabulsi notables sent an appeal to Istanbul demanding the secession from Beirut and the attachment of the Balqa and the district of Nazareth to the autonomous subprovince of Jerusalem.[17] This request came in the wake of two landmark events in the modern history of Palestine. First, the seventh Zionist Congress had just voted for Palestine as Jewish homeland in whose wake several Beirut based landowners—most notably Eliās Sursuq—obtained the governor general's permission to sell their vast land-holdings in the Balqa region to the Jewish National Fund. Second, Néguib Azoury had just published his controversial manifesto *Le Réveil de la nation arabe* in which he indicted Hamidian provincial rule and predicted a clash between Zionist settlers and Palestinian inhabitants.[18] After the Young Turk revolution, Azoury again called for the inclusion of the southern territories of the province of Beirut into an expanded province of Jerusalem, insisting that 'the progress of Palestine depend[ed] on this.'[19]

The regional challenges to Beirut's economic position and nationalist and decentralist movements in the Arab provinces after 1908 questioned anew the provincial boundaries in Bilad al-Sham. Advocates for a territorial merger between Beirut and Mount Lebanon grew more vociferous. At a time when international markets grew more competitive, some Damascene and Beiruti merchants also joined forces in infrastructural projects so as to increase local industrial output in tobacco, grain, cotton, silk, and other export-oriented goods. In both cases the fear of economic decline may temporarily have laid to

14 Rogan (1999: 55). See also Mundy (1996: 77–94). 15 Doumani (1996: 114). 16 Ibid. 176.

17 MAE, Nantes, CEB 1912, Beirut, 31 May 1906. The Ottoman government turned down the appeal.

18 Néguib Azoury, *Le Réveil de la nation Arabe* (n.pl., 1904).

19 *Thamarāt al-Funūn* (23 Sept. 1908), quoted in Khalidi (1997: 28).

rest previous rivalries and jealousies.[20] Nevertheless, considerations to join forces in the face of international economic challenges did not sweep aside the existing administrative geographies as points of reference for local reform plans and as ideally bounded future entities.

By the time Arab nationalist ideologies took root in the Arab provinces, urban—particularly *émigré*—intellectuals acknowledged distinct characteristic differences between the people of the mountain and the city, but at least one of them found solace in that 'the Lebanese and the sons of the *vilāyet* had become one with heart and soul'.[21] This nationalist retrospective implies that Ottoman administrative divisions had seriously affected the mentalities of their inhabitants and impaired a putative natural unity. Before 1914, however, there was nothing to suggest that the fusion of mountain and city—as was increasingly suggested by Christian and Muslim notables from 1913 onwards—was the only viable arrangement. For this idea to be implemented physically, the Ottoman Empire first had to be defeated in the Great War.

'Onto a Sea of Bureaucrats'

One of the immediate effects of the creation of a provincial capital on the city of Beirut was the mushrooming of administrative services and the expansion of the imperial bureaucracy staffed by salaried officials. At the turn of the century, the city accommodated local and imperial bureaucrats not only of the provincial capital of Beirut, but also many from the *mutaṣarrifiyya* of Mount Lebanon, most notably the Arslāns from the nearby town of Shuwayfat who were notoriously fishing for positions in Beirut.

A rough estimate based on the Ottoman yearbook of the province of Beirut for 1310 (1892/3) lists almost 200 imperial appointments in Beirut alone. Twenty-five police officers and over 200 gendarmes maintained public order in the city. Moreover, innumerable former, present, and future, permanent and elected members on local and provincial councils of the departments of health, education, justice, police, benevolent endowments, *sicill-i aḥvāl*, and public works populated Beirut.

Other people worked—these bureaucrats had a career. Ottoman bureaucrats had in common specific employment patterns, daily routines through fixed or flexible office hours, and a distinct self-interested identification with the Ottoman state.[22] In *fin de siècle* Beirut there was no residential segregation

[20] Haddad (1998: 129–53).

[21] Amīn Rīḥānī, *al-Qawmiyyāt*, quoted in Hakim-Dowek (1997: 270).

[22] On the everyday life of Ottoman bureaucrats, see Dumont and Géorgeon (1985: 125–83), and Findley (1989).

between Ottoman officials and the local population. State officials rented private houses partially or fully. For example, between 1868 and 1892, two governors of Mount Lebanon resided on a floor each in the villa of the municipal member Yūsuf al-Judāy in Zuqaq al-Blat.

It was not unusual for unmarried Ottoman officials posted to the province to marry the daughter of a local notable. The imperial source of their local power would have made it a viable strategy of politically minded fathers to marry off their daughters to Ottoman career bureaucrats.[23] As individuals with ample time and relative wealth and standing, this prominent professional class of urban society had a tangible impact on daily life and sociability in Beirut. In his memoirs, the Lebanese president Bishāra al-Khūrī remembered the omnipresence of the Ottoman bureaucrat in Beirut's public life: 'when I was born into this world [in 1890] I opened my eyes onto a sea of bureaucrats'.[24]

Bureaucrats formed a conspicuous social group in Beirut distinguishable by their Ottoman civil service uniform. Dressed and *ad*dressed as *efendi*s, their corporate attire—black tailcoat and skin-tight, tailor-made trousers, white dress shirt, stand-up collars, bow tie, and the obligatory ruby-red fez matched with a well-kept beard or trimmed moustache—produced an angular facial and regular bodily appearance that radiated distinctly modern knowledge and authority.[25] The bureaucrats' uniforms were at marked variance from the ostentatious fashions of the day, described here by a British resident of the mid-nineteenth century:

> As the inhabitants grew wealthier, greater attention began to be paid to dress and fashion. The Europeans set the example, and Turks, Greeks, and Armenians followed it. Not that these latter gave up their Oriental costume, but this, in lieu of being some ordinary material, was now made of rich silk and satins. The Europeans promenaded in the latest Parisian fashions, and the natives in the richest Oriental robes.[26]

Growing prosperity and security made Beirut a time and a place for conspicuous consumption in which the body became one of the markers of cultural refinement while the local textile fashion rendered legible social hier-

[23] To marry into an Ottoman family from Istanbul meant upward mobility for Beirutis and was sought after. Likewise, urban notables from Aleppo, Damascus, Beirut, and Jerusalem intermarried happily. To marry someone from the lesser provincial towns, however, meant to marry down: 'Search Acre and Ruwwad rather than marry a man with children' (in Lebanese dialect '*Ubrumī ʿAkkā wa Rawwād, wa la takhdhī rijjāl ʿindū ulād*). See Freyha (1974: 5).

[24] B. al-Khūrī (1960: 30).

[25] Jirjī Zaydān confessed in his memoirs that during most of his early life in Beirut he 'was convinced that people who wore *bantalūn* [tight trousers] were of higher intelligence, wider knowledge and better judgment than those wearing the *sirwal* because most of them belonged to the educated people. But when I began to open my eyes and read a little of the scientific principles, this opinion of mine was somewhat weakened. I stopped being surprised any more when people wearing the *sirwāl* and the *qunbāz* kept up with those wearing pants and hats'. Philipp (1979: 156–7).

[26] Neale (1851: 210).

archy.[27] Significantly the representation of the self in the preceding quote was not so much conducted through imitation of Western tastes but rather through reinterpretation and elaboration of existing patterns.

In conscious contrast to a kaleidoscopic proliferation of local fashions, individuals in the civil service only distinguished themselves through an elaborate stratification of Ottoman ranks and medals conspicuously attached to the uniforms on chest and shoulders. As markers of authority, state insignia were worn at official commemorations and ceremonies, processions and music festivals, where they denoted status, integrity, and achievement. Particularly under Abdülhamid, occasions such as the arrival of a new governor general, the sultan's birthday, or the anniversary of his 'coronation' were important social events. Bureaucrats 'would spend the night before as excited as children, cleaning and ironing their ceremonial clothes and polishing their medals with oil'.[28] Local merchants and young professionals were attracted to these fine distinctions, as a cynical Gramsci also noticed of imperial Italy: 'Lawyers, professors and functionaries joined in with enthusiasm aroused by every new possibility of fishing for titles and medals'.[29] To the Ottoman government, however, its officials were the embodiment of imperial order in the provinces.

The Ottoman's Burden

Governors general held both the most powerful and arguably the most volatile position in the provinces. The Provincial Law of 1864 vested them with paramount authority over imperial staff and local councillors in their provinces.[30] Inside the imperial government, they reported directly to the Minister of Interior, but often the sultan, his Arab advisers, and grand viziers interfered. At the intersection of the imperial, regional, and the local level of decision-making the office of the governor general in Beirut, therefore, provides 'an ideal window' onto the Ottoman's own civilizing mission.

From 1888 to the Young Turk revolution of 1908, Beirut had ten governors general. Thus under Abdülhamid's rule, and particularly after the initial settling-in problems of the first three governors general, Beirut enjoyed a relatively stable provincial government by Ottoman standards with an average term of three years between 1892 and 1908 (see Table 1).[31] The first three governors general appointed to Beirut were experienced, elderly administrators of cosmopolitan background whose main task was to pacify the rural

[27] Bourdieu (1996: 18). [28] al-Barūdī (1951: 49–50).
[29] Gramsci (1977: 33). [30] Young (1906: i. 48–51).
[31] Beirut lacked one dominating figure compared to the provincial government in Damascus at the time which was dominated by the extended term of Nāẓim Pasha. See S. Weber (Ph.D. thesis, 2001).

Table 1. Ottoman governors general of the province of Beirut, 1888–1908

Name	Rank	Office held	Previous positions	Next position(s)
ʿAlī Riḍā	Pasha	Mar. 1888–Jan. 1889	Governor, Beirut (1868–9), governor general, Izmir, ambassador in Paris	Died in office
Ra'ūf/Ra'īf	Pasha	1889 (5 months)	Governor, Beirut (1877–9), governor, Jerusalem (1879–89)	Governor general, Bitlis
Aḥmad ʿAzīz	Pasha	Aug. 1889–Dec. 1991	Bosnian origin, favourite of sultan, governor general in Yemen	
Ismail Kemal	Bey	Jan. 1891–Aug. 1892	Governor general in Gallipoli	Governor general in Tarabulus Garb, Albanian political figure, died in 1920
Khālid Bābān	Bey	Sept. 1892–Aug. 1894	Kurdish, from Crete, amb. Teheran, 1st governorate	Istanbul
Naṣṣūḥī	Bey	1894–Dec. 1896	Governor in Beirut, 1883–7, governor general in Adana	Istanbul
Ḥasan Rafīq	Pasha	interim	Governor general and military general in Damascus, Young Turk investigator	
Ḥusayn Nāẓim	Pasha	1897 (3 months)	Istanbul municipality, police chief, client of ʿIzzat Pasha al-ʿĀbid	Governor general in Damascus, Izmir, Edirne
Rashīd	Bey	July 1897–1903	Council of State, Ministry of Interior, client of ʿIzzat, Taḥsīn Pasha	Governor general in Bursa
Ibrāhīm Khalīl	Pasha	July 1908	From Albania, governor general, Van and Sivas; client of ʿIzzat Pasha	
Ḥusayn Nāẓim	Pasha	Sept. 1908	Governor general in Salonika, Adrianople, Baghdad, educated at St Cyr, Paris	
Shukrī	Pasha	interim	Governor general in Damascus	
Meḥmed ʿAlī	Bey	1908 (14 days)		Governor in Jerusalem
ʿAlī Ekrem, ibn Nāmık Kemāl	Bey	1908 (13 days)	Governor in Jerusalem (1906–8)	Governor in Archipelago, Rhodes
Farīd	Pasha	1908 (14 days)		

Table 1. Cont.

Name	Rank	Office held	Previous positions	Next position(s)
Edhem	Bey	Dec. 1908–Sept. 1909		
Ḥusayn Nāẓim	Pasha	interim	Governor general in Damascus	
ʿAbd al-Raḥmān Nūr al-Dīn	Bey	1910–11	Teacher in Salonika, councillor of state	
Ḥāzim	Bey	Dec. 1911–Sept. 1912	Unionist, Anti-Beirut Reform Committee	
Edhem	Bey	Sept. 1912–Feb. 1913		
Ḥāzim	Bey	Feb. 1913–Sept. 1913		
Sāmī Bakr	Bey	Oct. 1913–Oct. 1915	Governor general in Trabzon	
ʿAzmī	Bey	1915–17	Governor in Tripoli, and Jerusalem	
Ismāʿīl Haḳḳī	Bey	1917–18	Simultaneously governor of Mt Lebanon	

population and achieve more efficient provincial taxation. ʿAlī Riḍā Pasha had been Ottoman ambassador to Paris, governor general in Izmir, and previously a popular governor of Beirut in the late 1860s.[32] Although less revered than ʿAlī Pasha, his successor, Raʾūf Pasha, also had strong credentials as one of Midḥat Pasha's law-and-order reformers and as 'governor of Beirut during the difficult times of the Russian War' before he assumed a long governorship in Jerusalem.[33] In Beirut, however, after only five months in office he found himself the victim of tensions between the sultan and the grand vizier, Kāmil Pasha.[34] When the third high-ranking pasha arrived in Beirut, ʿAzīz Pasha's reputation also preceded him. The British consul remarked that 'he has already won golden opinions from the population by his courtesy and genial manners. He appeared to be of great ability and intellect.'[35] ʿAzīz Pasha had been the original candidate for the post but rivalry between Porte and Palace in 1888 stalled his appointment.

In 1890, the British Consul General informed his ambassador in Istanbul of 'much improved government in Beirut' under ʿAzīz Pasha.[36] He was

32 *Lisān al-Ḥāl* (12 Jan. 1888).
33 PRO, FO, 195/1648, Beirut, 11 Mar. 1889, and Kushner (1987: 277–8).
34 BBA, YHUS, 224/47, 16 Apr. 1889 and 223/6, 3 Mar. 1889.
35 PRO, FO, 195/1648, Beirut, 30 July 1889.
36 PRO, FO, 195/1683, Beirut, 20 May 1890.

considered practically minded and 'ambitious to execute justice without fear or favour'. Mastery over consular circles in Beirut allowed him a free hand in the 'unruly' Nablus region where Protestant missions tended to regard with suspicion any Ottoman involvement from Beirut. On the contrary, ʿAzīz Pasha was praised for his *tour de force* through the western Balqa as he not only 'made it possible to track down a mob of bedouins that had robbed an English traveller of all his possessions' but ʿAzīz Pasha also 'effected the dismissal of the *qāʾimaqām* of Tiberias [held responsible for the attack]'.[37]

The memoirs of the fourth governor general, Ismail Kemal Bey, offer a rare and vivid account of the career path of an imperial bureaucrat in general and his perspective on office in Beirut in particular. He was considerably younger than his predecessors. In his early career, he was influenced by Midḥat Pasha, whom he served in junior assignments to the Danube and Damascus. Dissatisfied with the Ottoman civil service he retired in 1890 and pursued a career as industrialist and concessionaire. When defamers in the Ottoman government charged him with profiteering, the sultan used his secret service to clear his name before offering him various governorships. Only after considerable pressure from the Ministry of Interior and a promotion did he agree to be posted to the province of Gallipoli.[38] Two months into his appointment, he was suddenly posted to the governorate of Beirut at the sultan's behest, again, he insists, quite reluctantly.

Upon arrival in mid-winter 1892, however, he overcame his initial unwillingness. In his memoirs he remarks how deeply impressed he was with 'the importance and the beauty of his new assignment'.[39] He declared Beirut 'a source of opulence and an arena of learning'. He promised to 'speed up the progress of civilization and to proliferate the enlightened knowledge of this epoch'.[40] Other inaugural speeches by incumbent governors general shared the tone of Kemal Bey's civilizing mission. Ottoman officials found an 'already civilized' city brimming with cultural activity. The mandate was to accelerate Beirut's existing 'progress', rather than drag a reluctant city out of decline.

Relations between the Ottoman government and the provincial capital Beirut neither followed European colonial projections, nor, in fact, those of the Ottomans in more remote provincial capitals such as Baghdad and Sanʿa.[41] Beirut was viewed as a valuable asset to hold and rule, indeed, a 'jewel in the crown of the empire', while, all the more so, its province was treated as Beirut's

[37] PRO, FO, 195/1683, Beirut, 24 Apr. 1890.

[38] In the Ottoman bureaucratic ranking system, a *bālā* was between Bey and Pasha. See Kekule (1892) for a contemporary explanation of Ottoman ranks.

[39] Kemal Bey (1920: 193).

[40] MAE, Paris, CPCTB, vol. 37, 26 Jan. 1892.

[41] See Kühn (2002).

negation—an outback where strange rites and religions reigned and where much civilizing work was to be done.

For Ismail Kemal Bey arriving in Beirut was a double sort of home-coming. He confessed that he was positively touched to meet so many familiar faces in Beirut and Mount Lebanon. His old friend Vāṣā Pasha was governor of Mount Lebanon and an 'Albanian compatriot', at whose deathbed in Beirut he sat some months into his tenure.[42] The warm welcome of colleagues and friends from his time in the province of Damascus, where he had followed Midḥat Pasha immediately after parliament was abrogated, gave him a sense of continuity that he considered unusual for the Ottoman provincial administration.[43]

In contrast, when he was called to Damascus to replace temporarily an incapacitated colleague, he was appalled at the general disorder in the city. The very government buildings, military barracks, and schools that Midḥat Pasha had inaugurated back in 1878 were run down and in a state of neglect.[44] Kemal Bey blamed 'the separation of the two Syrian provinces' for this 'decay'. In his eyes the separation deprived Damascus of the sea and Beirut of the hinterland. This resulted in the 'paralysing of all works of economic development, which required unity of direction and administration'.[45]

In comparison to Damascus during the 1890s, Beirut's urban development was accelerating, not least through his own planning initiatives. Ismail Kemal was the first governor general since the creation of the province of Beirut to have deemed it necessary to break down the structures of the old city and redesign the flow of traffic. He encouraged the development of the port and planned for the piercing of two new streets connecting the port and the city centre. He also introduced reimbursement schemes for property owners affected by the demolition in the old city.[46] At the same time, he appealed to the urban notables to 'interest themselves in the affairs of the country, of which they were the leading inhabitants'.[47]

However, his tenure proved too short to see his ambitious urban restructuring projects materialize. When, after only seven months in office, the sultan assigned him to compose a report on the state of the empire, local notables and foreign consuls alike praised his leadership.[48] The municipality of Beirut regretted his departure. His memoirs proudly registered that 'the town of Beyrouth presented me with a souvenir album of photographic views of the place and its monuments bound in massive gold with an emerald in the centre'.[49]

[42] Kemal Bey (1920: 192). [43] Ibid. 193. [44] Ibid. 201. [45] Ibid. 202.
[46] PRO, FO, 195/1761, Beirut, 2 Aug. 1892. The scheme was only completed in 1894.
[47] Kemal Bey (1920: 194). [48] PRO, FO, 195/1763, Beirut, 2 Aug. 1892.
[49] Kemal Bey (1920: 206).

The nature of the gift and its value were expressions of the acute awareness of the municipality of their city as an artefact and their gratitude for the governor general who contributed to 'sculpting' it.

Centre–Periphery Relations in Lattakia

Under the first four governors general, the provincial capital Beirut functioned as the platform from where an Ottoman *mission civilisatrice* into the province was launched. In this regard, the ʿAlawi hinterland of Lattakia became a high-profile test case for both the application of the provincial government's 'benevolent reforms' and Abdülhamid's very own policies in his 'well-protected domains'. Like his predecessors, Ismail's main task was to pacify what the Ottoman government considered isolated and disintegrated mountain regions of the province.[50] On the governor general's obligatory provincial inspection tour, Ismail Kemal Bey visited the ʿAlawi mountain—or *Jabal Nuṣayrī*—to supervise cultivation of tobacco and the planning of railway tracks through the region.[51] He noted the 'unjust treatment of the *Nusairis*' by the local *qāʾimaqām*, and ordered him to treat them justly as a means 'towards attaching them to the government'.[52]

Considered heretics to Sunni Islam, the ʿAlawi community was subjected to various *tanẓīmāt* attempts at coercing them into Ottoman Hanafi Orthodoxy. Early in the nineteenth century, military incursions and punitive expeditions led to random Ottoman plundering, abductions, and executions, but did little to improve conditions for cultivation, trade, and travel.[53] In the early 1880s, the Ottoman authorities in Damascus still faced violent resistance to centralization policies in this region.[54] The heavy-handed policies against the ʿAlawis of the governors Aḥmad Pasha al-Ṣulḥ (*c.*1818–93), who was to be elected to Beirut's first provincial council and—succeeding him—Aḥmad Pasha Abāẓa who had been the first municipal president of Beirut between 1868 and 1877, appear to have had the support of Lattakia's urban elites. But their military interventions only hardened rural resistance to state centralization and suspicion towards the predominantly Sunni city of Lattakia.

The style of the Ottoman government's *mission civilisatrice* in ʿAlawi territory changed from the stick to the carrot in the late 1880s. When Lattakia's

50 On early 19th-century Ottoman policies towards the ʿAlawis, see Winter (2004).

51 Hartmann (1891: 166; 1895: 56–64). The author was a highly talented student of the leading German Orientalist of his day, Professor Heinrich Fleischer, at Leipzig. He was German consul in Beirut between 1867 and 1887 where he was part of the burgeoning literary circles and struck up a number of friendships among some of its members, such as the parliamentary deputy for Beirut, ʿAbd al-Raḥīm Badrān.

52 Kemal Bey (1920: 197).

53 Douwes (1993: 149–69).

54 MAE, Nantes, CEB 1882–1885.

jurisdiction changed over to 'enlightened' Beirut, its governor, Żiya Bey, built roads, civil schools, and Hanafi mosques, initiated large-scale educational programmes, and encouraged 'entry into the bureaucratic *efendiyya* class'.[55] Not obedience but conformity, not coercion but conversion, was the new way of pacifying this 'unruly region'. In order to inscribe its authority once and for all, the provincial government constructed administrative buildings, or *konaks*, schools in and around the troubled northern subprovinces in the head towns to mark the twenty-fifth anniversary of the sultan's accession to the caliphate.[56] The governor gained popularity among the ʿAlawis for granting them 'a full share in local administration and by promoting education amongst them'.[57] Under imperial instructions, Żiya Bey was

> active in inducing these Ansariehs [ʿAlawis] to embrace Sunni Islam. Apparently successful, 15,000 out of a total of about 60,000 have come forward and accepted the Muslim doctrines. The Sultan takes great interest in this movement and ten mosques and ten schools have already been erected at his expense. [And] the Civil List is funding another forty of each. The Ansariehs hope to be treated equally and not, as formerly, as pariahs by the bona fide Muslims, hence their large-scale conversion.[58]

What Protestant missionary activism was to the inhabitants of the southern subprovinces of Beirut, especially Acre and the Balqa, Ottoman administrators' proselytism was to the inhabitants of the northern subprovinces, especially the ʿAlawis. While the situation was far more complex, nevertheless, as part of the Ottoman government's pacifying mission, provincial inspectors ordered the prejudiced urban Sunni population to accept ʿAlawi converts to Hanafi Islam and to allow them to integrate into their society as legal equals.[59] The memoirs of Yūsuf al-Ḥakīm (b. 1879), a Lattakia-born career bureaucrat, add another dimension to Ottoman rule in the province of Beirut. He argues that, from the 1890s, governor appointments to Lattakia were settled in Abdülhamid's palace rather than in Beirut—undermining the very provincial order Hamidian governments sought to create. The ʿAlawi region was already renowned for the taste of its tobacco. Since the entire production had fallen under the international Tobacco Régie after Ottoman state bankruptcy in 1875, the region had been catapulted into the Ottoman political economy.

ʿIzzat Pasha al-ʾĀbid, the sultan's favourite adviser and notorious Damascene concessionaire, first secured the governorship for his son-in-law and then for

[55] al-Ḥakīm (1966: 98–9).

[56] As well as in Banias, Hosn al-Akrad, and Akkar, and the southern districts of Safad, Marj ʿAyun, Jenin, Tulkarm. PRO, FO 195/2075, Beirut, 2 May 1900.

[57] Douwes (1993: 167).

[58] PRO, FO/195/1723, Beirut, 10 Aug. 1891.

[59] Deringil (1998: 83).

his own son. The grand vizier Kāmil Pasha had his son appointed governor of Lattakia twice (1896 and 1905) while al-Sayyid Abū al-Hudā parachuted one of his clients into office in 1901.[60] After a controversy over the Tobacco Régie's buying and selling preferences, the governor was dismissed and replaced by an eager Muḥammad Arslān hovering in Beirut.[61]

The Provincial Council of Beirut

If the position of the governor general constituted the most powerful manifestation of direct imperial rule in Beirut, the provincial council was the most powerful manifestation of the stranglehold of Beirut notables over its administrative hinterland. The Ottoman Provincial Law had turned provincial capitals into powerful political centres where decision-making and lobbying converged. The most important decision-making body was the provincial council which convened regularly in the capital. Applications for concessions were reviewed in Beirut's provincial council. Taxes and revenues were assessed there. Land sales and property deeds were ratified there. Projects of infrastructure and public works throughout the province were decided there. Sites for industry were allocated by the provincial council and resolutions of all municipalities were checked by it.[62] In short, whoever sat on this general council for the province wielded a lot of power (see Table 2).

The *muftī* and *naqīb al-ashrāf* of Beirut were *ex-officio* council members, as were the imperial bureaucrats sent from Istanbul—the governor-general, the judge (*nā'ib*), the treasurer (*deftardār*), and the secretary general (*mektūbci*). The remaining six members were elected. The law explicitly required parity between Muslims and minorities but remained vague as to the geographical distribution of the representatives in the subprovinces.[63] In Beirut's first provincial council, three members were Beirut notables of at least the second generation.[64] Another member, Aḥmad Pasha al-Ṣulḥ, was a provincial notable originally from Sidon before he took residence in Beirut in the early 1860s.[65] His father had sent Aḥmad for military training to Istanbul when the Egyptian

60 al-Ḥakīm (1966: 76–8). Likewise, Tripoli, Acre, Haifa, and Sidon were also places of extensive palace intervention. See MAE, Nantes, CB 1880–97, carton 279.

61 After his death in Istanbul during the Young Turk revolution, his cousin Amīn Arslān succeeded him.

62 Young (1906–7: i. 62–5).

63 'Idare ʿUmūmī Vilāyetler, Chapter III, Art. 25', BBA, YEE, 37/47/47–112, tr. into French, in Young (1907: i 38).

64 Sursuq, Bayhum, and Qabbānī were established Beirutis. French consular reports list Jirjī Naqqāsh instead of Eliās ʿArab as elected member.

65 Aḥmad Pasha al-Ṣulḥ's son joined Buṭrus al-Bustānī's newly opened *madrasa al-waṭaniyya* in Beirut in the mid-1860s (see Ch. 6).

TABLE 2. Members of the administrative council of the province of Beirut

Institution/Year	1305: 1888	1310: 1892	1318: 1899/1900	1319: 1900/1
Governor general	ʿAlī Pasha	Khālid Bey	Rashīd Mumtāz Bey	Rashīd Mumtāz Bey
Chief judge	Ismaʿīl Rāmiz Bey	ʿAbduh Kamāl al-Dīn	Aḥmad Shukrī	Aḥmad Shukrī
Treasurer	Muḥammad Sharīf	Hanīf	Edhem	Edhem
General secretary	Fikret Bey	ʿAbdallah Najīb	Faṣīh Bey	Maḥmūd Bey
Muftī	ʿAbd al-Bāsiṭ Fākhūrī	ʿAbd al-Bāsiṭ	ʿAbd al-Bāsiṭ	ʿAbd al-Bāsiṭ
Naqīb al-ashrāf	Shaykh ʿAbd al-Raḥmān Naḥḥās	ʿAbd al-Raḥmān Naḥḥās	ʿAbd al-Rahmān Naḥḥās	ʿAbd al-Raḥmān Naḥḥās
Elected members:	Aḥmad al-Ṣulḥ	Ḥasan Bayhum	ʿAbd al-Qādir al-Danā	ʿAbd al-Qādir al-Danā
	Saʿd al-Dīn Qabbānī Pasha	Saʿd al-Dīn Qabbānī Pasha	Amīn Mukhayyish Pasha	ʿAbd al-Raḥmān Bayḍūn Pasha
	Muḥammad Bayhum	Miṣbāḥ Ghandūr	Ḥasan Bayhum	Arslān Dimashqiyya
	Yūsuf Sursuq	Nakhla Tuwaynī	Jibrān Tuwaynī	Jibrān Tuwaynī
	Yūsuf Naṣr	Eliās al-ʿArab	Ibrāhīm Thābit	Ibrāhīm Thābit
	Eliās al-ʿArab	Mikaʾīl Farʿūn	Salīm Muṣaddiyya	Yūsuf Farʿūn

Institution/Year	1322: 1904	1324: 1906	1326: 1908
Governor general	Ibrāhīm Khalīl Pasha	Khalīl Pasha	Khalīl Pasha
Chief judge	Muḥammad Tawfīq	Muḥammad Tawfīq	Amīr Khalūṣī
Treasurer	Vacant	Shawqī Bey	Mālik Bey
Secretary general	Maḥmūd Bey	Maḥmūd Bey	Aḥmad Bey
Muftī	ʿAbd al-Bāsiṭ Fākhūrī	Vacant	Vacant
Naqīb al-ashrāf	ʿAbd al-Raḥmān Naḥḥās	ʿAbd al-Raḥmān Naḥḥas	ʿAbd al-Raḥmān Naḥḥās
Elected members:	Amīn Mukhayyish Pasha	ʿAbd al-Raḥmān Bayḍūn Pasha	ʿAbd al-Raḥmān Bayḍūn Pasha
	Arslān Dimashqiyya	Arslān Dimashqiyya	Arslān Dimashqiyya
	Rashīd Bayhum	Rashīd Bayhum	Rashīd Bayhum
	Iskandar Tuwaynī Bey	Najīb Ṭrād	Najīb Ṭrād
	Bishāra Ṣabbāgh	Nadra Mutrān Bey	Nadra Muṭrān Bey
	Najīb Hānī	Najīb Hānī	Najīb Hānī

army conquered Bilad al-Sham in 1831. Ṣulḥ returned to Beirut with the Ottoman army after the Egyptian withdrawal and joined the provincial administration serving as governor in Lattakia and Acre. His marriage to the daughter of the Damascene mufti, Ḥasan Taqī al-Dīn al-Ḥisnī, made him a major player in the late Ottoman politics of notables and the linchpin of the short-lived Syrian reform movement under Midḥat Pasha's rule between 1878 and 1880.[66]

[66] On the movement, see Steppat (1969).

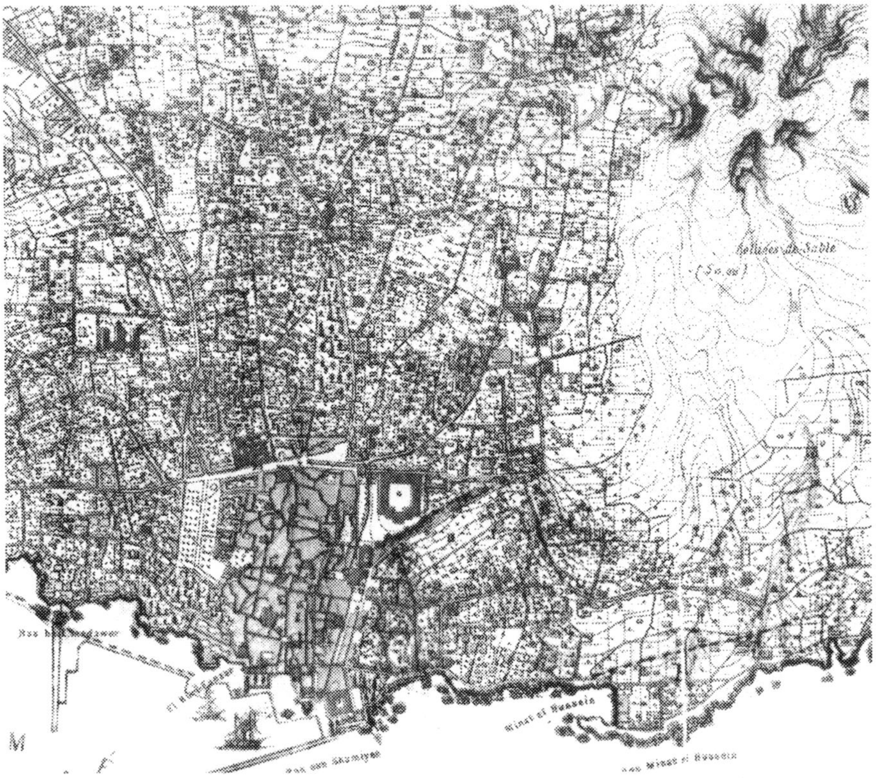

Map 3. Map of Beirut, 1876 (excerpt from Llöytved Plan)

Prominent members like the Bayhums, Dimashqiyyas, Mukhayyishs, Ṣabbāghs were notables, merchants, and entrepreneurs who were active in development projects across the Arab provinces. Their administrative positions allowed them to be inside the provincial decision-making apparatus and wield extensive powers in the process of Beirut's 'financial capitalization'.

The families of most members of the Beirut provincial council had been involved in the petitions for the capitalization of Beirut since 1865. They will reemerge in the narrative of this book—be it as local investors, municipal members, newspaper editors, propertied merchants, career bureaucrats, or party politicians. In all cases, they had established for themselves a privileged position to impose their vision of *fin de siècle* Beirut on the physical environment of a provincial capital. The geographical distribution of members of Beirut's provincial council is testimony to the extent of the capital's dominance. The records available suggest that in twenty years all but a handful of members were from Beirut.

Thus, the particular centre–periphery relations in late Ottoman Beirut defied polarization into a binary imperial and local antagonism. Instead, the imbrication of imperial and local structures of decision-making helped shape Beirut's regional trajectory as a political and economic centre within the larger Mediterranean economy. Local interest groups not only depended on, but also sought, the presence of Ottoman imperial power in Beirut. The particular structure of the Ottoman provincial administration manned by imperial bureaucrats and provincial councillors from the capital was to play an important role in capitalist urbanization as well as the production of dominant and marginal spaces in the city and province of Beirut.

Before I turn to these themes, the remainder of this chapter will examine the extent to which this new administrative entity was incorporated into the political discourse between the 1908 revolution and the First World War. Far from being dismissed as a Hamidian construct of provincial divide and rule, under the Young Turks the province of Beirut was seized by a new breed of local politicians as a central rallying point for provincial self-determination in Ottoman parliament and local parties. What is surprising, given the myth of the deep-rootedness and the evolutionary narrative of the Lebanese nation state, is that in the political imagination of Beirut's Muslims and Christians alike, the political entity of the province of Beirut was as viable and as legitimate as the *mutaṣarrifiyya* of Mount Lebanon. Expressed more succinctly, historically the dissolution of Beirut's provincial entity was as unpredictable at the onset of the First World War as was the final shape of the post-war Lebanese nation state.

City and Province after the Young Turk Revolution

Characteristically cynical of euphoric new beginnings in the Middle East, Elie Kedourie declared 'that the Arabic-speaking provinces on the eve of the coup d'état of July 1908 were quiescent'.[67] This view belittles the fact that the period from 1908 to the suppression of the 'Reform Committee for the Province of Beirut' in April 1913 witnessed mushrooming electoral activity and ideological formations.[68] In Beirut and Bilad al-Sham more generally, a new type of political leadership—the '*zaʿāma*'—emerged that was to dominate national politics for the rest of the twentieth century. During this crucial period in Lebanese politics, Salīm ʿAlī Salām (1868–1938) soared from relative political obscurity to an internationally fêted power broker. His meteoric rise was made possible by the new local style of party politics—communal bosses (*zaʿīms*) and

[67] Kedourie (1974c: 128). [68] Samneh (1920: 55–96).

clientelism. After the Young Turk revolution the Salāms emerged as Beirut's dominant and archetypal family of *zaʿīms*.[69]

The notables' 'inherited' honour and nobility—whether through genealogy, wealth, or 'brave' acts of violence—allowed for a cross-confessional elite solidarity that balanced social order with confessional commitment. In the rare events of subaltern, urban violence in late Ottoman Beirut, the notables activated this system of social control and mediated between warring factions to re-establish public order and confessional coexistence.[70]

The *zaʿāma* differed from the politics of notables of the eighteenth- and nineteenth centuries in that a *zaʿīm*'s political authority was based on the interplay between a property-based electoral system and control over street politics. The fall of the Hamidian regime in 1908 paved the way for political bosses to mobilize the urban population through horizontal ties of consociation and vertical ties of patronage on the one hand and through conflicting and overlapping ideologies of nationalism, provincialism, and Ottomanism on the other.

Patronage relied less on physical coercion or access to state power alone, but crucially on the *zaʿīm*'s ability to build a loyal electorate through a party, a movement, a welfare organization, or a community-based clientele. What also distinguished a *zaʿīm* from other notables was the respect (*iḥtirām*) attached to his role. Like other notables, a *zaʿīm* inherited nobility, but someone like Salīm Salām 'asserted himself in violent and heroic acts against his enemies' or, indeed, against Ottoman and later French authority.[71]

In the wake of the Young Turk revolution, rural, non-Beiruti notables—like Kāmil Bey of the Shia al-Asʿad clan, the Druze notables of the Arslan family or the ʿAbd al-Hādīs of Nablus—seized the new paths to power and replaced the disgraced so-called 'Hamidian Arabs' of the provincial capital.[72] These families hailed from mountainous regions whose respective communities had been marginal in Beirut politics before the revolution. Thus the outer edges of the province—the districts of Lattakia in the north and of Acre, the Balqa and Marj ʿAyun in the south—entered more directly into the orbit of imperial politics.

In terms of Ottoman centre–periphery relations the purging of Hamidian appointments in Beirut's provincial administration possibly constituted one of the revolution's most significant points of rupture as layoffs and new appointments constituted the 'driving force of the process of politicisation'.[73] In particular the systematic posting of the first generation of Arab graduates from the

69 Johnson (1986). 70 Johnson (1986: 47–50). 71 Johnson (2001: 35).
72 Hanssen (2002: 70–4). 73 Kayali (1997: 58–9).

Imperial Civil Service School (*mülkiye mektebi*) to district offices across Bilad al-Sham helped to politicize the provinces.[74]

The Hamidian era was the era of provincial capitals.[75] Driven by competent provincial governors like Midḥat Pasha, enthusiastic municipalities, a demanding Arabic press, and able engineers, cities like Baghdad, Izmir, Jerusalem, Damascus, and Beirut were turned into self-consciously modern cities and relay stations for the systematic Ottomanization of Arab provinces. The Young Turks did not abandon Beirut. However, no new projects of urbanism were carried out in Beirut until the wartime destruction of the old city in 1915–16.[76]

The attention of the Young Turk governments shifted beyond the provincial capital and into the administrative hinterland of Beirut. The Committee of Union and Progress (CUP) opened party offices in a host of towns on the district level in an effort to mobilize the provincial populations more directly. The political voices of the district governors themselves grew louder after 1908. Many latter-day nationalists launched their political careers on Ottoman district assignments. The amirs Muḥammad and Amīn Arslān in Lattakia, nationalist martyr Shukrī al-ʿAsalī, and *mülkiye* graduate Amīn ʿAbd al-Hādī made their debuts as *qāʾimaqāms* of Nazareth and Tiberias respectively before winning parliamentary seats or imperial office in Istanbul a decade later.[77]

Another *mülkiye* graduate, Néguib Azoury, owed his 1907 appointment as *qāʾimaqām* in Jerusalem less to his education than to his connection with the powerful Malḥamas in Istanbul.[78] In fact, French observers considered his appointment an imperial 'sinecure rewarding Azoury for giving up Young Turk activities and declaring his loyalty to the sultan'.[79] Under the Young Turks he became an uncomfortable spokesperson for Arab secession from the Ottoman Empire.

As political parties proliferated in Istanbul and the provinces, ideological differences emerged not just between supporters of the sultan and the CUP but also between different strands of Young Turk thought. Professional associations mushroomed in Beirut and Damascus. Merchants, pharmacists, lawyers, and urban craftsmen formed social clubs and lobby groups. The three pre-war parliamentary elections in 1908, 1912, and 1914 saw liberal, unionist, and decentralist candidates vie for votes.

The 1912 parliamentary elections, in particular, were a landmark event in Arab politics. Conducted in the wake of the Ottoman–Italian war and the

74 Blake (Ph.D. thesis, 1991). 75 This is one of the central tenets of Hanssen *et al.* (2002).

76 This was contrary to Young Turk Damascus where public construction thrived once again. See Weber (1998: 292–343). 77 See Cankaya (1968–9: iii. 740, 934, 943, 1195).

78 Wild (1981: 93). 79 Consul Boppe, quoted in Kedouri (1974*b*: 111).

Italian bombardment of the port of Beirut in 1911, government and opposition candidates went on large-scale election campaigns across Bilad al-Sham. Shukrī al-ʿAṣalī, parliamentarian for the province of Damascus, and Kāmil Bey al-Asʿad, candidate for the province of Beirut, were joined by other young opposition politicians, such as ʿAbd al-Raḥmān Shahbandar, ʿAbd al-Hamīd Zaḥrāwī, and Muḥammad Kurd ʿAlī, on their tours. Journalists followed their trail to Beirut, Baalbek, Damascus, Homs, and Aleppo and reported the effects their speeches had on crowds. In many ways, these party-based election campaigns in 1912 prefigured the mass politics during the Faysal period whose diverse manifestations James Gelvin has painstakingly documented.[80]

At the time, however, such popular mobilization was unprecedented. They were the 'first in the history of the region in which voters had a choice of supporting or opposing a party in power'.[81] Significantly, these elections also signalled the subtle but significant gravitational shift in provincial politics away from the capitals.[82] The Young Turk government actively sought to bypass Beirut and manipulated the electoral boundaries in the province in order to avoid the prospect of defeat at the hands of the popular opposition groups around Aḥmad Mukhtār Bayhum and Salīm Salām, Michel and Yūsuf Sursuq.[83] The ensuing election victory proved short-lived for the CUP whose violation of the administrative integrity backfired heavily when provincial self-determination became the battle cry of the 1913 reform movement.

One beneficiary of the government's electoral interference was the Shiite notable Kāmil Bey al-Asʿad—a new type of provincial politician with a rural power-base.[84] In 1909, Kāmil Bey was elected onto the provincial council, taking the Sidon seat of Riḍā Bey al-Ṣulḥ who had become an Ottoman parliamentary deputy in Istanbul.[85] Kāmil Bey moved his residence to Beirut, delegating the affairs in Jabal ʿAmil to family members. His successful re-election in 1912 followed his last-minute abandonment of the *Entente Libérale* in favour of the ruling CUP.[86] Having ingratiated himself with the CUP, his third candidacy in 1914 also proved successful.

[80] Gelvin (1998). In fact, many of the political phenomena of the Faysal period were a continuation of the party politics that developed in the wake of the Young Turk revolution. See also below, Ch. 9.

[81] Khalidi (1984: 461). [82] Ibid. [83] Kayali (1997: 119).

[84] Kāmil Bey hailed from an established landowning family in Jabal ʿAmil which had been awarded a *shaykh*-ly title by the Ottoman government in recognition of their campaigns against Aḥmad Pasha al-Jazzār and his successors in Acre. See Abū Saʿd (1997: 78).

[85] Riḍā al-Ṣulḥ (1857–1935) was the son of Aḥmad Pasha al-Ṣulḥ and the father of Riyaḍ al-Ṣulḥ, the charismatic leader of the independence movement during the French mandate and prime minister during early Lebanese independence. On the rivalry in Sidon between Riḍā al-Ṣulḥ and Kāmil al-Asʿad, see Ṣafā (1998: 212–15). [86] Ibid. 264.

Salīm ʿAlī Salām was the most prominent beneficiary of the sea change brought about by the revolution of 1908. His father had been a second-tier merchant upstart from Ras Beirut with business ties in Damascus, Aleppo, Jaffa, and Alexandria. Business fortunes allowed him to move to a large building complex in Musaitbeh south of the old city. After Abū ʿAlī's prestigious marriage to the daughter of Beirut's two leading Sunni *ʿulamāʾ* families (the Barbīrs and the Aghars) propelled the Salams into the top ranks of local respectability, his son Salīm turned the family residence into a palatial building complex from where national *zaʿīm* politics were conducted until his son Ṣāʾib's death in 2000. Although during the Hamidian period Salīm Salām had taken over and expanded his father's business into a profitable enterprise, his only public posts recorded in the Ottoman *Salnāmes* until 1908 were memberships of local agricultural and hospital committees.[87] Salīm Salām's break into political prominence came with the revival of the Sunni philanthropic society '*jamʿiyyat al-maqāṣid al-khayriyya al-islāmiyya*' in 1907/8.[88] Two years later the governor general, Nāẓim Pasha, appointed him to the presidency of both the society and the municipality. On the basis of these two pivotal positions Salim advanced as an indispensable force in Ottoman provincial politics. The watershed events of 1911–12—the Italian invasion of Ottoman Libya, the Balkan crisis, and the election defeat of Ismail Kemal Bey's *Entente Libérale*—had politicized Salām who saw the integrity of the Ottoman Empire threatened by internal and external crises. He was elected to the Ottoman parliament in 1914 on the platform of forming a reformist Arab block but this was nipped in the bud by the beginning of the First World War.[89]

Al-Asʿad and Salām were both relative upstarts in Beirut politics. But there were also significant differences between these two shooting stars of the Young Turk period. While Salam was bound to Beirut's political system by marriage, business, and municipal office and quickly rose to become the leading Sunni politician in the Young Turk period, the Shiite al-Asʿad remained an outsider in Beirut's political economy. On the one hand, he continued to be viewed with suspicion, on the other he was not bound by the informal web of obligations that regulated Beirut's particular blend of politics of notables. His rural power base allowed him to break agreements with fellow Beiruti politicians with relatively little social consequence. Moreover, while Salam was reluctant to abandon his affairs in Beirut for a post in Istanbul, al-Asʿad went out of his way to remain in Istanbul where, after the coup d'état of 1913, his CUP affiliation was far more appreciated than in *Entente*-held Beirut.

[87] *Salnāme—Bayrūt Vilāyeti*, 1328 (1908/9).

[88] Shubārū (2000: 64). See also below, Ch. 6.

[89] MAE, Nantes, CB, 1904–1914, carton 361, Beirut, 23 Apr. 1914.

The Reform Committee for the Province of Beirut

The reformers in Beirut once again had the benefit of a favourable ear inside the government in Istanbul when old friends of Beirut, Grand Vizier Kāmil Pasha and the leader of the *Entente Libérale*, Ismail Kemal Bey, returned to power at the Sublime Porte in June 1912. Kāmil Pasha encouraged Beirutis to submit a provincial reform proposal. In return, Salīm Salām, Aḥmad Mukhtār Bayhum, the Sursuqs, and, notably, Kāmil Bey al-Ṣulḥ, the other son of Aḥmad Pasha al-Ṣulḥ, mobilized the streets in support of Kāmil Pasha and backed the provincial assembly,[90] which the sympathetic governor general, Edhem Bey, called for the first time in the history of the province of Beirut on 14 January 1913. Nine days later, however, Kāmil Pasha's government in Istanbul was overthrown. From our provincial perspective on Ottoman political machinations, one of the reasons for the storming of the Sublime Porte by CUP officers on 23 January may have been the grand vizier's encouragement of rights of provincial self-determination.[91] What deserves special attention is that Beirut's reform discourse was framed neither by an urban nor a national unit of political representation but by a provincial unit. As a way out of the Ottoman crisis in general and the threat of foreign occupation of Bilad al-Sham in particular, Salīm Salām advocated reform on the level of the 'Ottoman community of provinces' (*laysa fī wilāyatuna faḥasab bal fī jamīʿ al-wilāyāt*).[92] In his view, only if this proposal was heeded by the Ottoman government could the growing popularity of secessionist ideas be countered. In other words, the integrity of the constituent provincial structure was crucial to the integrity of the empire as a whole.

The founding meeting of the 'Reform Committee for the Province of Beirut' took place in the municipal building on Sunday, 31 January 1913.[93] Its eighty-six members submitted a fifteen-point plan, which was adopted in the concomitant third session of the General Assembly of the province of Beirut.[94] They presented their project of provincial reforms based on the 'fundamental disposition [that] the Ottoman government is a constitutional parliamentarian government'.[95] The project acknowledged the authority of the imperial government in foreign, economic, and military affairs, but insisted on the integrity of the provincial form to which reforms must be applied. Arabic was demanded as the official language. A general council of thirty members elect-

[90] Aḥmad Mukhtār Bayhum, 'Movement Beni', *al-Ittiḥād al-ʿUthmānī* (19 Dec. 1912), Salīm ʿAlī Salām, 'Les Reformes Decentralistes', *al-Ittiḥād al-ʿUthmānī* (23 Dec. 1912); in MAE, Nantes, CB, 1904–1914, 361. See also Salām (1981: 130).

[91] A more direct cause seems to have been the loss of Salonika to Greece that month. See Kayali (1997: 130).

[92] Salām (1981: 129).

[93] Ibid. 133.

[94] For the names of the members, see Hanssen (D.Phil. thesis, 2001: annex).

[95] Saʿadūn (1994: 40–1).

ing Muslims and Christians in equal halves should be convoked regularly. It should be vested with more legislative power *vis-à-vis* the governor general—in particular regarding loans, concessions, and shareholding companies. Foreign officials should be allowed to staff certain posts in the provincial administration for the benefit of improving services.[96]

With the proclamation of this comprehensive Decentralist Manifesto, the once awkward construct of the province of Beirut became a political stake in Ottoman–Arab politics and elicited support from people across the provinces of Beirut, Syria, and Baghdad. The proposal of Salīm Salām and his allies to open up the provincial council to the large number of non-Beiruti notables who had been hitherto underrepresented and denied access was an effective strategy to reach out and mobilize the province. Relinquishing Beiruti's near monopoly on the provincial council paid off, as people across the provinces rallied in support of the reform movement in their towns and districts.[97]

Recognizing the momentum in the provinces, a commission of the Ministry of the Interior inspected the reform proposals and submitted a counter-draft to the sultan.[98] When the new governor general, Abū Bakr Ḥāzim Bey, arrived in Beirut, he quickly closed the Reform Club's salon near Bab Idriss. In protest, Beirut's chamber of commerce dissolved itself, municipal and provincial council members such as Salīm Salām resigned, and a general strike was called, after a defiant meeting was held at the Syrian Protestant College.[99] In response, Ḥāẓim Bey arrested a host of rebel notables.[100] The direct test of strength between Beirut's notables and the governor general was won by the former who managed to have Ḥāzim Bey recalled. However, this episode caused insurmountable suspicion between the CUP government and the reformers in Beirut.[101] With opposition voices calling for foreign intervention growing louder and the Arab Congress about to commence in Paris, the stakes were rising and the rift in Ottoman–Arab unity was growing larger. It reached its tragic pinnacle with Cemāl Pasha's hanging of over thirty opposition leaders during the First World War.[102]

[96] *Le Réveil* (20 Feb. 1913).

[97] *al-Mufīd* and *al-Ittiḥād al-ʿUthmānī*, the most committed newspapers of the reformers' cause, carried weekly updates of pro-reform manifestations in the Arab provinces. See Khalidi (1981).

[98] *Le Réveil* (13 Mar. 1913). The new provincial law turned out to be more centralist than the existing one and subsequently fuelled opposition dissent. See Findley (1986: 3–29).

[99] Petitions from across the province were published in *al-Iṣlāḥ* and *al-Ittiḥād al-ʿUthmānī*. For example, on 16 Apr. 1913, fifty-two Muslims and Christians of Haifa wrote a protest note against the dissolution of the Reform Committee: 'We admire the courage of the Beiruti reformists who have just added a beautiful page to the History of the country!' Centralist newspapers in Istanbul, such as *Tanin* and *La Turquie* published anti-reform petitions.

[100] Salibi (1976: 208).

[101] See below, Ch. 9.

[102] For the list of martyrs hanged on Sahat al-Burj in 1915–16, see Hanssen (D.Phil. thesis, 2001: Annex).

Bayrūt Vilāyeti: *Ottoman Wartime Ethnography*

During the First World War, the incumbent governor general ʿAzmī Bey called two General Assemblies, for the first of which extensive minutes are available.[103] This meeting brought thirty-two deputies from the districts of the province together in the capital in order to discuss conditions and developments. The delegates brought a variety of issues in their constituencies to the attention of the capital bureaucrats. The minutes of the meeting reveal the assertiveness with which hitherto unknown notables from minor towns put forward their constituency's demands for infrastructural, agricultural, educational, and financial improvements.

The governor general set up planning committees in which lesser provincial notables were introduced to Beirut politics. Under the presidency of Muḥammad al-Jisr, a Tripoli notable and son of a revered Islamic scholar, deputies from Haifa, Tyre, Acre, Bani Saʿab, Tiberia, the remote Akkar region, and Safita voted on changes to the provincial laws, revised statistical procedures, challenged property divisions used for taxation, called a provincial survey of Ottoman schools, and demanded a provincial, public library.[104]

As a consequence of the two meetings, the governor general ʿAzmī Bey commissioned two Ottoman officials of the education department to study the wartime conditions of the people of the province of Beirut. The two individuals selected belonged to a new kind of provincial elite that came through the ranks of the Hamidian school system.[105] Armed with an imperial *passe-partout*, Rafīq Bey Tamīmī, a Nablus-born employee at the Ministry of Education with links to the secret Arab nationalist society *al-Fatāt*,[106] and Bahjat Bey, an Aleppo-born lawyer, journalist, and teacher, were in a position to admonish hitherto untouchable notables and powerful merchants 'for their oppression and greed', their acts of injustice being considered all the more despicable and treasonous in the hard times of war.[107]

The two volumes of *Bayrūt Vilāyet-i* were shot through with paragraphs on the morality of progress as well as with the desire to penetrate the 'unknown regions' of the provincial periphery.[108] During their two eight-week trips,

[103] *Bayrūt Vilāyet-i meclis umūmisinin 1330 [m.] senesi ictimāʿında itiḥāz eylediği mükarirat* (Beirut, 1915); *Bayrūt Vilāyet-i meclis umūmisinin; üçüncü devre-i ictimāʿında ceryan eden muzakeratin ẓābitdir, 1331 [m.]* (Beirut, 1916). [104] *Bayrūt Vilāyet-i meclis umūmisinin 1330.* [105] See Fortna (2001).

[106] Born in 1886, Rafīq Bey Tamīmī graduated in history from the Faculty of Arts in Paris in 1909. See Gilsenan (1996: 333 n. 3).

[107] Born in 1891, Bahjat Bey was educated at the Law Faculty in Istanbul and served on various courts across the empire before turning to journalism. He came to Beirut to join his co-author at the *sulṭaniye* school where he taught philosophy and literature. See Doumani (1996: 150, 292 n.).

[108] Gilsenan (1996: 69–74).

Rafīq Bey compiled, in unprecedented detail, information on geography, population statistics, history and archaeology, education, agriculture, commerce, public works, and industry. He studied the problem of emigration, blamed the 'backward' state of many outlying regions in the province, and recommended 'better guidance' by the state. His observations were complemented by Bahjat Bey's survey on the people's traditions, morals, hygiene, dialects, literature, and fine arts, especially the scientific movement and publishing world, 'the conditions' of heterodox sects, and ethnic groups such as the ʿAlawis, the Ismaʿilis, and Turkmans.[109]

The work for the promised third volume on Beirut may have been prevented by the war, but from the outset the mission was designed to shed light on what were considered the more obscure corners of the empire. The two volumes represented a break with previous structures of provincial knowledge culled from Ottoman yearbooks that had merely reproduced statistics and legal texts. The detailed and evaluative narrative of *Bayrūt Vilāyeti* reported on complaints and petitions against social injustices from towns and villages, and the authors often sided with the aggrieved peasants against the moneyed elite.

Previous provincial inspection tours and committees of improvement were conducted in the main by military or high imperial officials, not teachers from the region. Previous inspectors during the *tanẓīmāt* period tended to take sides with the existing local elites where and when challenged by uprisings from below.[110] Bahjat and Tamīmī's enlightening panacea was primary schooling. They sharply criticized the Young Turk government for failing to provide public education and thus to lift the provincial peripheries out of their assumed backwardness.[111] Stability and order alone were no longer sufficient requirements for a lasting improvement of the provincial conditions and a lasting popular identification with a reinvigorated Ottoman empire. The role and legitimacy of the state was contingent on its ability to imbue its people with modern forms of knowledge.

Conclusion

The point of departure of this chapter was 1888, the year Beirut was made an Ottoman provincial capital. The choice of the Ottoman provincial capital as the principal unit of analysis consciously steps out of the geographical confines

[109] Bahjat and Tamīmī (1987: i. 4). [110] Hanssen (2002: 58–61).
[111] Bahjat and Tamīmī (1987: ii. 194).

of previous national histories of Lebanon. Istanbul was the main point of reference for urban notables and political culture. Conversely, Ottoman imperialism crystallized as much out of an adaptation to political changes in Europe as to political changes in the provinces. Local reaction to the implementation of the new provincial boundaries suggests that an acute awareness of the importance of the spatial structure of the Arab provinces during the late Ottoman empire may have fed latter-day territorial nationalisms.

Certainly spatial and territorial awareness pre-dated the nation state as it emerged after the First World War. My insistence that, in the late Ottoman period, provincial boundaries mattered to the people living within them is not because we should 'assume that boundaries were literally fixed and provinces well-defined [so as to] project the limits of modern states into the past'.[112] On the contrary, provincial boundaries were challenged or defended because they affected taxation, infrastructure, welfare, and ultimately political identities of the day, irrespective of whether they came to delineate nation states or not.

The territorial boundaries of the province of Beirut ceased to exist on 29 August 1920. In a hastily drafted Arrête No. 320, the thirty-two-year-long chapter of the province of Beirut was closed just two days before the French mandate officially began.[113] In the driest of official languages, the French High Commissioner, Henri Gouraud, quietly committed this late Ottoman territorial construct to the scrapyard of history. Although some Beirutis continued to resist the chopping up of the province of Beirut by the mandate powers, in hindsight 'History' had moved on and so had the dominant Lebanese agendas. Even the 1936 'people of the coast' movement no longer based their short-lived agenda on the same boundaries as the 1913 Reform Committee of the Province of Beirut.[114] The historic merger of coastal districts, the Mountain, the Biqaʿ valley formerly under Damascene jurisdiction, and Bilad Bisharri in the south into one Grand Liban in 1920 was clearly neither the revival of an ancient Phoenician geography[115] nor, in fact, the natural outcome of the *mutaṣarrifiyya* experience of Mount Lebanon.[116] The eventual shape of the Republic of Lebanon was the product of conjectures, negotiations, and compromises during and immediately after the First World War, which could draw on a whole arsenal of different social currents and counter-currents, geographical models, and political ideas for Lebanon that mushroomed from the mid-nineteenth century onwards.[117]

112 Barbir (1980: 16). It is crucial to resist the teleological temptation to reify Ottoman provincial borders as natural precursors to national ones. See Fattah (1997: 1).

113 Haut Commissariat de la Republique Française en Syrie (1925), *Récueil des actes administratives, 1919–1924*, i (Beirut), 136.

114 See Shehadi (1987).

115 Salibi (1988: 178–9).

116 As argued by Akarli (1993).

117 Hakim-Dowek (D.Phil. thesis, 1997).

Far from a *cul-de-sac* of history, the legacy of the Beirut province lies in remembering historical roads not taken. It is precisely the legacy of the Ottoman province of Beirut that allows us to historicize the political emergence of Lebanon and Beirut as the Lebanese national capital in the twentieth century while at the same time rescuing its urban history from 'inevitablist' appropriations of state nationalism.

3

Capitalist Urbanization and Subaltern Resistance

As long as there exists a state power capable of maintaining a semblance of order, direct domination was less important. This changed with the predominance of capital exportation when much greater vested interests are at stake. When railways are built in a foreign country, when land is expropriated, when ports are constructed and mines are founded, the [investment] risk is far greater than buying and selling mere merchandise.[1]

Rudolph Hilferding was arguably one of the most influential Marxist theoreticians of the nexus between capitalism and colonialism and was in many ways the 'missing link' between Marx and Lenin. According to Hilferding, the sheer volume of financial capital moved around the globe and into the colonies by large investment companies raised the economic stakes of European imperialism. These higher stakes—so his analysis continued—inevitably led to 'ever more pressing attempts to impose on [colonial] countries legal systems appropriate to capitalism, regardless of whether existing rulers are retained or destroyed'. Each European power tried to monopolize a share of the colonial market through military conquest, trade tariffs, and economic dependency. During the Great Depression of 1873–96—the 'highest phase of capitalism'—this practice not only exploited economic resources and destroyed social relations in the non-European world, but Hilferding argued prophetically in 1910 that it was also bound to cause wars inside Europe.[2]

The link between capitalism and colonialism is the subject of continuing debate amongst the historians of metropolitan Europe and the colonial

[1] Hilferding (1968: 436). See also the discussions of Marxist writings on the link between capitalist expansion and imperialism in Owen and Sutcliffe (1972). Robert Brenner's important critique of the tendency of both modernizationists and Marxists to overlook the internal social and economic conditions for historical change strengthens this chapter's critical account of local capitalist agency and underlying class formation and conflict in 19th-cent. Beirut. See Brenner (1977: 25–91).

[2] Hilferding (1968: 437).

world.[3] In the case of the Ottoman empire, European powers forced the government to lift its trade tariffs in 1838. In spite of this the integration of the Eastern Mediterranean into the world-economy and European financial capitalism 'could not readily proceed through an alliance between the dominant interests in the center countries and those social classes in the periphery whose interests lay in the same direction'. Instead, provincial merchants and export-oriented landlords operated through, and within, Ottoman state structure.[4]

In a comparative perspective, the societies of the Ottoman empire in the nineteenth century experienced capitalist and colonial expansion differently from other peripheral regions in the world-economy. For one, the size of the empire meant that Ottoman territories became peripheralized at different times and in different places. Moreover, state bankruptcy in 1875 and the subsequent financial control by the European-controlled Public Debt Administration (PDA) neither turned the Ottoman empire into a formal colony, nor integrated it into the 'informal empire' of one particular imperial power.

Notables, Entrepreneurs, and Shareholders Capitalize on Beirut

Economic historians of Europe link the origins of organized export capital—that is to say, state-protected shareholder companies investing abroad—to 'the unprecedented disturbance and depression of trade' in Western economies between 1873 and 1895/6.[5] Historians of the Ottoman empire, too, look at the bankruptcy of the Ottoman state in 1875 as the culmination of the empire's integration into the world-economy.[6] As a way out of the financial crisis a six-plus-one nations PDA was set up to monitor Ottoman fiscal policy. In order to service the Ottoman debt, the PDA farmed out tax monopolies to European public/private companies that siphoned off taxes on spirits, salt, hunting and fishing licenses, silk, and tobacco. Determined to modernize the empire but crippled by debts and fiscal obligations, the Ottoman government took to selling concessions and granting contracts to international construction companies as a way to stimulate as much as possible the development of public utilities, regional and urban transport systems, and infrastructural projects with the limited funds available.[7]

[3] See e.g. Marseille (1984), and Saul (1997). [4] Pamuk (1988: 131).
[5] Hobsbawm (1995: 35). [6] See Kasaba (1988). [7] Verney and Dambmann (1900).

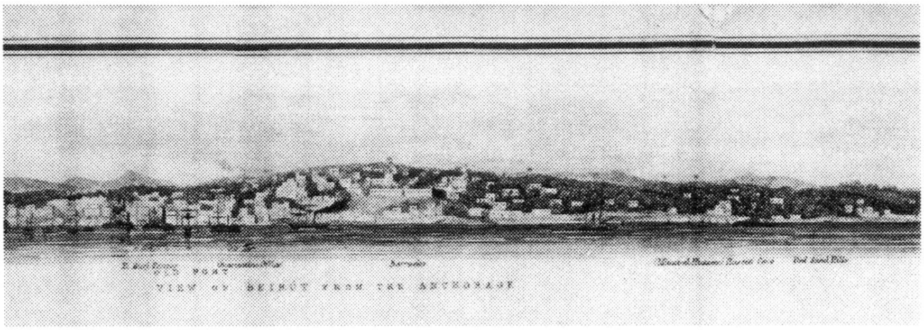

FIG. 2. Beirut seen from the sea in 1859 (Excerpt)

It will be shown in this chapter that, in Beirut prior to 1888, locally funded shareholders were attempting to develop projects, such as the enlargement of the port or the construction of a rail-link between Beirut and Damascus, but they failed due to the magnitude of the cost involved. At the same time, foreign companies were far less willing to invest in Beirut before it was a provincial capital. Nevertheless, it is significant for both this study and an understanding of capitalism in non-Western regions more generally that international construction projects were conceived first in the cities and towns of the 'peripheral' regions of the world-economy and not in the palatial environs of Paris, Brussels, London, or even Istanbul. Not only 'natural advantages', but—crucially—local agency also played an important role in the choice of investment sites.

A new dimension of inter-urban rivalry to attract large-scale finance capital eventually favoured capital Beirut over other port-cities, in particular Haifa and Tripoli. Beirut owed its success to two factors: the shift from a 'merchant republic' to a port-city and provincial capital on the one hand, and to the acute sense of political geography of its intermediary bourgeoisie and foreign residents and their intimate contacts in Istanbul on the other. The unfolding 'financial capitalization' operated within the political economy of the Ottoman state.

Under these conditions, Beirut's authorities and merchant elites averted a wholesale surrender to international capital and instead, by and large, managed to twist capitalist penetration to enhance their own vision for the city. The fear that Beirut would turn into a mere stepping stone for international trade—or of Beirut becoming a 'colonial bridgehead'—united Ottoman governors, the municipality, and merchants. The ultimate resort of resistance to the human cost of the 'financial capitalization', however, was repeated industrial action.

Concerted strikes by port and gas workers were declarations of 'the right to the city'—of reclaiming the city of Beirut from the control of international investment companies.[8]

'The Bride Among the Ports of the East'

In the first half of the nineteenth century Beiruti merchants and notables had frequently attempted improvements to the harbour walls and arcaded warehouses. These remained piecemeal repairs but appeared to maintain existing trade volumes.[9] The initial idea for a large-scale port enlargement project was conceived by a French naval officer in the aftermath of the civil war and designed by the French chief engineer of the Suez Canal, Stoeklin, in 1863.[10] The capsizing of the Messageries Maritimes steamship *Jourdain* in anchorage in February that year had impelled the local agent of this Marseilles-based company, Edmond de Perthuis, to act.[11] The envisaged plan was not only to enlarge the port ten-fold, but it was also the ambition of de Perthuis—the most powerful foreign resident in Beirut during the second half of the nineteenth century—to create a direct link between his shipping company and his road enterprise which had recently connected Beirut and Damascus.[12] This scheme would effectively give him a monopoly over all modern transport and travel facilities between the coast and Damascus. Although at the time the project remained in the office drawers of the road company and the imperial government in Istanbul, it was to be the basis of subsequent extension plans and the subject of bitter disagreement with the municipality of Beirut.

Ten years after the provincial authorities in Damascus had dropped renewed Beiruti initiatives for port enlargements,[13] the issue was raised publicly again under Midḥat Pasha's forceful governorship between 1878 and 1880. Encouraged but alerted by the governor general's development project of Tripoli's port which connected port and commercial centre of a rivalling town, Beirut's newspaper *Lisān al-Ḥāl* published a series of anxious articles reminding the Ottoman government of its commitment to Beirut's economic progress and urban improvement.

Midḥat Pasha urges everybody to participate in urban reforms. He has experience from travelling extensively in European cities and has inaugurated many new ports and roads, as well as spacious parks that fill everybody's hearts. Therefore the people of

[8] Lefebvre (1968). [9] Seeden and Thorpe (1997–8: 221–54).

[10] For the original map and options, see PRO, FO 78/1769, 2 Dec. 1863.

[11] See photograph of the wreckage, dated 22 Feb. 1863, and signed by de Perthuis, in Debbas (2001: 11).

[12] Tresse (1936: 248). [13] MAE, Paris, CCCTB 1868–1888, Beirut, 10 July 1868.

Beirut embrace his concern for the construction of a new port. They are aware of the honey inside this beehive. . . . Since the people of our *julia felix* know that it was a commercial centre since ancient times, the construction of the new port will return commercial activity to our city. What they invest will in a short period of time generate high interests.[14]

And a couple of months later, reports on the poor condition of Beirut's roads and port compared to Tripoli's development returned, prompting a research committee to assess costs and location of a port project for Beirut.[15] According to one source from the governor general's camp, when Midḥat Pasha finally turned his attention to Beirut in December 1878, the economy reacted instantly and the value of real estate briefly sky-rocketed by 40 per cent.[16] But the financial obstacles remained insurmountable as the Beirutis were unwilling to pay new consumption taxes to implement the project.[17] Instead, the French consul warned his Foreign Minister in Paris that the local inhabitants believed the Ottoman treasury should spend its revenue on more pressing issues.[18]

Given such popular reluctance, merchants and municipal members formed a lobby group whose members raised some 20,000 lira of private funds for the port project. *Lisān al-Ḥāl* broke down the contribution of the ten members and praised the individuals with characteristic panegyrics: 'We have the right to be proud of these businessmen. We can be reassured of their determination and strength in the service of the homeland (*waṭan*).'[19] Having thus identified and advertised the heroic deeds of the investors, the editor of *Lisān al-Ḥāl* specified their plan of action:

Now that the Porte has removed the obstacles many of the local notables and municipal members decided to meet under the leadership of Ra'ūf Bey [the governor of the subprovince of Beirut] to determine a place for the construction of the new port. They picked a site on Rās al-Shāmiyya near Khān Anṭūn Bey stretching to the building of the Mudawwar [family]. The decision was taken that the costs were balanced in annual instalments over four years by issuing at least 15,000 shares at 20 lira per share. It was upon the municipality to contribute to the company by holding 2,500 of its shares. If

14 *Lisān al-Ḥāl* (7 Mar. 1879). 15 *Lisān al-Ḥāl* (3 May 1879). 16 Clician (1909: 180).

17 According to *Lisān al-Ḥāl* (7 Mar. 1879), 'their value will amount to 10,000 lira, plus the average tax on passing goods amounts to 15,000 lira, but it is hoped this income will increase shortly after the construction of the port from the taxes raised then. [The municipality guarantees] to pay 6% of interest annually, through consumption tax, and 1%, through amortization, of the originally invested capital.'

18 MAE, Nantes, CB 1882–1912, carton 313, Beirut, 8 June 1879.

19 *Lisān al-Ḥāl* (7 Mar. 1879). The municipal president, 'Ibrāhīm Fakhrī Bey, [pledged] 2,000 lira, Khawāja As'ad Malḥama 500 lira, al-Sayyid Ayyās 2,000 lira, Khawāja Bustrus 3,000 lira, Sādāt Bayhum 2,000 lira, Khawāja Jirjī Tuwaynī 1,000 lira, Khawājāt Ra'ad and Hānī 500 lira, Khawājāt Sursuq 3,000 lira, Khawāja Nakhla Mudawwar 500 lira and Khawāja Yuḥanna Abkārius, 500 lira.'

the population wants to participate, the director of the company is obliged to offer options on one third of the shares. Those present at the meeting should not hold more than 950 shares each, [in other words invest more than] 19,000 lira. . . . This we ask from the buyers and sellers for sake of the success of the port. Then we can rightfully say that the city of Beirut is the bride among the ports of the East and the beauty spot in Syria.[20]

The municipal officers met in May 1878 and completed a seven-point draft position for negotiations with European financial capitalists. The committee insisted on an Ottoman company whose 'head office will not be outside Beirut but inside it'. It was to be financed by municipal taxes on visitors to the city. In return 'the company has the right to levy taxes on everything that is imported to the city on the condition that the municipality has knowledge of all income'.[21] The municipality would yield the territory of the prospective landfill to the company. However, when Midḥat Pasha resigned, the entire enterprise was shelved once more.[22]

The idea of the port project received a new injection of optimism after 1883, when de Perthuis's lobbying tours to Paris and Istanbul achieved the financial commitment of a number of large banking houses. In 1886 the Beirut port company was founded in Paris with the financial backing of the Ottoman Imperial Bank (BIO), the Comptoir d'Escompte, the Banque de Paris et des Pays-Bas, and the Messageries Maritimes. Edmond de Perthuis was closer than ever to attaining his cherished prize when, on 19 June 1887, the minister of public works signed away the concession to the Baalbek-born and Beirut-based Joseph Efendi Muṭrān (d. 1899).

The Ottoman government's granting of the port concession to Joseph Muṭrān 'and his associates'[23] signalled Abdülhamid's policy of favouring Ottoman subjects in general, and loyal Arabs in particular, over foreigners.[24] This policy represented a potent counter-measure against the international PDA's growing fiscal control over the productive sector of the Ottoman Empire. Sultan Abdülhamid also used concessions as a political tool to buy out Young Turk opposition. Natural resources had become a political bargaining chip for the sultan and a means to manufacture loyalty.

20 Ibid. 21 *Lisān al-Ḥāl* (26 May 1879).

22 In 1880, the municipality asked the Porte for better conditions than were offered by the French port company. Ismail and Chehab (1976: xiv. 143, 204–5).

23 These were probably his in-laws, Najīb and Salīm Malḥama. M. Dumast, 'Le Port de Beyrouth' (typewritten manuscript kept at the German Orient Institute in Beirut, n.d.), 6.

24 Prior to his reign, the Ottoman government tended to give concessions directly to foreigners, e.g. the concession for operating the supply of drinking water in Beirut in 1871. See MAE, Nantes, CB 1895–1914, carton 348, Exposé dated Beirut, 13 Feb. 1913.

Between 1887 and 1889, Joseph Muṭrān obtained two more imperial concessions—one for a tramway in Damascus and one for a railway between Damascus and Hawran.[25] For Beirut his concession proved an auspicious pointer and *Lisān al-Ḥāl* expressed its gratitude to 'our friend' Muṭrān.[26] He was one of the first of a series of Beiruti merchants who dominated the Ottoman concessionaire business under Abdülhamid II. Muṭrān was part of a merchant elite who moved between Beirut, Damascus, and Paris, and in Istanbul between the palace, the Ministry of Public Works, and the international Public Debt Administration. Once these individuals had bought the concession, they were free to sell it to foreign bidders, and Muṭrān quickly sold his concession to de Perthuis's investment company for 600,000 French francs at some considerable margin of profit. Under these conditions, the concession business soon developed into an 'emerging market' for Ottoman merchants with relatives in powerful government positions.

The political economy of the concession business differed considerably from previous forms of capitalism in the Ottoman empire, although both the Mediterranean merchant and the Ottoman concessionaire maintained their roles as socio-economic intermediaries. Here it was not merchandise or raw material that was shifted, such as silk or cotton, but capital and know-how. The concession business demanded greater liquidity, international banking credibility, and far better connections in Istanbul on the part of the local buyer.

The port company's finance capital was set at 5 million French francs (Ff) and divided into 10,000 shares at 500 Ff. When the shares were tendered, *Lisān al-Ḥāl* urged Beirut's inhabitants to seize the opportunity:

> We appeal to the local people to move quickly to register their names before the chance has passed because after the completion of the open registration, the group of shareholders will raise the original value according to the importance of the operation and its achievement. We seek to increase the importance of the [local] capitalists [*asḥāb al-māl*] for these shareholders have a special feeling for Beirut [and can] avoid a majority of shareholders whose interests are contrary to Beirut.[27]

Again, the newspapers published the names and amounts invested by Beiruti shareholders. Thus the readers learnt that the Sursuqs invested 25,000 lira (*c.*625.000 Ff) and the Ayyās 20,000 lira in port company shares. The port company's overwhelming financial power, both local and international, was

25 Weber (1998: 292–343).
26 MAE, Paris, NSTSL 1909, vol. 112, Beirut, 19 Feb. 1909.
27 *Lisān al-Ḥāl* (2 July 1888).

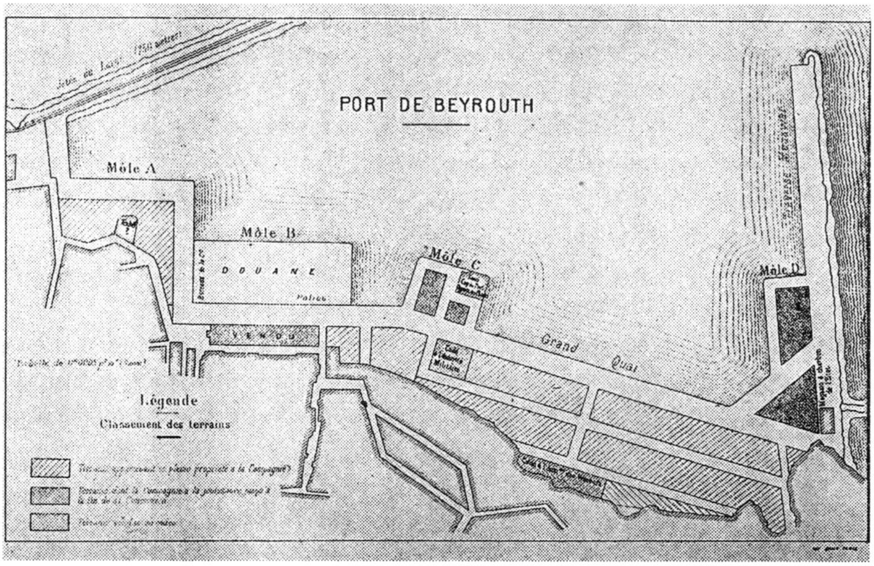

MAP. 4. Port enlargement plan

barely checked by the stipulation that the port company's tax scale was accountable directly to the Ministry of Commerce and Public Works in Istanbul.[28]

Work on the harbour basin started in January 1890 (see Map 4). Under the supervision of Henri Garreta, an experienced engineer of bridges and roads, French building companies set about to dig out the basin and create a landfill for the quays. The remains of the Crusader castle, the twin towers of the port, and the old lighthouse were razed to the ground to level the surface.[29] An employee of one of the French construction companies acknowledged the symbolism of the act of erasing these historic monuments. In a brief, private moment the engineer admitted doubts about the destruction of three of Beirut's most distinctive landmarks: 'It may appear a little savage to destroy the ruins which gave Beirut's entrance a picturesque aspect. For my part, I would not have dared to take the initiative of such a proposition.' But he instantly found solace in the excuse that 'at Beirut nobody attributes to them the least importance, one considers them ugly, without character'.[30]

[28] PRO, FO, 195/1843, Beirut, 28 March 1894.

[29] A year earlier the imperial lighthouse board decided to pull down the other lighthouse in Ras Beirut and replace it with a higher one. Newly built houses had obstructed the view from the port to the lighthouse. PRO, FO, 195/1648, Beirut, 28 May 1889.

[30] Quoted in Thobie (1977: 175. n. 235). Indeed, neither *Thamarāt al-Funūn*, nor *Lisān al-Ḥāl* appear to have complained too much at the time.

The port company effectively held a monopoly over all commercial access to the sea within Beirut's radius of five to seven kilometres. This led to frequent conflict with the British water company based as of 1896 on the northern border of the district of Beirut. It also criminalized the pursuit of the livelihood of local fishermen based in the Druze fishing harbour in ʿAyn al-Mreisse and at the bay of St Andrew just east of the port. Prior to the privatization, these natural fishing bays had been alternative, small-scale outlets for local consumption.[31] In fact, the status of de Perthuis's company turned the port into extra-territorial property over which the city authorities had no say. The only aspects de Perthuis could not (yet) legally control were the port workers and the customs officials. When the company started to operate in June 1893, as I will demonstrate shortly, these were the first flash points of discontent.

The Logic of Capitalist Expansion

Within decades of its invention in 1832, the railway spearheaded European access to much of the globe and fundamentally restructured the perceptions of distance and time.[32] The construction of railways in non-European regions not yet formally colonized was the subject of intense rivalries between financial capitalists and national governments in Europe from the 1870s onwards.[33] In Bilad al-Sham during the 1890s capitalist interests shifted from the coast to the development of railways and carriage ways that aimed at making the wealth of natural resources in the vast inland regions accessible to profitable trade (see Map 2). Numerous engineers and Orientalists were dispatched from Europe to explore and report on the topographical and geological qualities of the territories.[34]

The restructuring effect of the railway on the regional economy was not merely externally imposed by European colonialism on an unaware local population, but like in the 'prehistory' of the port enlargement of 1890–3, local notables possessed an arsenal of strategies to push their self-interest. The Beirutis, in particular, were able to play off the British against the French and tip the scales of the evolving urban rivalry towards a railway endpoint in their

[31] In 1899, Abdülhamid II issued an imperial decree, enforcing existing regulations, decreed that all fishing boats, foreign or native, required a licence of 10 piastres to fish in 'Ottoman waters' (*sic*). PRO, FO, 195/2049, Beirut, 13 June 1899.

[32] For a study on the Middle East railway network, see Khairallah (1991).

[33] See Hobsbawm (1995).

[34] See e.g. the study and the railway map drawn by the German Orientalist Martin Hartmann (1895: 56–64).

own city. They understood very well the importance of the expanding regional network of transportation and used the provincial council to argue for a connection between Beirut's port and the hinterland by railroad.

In terms of the topographical conditions between Beirut and Damascus, a railway between the two cities was by no means a natural choice. The lines would have to pass over two mountain ranges and a 1,500-metre summit. Thus it is not surprising that in a preliminary study on Syrian railway networks in 1887–8, Edouard Coze, the future technical director of the Beirut gas company, did not even mention the possibility of a Beirut–Damascus line and instead suggested other coastal cities like Tripoli as possible railheads.[35] Coze's may also have been a counter study to an earlier feasibility study by the Beiruti engineer of the province of Syria, Bishāra Dīb who was advocating a railway network that centred around Beirut. To this effect Dīb had passionately appealed to the governor general, Aḥmad Ḥamdī, Pasha in Damascus:

> We cannot wait until the foreign capitalists take over, we need to form subscription committees in Beirut, Damascus and elsewhere to raise a good part of the necessary sum of money. With your presence in Syria, Ra'ūf Pasha, the former governor of Beirut as minister for public works and the integrity of the notables of Beirut it is possible![36]

Again, the local plan was not immediately adopted but served as the base for future Beiruti lobbying. In early 1890, Coze relaunched his quest of a *tête de la ligne*, or railhead, in Tripoli for the 'Carriage Company operating from Tripoli to Homs and Hama'.[37] It was supported by Tripoli's governor and local notables who set up their own investment fund.[38]

Another challenge to Beirut was the struggle for the Haifa–Damascus rail-link in the 1880s, which was conceded to a group of Damascene and Beiruti merchants and which had been driven by the British adventurer Lawrence Oliphant.[39] This project was favoured by a more level topography.[40]

[35] Undated report, 'La Syrie, considérations générales sur l'étude des chemins de fer et sur leur développement, 1888', quoted in Thobie (1977: 170).

[36] 'Report of the Chief Engineer of the Province of Syria', Beirut, 7 July 1884. Quoted by Thobie (1977: 165).

[37] Since 1883 it had existed as a shareholding company in which Sultan Abdülhamid himself held 250 shares. See Eldem (1998: 154).

[38] MAE, Paris, CPCTB 1890, vol. 35, Beirut, 26 May 1890. Because of this rivalry, according to the French consul general, 'la Lutte existe bien ici entre de Perthuis et Coze, directeur de gaz et promoteur de la ligne de Tripoli'.

[39] In 1882, the sultan also granted a concession for a railway from Acre to the Jordan river to Muḥammad Sa'īd Pasha of Damascus, the Commander of the Pilgrimage, Muḥyī al-Dīn Ḥamāda, Yūsuf Sursuq, Jirjī Mūsa Sursuq, Michel Jirjī Tuwaynī, and Ḥannā Khūrī. In 1884, the palace granted permission to construct a railway bridge in the district of Acre. BBA, Istanbul, YHUS, 179/135, Beirut, 21 Oct. 1884. See also Ismail and Chehab (1976: xiv. 450, Beirut, 29 Jan. 1883).

[40] MAE, Nantes, CEB 1883–85, Beirut, 5 Mar. 1884.

Oliphant's designs for the Haifa–Damascus rail-link rang alarm bells in de Perthuis's camp for he feared that a railhead in Haifa would preclude a railway line to and from Beirut and ultimately jeopardize his plans for the enlarged Beirut port. De Perthuis and a group of export merchants of Beirut intervened. They realized that the project threatened to divert the export of wheat from the Hawran from the port of Beirut to the port of Haifa.[41] The provincial council protested to the governor general of Beirut and the palace. With skilful manipulation, resourceful tactics, and inside knowledge of how to persuade the sultan, they pointed out that the land through which the rival-railway was to pass belonged to the sultan. The swift intervention of the council proved successful.[42] The construction of the British line, which started in 1892, was halted in 1898 after only eight kilometres had been built.[43]

A number of municipal members, provincial councillors, and merchants of Beirut convened in the residence of Muḥyī al-Dīn Bayhum in early February 1890 for a conference on the railway issue.[44] The host, an original municipal member for the first seven years and the head of the Bayhum family, opened the meeting by calling on the audience to support his struggle to make Beirut the railhead of the first prospective railway in Bilad al-Sham. He reminded those present that it was a pressing issue for the Beirutis to offer financial support to Bishāra Dīb's project.[45] The meeting decided to appoint a committee steered by Muḥammad Ayyās to conduct an inquiry into the financial implications of a local investment fund. *Lisān al-Ḥāl*, whose editor, Khalīl Sarkīs, was himself a member of the committee meeting, supported Muḥyī al-Dīn Bayhum's initiative but in his newspaper warned the public of the financial sacrifices it entailed for the population:

41 FO, 195/1683, Beirut, 29 Oct. 1890.

42 BBA, Istanbul, YHUS, 267/115, Beirut, 15 Dec. 1892.

43 Fawaz (1983: 70).

44 *Lisān al-Ḥāl* (13 Feb. 1890). The Bayhums were the most in fluential family of notables in late Ottoman Beirut. Muḥyī al-Dīn was a cousin of the poet Ḥusayn Bayhum (1833–81) and Muḥammad Muṣṭāfa, a member of the municipal council and the chief merchant of the family. After Ḥusayn's death, Muḥyī al-Dīn emerged as the head of the family. His daughter married Aḥmad Mukhtār Bayhum, another family member who sat on Beirut's municipal council, and a leading reformist in the Young Turk period. Muḥyī al-Dīn was a member of the Syrian Scientific Society of 1867–9 before he was appointed mā'nicipal president briefly in 1877. He then became a member of Beirut's subprovincial council (*majlis al-liwā'*) between 1879 and 1885 and sat on the provincial education council.

45 *Lisān al-Ḥāl* lists the following individuals as present at the meeting: 'Ibrāhīm Thābit, Hajj Ibrāhīm Tayyāra, Eliās ʿArab, Bishāra Arqāsh, Bishāra Dīb, our Jews [sic] the Bayhums, Jabbūr Ṭabīb, Jirjī Tuwayni, Jirjī Mūsa Sursuq, Khalīl Sarkīs, Rizqallah Khadrā', Rashīd al-Muṭrān, ʿAbd al-Qādir al-Qabbānī, Muḥammad Ayyās and son, Muḥammad Badrān, Muḥammad Shakhībī, Muḥammad Dāʿūq, Muḥyī al-Dīn Ḥamāda, Muḥyī al-Dīn al-Qāḍī, Miṣbāḥ Ghandūr, Najīb Mudawwar, Nakhla Farʿūn, Yūsuf Bījī. Others were invited, but they excused themselves for health reasons.'

We will soon see success or failure of preserving our central position (*markazuna*) and wealth. . . . Remember, the distance between Beirut and Damascus is 180 km and the distance from Hawran to Damascus is 70 km. The construction of one kilometre costs roughly 4,000 lira, so what is needed are 1,000,000 lira. Having said this, the backdrop is that Beirut and the committee members can only raise a maximum of 150,000 lira. This is completely insufficient, because we would have to pay [this amount] for at least six years. It is well-known that Beirut pays 15,000 lira annually in *virgu* taxes. Even if the property owners were to pay double that amount it would take over fifty years.[46]

It became clear to the committee that the financial resources for such a vast infrastructural project were not available in Beirut. The municipal and provincial budgets were fully spent. Nevertheless, under the direction of Ḥasan Bayhum, whose position on the provincial council and whose thriving grain trade in Hawran would have made him a leading lobbyist, the Bayhums constituted the 'Société anonyme ottomane de la voie ferrée de Beyrouth à Damas' and applied for an imperial concession in Istanbul which the sultan granted to Ḥasan Bayhum for ninety-nine years on 3 June 1891.

The Beirut–Damascus and the Damascus–Hawran railway plans were thus in the hands of two Beiruti concessionaires, Muṭrān and Bayhum. In 1892, Bayhum sold his company to de Perthuis who merged the Beirut–Damascus Road Company with the 'Société de la voie ferrée de Beyrouth-Damas'. A year later the two concession companies of Joseph Muṭrān and Ḥasan Bayhum were merged into the renamed 'Société anonyme ottomane des chemins de fer de Beyrouth–Damas–Hawran et Birecik sur l'Euphrate'.[47]

As a consequence of these developments, de Perthuis finally held the reins of what had been four separate road and railway concessions, while the Beirutis had irrevocably established their city as the dominant political and economic centre of Bilad al-Sham. In the short term, the railway company had to run the enterprise at a considerable loss, even jeopardizing the profitable road company.[48] Ultimately, however, the turn of events only revealed that Beirut's merchants wielded enough powers of persuasion to ensure the creation of an uneconomic enterprise for the underlying purpose of depriving rivals from capturing the trade of the hinterland.[49]

[46] Ibid. Khalīl Sarkīs was born on 22 Jan. 1842 in the Christian village of ʿAbay in Mount Lebanon. After his father died, he moved to Beirut with his three sisters in 1850 where he received his primary education at the American seminary under the aegis of Anglican missionary William Thomson and Khalīl al-Khūrī. For more biographical details on Khalīl Khurī and other Beirutis in this chapter see Hanssen (D.Phil. thesis, 2001: Annex).

[47] BBA, Istanbul, YHUS, 269/7, Beirut, 21 Jan. 1893.

[48] Thobie (1977: 164).

[49] Özveren (Ph.D. thesis, 1990: 179).

Like de Perthuis's port company, the railway company was forced to borrow heavily from the BIO. Thanks to financial injections, construction work crossed over mountain tops, numerous bridges, two viaducts, and through 300-metre tunnels, going ahead at a considerable pace. On 8 August 1895, attempting to coincide with the sultan's anniversary, the inauguration of the connection between Baramke in Damascus and Qarantina in Beirut was staged as grand, citywide celebrations in both cities. At ten miles per hour, the trains took nine to ten hours to cross Mount Lebanon, four to five hours less than the carriageway.[50] It was presented in the press as a great success for industry and modernity. In the years to come, other inland cities were connected to this railway line: Hama, Rayak, Baghdad, and, after 1902, a direct Istanbul–Hijaz connection converged with the Beirut–Damascus line at Baramke station, Damascus.

The capitalist logic of railway expansion, which purported to serve the rational requirements of transport and communication between various parts of the region, was also a strategy that served the dominant economic interest of European companies and local merchants. In the next section, I turn to the effects of infrastructural integration inside the city of Beirut; that is, the capitalist development of certain parts of town and the underdevelopment of others. To apply Lefebvre to Beirut once more,

> '[c]ontradictions [of capitalism] are no longer situated between town and country. The principal contradiction occurs and situates itself inside the urban phenomenon between the centre of [political] power and other forms of centrality, between the centres of wealth and the [inner-city] peripheries, between integration and segregation.'[51]

City of Lights

The number of foreign residents in Beirut grew considerably during the 1890s. The population of the French 'colony' alone rose from 600 to 1,400 between 1891 and 1897.[52] The main thrust of French intervention in Beirut and Mount Lebanon had been cultural in general and religious in particular. The educational policies of Catholic Jesuit circles, which addressed particularly the Maronite community, had long constituted a most reliable avenue of French

[50] This rendered travel between Damascus and Beirut faster than travel between Beirut and the more accessible neighbouring coastal towns of Haifa or Tripoli.

[51] Lefebvre (2003: 225).

[52] Ismail and Chehab (1976: xvi. 430), and MAE, Paris, CCCTB, vol. 12, Beirut, 13 Aug. 1897.

colonial designs.[53] In Beirut, this policy culminated in the founding of the Université de St Joseph in 1875 and the Faculté de Médicine in 1883. If this approach was never entirely abandoned, the dominant role of the Jesuits was superseded by a policy of supporting French economic investments in the entire region of Bilad al-Sham, relegating somewhat the primacy of the Christian Mount Lebanon in the French foreign ministry.[54] French, let alone foreign companies more generally, constituted a far from homogeneous and unified interest group. In fact, foreigners struggled among themselves and often were bitter personal enemies. Eugène Melchior Vicomte de Voguë, himself a leading advocate of French colonialism and *connaisseur* of Syria, once summed up this conflict as polarized between 'those of Notre Dame (Christian loyal, and backward looking), and those of the Eiffel Tower (Republican, anti-clerical, and idealist, who wilfully ignored the past)'.[55] Edouard Coze came close to the Eiffel Tower archetype. This newly arrived, resourceful, and progressive engineer was the bitter enemy of Count de Perthuis whose increasing possessiveness of Beirut as his 'fiefdom' and whose Orléanist tendencies and arrogant expatriate conservatism offended the sensibilities of French modernists like Coze.[56]

Unusually, the concession to build a network of gas lighting in Beirut had been given to a foreigner back in December 1885. In January 1887, 'la Société anonyme ottomane du gaz de Beyrouth' was created and consisted of a seven-member board, three of whom were also European BIO executives. Emile Coze represented 'la Société de gaz du Nord et de l'Est de la France' in Beirut, while in the early years the only Ottoman member of the board was the merchant and municipal member Mūsā de Frayj. The company quickly set about building a gas factory near the quarantine, a depot east of the main square, Sahat al-Burj, and some twenty miles of underground pipelines. By 1889 some 600 gas lamps were installed along the main streets and throughways of the city.

As with the port and railway companies, early optimism quickly faded with the realization that the income could not cover the expenses, let alone generate profit. A fortnight after promoting the gas company in a spectacular light show at a party in his home in Zuqaq al-Blat, Mūsā de Frayj and Emile Coze met to discuss ways to improve the company's services and the payment of municipal arrears to the company with the leading municipal member, Muḥyī al-Dīn

[53] Spagnolo (1973: 563–84). [54] Shorrock (1975). [55] Rabinow (1989: 116).

[56] Ismail and Chehab (1976: xvi. 18, 26 May 1890). Coze was the author of *La Syrie et le Liban* (Lyons, 1922) and board member of a British–Egyptian trading company.

Ḥamāda.[57] In subsequent years, the gas company was unable to maintain even these standards. At a public hearing, the municipality complained that the light the gas company produced was too weak to light up the street and that at least 300 more lamp-posts were needed.[58] Over the next few years the company did install another 1,000 lamps across the city, but tensions between the foreign investors and the municipality continued throughout the Ottoman period. As with the previous investment companies in Beirut, the gas company saw no other way out of the crisis than to borrow money from the BIO. Between 1895 and 1903, the Beirut gas company was effectively run from the BIO head offices in Istanbul.[59] Thus, in the 1890s, the BIO assumed financial control over all French infrastructural investment projects.

The gas company witnessed a significant change from the familiar pattern of BIO absorption when in 1903 Ibrāhīm Ṣabbāgh took over the company in a veritable financial coup.[60] A Beiruti banker and shareholder in both the BIO-controlled gas and the railway companies, Ṣabbāgh was also the president of the Ottoman Chamber of Commerce in Paris and executive member of a host of international banks.[61] With the help of political allies in Istanbul, he took the BIO to court. He demanded a two million francs reimbursement for his stakes in the railway company on the pretext that the agreement was signed in Paris and not, as stipulated, in the Ottoman capital. The case was settled in Ṣabbāgh's favour and he received the BIO's entire stock of gas company shares.[62]

Just before his death in 1909, he and his brother Eliās took over the British-owned 'Beirut Waterworks' which had supplied the city with water from the nearby Nahr al-Kalb since it bought the concession from the French entrepreneur Thévenin in 1871.[63] Although the extent of their influence was exceptional, Ṣabbāgh and his family members on the board of directors formed part of a growing group of Beiruti merchants who moved beyond the geographic boundaries of Eastern Mediterranean trade, and whose radius of activities can

[57] *Lisān al-Ḥāl* (16 Dec. 1889). Mūsā Frayj was made marquis by the Vatican in the 1870s, either because of his trade connections to Austrian Trieste or for his generous support for Beirut's Cappucin church in Beirut. Mūsā's father Yuḥannā had come to Beirut in 1860 via Palestine and Damascus.

[58] *Thamarāt al-Funūn* (1 Jan. 1894).

[59] MAE, Nantes, CB 1863–1914, carton 330, Beirut, 8 Sept. 1907. It obtained an extension of thirty-five years for the operation of the Beirut gas works.

[60] The Sabbaghs were Greek Orthodox, originally from Homs, later Marj ʿAyun. In the 18th century, the Ṣabbāgh family moved from Acre (where one Ibrāhīm Ṣabbāgh was Ẓāhir al-ʿUmar's doctor), then to Shuwayr, and later Beirut.

[61] Thobie (1991: 407–40, esp. fig. 18.5). Ibrāhīm Ṣabbāgh made his fortunes in Beirut's silk and linen trade in the 1880s. Based on their shares in the gas company, Ibrāhīm and Eliās founded the banking house Ṣabbāgh and Co. in Paris in 1903.

[62] Thobie (1993: 144).

[63] al-Wālī (1993: 204).

no longer be grasped in the familiar parameters of local merchants or urban notables. The Ṣabbāghs, like the Malḥama family below were international power brokers.

Vehicles for the Mobilization of Urban Space

On 28 September 1905 the French journal *Stamboul* published an advertisement for a newly founded company, the 'Société Anonyme Ottomane des Tramways et de l'Electricité de Beyrouth'. It tendered 20,000 shares at 100 francs each. The list of executive board members introduced the Malhama family to the international world of finance.[64] Najīb Pasha Malḥama was named as the president, and his brothers, Philippe Efendi and Ḥabīb Efendi, as well as Najīb's father-in-law Salīm Raʿad—the original concession holder—shared the board with old hands who were already executive members in various companies.[65]

The foundation of this new infrastructural investment company presents a new variation on the theme of a systematic European investment in the urban fabric of Beirut. As ministers of state and palace favourites, Salīm and Najīb Malḥama had managed to place family members and loyal allies inside the government. The main legislative body of the Ottoman state, the Council of State, functioned as the arbitrator of provincial development projects. Investment projects from international companies depended on its approval. Councillors of state thus became the investors' best friends.

The novelty of the tramway project was that Salīm Raʿad passed his concession on to an in-law who founded and presided over the company himself before merging with the existing Beirut gas company. This business strategy secured considerably more profit than Joseph Muṭrān's sale of the railway concession a decade earlier. The Beiruti concession holders had become international players in the quest for the 'financial capitalization' of their city.

The origins of the idea were probably in the successful operation of the tramway of Tripoli initiated by Midḥat Pasha in 1878. In Beirut action was only taken after the creation of the province of Beirut. In 1891, the provincial engineer Bishāra Dīb asked the governor general, Ismail Kemal Bey, to grant a 'tramway concession for the best suited throughways in the quarters of Beirut'.[66] Despite the governor general's approval, the plans evaporated somewhere between Istanbul and Beirut. Some fifteen years later an imperial

[64] Ch. 4 of Hanssen (D.Phil. thesis, 2001) traces this Maronite family's rise from 17th-cent. warlords to Hamidian ministers.

[65] MAE, Nantes, CB 1863–1914, carton 330, 'Stamboul' article enclosed.

[66] *Thamarāt al-Funūn* (5 Dec. 1891); quoted in al-Wālī (1993: 186).

concession was granted to Salīm Efendi Raʿad, a councillor of state at the Sublime Porte, Aleppine of origin but member of a wealthy Beiruti merchant family with considerable property in Beirut.

Raʿad immediately took two foreign engineers to inspect the site and conduct a feasibility study on Beirut. They noted the difficult and uneven terrain, but figured that modern technology could overcome these problems. The existing, prosperous business of horse-drawn cabs convinced them that there was a market for connecting the burgeoning outer-city quarters to the port and city centre. Although construction costs were estimated to be in excess of twelve million francs, the project had every prospect of profit. The only problem they figured was the source of energy—whether to use water generation from the distant Nahr al-Kalb whose exploitation belonged to a British company, or coal, petrol, or gas driven engines.[67]

The Malḥamas preferred a third option. They decided to expand their business to electric lighting for Beirut, an aggressive move against Ṣabbāgh's existing company that was probably a calculated confrontation to up the price for an eventual take-over. Predictably, their proposition to tie up the tramway with an electric lighting venture was contested by the existing gas company when the Ṣabbāghs launched a legal offensive claiming contravention of the stipulations of their concession and ultimately bought up the Malḥama's company at one million French francs in March 1907.[68]

In return for a ninety-nine-year concession which was granted halfway through the construction in 1908, the Ottoman minister of public works obliged the tramway company to pay the municipality some 6,000 napoleons (*c.*6,000 lira) for the necessary property expropriations and loans for street widening.[69] After an enthusiastic start, the works slowed down due to growing 'prevarication'—as the French consul called it—by the municipal members and the Beiruti newspapers 'that have captured public opinion'.[70]

In fact, the population as a whole was discontented. The expropriation loans turned out to be far from sufficient for the municipality to finance the reparations for those inhabitants affected by the ensuing house demolitions. It became necessary for the provincial council to intercede and write a memorandum to the Ministry of Public Works that pointed out the misfortunes that had befallen the city of Beirut at the hands of ill-conducted engineering work. Ever the voice of the city, *Lisān al-Ḥāl* covered the conflict in its local news section

[67] PRO, FO, 195/2217, Beirut, 11 Sept. 1905.

[68] Ibid. 'Quarterly Report', Beirut, 10 Aug. 1906. MAE, Nantes, CB 1863–1914, carton 330, Beirut, 8 Sept. 1907.

[69] MAE, Paris, NSSTSL 1902–1907, vol. 46, Beirut, 19 Sept. 1907.

[70] MAE, Nantes, CB 1863–1914, carton 330, Beirut, 18 Nov. 1908.

and argued that the root problem lay with the formulation of the concession itself:

The provincial authorities have designated a commission of notables to examine the negative effect of the tramway lines on the inhabitants and passers-by. A petition signed by 7,000 people of the town demanded that the provincial authorities deal with the dangers which may result in the installation of this form of traffic, especially on double tracked streets and the narrow streets where walking is seriously impaired and a source of unforeseen dangers. . . .

We have been wondering when the trenches and the banking on both sides of the tramway will be completed and whether the carriages will start running this season. We are worried that the stipulations of the company are too vague and that the inconsiderate conduct of the company regarding street enlargement and paving on both sides of the tracks remains unaddressed.[71]

The tramway, whose construction had been inaugurated amidst great pomp in honour of Abdülhamid's birthday on 1 September 1907, was opened to the public only fifteen months later. The initial problems had been laid to rest and many streets had been aligned, paved, and widened alongside the rails. Five lines were opened. One connected the pine forest, through the quarters of Bashura, Ras al-Nabaʿ past the military hospital and Khan Fakhrī Bey. Another ran from the lighthouse in Ras Beirut to the port. A third offered a fast way around the old city centre by running along the traces of the old city walls towards distant Furn al-Shubbak. The fourth line ran from behind the Petit Serail through the old town to the former Bab Idriss and linked up there to the third line. The fifth line passed from Sahat al-Burj through the wealthy Christian quarters of Mudawwar and Rumayl to Beirut River in the east[72] (see Map 5).

The tramway had far-reaching consequences for those outlying quarters and quasi-rural hamlets that it connected to the city centre. At the same time, that city centre was quickly turning into 'the old part of the town, which was a labyrinth of dark narrow alleys inhabited by poor Muslims' encircled by modern transport.[73] The tramway galvanized urban development along its tracks analogous to the way the port and the railway tied international and regional trade to the city.[74] When Coze's long-planned Tramway Libanais between Beirut and Sidon began to operate its regional network in the 1910s, the link it created between the villages of Sin al-Fil,[75] Furn al-Shubak, and Shiyyah on the

[71] MAE, Nantes, CB, 9 July 1907, enclosure: translation of undated *Lisān al-Ḥāl* article.

[72] PRO, FO, 195/2245, Beirut, 19 Sept. 1907.

[73] PRO, FO, 195/1761, Beirut, 2 Aug. 1892.

[74] Ilbert (1996) observed similar effects of the tramway for Alexandria.

[75] BBA, Istanbul, CL, 7/292, Beirut, 12 May 1915.

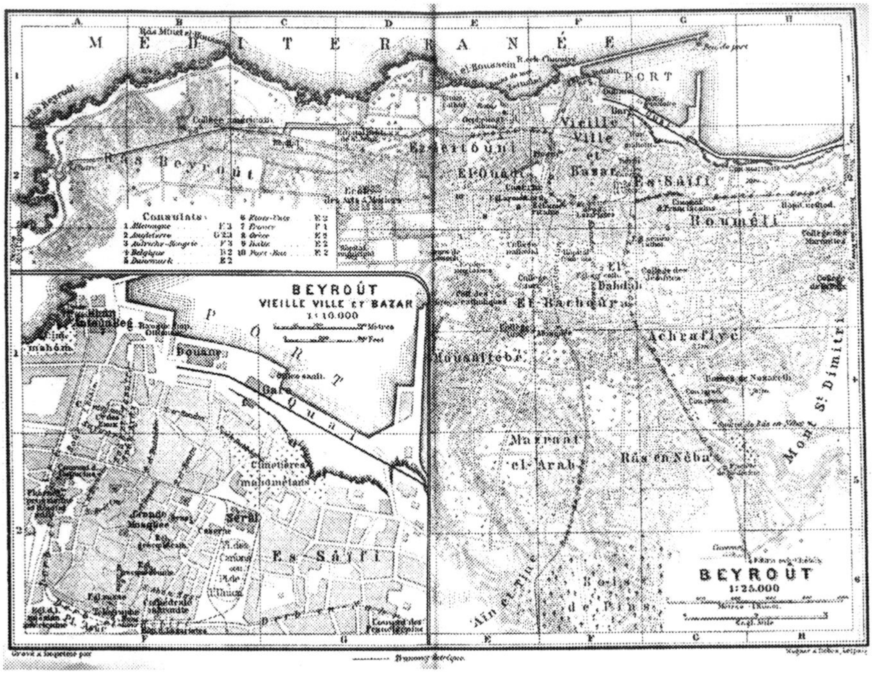

Map. 5. Baedecker Map of Beirut, including the five tramway lines, 1912.

one hand and Sahat al-Sur on edge of the city centre on the other, played a catalyst role in the development of these settlements.

The tramway and the extramural construction boom also attracted land speculators from abroad. News of the construction of the tramway lines reached Cairo and in 1906 a British development company sent Wilcocks, one of the chief engineers of the first Aswan dam, to study the terrain. He identified 'an area of vast sand dunes called al-Jinah' as the most profitable investment site on account of its location on the border separating the territory of Mount Lebanon and the province of Beirut. Legally in the mountain district of Matn-Sahil, some of the plots of the area belonged to 'rich personages' of Beirut. Wilcocks speculated that Beirut's vast expansion would push up land prices in this area where land was still cheap in the foreseeable future. His proposal for apartment blocks for Beirutis who would take advantage of the connecting tramway and the security of the area compared to the bustling city was taken up by the Cairo-based, Anglo-Belgian Entreprise and Development Co. But attempts at land purchases appear to have been thwarted by the ruling of an Ottoman court that *mīrī* land (state-owned property) represented part of 'local heritage that could not be sold *en bloque* to isolated investment companies'.[76]

On the edge of the 'old city', Sahat al-Sur and Sahat al-Burj became the main two traffic centres.[77] For a two-hour journey from Beirut River, the city's eastern border with Mount Lebanon, to the lighthouse in Ras Beirut the passengers would have to change lines on Sahat al-Sur. Inner-city distances were covered more quickly and demanded less effort. At least in theory, the introduction of scheduled transport services regulated the organization of time in Beirut more rigidly. In practice, however, the system of timetables and stops was undermined by passengers who stopped the carriages between stops and forced them to wait for them to embark and disembark. The new dimensions of geographical mobility of Beirut's population caused considerable strains on public security in Beirut. For some older Beirutis the tramway even gained the epithet Satan's wheels, 'Dūlāb al-Shaytān'.[78]

However, superstition was much less the root cause of anxiety than accidents and tangible unrest along the tramway tracks.[79] There were incidents of hijacking carriages and boycotts by passengers in the Mudawwar quarter and elsewhere.[80] Occasionally, tramway passengers molested the passing pedestrians, or a passing of the one or two-carriage tramway—strictly gender-separated—was attacked by agitated coffeehouse guests along the lines.[81] The tramway became a constant source of conflict over access to modern amenities. The French consul cabled an exasperated report to Paris in 1910 complaining that 'for some time now, disputes and riots occur on the electric tramway in Beirut. . . . I myself have seen a passenger who was thrown out of the carriage for refusing to pay for his seat run after the tramway firing revolver shots.'[82] Such incidences challenged the technological achievement of the age as much as urban security in general. They generated heavy criticism against the local police force and, indeed, led to a doubling of numbers of policemen to fifty officers.[83] The very bourgeois order the tramway had heralded appeared constantly under threat from malicious acts of deviance and contributed to the general sense of unease amongst the well-to-do of Beirut.

[76] MAE, Nantes, CEB 1894–1911, Beirut, 7 Jan. 1907. Little information on the link between infrastructural development and land speculation exists in Beirut. On the Jinah project, see PRO, FO, 195/2217, 'Quarterly Report', 10 Aug. 1906.

[77] For a comparison of both squares, see Ch. 9.

[78] al-Wālī (1993: 187).

[79] Writing from Egypt, Dr Shiblī Shumayyil (1850–1915), leading Darwinist in the 1880s, socialist in the 1890s and decentralist activist in the 1900s, called the tramway an 'Angel of Death' in *al-Muqaṭṭam* (17 Mar. 1898). See Shumayyil (1991: 28).

[80] MAE, Nantes, CB 1905–1914, carton 253, undated enclosure, 'Rapport adressé à la direction par le service de l'exploitation des Tramway Libanais' (1909).

[81] al-Wālī (1993: 187).

[82] MAE, Paris, NSTSL 1910, vol. 113, Beirut, 25 Apr. 1910.

[83] Ibid.

The tramway was an arena as well as an instrument of mobilizing labour and of public protest. Soon the tramway became such a popular means of transportation in Beirut that the guild of coachers who until then had conducted the mainstay of public transportation in Beirut began to mobilize resistance against their new rivals.[84] Likewise, a decision by the company to raise the fare was received by an organized passenger boycott. Those Beirutis who chose to ignore the boycott were jeered by the crowd.[85] Such popular unrest and civil disobedience also signified resistance against a sense of intrusion into the people's organization of private life by external agencies. Families who happened to live on the tramway line suddenly found themselves exposed to journeying crowds. As a passive form of protest against the imposition of an external rhythm by the tramway, they moved out of their houses towards infrastructurally more remote areas of the city.[86] Often businesses and shops attracted by the exposure and easy access moved in.

The everyday life in Beirut was beginning to be shaped by its modern infrastructural investments. Until 1888, the municipality of Beirut and Ottoman authorities had struggled to optimize the port facilities *for* the city centre. With capitalist urbanization, however, commerce, transport, and communication were conducted around and even *against* the original centre. The centre continued to exist as a place of small-scale commerce and dwelling, but that place was perceived of more as an obstacle to, rather than an object of, urban improvement. Wealthy merchants moved their offices to the edge of the city centre where new, aligned bazaars were being built. At the same time they moved their residences to the new, spacious quarters overlooking the city centre and the Beirut bay.

Spaces of Resistance

Space is fundamental in any exercise of power.[87]

Capitalist intervention in Beirut's urban fabric was powerful but not triumphant. The weak financial structure of international investment companies may account for their harsh bargaining course against the municipality and the severe working conditions imposed on its labour force. Certainly, the highly speculative nature of the public works projects that developed after the 'political capitalization' of Beirut left both the municipality and the companies

[84] al-Wālī (1993: 188). [85] Ibid. [86] Ibid. 187. [87] Foucault (1980).

virtually paralysed. In this section I argue that the urbanization of Beirut after 1888 also created its own forms of opposition.

On the Waterfront: 'You are not in France here, you are in Turkey'

On the morning of 18 June 1893, Captain Phalix and his crew were in for a shock when they steered their richly laden Messagiers Maritimes vessel, the *Yang Tse*, into Beirut harbour. The new port was still not fully operational, but the *Yang Tse* was poised to enter the annals of the port company as the first ship to enjoy the services of the new customs office and the new haulage services of MM Estier et Frères, a Marseilles-based subcontractor that de Perthuis had employed to improve the efficiency standards of his company. The company director seemed to have anticipated trouble but the chief of police rebuffed his request for an escort.[88]

When a boat of Estier et Frères set out to unload the merchandise of the ship several hundreds of the local port workers took it as a signal for a timed attack on the French-held offices at the customs and the approaching ship. The furious protestors destroyed the furniture of the offices and threw the boat's merchandise overboard. Captain Phalix made for the port where the police finally intervened but could do little to quell the anger of the port workers. Instead the hapless captain was arrested and brought to the Serail prison where he remained on charges of threatening the port workers with his pistol.[89]

Captain Phalix had become the unwitting victim of a simmering conflict between the local authorities and the director of the port company that had started three years earlier and grown intense in the run-up to the opening of the new port facilities. De Perthuis had incurred the wrath of a humiliated municipality when his newly privatized customs regime closed a small pier for regional and local boats, which effectively deprived the municipal budget of revenues accrued from minor quantities of merchandise.[90] In another act of managerial streamlining, in May 1893 the efficient and generally liked head of Beirut customs, Wafiq Bey, a son-in-law of the late Midḥat Pasha, was sacked and replaced by a less experienced Ottoman official. His surprising dismissal generated speculations that de Perthuis's middlemen in the capital had discredited him because of his criticism of the port company's French ownership, the increased tariffs, and the port workers' pay.[91]

88 MAE, Paris, CPCTB 1892–3, vol. 37, Beirut, 8 July 1893. 89 Ibid.

90 PRO, FO, 195/1683, Beirut, 24 May 1890.

91 PRO, FO, 195/1801, Beirut, 18 May 1893. In 1907 the salary was $^{3}/_{4}$ mecidiye (3 fr 20c) per day.

More important still, the port company had also replaced local labour with that of other coastal towns in the Levant.[92] These new migrant workers were probably more economically desperate than professionally qualified and had no choice but to subject to the mechanized rules of conduct the company imposed on them. The Règlement du Port et des Quays de Beyrouth sought to overcome lack of experience and qualification in the new workforce by strictly regimented working order.[93] Unable and unqualified to exercise any other work, the sacked local port workers who—unlike the imported labour—were organized in two guilds—the lighters and the porters—turned to the governor general for help.[94] Khālid Bey, the governor general, rendered his full support to the cause of the lighters and the porters.[95] Khālid Bey justified his confrontation with de Perthuis by insisting that the Council of State's ruling of opening tender to workers applied only to local and not to imported labour. He insisted that the port company should not compete with the existing port workers' guilds. In mid-June, he urged de Perthuis to re-employ in his company all those porters who had worked under the previous customs regime. It was de Perthuis's categorical refusal that caused the port workers to attack the unsuspecting crew members of the *Yang Tse*.

Supported by the governor general who demanded that the customs office allow all unemployed porters to enter its premises, an angry crowd occupied the port buildings shouting at the company: 'You are not in France here, you are in Turkey. You are not the masters.'[96] Commerce in the port of Beirut came to a halt. De Perthuis complained vehemently to the governor general against what he considered 'acts of piracy' and against Khālid Bey's irresponsible tolerance of it. But the governor general's protection of the port workers earned him the backing of the sultan who had been visited by the port workers' representative Faḍlallah Bey Sayyūr, a Greek Orthodox merchant and agent of the Khedival Lines. The sultan was persuaded and decreed that the company should re-employ port workers.[97]

Beiruti resistance against the port company drew wider circles. Soon, the port company's new tariffs on anchorage and mooring, although ratified by the Council of State in Istanbul, incensed local and foreign merchants alike. These merchants forged an unlikely alliance of purpose between them and the

[92] PRO, FO, 195/2245, Beirut, 11 July 1893.

[93] MAE, Nantes, CB 1882–1912, carton 313, undated enclosure.

[94] Scattered British consular reports speak of a total of 400, mainly Muslim porters (possibly former Druze fishermen from nearby ʿAin Mreisse), but also mention Maronites working in the port.

[95] MAE, Paris, CPCTB 1892–3, vol. 37, Beirut, 8 July 1893. [96] Ibid.

[97] MAE, Paris, CCCTB 1888–94, vol. 10, Beirut, 5 July 1893.

strikers who—according to the usually snobbish language of the British consul general—'belong to the lower classes, blacksmiths, boatmen, porters, smugglers, port loafers, not to mention the scum and riffraff which are always to be found in seaports of the Levant'.[98] When the port company started collecting higher taxes a year later, the Beirut merchants took part of their goods—sugar, rice, and coffee—to Tripoli and Haifa.[99] This *de facto* boycott of the port put de Perthuis in conflict with his subcontractors, Estier et Frères. De Perthuis had lured them to Beirut promising them the lucrative business of a monopoly on loading and unloading. The opposition from the local authorities, the merchants, and the guilds forced the company to leave Beirut after only a few lacklustre months.[100]

The port workers won an important victory. But the British consul already anticipated in 1894 that, once Beirut became the railhead, the merchants would be forced to take their business back to Beirut. And, indeed, when the Beirut–Damascus railway opened its services, the embattled port company found the long awaited relief. De Perthuis may have been made to retire from active office by his financiers, and the railway company was to run long years of losses but the port/railway combination saved the day for both works in the long term. At the same time, the leverage and margin of local protest against the effects of the infrastructural projects lay precisely in the immovability—or, in Harvey's terminology, 'the spatial fix'—of these capitalist projects.[101] In contrast to trade based on free exchange of commodities, which was characteristically a much more 'promiscuous' business, the physical fixity of a port or a railway tied financial capital hook or crook to the city in which it was invested. As long as the Ottoman state was unwilling to surrender to the demands of finance capital, this would give some protection to the rights and job security of the workers.

Labour protests grew louder and more violent again after Abdülhamid II was ousted in 1908–9. Despite the different circumstances, the demands of the workers were very similar to the ones of the 1890s. In 1908, industrial action in Beirut had the support of a number of local journalists, some of whom had probably joined the recent formation of a socialist movement.[102] The workers used the medium of the newspaper to advance their aims. While the press in Beirut had been largely silent on the strike action in the 1890s, in the direct

[98] PRO, FO, 195/2140, Beirut, 7 Sept. 1903.

[99] MAE, Paris, CCCTB 1895–1911, vol. 11, Beirut, 8 Jan. 1895.

[100] MAE, Paris, CPCTB 1892–3, vol. 37, Beirut, 8 July 1893.

[101] Harvey (1999).

[102] According to Samneh (1920: 57), 'a socialist demonstration took place on a Lebanese beach [south of Beirut] on May 7, 1907 [that included] ardent speakers . . . the likes of Daoud Bey Naqqash, Sulayman al-Boustani and Zehrawi Efendi'. See also Ḥanna (1983).

aftermath of the April revolution in Istanbul, journalists came out in strong support for the workers' cause.

In a public address to the governor general, the port workers appealed to Ottoman law to prevent their 'eradication'. They published their complaints in Arabic and in French in *al-Ayyām*:

> We, the undersigned, Ottoman boatmen of Beirut have the honour to expose the following:
>
> The company of quays and warehouses of Beirut whose resources and powers are ever increasing is in a position to transform the slightest desire into reality. We unfortunate workers who earn just enough not to let our large families die of starvation are unable to defend ourselves. . . . A good number of us were arrested and thrown into prison and others had their boats confiscated and thrown out of the port to the open sea where they are exposed to great dangers. But all this is not enough. They have mobilized gangs who threaten to shoot at anyone who tries to salvage their belongings on the port premises. Such acts of aggression are not approved by our laws and all principles of government condemn them. It is directed purely at eradicating us. . . .
>
> As a consequence, we declare that if we do not obtain guarantees for our people and our rights and if the arbitrariness of the company is not put to a stop, we find ourselves obliged to defend ourselves to ensure the subsistence of our families who consist of over 20,000 people and to take all measures the law offers us to address higher places [in Istanbul].[103]

The workers made reference to their growing number—20,000 men, women, and children—to show the justice of their cause and to threaten the companies. And, indeed, in October 1908, they were joined by their comrades working in the railway and gas companies.[104] After the proclamation of the constitution, the port workers renewed their claims by adopting the very language of universal principles enshrined in the Ottoman constitution. Apart from previous demands for a pay rise, 'with a violence unknown before' the strikers now refused forced retirement, rejected all outside interference in the operation of their guilds, and 'claimed the right to designate their own successors from amongst their family'. Moreover they now categorically objected to 'the legitimacy of their foreman's punishment'. Encouraged by the news that port workers in Istanbul, Izmir, and Salonika had also gone on strike, the Beiruti strikers 'appealed to the patriotism of the Beirutis to support them in their struggle against the increasing intervention of foreign elements in the affairs of the city'.[105] In *al-Aḥwāl*, for example, they released the following statement:

[103] MAE, Nantes, CB 1882–1912, carton 313, undated enclosure.

[104] MAE, NSTSL, vol. 111, Beirut, 8 Oct. 1908. This was Beirut's first general strike.

[105] Ibid., enclosed letter to Istanbul, dated Beirut, 17 Aug. 1908.

The port workers of the customs office

In the name of justice and liberty . . . We have inherited our work from father to son. It has become ours over generations. Owing to lack of other knowledge we have no other way of earning our daily bread. Now we have fallen under the yoke of the port company, Ottoman in name but actually French and this in spite of us and the local merchants.

The ways in which the company has obtained this concession are well known!

We have suffered much: through the extra work we were forced to do, through the paucity of porters, and finally through the mediocrity of our salaries and the unbearable arbitrariness we are subjected to.

We are tired of this state of affairs, tired by our own complaints and cries which we voice without ever being heard—the reason is well known!

Today, when the word liberty reverberates throughout the world, do our comrades have the good fortune to obtain something of this liberty?[106]

Encouraged by the apparent success of the port workers' strike, the gas workers, too, staged a strike on 2 October 1908. They elected Mikā'il Ghabrīl and Elias Ṭrād, both Greek Orthodox members of the Ottoman commercial court, who later became involved in the Beirut Reform Committee, one Aḥmad ʿAbd al-ʿĀl and the company's engineer Elie Qaykānū,[107] as their representatives to negotiate their demands. Their opening positions were a 50 per cent increase in salary, a thirteenth salary payment at the end of the year and a bi-annual adjustment for inflation of 10 per cent, cumulative fifteen days holiday and rest days after night work, free medical care and continued payment three and a half months into the illness, payment of pensions identical to the railway workers, job security granted by law, ten-hour working days with double salary for extra hours, night work, and on holidays, and a company loan scheme. After four days of strikes that left the city dark at night, the general director of the gas and electricity company was willing to enter into negotiations. In a meeting with workers' representatives he offered a 20 per cent increase for those whose salary was below 201 piastres per month and conceded to those operating in the city on most other issues but refused to make concessions to those in production in the factory.[108]

The general enthusiasm and optimism after the Young Turk revolution notwithstanding, the port workers became ever more exposed to the dictates of foreign companies, the Ministry of Commerce and Public Works and the

[106] Ibid., enclosure *al-Aḥwāl* (12 Aug. 1908).

[107] Ismail and Chehab (1976: xviii. 110–16); and Thobie (1993: 149).

[108] Thobie (1993: 158). On 17 Sept. 1909 the workers posed an ultimatum, 'demanding a reduction of their daily work to eight hours, an increase of salary by 30%, regular holidays, and in case of illness, payment of half the salary for 6 months'. MAE, Paris, NSTSL, vol. 112, Beirut, 30 Sept. 1909.

Council of State—all institutions whose members represented financial stakes and vested interests in large-scale investment schemes. By way of contrast to the paternalistic but largely sympathetic approach of Sultan Abdülhamid, the officers of the Committee of Union and Progress (CUP) had less personal indulgence for the fate of a few workers who were seen as threatening precisely that Ottoman union and progress. In September 1908, the new Young Turk Minister of Public Works outlawed all strike activities and trade unionism by workers employed in public service companies.[109]

Strikes were never entirely rooted out as working conditions continued to deteriorate. Between 1910 and 1914, numerous reports of industrial action by the Beirut workforce reached the European foreign ministries and again distinguished local lawyers and negotiators supported the strikers' demands. Following the September 1908 law, the CUP moved to protect more rigorously the interests of the European investment companies and—as Hanna has shown—abandoned the previous government's relative protection for Ottoman workers.[110]

At a more fundamental level, two notions of the production of space clashed during strike action: In Beirut of the 1890s and 1900s, capitalist development imposed on the Ottoman state the role of controlling and encouraging the establishment of a new inter-regional division of labour. The projected space of capitalism encroached upon the inherited space of working-class families, whereby the former came into more or less violent conflict with those who resisted this kind of manipulation.[111]

Conclusion

Lewis Farley, the lonely BIO accountant I introduced in Chapter 1 as the harbinger—or siren—of capitalist investment, would have felt vindicated at the end of the nineteenth century, had he not been forced to return to London in 1858. Not only did his successors at the bank push the 'financial capitalization' he had called for in his memoirs, but the BIO also held a major share in all of Beirut's capital investments.

The way the Beirutis related to their city, struggled for a provincial capital, and attempted to consolidate their city's status and economic capacities under increasing pressures from encroaching investors and creeping colonialism was

[109] MAE, Nantes, CB 1895–1914, carton 348, enclosure, *Stamboul* (13 Oct. 1908).
[110] Ḥanna (1973: 18–19). [111] Lipietz (1980: 74).

arguably the single most important factor shaping the particular trajectory of Beirut in the nineteenth and early twentieth centuries. Under the restructured Ottoman provincial rule foreign powers largely remained outside the institutions of formal decision-making in Bilad al-Sham while international banks and companies invested almost 70 million French francs between 1888 and 1914. Investments in urban infrastructure in the 1890s and 1900s brought about an immense urban transformation. Owing to the regulating impact of the Ottoman administration, the municipality, and the participation of the local merchant community, the intense period of 'financial capitalization' did not turn Beirut into an outright colonial city. Even though *fin de siècle* Beirut must have been one big building site during this time, foreign capital and physical occupation failed to bifurcate the urban structure into a new 'European' town and an old 'Oriental' centre.

The production of *fin de siècle* Beirut as a beacon of modernity, order, and technological progress was a complicated and contentious process. As trade figures for Beirut's port show, French investment in urban facilities proved slow to amortize.[112] The fear that prosperity might prove ephemeral had permeated the local petitions for a provincial capital. It also gripped the investment companies in the 1890s and led to fierce negotiations with urban notables and municipal authorities in Beirut. In contrast to these negotiating practices, actual physical resistance was exercised only by workers whose livelihood and social space were destroyed by the effects of capitalist urbanization. The Beirut port workers' strike happened almost exactly a year to the day before the dockers of Istanbul went on strike.[113] As in Istanbul, the *casus belli* was the arrival of one of the first ships after the new port regime was introduced. It signalled to the protestors the encroachment of an international company on the workers' livelihood in the name of modernizing port facilities.

The Ottoman labour historian Donald Quataert has shown that, in the Istanbul case, the struggle 'contributed to the erosion of popular support for the government of Sultan Abdülhamid II'. In contrast, it appears that in provincial Beirut the support of the sultan for the strikers briefly made him a popular figure. At least for the duration of the Hamidian regime there existed a measure of local cooperation between merchants and port workers against the foreign logic of finance capital.

The workers demanded their right to the city at the particular point in time when their social space was threatened by the effects of the political capitalization. Beirut generated a unified struggle for its regional ascendancy, but after

[112] Issawi (1988: 51–4); Kalla (Ph.D. thesis, 1969); Owen (1981). [113] Quataert (1983: 97).

1888 it also began to feel the strains of physical and social boundaries inside the city itself. The spatial effects of the tramway traced here were important for the development of an urban consciousness which was determined as much by access to urban space as to modes of production *per se*.

In Beirut's particular development after 1860, actual class consciousness crystallized not in the context of major social conflict and nationalist upheaval over access to means of production, as Lockman and Benin argue convincingly for industrializing Egyptian cities.[114] In the relative political stability of late nineteenth-century Beirut even as the city underwent immense urban construction, class consciousness emerged in the struggle over the production of space. This occurred through processes of urban reform and social exclusion. In the next two parts I will locate the ways these processes were driven by competing foreign, imperial, and local civilizing missions and how they produced urban politics of difference.

[114] Lockman and Benin (1988).

II

Mediations

In Beirut each thought inhabits a mansion.
In Beirut each word is a drama,
In Beirut, thoughts deliver filibusters of the mind,
and caravans bear priestesses and sultans' wives.
Let her be nun or sorceress or both,
Or let her be the hinge
Of the sea's port or the gateway to the East,
Let her be adored or let her be cursed, let her be thirsty for blood or holy water,
Let her be innocent or let her be a murderess.

(Tuéni 2001: 302–3)

4

War, Health, and the Making of Municipal Beirut

Municipal governance was established in Beirut in the wake of the civil war in Mount Lebanon of 1860. The urgency of the post-war crisis made it the first municipality in the Arab provinces of the Ottoman empire and possibly the second after the 1854–6 model of Galata/Pera. It was during Fuad Pasha's extended pacifying mission in Beirut that the idea of a permanent municipality as an Ottoman institution for urban management materialized. And it did so in the specific context of a discourse of urban sanitization that conflated cleanliness, social behaviour, and public hygiene.

In Beirut as elsewhere, the municipality was an 'amphibious' institution where definitions and regulations of a distinctly urban experience of modernity were played out between imperial and local domains. The 1864 Provincial Law called for the official application of Istanbul's municipal model to the provincial cities and towns of the empire: 'each village shall have a municipality'.[1] While this law was more a declaration of intent, the 1867 law fine-tuned the workings of the municipality in a detailed fashion. These stipulations were reviewed and amended in 1877,[2] were translated into Arabic by Nawfal Efendi Naʿmatallah Nawfal, and published in full length in Beirut's press.[3]

The 1877 Municipal Law excluded foreigners from membership of the council. It applied empire-wide to every city (*şehir*) and small town (*kaṣaba*). Cities with a population in excess of 40,000 were to establish two municipal councils, as was attempted briefly in Beirut in 1909. Moreover, the municipalities were assigned clearly defined—if indiscriminately enumerated—duties

[1] 'Her köy bir belediye dairesi sayılır', quoted in Ortayli (1974: 166).

[2] For the original text of the 1877 *Belediye Kānūnu*, see BBA, YEE, 37/302/47–112 (1877).

[3] *al-Jinān*, 9 (1878), 44–8, 93–7, 131–4 and *Thamarāt al-Funūn* (14 Jan. 1878). Naʿmatallah Nawfal was the official translator of the Ottoman constitution *al-Dustūr*, Beirut, 1883–4 [1301h].

which can be arranged into five categories: urban planning, market control, health, public morality, and public welfare.

Taken together, I would argue, these competences provided the provincial municipalities with a powerful mandate to intervene in daily life and revolutionize Ottoman towns and cities. On the other hand, the municipal mandate's legal consecration established a normative order which constricted the daily practices of the municipality and exposed it to popular and foreign criticism. As a consequence of this intricate web of mandate, norm, and practice, the Beirut municipality became a prime site of the politics of urban space after 1860.

In particular, as I will argue in this chapter, the evolution of the municipality's health mandate fundamentally restructured urban life before being challenged by colonial medical institutions in *fin de siècle* Beirut.

The Origins of the Municipal Idea in Beirut

In 1868, Shaykh Ibrāhīm al-Yāzijī gave an influential speech on classical medicine. Addressing the Syrian Scientific Society in Beirut, he advocated respect for classical scholars like Ibn Sīnā. The Arab world, he argued, could look back on a rich heritage of medical expertise since the times of the Abbasids. However, he held that the appearance of new conditions for the spreading of disease necessitated innovation in hygiene and medicine.[4] Such lectures were an important reminder that, in the Arab–Ottoman world, scientific traditions and medical epistemologies existed prior to the onslaught of colonial medicine.[5]

New epidemics were a common occurrence in the Ottoman empire as in Europe and urgently required scientific collaboration. Between 1700 and 1842 the plague raged forty-one times in Bilad al-Sham.[6] Neither the Graeco-Arab medical traditions passed on from generation to generation, nor the *maghriba*s (ambulant paramedics), *miqbaʿa*s (traditional dermatologists), could help.[7] Neither miasmic explanation nor charity could purge this lethal danger from society. With the blatant impotence of classical and popular cures, Christian priests and Muslim shaykhs exercised paramount medical power due to their unquestioned religious authority and scriptural knowledge. Until the early

[4] Ibrāhīm al-Yāzijī, 'Fī al-ṭibb al-qadīm', in Y. Khūrī (1990: 121–5).

[5] See Fanon (1967: 121). [6] Panzac (1985: 30–4).

[7] For a discussion of early 19th-cent medical professions by contemporary sources, see Sehnaoui-Salam, (MA thesis, 1981), 41–4.

nineteenth century, they were in a position to link the spread of the plague to divine intervention by vesting plague visitations with a religious function and metaphysical causality. Popular fear of provoking the wrath of God by misbehaviour was an important component of the moral and social structure of everyday life in Beirut as elsewhere.

Generally, measures taken by political authorities were incomplete and not followed up systematically. More importantly, in the absence of a single regulatory urban institution like the municipality, isolated preventive measures taken by individuals or communities would be ignored by others. With no cure on the horizon, Beirutis habitually fled and took refuge in the monasteries of their particular denominations or with relatives outside the city. Thus in an 1810 poem on the plague, Niqūla Turk advises 'if the plague has reached a place—flee if not hide behind a well-closed door'.[8]

In the 1830s a new generation of local doctors was trained. Since the Egyptian occupation, the authorities in Mount Lebanon began to send a steady stream of medical students to Cairo to study with Clot Bey, the director of the medical academy in Cairo.[9] Others went to Istanbul. They constituted a lasting scientific network which stood at the centre of the struggle against epidemics and infectious diseases. Most came back to Bilad al-Sham, and Beirut in particular, where they became leading figures in various medical fields.

The Ottoman quarantine system banished the plague to the frontiers of the Ottoman empire by the 1840s.[10] While Baghdad, the Arabian peninsular, and Kurdistan continued to experience outbreaks of the plague throughout the nineteenth century, the plague was rooted out in Bilad al-Sham. But a new disease emerged in 1821 that appeared equally as devastating as the plague—cholera. The urban struggle against this epidemic had far-reaching consequences for the relation between individual, society, city, and the state. Institutional medical knowledge and techniques of social and urban planning developed in nineteenth-century Beirut to a large extent in the context of the experience of cholera.

With the advent of the *tanẓīmāt*, Ottoman and Egyptian sanitary techniques changed in ways not dissimilar to—and influenced by—those of European states discussed by Foucault[11] and more recently by

[8] Tr. from the French in Panzac (1985: 577–8). On the work of Niqūla Turk as an early Arab historian, see Philipp (1984: 161–75).

[9] D'Armagnac (1985: 56). On early medical missions to Cairo, see S. al-Khūrī (1992) and Ḥaqqi (1970: 573–9).

[10] See Panzac (1985).

[11] '[A]n epidemic has a sort of historical individuality, hence the need to employ a complex method of observation when dealing with it.' The scale of the undertaking made the central state the only viable coordinator of the operation. Foucault (1986: 25–6).

Rabinow[12] and Fassin,[13] who insist on the uniquely global, historical experience of pandemics. As European medical missions were dispatched to explore the zones of germination, explanatory paradigms leapt first to the social level of analysis, identifying disease among the urban poor, and then—towards the end of the nineteenth century—to the civilizational level.

In the wake of European colonial expansion across the Mediterranean, proneness to infection was no longer identified as divine retribution but increasingly as scientific evidence for Oriental backwardness and racial inferiority.[14] As in nineteenth-century France, in the Ottoman empire fields of medicine and public hygiene began to necessitate the collaboration of legions of engineers, architects, inspectors, and administrators. Public hygienists generally became part of the political process of state centralization on the one hand and imperial civilizing missions on the other. The very statistics and population censuses introduced in order to establish reliable data to plan new systems of taxation and military conscription came to be used effectively for medical and demographic surveillance.[15] Missionary charity for Beirut's Christian communities and *ad hoc* post-occurrence measures were complemented by the establishment of permanent Ottoman institutions of public health for urban society as a whole.

Protecting the City: the Quarantine and the Cordon Sanitaire

Beirut got off relatively lightly from the ravages of the first cholera pandemics of the 1820s and 1830s, thanks in great measure to the quarantine built by Maḥmūd Nāmī Bey in 1834/5.[16] Travellers to Beirut during the first half of the nineteenth century concurred that the city compared favourably to other Syrian towns: 'With the exception of dysentery and some pernicious fevers which develop during strong heat waves in the vicinity of rivers and stagnant water, there are few grave illnesses to worry about.'[17] The quarantine was a highly tangible and contested sanitary measure, which often necessitated military enforcement. It was also a novel means to condition access to the city on medical inspection and on temporary isolation of the body from the environment. By setting up quarantines, the Ottoman empire became a transconti-

[12] 'The worldwide spread of cholera demolished one by one the criteria of the classical science of epidemics'. Rabinow (1989: 34).

[13] See Fassin (1998).

[14] S. Bayly (2002: 285–309).

[15] On the emergence of Ottoman state statistics, see Karpat (1992: 283–95).

[16] *Administration Sanitaire de l'Empire Ottoman* (1906: 7). On the plague in Beirut in 1831, see Michaud and Poujoulat (1833: ii. 295).

[17] Blondel (1840: 46).

nental sanitary bulwark and found itself at the centre of the European discourse on hygiene.[18]

The 1865 cholera epidemic swept from Mecca to an ill-prepared Beirut and cost an estimated 3,000 lives, mainly poor inhabitants who had no place to flee.[19] The more fortunate ones took refuge with relatives in Mount Lebanon. But the exigencies of international trade and political order forced both the imperial government and local merchants to protect Beirut pre-emptively from epidemics and from abandonment. To this effect the foreign community and the Ottoman government colluded to pave the way for a more effective implementation of a *cordon sanitaire*.

Beirut was again affected by cholera during the 1875 pandemic. This time, the disease was believed to have entered the city from the sea. Although some improvements had been made, the quarantine still proved untrustworthy and fatally ineffective to protect the city. All but 15,000 poor inhabitants fled the city and up to thirty residents died on a daily basis.[20] A first of many commissions of inquiry into the state of the quarantine was set up when the medical crisis abated at the end of the summer. In July 1876 the municipality announced in the recently launched newspaper *Thamarāt al-Funūn* that it planned to destroy the old quarantine premises near the port and was looking for a new, larger area outside the city.[21] Although it appears from later developments that it remained in place, the commission's work laid the foundations for an effective protection of the city the next time cholera came Beirut's way in 1882.[22]

The urban expansion of Beirut's built-up area pushed the city to the geographic borders with Mount Lebanon. As it rapidly expanded eastwards, private residences also moved ever closer to the sanitary compound on Beirut's east coast. Consecutive Ottoman governors in Beirut appealed to the Sublime Porte to be allowed to move the quarantine. In 1891, the governor general of Beirut, ʿAzīz Pasha, cabled Kāmil Pasha in another attempt to transfer the quarantine from the Rumayl quarter.[23]

Instead, the imperial government set up a commission, consisting of one Dr Deluciano, health inspector Niẓām al-Dīn Bey, Dr Adīb Qaddūra—recently graduated from the American medical college in Beirut—and the provincial engineer Bishāra Dīb. The proposal to transfer the quarantine to offshore

[18] See Panzac (1986). [19] Jessup (1910: 289). On cholera in Mecca, see Kuneralp (1989: 69–81).
[20] MAE, Paris, CCCTB 1868–1888, Beirut, 4 Aug. 1875. [21] *Thamarāt al-Funūn* (13 July 1876).
[22] See next section.
[23] MAE, Nantes, CEB 1890–1891, Beirut, 4 May 1891. PRO, FO, 195/2056, Beirut, 24 June 1899. PRO, FO, 195/2075.

islands near Tripoli or Tartus and the bay of Mersin were quickly dismissed by the local government since it would jeopardize Beirut's position as the dominant port-of-call on the Eastern Mediterranean.

In the most comprehensive and intrusive survey of Beirut's sanitary conditions conducted in the Ottoman period, Dr Benoît Boyer warned that 'in ten years, the lazaretto will be in the middle of the city'.[24] Composed in the wake of Beirut's port enlargement and railway construction which drastically increased the number of visitors and pilgrims in transit, the report deplored the quarantine's insufficient surveillance and reiterated emphatically the necessity to 'transport the quarantine elsewhere and to deliver a city of 120,000 inhabitants from the perpetual nightmare of cholera'.[25]

After 1888 the municipality had begun to develop the area around the quarantine into an industrial zone 'destined very soon to raise on its territory a working-class population of relative density', and into what Boyer prophetically called 'one of the future quarters of Beirut'.[26] In 1900, a British report by Dr Vitalis admonished that '[t]he position of the Beirut lazaretto between the gasworks, and the public slaughter house and in close proximity to the railway station has caused a standing menace to the health of the town'.[27]

Despite these appeals, a joint European and Ottoman health inquiry conducted in 1905 considered cholera under control and the proximity of these constructions no longer a health hazard *per se*. The health inspectors were much more confident in the existing location than Boyer had been a decade earlier.[28] They raised more concern about encroaching private residences, the prospect of a hotel construction nearby, and the permeability of the isolation procedures inside the compound. The report therefore proposed to speed up the internal human circulation, to enforce the separation of passengers in the compound, to monitor more strictly the movements of the quarantine's staff and 'make provisions to expropriate land to the east and south of the lazaretto'.[29]

The dilemma the Ottoman government faced with regard to maintaining public health was largely financial. The modifications called for in the above report, for example, required credits in the region of 2,000 Ottoman gold lira (*c*.£2,000 sterling).[30] Financial malaise became very apparent in an episode in 1910 when two cholera cases were suspected inside the quarantine itself. It prompted the Ottoman governor to hold two meetings on the state of hygiene in Beirut. In the first one with his staff, the director of the Ottoman Bank declared that the treasury of the municipality was too depleted to take even the

[24] Boyer (1897: 154). [25] Ibid. [26] Boyer (1897: 2).
[27] PRO, FO, 195/2075, Beirut, 13 June 1900.
[28] *Administration Sanitaire de l'Empire Ottoman* (1906: 8, 36). [29] Ibid. 13. [30] Ibid. 40.

most urgent sanitary measures. He estimated that the municipality needed at least ten million piastres to improve urban conditions and complained about the difficulty of collecting dues from foreigners. At a second meeting the next day, forty of the city's elite gathered to appoint a committee consisting of Professors de Brun from the French Medical Faculty and Graham from the Syrian Protestant College, the director of the Ottoman Bank, and the director of the Water Company to oversee preventive cholera preparations.[31] Foreigners, and especially foreign doctors, were an integral part of Ottoman health preparations. But at the governor general's suggestion that a new loan to step up sanitary measures was necessary and that the foreigners had to pay their share, one of them intervened brusquely arguing that 'the 2,000 Europeans would not make a great difference in revenues in a city of 180,000 [*sic*]'. The governor retorted that this was irresponsible because new regulations were urgently needed. No agreement was reached and the issue was assigned to the new committee.[32]

In the imperial languages of the British, French, and Ottoman sanitary reports, the quarantine was treated as an ideal urban microcosm. The functional requirements of human circulation and regulation as well as spatial and social segregation reflected the accepted norms in Ottoman and European urban discourse in the nineteenth century and affected the production of space in Beirut itself. The quarantine and *cordons sanitaires* introduced to Beirut a sense of siege. The inherently political nature of the sanitary discourse introduced public health, social hygiene, and urban pathology as constantly elusive measures of modernity in the eyes of the authorities and the foreign experts. Certain diseases like the plague were effectively rooted out, yet the prevention of illness could never be complete. Urbanization generated new conditions for new diseases, new languages to identify them, and new techniques to isolate them.

Rotten from Within? The Municipality Takes Centre Stage

Cordons sanitaires and the quarantine were only one set of strategies, albeit the most conspicuous and symbolic, by which the Ottoman government addressed urban hygiene in Beirut. Following the experience of recurring cholera, typhoid fever, and other infectious diseases, European, Ottoman, and local medical staff realized that quarantine tactics alone were insufficient. As in other Mediterranean cities, disease came to be located within the city.

[31] French Consul in Beirut to the Minister of Foreign Affairs, 19 Nov. 1910, MAE, NSSTSL 1908–1914, vol. 428. [32] Ibid.

Beirut's children had been vaccinated by the Austro-Italian doctor Pietro Laurella against smallpox since the early part of the nineteenth century.[33] After the civil war, schools and private houses were inspected for influenza and other common infectious illnesses.[34] Sewage ditches were dug out to manage seasonal flooding.[35] Cattle were forbidden to enter the city centre by municipal decree,[36] and ambulant merchants were banned from bartering in public passages.[37] Public health became a powerful restructuring device of the everyday life and a source of constant transgression in the city.

The presence of foreign missions in Beirut placed extra pressure on the Ottoman provincial government to perform and offer modern urban services. Meanwhile long-standing missionary schools, convents, and the specially dispatched relief agencies provided medical charity for their respective communities as best they could.[38] The Lazerist Sœurs de la Charité order, for example, had provided free beds for the sick and wounded since 1860.[39] Another local Florence Nightingale, Emilie Sursuq, who founded the society for the sick and needy, *iḥsān al-zahrā'*, in 1880 was favourably mentioned in most Arabic and European travelogues and diaries.[40] And as the culmination of fifty years of foreign medical relief, the American consul in Beirut founded the Red Cross chapter in Beirut in the early 1900s.

However, after the civil war in Mount Lebanon and Damascus, Ottoman institutions assumed responsibility for the health of the city as a whole. Fu'ād Pasha and subsequent Ottoman governors appreciated international relief efforts in Beirut, but they realized that charity alone could not and should not remedy the structural problems of urban management in the face of post-war reconstruction challenges. Buṭrus al-Bustānī, too, recognized the structural dependence that foreign, non-governmental charity might entail. In *Nafīr Sūriyya* he warns:

What is the state of these many poor ones who have been hurled at the mercy of philanthropists (*ʿalā aktāf al-ajāwid*) by the workings of the age (*ṣarrūf al-dahr*) and by the destitution of the time (*dawāhi al-zaman*)? . . . This has kept many people at the gates

[33] Kornrumpf (1998: 209–10). Pietro was probably the father of George Laurella, a Beirut municipal member between 1868 and 1877. See Ch. 5.

[34] *Thamarāt al-Funūn* (13 Feb. 1890).

[35] *Thamarāt al-Funūn* (21 Nov. 1878).

[36] *Thamarāt al-Funūn* (25 Oct. 1878).

[37] *Thamarāt al-Funūn* (26 Dec. 1878).

[38] Fawaz (1994: 135). See also Farah (2000: 632–4).

[39] The founder of the hospital/orphanage, Sister Gélas (1811–97), was treated like a saint by the Beirutis for her altruism. She had arrived in Beirut from Izmir in 1847 and was instrumental in combating the three epidemics (typhus, smallpox, and cholera) that rocked Beirut a year later. Her order bought a large plot of land between Sahat al-Burj and Sahat al-Sur. The Sœurs de la Charité and their resident doctor Sucuet, played an important role in health care during the aftermath of the civil war in 1860. S. al-Khūrī (1992: 304–6).

[40] e.g. in S. al-Khūrī (1992: 415); and in Kremski's letters, edited by Ḍāhir (1986).

of charities (*al-iḥsanāt*) and multiplied their calamities. Who guarantees us that these gates will remain open and won't be blocked by iron bolt and brass lock before the end of the winter.[41]

Fuad Pasha did not need to look far for alternatives. Probably even before his arrival in Beirut, the governor of Sidon, Aḥmad Pasha, had set up a relief council (*majlis al-iʿāna*) under the leadership of one Nāẓim Bey and Muḥyī al-Dīn Bayhum. This council was responsible for coordinating the provision of shelter, food, and medication to the refugees,[42] for it had become clear 'that the accumulation of refugees in Beirut has become the reason for the occurrence and spread of many diseases'.[43]

In post-war Beirut, the putative umbilical link between the Ottoman idea of the municipality, relief, welfare, health, government responsibility, on the one hand, and the attainment of 'modernity', on the other, dominated the pages of Beirut's first newspaper *Ḥadīqat al-Akhbār*. Health conditions and the general state of Beirut's urban services, such as housing, street repair, law and order under the conditions of large-scale immigration were linked to the destiny of the Ottoman state. In a strikingly euphoric article (given the recent massacres in the Mountain) in November 1860 about the opening of the new telegraph line between Beirut and Damascus, its editor, Khalīl al-Khūrī, reported enthusiastically on the recent establishment of a 'health council for urban cleaning' (*majlis al-ṣaḥḥa li al-tanẓīfāt*). Khalīl al-Khūrī's assumption was that a healthier city would root out once and for all the social ills that led to the civil war. His article also contains the first mention of the impending formation of a municipal council, or *majlis al-tanẓīmāt al-baladiyya*, as it was originally called, for Beirut which 'was to be charged with establishing and executing all things pertaining to the public good of the city'.[44] Underlying municipal projects of urban rehabilitation was the recurring formula of *al-tanẓīf*, 'cleaning' or 'cleansing'.

In the absence of a legal ruling on the rights and duties of the municipality in the early years, most of the 'cleansing' measures were initiated by the governor of Sidon which the municipality seems to have fully endorsed. Both councils were promoting urban rehabilitation, prophylactic sanitary measures, and

[41] Buṭrus al-Bustānī, *Nafīr Sūriyya*, sixth issue, Beirut, 8 Nov. 1860, 31. The page numbers refer to the version edited by Y. Khūrī (1990).

[42] In May 1861, Nāẓim Bey proposed to found an asylum for widows and orphans in the old quarantine (*dār al-shaqāfa*), *Ḥadīqat al-Akhbār* (16 May 1861). [43] Ibid.

[44] The health council had been formed by three doctors in the service of the Ottoman health department, Dr Roussiniyan, Ibrāhīm [Nāẓim] Bey, and M. Colmant, 'the principal medical officer of the French expedition', *Ḥadīqat al-Akhbār* (29 Nov. 1860).

medical treatment: fresh water supply, rain drainage, street alignment, construction of pavements, and child vaccination.[45]

With Fu'ād Pasha's mission, security returned but anxiety prevailed. In the 1850s, 'life and property [had been] perfectly secure in Beyrout. Murder, robbery, and other crimes, so frequent in European cities, are here unknown.'[46] After the war, however, reports of criminal attacks on local and foreign residents punctuated the pages of *Ḥadīqat al-Akḥbār* next to lists of exiled war criminals. Despite the editor's appreciation 'that [governor] Aḥmad Pasha has turned Beirut into a city of order and style, acts of crime still happen here and there at night'.[47] Bustling intramural squares, like Saḥat al-Samak and Saḥat al-Qamḥ, were identified as particularly notorious spots. All along, the same discourse of 'social cleansing' pervaded urban management:

> the rehabilitation and cleansing of the city of Beirut continues to concern us. We begin to see that its streets have been rid of squalor (*al-awṣākh*) and that a better manner of order (*al-tarṭīb*) than before has been achieved. The majority of streets in the bazaars that were not paved are now paved . . . Likewise roads outside the city have been repaired. This raises our hopes that Beirut may prosper daily in terms of embellishment and organization so that one day it may become the most beautiful resort on the Syrian coast.[48]

The commercial and aesthetic imperatives of the advent of a new age extended the semantics of cleanliness to the social milieu for the rest of the Ottoman period and beyond. In the tense atmosphere of post-war Beirut, the Ottoman governor developed a distinct paranoia against certain traditional pastimes and social activities and issued *ad hoc* rulings to prevent havoc and feuds. For fear of violent escalation, the popular javelin game in the pine forest was forbidden.[49] Moreover, the governor forbade gambling in 'social places'. He threatened to arrest and to publish the names of the culprits, if caught red-handed gambling 'in such ugly abode[s]'.[50] Nor would foreigners be exempt from 'social cleansing'. In March 1861 the governor in Beirut, Ahmad Pasha, publicly pledged to act to cleanse the city of unwanted guests:

> Considering the amount of base scum (*al-aṣāfil wa al-ajlāf*) who arrive at Beirut, the governor has issued a decree that allows the authorities to search foreign ships, to

[45] In early Feb. 1861, the municipal council approved a proposal by the health council to carry out city-wide vaccination in Beirut. A council of doctors met twice a week in government offices to vaccinate the children against smallpox. After the vaccination, they were given a health certificate. *Ḥadīqat al-Akhbār* (14 Feb. 1861). [46] Farley (1859: 59). [47] *Ḥadiqāt al-Akhbār* (8 Aug. 1861).

[48] *Ḥadīqat al-Akhbār* (4 Apr. 1861).

[49] However, in the early 20th cent. the javelin game was still one of the most popular sports in Beirut. See al-Barghūtī (2001: 126). [50] *Ḥadīqat al-Akhbār* (24 Jan. 1861).

inspect passports of every inbound passenger and to prevent entry to anyone with insufficient documentation, in order to cleanse Beirut from the human rabble (*li al-tanẓīf min al-awbāsh*).[51]

Public health concerns grew proportionate with the size of the population and the level of urban densification, but after the civil war of 1860 ideas and practices of urban pathology entered the public debate about the planned, open city whose 'public health' language expressed concerns for tourism, commerce, and state finance. The city centre in particular became identified as a site of danger and insecurity in newspaper articles whose editors employed hygienic metaphors to define the problem. Public health not only provided new vocabulary to describe, identify, and tackle social problems, it appeared to form 'the ultimate language of the social'.[52]

In the aftermath of the British occupation of Egypt in 1882 a new cholera epidemic reached Beirut from Alexandria. But Beirut's municipal health authorities were better prepared than during the previous outbreak in 1875. The Ottoman correspondence between Beirut and Istanbul betrays a sense of urgency about the matter. The imperial authorities realized that people fled the city and the damage to trade and property was considerable. Abandoned shops and houses were looted and bread prices jumped as Beirut's wheat market was running out of supplies.[53] Isolationary measures were stepped up to protect the city, despite the destabilizing effects on international commerce and despite vocal French consular protests. The municipality convened a medical meeting between the governor, Dr Nakhla Mudawwar the municipal doctor, Dr Milḥim Fāris a prominent local practitioner, Dr Wortabet a local doctor at the Prussian hospital and professor at the Syrian Protestant College, and the long-term French resident Dr Sucquet, director of Beirut's quarantine since 1847. The medical commission cabled a request for a *cordon sanitaire* at a five-mile radius around the border of municipal Beirut to the imperial health directorate in Istanbul which was instantly granted.[54] The medical commission issued a detailed twelve-point plan that stressed the need for prophylactic measures, such as daily street-cleaning and inspection tours of places of sale and storage of food-stuffs, improvement of the quarantine's architecture, and containment of the sudden immigration of Egyptian ʿUrābī supporters exiled after the British invaded their country. The measures proved successful, although urban expansion rendered a complete isolation of the city difficult to maintain as

[51] *Ḥadīqat al-Akhbār* (17 Jan. 1861). Ch. 7 deals with how such representations paved the way for a new discourse of public morality in Beirut. [52] Fassin (1998: 39–40).

[53] BBA, YAHUS, 174/43, Beirut, 16 Oct. 1883. [54] Ibid.

Beirut's outskirts and the surrounding villages of Mount Lebanon already began to merge into one. Despite these adverse conditions, no cases of cholera occurred in Beirut and the *cordon* could be lifted after a week.[55]

The Ottoman administration in Beirut realized after the 1882 *cordon* against cholera that routine urban surveys were necessary to identify health hazards. The administrative yearbook for Syria in 1885 included for the first time a detailed list of all occurrences of diseases and illnesses by kind and location in the province.[56] The 1882 epidemic proved to be the last major outbreak around Ottoman Beirut. New rumours of an outbreak of cholera in Toulon in 1884 compelled the imperial health directorate to close the ports of Izmir, Trabulus Gharb, and Beirut.[57] The concerted action proved successful.

By the time cholera raged in Tripoli and Lattakia in 1890–1 Beirut had become vested with sufficient medical knowledge and administrative mechanisms to deal with cholera threats. The timing of Beirut's immunity to cholera was no coincidence. As a provincial capital, it received more direct attention from the imperial government and better provincial funding for urban services. Conversely, while improved public health favoured foreign economic investments in capital Beirut, towns lower down in the provincial hierarchy continued to suffer outbreaks of contagious diseases.

After the creation of the province of Beirut the *ad hoc* health commission which had been founded during the 1882 crisis was absorbed into the new administrative structure to support the work of the health inspector.[58] This partly foreign, partly Ottoman, partly local health organization was instrumental in planning the successful *cordon* around Beirut in 1890–1.[59] A few months later the members were dispatched to Acre to investigate reported cholera cases in this new dependency of Beirut.[60] In the provincial capital, schools and public buildings were more regularly inspected, clinics set up and invested with new medical equipment. A municipal women's hospital was set up in Beirut: 'a hospital with a capacity of 25 beds which was opened in the summer of 1891 is now in a position to have instruments and medication to carry out surgery'.[61]

In sum, two themes have emerged from this subplot to the municipal workings of a provincial capital. First, foreign health experts have cooperated with Ottoman institutions. As long as the common goal was to protect Beirut's

55 MAE, Nantes, CEB 1883–1885, Beirut, 14 Aug. 1883.
56 *Salnāme—Sūriye Vilāyeti* (1302/1885), 258 ff.
57 BBA, YAHUS, 179/11, Beirut, 1 July 1884.
58 *Lisān al-Ḥāl* (15 Oct. 1888).
59 BBA, YAHUS, 265/40, Beirut, 28 Sept. 1892.
60 BBA, YAHUS, 262/24, 2 July 1892, and YAHUS, 262/33, 5 July 1892.
61 *Salnāme—Bayrūt Vilāyeti*, ii (1310/1893), 144.

health from outside threats, the hygienists of the foreign medical schools and hospitals joined the fray on a more or less equal footing. Indeed, they effectively served to enhance 'Ottoman civilization'. However, this partnership was to change, or at least, there were ulterior dynamics at work, too, which emerged when causes of disease were located inside the city itself. Second, the 'cleansing' discourse and hygienic measures did not create a clean city, but a stream of municipal intervention backed by imperial legislation in the everyday life of the city.[62] As I argue in the following section of this chapter (in Didier Fassin's words), 'it is remarkable, in fact, that it is not the normalization of behaviours and processes, as a Foucauldian analysis would claim, but rather the manner in which social problems find not their solution, but their most authoritative expression in the language of public health.'[63]

From Public to Colonial Health: Entering the House, Body, and Mind

Throughout the nineteenth century, religious, economic, and educational 'interests' motivated French interventions in the Levant. In terms of religion, the lasting myth of ancestral links between Maronites and France was first created in the 1840s.[64] This myth has fed the French policy of minority protection for the Catholic communities ever since, although the growing economic and political attraction of the Syrian hinterland increasingly overshadowed the religious justification for French intervention. After the demise of the French share in the silk industry of Mount Lebanon in the 1880s, large-scale infrastructural investments provided a new avenue for Belgian- and French-led economic modernization in Beirut.[65]

As a provincial capital that attracted this kind of international investment, Beirut's public health management spun out of the control of a financially troubled municipality. From the 1890s onwards, French and British medicine began to impose a new logic of public health that challenged the role the municipality of Beirut had acquired in the 1880s. Significantly, this sea change occurred at the particular point in Beirut's history when economic stakes grew and large-scale foreign investment required stable health conditions. The spatial fix of capitalist urbanization reinforced the colonial grip on the city. This

[62] The Sultanic Medical Law was published in Arabic in *al-Jinān*, 3 (1872), 406–8. The imperial quarantine regulations (*Ḳarantīna niẓāmeti*) were later published in an abridged version in *al-Jinān*, 13 (1882), 702–3. [63] Fassin (1998: 40).

[64] Hakim-Dowek (D.Phil. thesis, 1997), esp. ch. 2: 'The French Dimension'. [65] See Ch. 3 above.

section examines how the medical field became a quasi-official conduit of colonialism in Bilad al-Sham as the health discourse mutated from the physical to the mental sphere, from sanitation to sanity.

The creation of an open, healthy city became the normative concern of urban planning and the proactive task of Beirut's municipality. In the course of the second half of the nineteenth century, the municipality treated slaughterhouses, tanneries, and Muslim and Christian burial grounds with the same logic of hygiene by systematically moving them out of visual and olfactory range.[66] Death was incongruous with notions of revival in modern urban design. In a series of titanic, antiseptic efforts, the peace of all but a few of Beirut's twenty-four graveyards was broken by the early twentieth century.

The most symptomatic of these desecrations was the evacuation of one of the oldest and largest cemeteries of Beirut in 1911–13. Urban development had turned *Maqbara al-Khārija* into prime real estate centrally located between the seat of government on the main square, Sahat al-Burj, and the newly enlarged, French-held port facilities. The transfer exposed the appropriation of the logic of public hygiene in Beirut in the service of ulterior, capitalist aims. The added moral incentive was the dispersal of illicit brothels that had recently migrated to the cemetery's fringes.[67]

Public Hygienists in Beirut: The New Faces of French Imperialism

When an outbreak of typhoid in 1895 caused the death of 105 inhabitants, the French hygienist Dr Benoît Boyer subjected Beirut's households to the most extensive and intrusive survey of the Ottoman period.[68] Based on this statistical survey, Boyer demanded drastic measures of urban reform, a sharp increase in municipal interventions and public investments in hygiene. In his book *Les Conditions hygiéniques actuelles de Beyrouth*, the urban fabric as a whole was treated as pathological. Urban infrastructure, daily social practices, and individual eating habits alike came under scrutiny as the potential causes of an imminent health catastrophe.

Boyer's study on Beirut deserves special attention because it marks a turning point from long-standing Christian charity work to scientific intervention in the city.[69] It also marks the entry of the French Medical Faculty in Beirut into the struggle for a healthy city, thereby moving French officials into the realm of

66 *Lisān al-Ḥāl* (26 Feb. 1883).

67 Barūd (1971: 5). See also Jabr (2000).

68 See Boyer (1897).

69 On the switch from evangelical to secular/scientific modernity among the Protestant missionaries, see Makdisi (1997: 680–713).

governance. That Boyer's study in public health should become the earliest European-language analysis of urbanism, architecture, and everyday life in Beirut reflects the impact of medical knowledge on late nineteenth-century processes of colonialism and urbanization. In Boyer's 1897 *Les Conditions hygiéniques*, Beirut-as-narrative (published by a major publishing house in Lyons, no less) appeared for the first time in the European world of books, text references, and libraries. Books like his and Vital Cuinet's geographic survey a year earlier would provide the stock of knowledge and experience on which colonial planners were to draw a generation later.

Boyer's narrative embodied the *fin-de-siècle* tensions between scientific knowledge, secular authority, and imperial power on the one hand and physical vulnerability, colonial anxiety, and bourgeois anxiety that sustained colonial bio-politics more generally in the Mediterranean between 1890 and 1920.[70] The interest in health, survival of the species, and vitality of the social body was especially marked in the city of Beirut, where just fifteen years earlier, Darwinian theories had caused a huge stir, and where buried forefathers were physically uprooted to make room for a prosperous future.

Dr Benoît Boyer came to Beirut with strong recommendations from the Hospice Civil de Lyon where he graduated in 1881. Significantly, neither he nor his successors were practitioners of tropical medicine—a prerequisite for French doctors wanting to serve in more distant colonies. He was hired as professor of therapeutics and hygiene at the French Medical Faculty on the Ashrafiyya hills above Beirut and served from 1889 to 1897. A number of his local medical students, who helped him conduct research on climate and morbidity statistics, later went on to become medical authorities in their own right.[71] The discourse of urban pathology of *Les Conditions hygiéniques* treated the city as a bodily structure prone to morphological aberration. It divided cities into different *milieux* and proposed planning measures aimed to separate the 'healthy' from the 'foul' in the name of 'public welfare'.[72] The distinction between the 'old' and the 'modern city' set the tone for Boyer's subsequent sanitary explorations of Beirut: 'In the bazaar of Beirut one recovers the descriptions of all the authors of the Orient; the narrow, tortuous and busy streets, the beasts of burden on the slippery pavements and the vaulted, decaying houses.'[73]

70 Bayly (2002: 285–309). 71 See Université St Joseph (1908).

72 On the discourse of urban pathology, see also Lefebvre (1968: ch. 6) and Rabinow (1989: 30–46).

73 Boyer (1897: 4). That scientific discourse should reproduce the images found in literary works confirms the citationary nature of Orientalism. See Mitchell (1990: 129–50).

Although Boyer acknowledged the efforts of the municipality to 'implant two great arteries' to revive the ageing body of the city centre and 'give a little air and light to this entirely depraved quarter', what was urgently needed, according to Boyer, was a total 'gutting (*éventration*) of the bazaar'.[74] This powerful image of literally 'disembowelling' Beirut's old city was the first time such a radical measure was suggested in public and flew in the face of cautious, contemporary negotiations between residents and the municipality over a contested street alignment project in Suq al-Fashkha.[75]

A master plan guiding the work of armies of successive administrators, engineers, hygienists, and architects would overcome—in Boyer's penchant for the prophetic—the constant quarrels between elected council members and the reversals of decision from one Ottoman governor to the next. In this sense, Boyer's work and text anticipated the large-scale urban projects of the mandate period as well as the present age of Solidere when the powers of the municipality were severely curtailed by the perceived exigencies of rapid development.[76]

In contrast to the old city, 'the modern city which stretches around this primitive nucleus' offered 'delightful attractions'. However, the author insisted the new quarters required cosmetic operations if Beirut were to live up to its potential to become a truly great city. 'As for sewage matters', Boyer bemoaned that, in the majority of quarters, the 'fixed cesspool system', invariably placed in the house, the garden, or the street, caused the putrefaction of the soil. Once the cesspools were filled up, either the owners spilt the content onto the streets and down into the sea, or half-naked workers disposed of the fetid excrement in bucket loads. Boyer was disgusted: 'this absolutely barbarian way of waste disposal must disappear'.

The image of excrement gushing down the slopes of the city towards the port was a powerful one that called for a higher order of civilization to take charge. Boyer incorporated European class- and gender-based notions into his racialized portrayal of Beiruti 'Orientals'. This emerges most clearly in his depiction of tuberculosis, the centrepiece of his description of morbidity in Beirut. Boyer dedicated an inordinate amount of attention to tuberculosis, whereas he treated cholera, typhoid, and other fatal diseases rather cursorily.[77] Tuberculosis rose steeply over the course of the nineteenth century. According to Dr Sucquet, TB was 'virtually unknown' in the country in 1847, whereas by

[74] Boyer (1897: 5). The powerful term '*éventration*' may have been adapted from Baron Haussmann who used '*éventrement*' in his memoirs—published in 1890–3—to refer to his efforts to rebuild a modern Paris between 1853 and 1870. [75] See Ch. 8. [76] Ghorayeb (1998: 106–21).

[77] At the end of this section, Boyer informs the reader that this section was made publicly available in Arabic in the local francophile newspaper *al-Bashīr*.

the turn of the century it was killing hundreds. The cause for this was in the 'current social conditions [that] shed light on this etiology'.[78] Primary among these social conditions was the 'psychology of the Syrian'. By appealing to psychology, he reconciled the mid-nineteenth-century discourses of emotionality and passion with the notion of contagion, which had taken centre stage by the end of the century. Boyer writes:

> Consider the alcoholic and venereal excess, long night-outs, the emotions of gambling, the maneuvers of masturbation—repeated up to 15 times per day—and one will not be surprised that the psychological misery of these overworked youths, debilitated by constant heat and chronically fainting of hunger, one fine day manifests itself in a fast-spreading tuberculosis affliction.[79]

Like the consumptive in mid-nineteenth century France, the infantilized 'Oriental' was seen as prone to bouts of passion and heightened emotion. It was but a short step for Boyer to transpose the romanticism around tuberculosis in France to the exoticization of the consumptive in Beirut. In both cases, tuberculosis took root in a weak, effeminate, and over-sexualized body that was unable to bear up to the social transformations of the second half of the nineteenth century. Entering through the door of passion, the disease was then transmitted within the family, the primary social unit. Personal excess was mirrored in excessive and obsessive material concerns: 'In his quality as an Oriental, the Syrian loves luxury, splendor and ceremonial. External appearance and ostentation of wealth is the object of particular attention. Above all, the Syrian lives for the gallery; nothing is too dear to him to attract the admiration of his neighbour.'[80]

Young family members of the social elites were diagnosed as particularly prone to conspicuous consumption and Europeanization. Of their salary of 50 francs, they spent up to 15 francs on luxury cigarettes, 'and every Sunday they parade in their carriages or on their horses in a suit to match their aristocratic aspirations. In order to maintain their station, they blackmail and suck their parents dry while economizing on a healthy diet'.[81] The Beiruti 'Oriental' lived above his station, both in terms of expenditures and social character. Boyer's consumptives had partaken of too many of Beirut's urban pleasures. They existed in

[78] Boyer (1897: 119).

[79] Ibid. 120, 127. One may wonder how Boyer obtained his data. But as Michel Foucault has argued, 'the war against onanism, which in the West lasted nearly two centuries', was driven by parental and medical fear that 'this sexual activity posed physical and moral, individual and collective dangers' of human degeneracy and social morbidity (1976: 104). As Eugene Rogan has recently discussed, in the 1880s the Victorian *Journal of Mental Science* identified masturbation as a prevalent pathogen of madness. These pseudo-scientific notions were then imported to Beirut and Cairo through early mental asylums. Rogan (2002: 104–25).

[80] Boyer (1897: 119). [81] Ibid.

the liminal and unviable—in the literal sense of unlivable—space between a non-European pre-modernity and the city's all-too-real contemporary modernization. Apparently, Beirut was a threat unto itself not because of some ontological flaw or irredeemable alterity but because they had become too accustomed to European habits, more similar to Europeans than was good for them.[82]

Boyer viewed tuberculosis, like hysteria and neurasthenia, as physical symptoms of social diseases with distinctly feminine underpinnings.[83] This explained why 'Orientals' were victims of the disease—and also why women were at even greater risk of disorders afflicting the nervous system. Their conditions owed much to the effects of 'new more or less relaxed morals, material preoccupations and depravation to which women are subjected in order to satisfy the caprice of their outfit'.[84] These new conditions, he continued, 'lead us to anticipate an increase of these manifestations of hysteria'.[85] With these categories, science and hygiene recast a gender hierarchy in terms of the medicalized control of the female body. Although it is unclear how the municipality reacted to his study, most of Boyer's recommendations were not immediately implemented. Some of his recommendations anticipated those of the French mandate. The first concerted efforts of 'disembowelling' the old city, for example, were only undertaken during the First World War and completed by the French colonial government in the 1930s.[86] Some aspects of his study, however, impacted the daily lives of Beirutis more immediately, particularly his demands for a sanatorium in Mount Lebanon.

More generally he introduced a new scientific discourse on the absence of hygiene which was chronically 'unstable, sliding between the social, moral and psychic domain'.[87] In particular Benoît Boyer's social language of hygiene underwent multiple semantic slippage in the way his treatise dealt with inner-city conditions. Morbidity was linked to morality and seamlessly interlaced with pseudo-psychological observations in the search for particular root causes of universal urban maladies such as typhoid and tuberculosis. Boyer, himself, died a martyr to the cause of public health in 1897, ironically from the same disease he had urged the Beirut municipality to take preventive measures against two years before. But the legacy of his spadework and the work of the French Medical Faculty lived on when France was given the League of Nations mandate to 'prepare' Lebanon and Syria for independence.

[82] See also Bhabha (1997).

[83] For a contemporary Orientalist view on female hysteria in the Ottoman empire (*raḥm illeti*) and the 'female science' of medical magic (*'ilm al-rukka*), see Stern (1903: 241 and 289 ff. respectively).

[84] Boyer (1897: 130). [85] Ibid. 131. [86] See Davie (1996).

[87] Stallybrass and White (1986: 130).

Mind Games

At precisely the time of Boyer's research, a case of female 'hysteria' shook bourgeois Beirut. It is unclear but very likely that this particular case of a Druze princess in the early 1890s who suffered mentally from resisting an arranged marriage affected Boyer's research. Its repercussions were certainly felt in the heart of the imperial government in Istanbul and almost brought down the governor of Mount Lebanon, Naʿūm Pasha. The tragic story Engin Akarli has recently extracted from the Ottoman archives in Istanbul is an intricate web of family politics and patriarchy, of sultanic patronage and missionary influence.[88]

Caught up in these high politics stood a young woman, Najlā Arslān, who had fallen in love with Majīd, a paternal cousin who studied at a missionary school in Beirut. The romance turned sour when they decided to get married. Her father felt betrayed by his only child for he had promised her to the son of the family's political boss, Muṣṭafa Arslān. Father and uncle decided to break her resolve by placing her under house arrest. After her dramatic escape and recapture, Najlā petitioned the sultan in Istanbul, pleading for imperial support against her unlawful confinement:

> I am twenty-five years old and a mature adult. Yet, my family insists that I marry a person whom I do not want to marry. I cannot find any refuge or helper but Your Compassionate Imperial Majesty. Please rescue me from the torment and oppression to which I am subjected and which endangers my life just for having a wish in perfect accord with the *sharīʿa*![89]

Istanbul referred the case back to Naʿūm Pasha who refused to act against Muṣṭafa Arslān who was an important pillar in his administration's delicate balance of power.[90] After a year of confinement high up in the Shuf Mountains, news spread to Beirut that Najlā had suffered physical and mental abuse. Pressured into reluctant action and alarmed by the sorry turn of events, Naʿūm Pasha suddenly did a volte-face. He ordered her release and forced the marriage consent of Najlā's father. By this time, however, Najlā bore 'signs of psychological disturbance' that certified her of unsound mind.

Her story had become a medical case and, in the wider picture, a bone of contention between family authority and state welfare. Although Naʿūm Pasha refused to interfere in the 'local customs' of the Druze community at the beginning of this case, he now ordered that the woman be taken out of the family's

[88] I am indebted to Engin Akarli's kindness in making available and discussing his article prior to its publication. [89] Akarli (forthcoming). [90] Akarli (1993: 53–7).

custody and submitted as a patient to the care of the medical profession of the state. She was shipped to Istanbul where the sultan personally attended to the well-being of the provincial princess: she was diagnosed with 'mania' and delivered to the leading mental hospital in Istanbul.

The case disappeared into the anonymity of the Ottoman archives and with it the voicelessness of Najlā Arslān. 'Modern science' may or may not have cured her medically, but socially she remained a dependent outcast, now so with the official stamp of the state. I would argue that this episode was by no means unique. Her case merely anticipated a more systematic victimization inherent in the unresolved relationship between the imperial state and local customary patriarchy.

Najlā was of the first female generation who were victims of the city's cultural contradictions: on the one hand, the failure of Beirut's nascent middle class to emancipate itself from the honour dictates of the *al-khāṣṣa* establishment as the latter successfully absorbed bourgeois aspirations into their power base; on the other, the teasing possibility to live out the popular fictional romances of Beirut's press.

In the 1870s and 1880s, serialized romance novels in Buṭrus al-Bustānī's *al-Jinān* in particular shook the certainties of family patriarchy. His son Salīm al-Bustānī and Nuʿmān al-Qaṣāṭlī crafted storylines in which women—whether educated and urban or respectable and rural—were independent and sexually desirable. The plots' suspense was generated by the complex subjectivities of the main characters, as well as the possibility, search and consummation of true love, as love sickness, depression and death are ever looming.

We do not know whether the tragic case of Najlā in any way influenced the establishment of the psychiatric asylum in Mount Lebanon in 1900. At the height of the political crisis triggered by her nervous breakdown in 1896, the assailed Naʿūm Pasha had encouraged the idea of a mental hospital.[91] Certainly, the individual case of Najlā coincided with a concerted Hamidian effort to assume medical responsibility over Arab provincial subjects by establishing hospitals for the 'alienated' (*mustashfā al-ghurabā'*) in each of the provincial capitals of Bilad al-Sham.[92]

Shortly after Najlā was sent for treatment in Istanbul, the Swiss Quaker and founding director of Broumana High School, Theophilius Waldmeier, and his wife founded the Lebanon Hospital for the Insane high above Beirut off the

[91] Rogan (2002: 117).

[92] As Robert Blecher (Ph.D. thesis, 2002) has argued, '[G]iven that the hospital[s] carried the term *ghuraba'* one might infer that the hospitals were sites not just of pathological but also of social exclusion.'

Damascus road in the reclusive village of ʿAsfuriyya.[93] Built on a plateau, a high wall encompassed different quarters, one for women, one for men, each containing separate wards and generous walkways.[94] The local population was impressed by the orderliness and cleanliness of the architecture and an anonymous chronicler hailed the institution as 'one of the greatest works honouring humanity'.[95] Patient numbers rose from fourteen in 1900 to sixty-three in 1905 to over a hundred in 1910. Successive Ottoman governors commended the hospital and committed funds for those suffering individuals who were too poor to pay for their treatment. In the absence of a *bimāristān* which had fulfilled the task of providing shelter for outcasts in the great Arab cities for centuries, the Ottoman government happily supported the hospital in this way to cleanse Beirut's streets from unwanted and unaccountable elements of society.[96]

Indeed, Waldmeier's private mental asylum quickly became accepted as the epitome of modern science and quickly challenged the monopoly formerly held by religious institutions over the proper treatment of the insane. This was not so much a result of the hospital's curing rate, which averaged a respectable 50 per cent in the first two decades. Rather, the hospital's popularity owed much to the public endorsement by the medical professors at the Syrian Protestant College and Waldmeier's 'public relations campaign in and around Beirut which pitted the modernity of the age against the alleged timelessness of local habits. From the outset the hospital linked the medical to its civilizational mission—to provide "an object lesson in the rational treatment of the insane"'.[97]

Given the general lack of medical treatment in early psychiatry, the hospital's actual therapy accorded to the patients could apply little of the scientific rhetoric used to discredit 'local treatment' as 'superstitious' and 'repressive'.[98] These men of science both took madness out of the hands of religious men—strawmen of a spurious argumentation—and out of the domestic sphere. The authoritative claims of science gave hope of 'cure' to the 'illness' and made the asylum the natural place for caring families to take the mentally ill.

As a private institution where patients were submitted by relatives, rather than by the authorities, it was also used by local society as a dumping ground for unwanted and uncontrollable family members. In one *cause célèbre*, the prolific feminist writer Māy Ziyāda was submitted to the hospital on spurious

[93] Rogan (2002: 114–21).

[94] Waldmeier 'was a great admirer of the Quaker William Tuke, and he styled his hospital on Tuke's York retreat, which Foucault described in terms of a "moral and religious segregation which sought to reconstruct around madness a milieu as much as possible like that of the Quaker community."' See Rogan (2002: 114).

[95] Hishshī (1973: 133).

[96] Stern (1903: i. 110–13) mentions Ottoman and missionary hospitals for outcasts in Izmir, Damascus, Baghdad, and Jerusalem.

[97] Harry Thwaites in Rogan (2002: 118–19).

[98] Stern (1903: 111).

grounds by her own cousins in 1936 over what appears to have been an inheritance scheme. Only recently has this remarkable author and *salonière* been restored to the canon of the Arabic revival movement—notably when the discovery of the original medical report of her doctors debunked the myth of her insanity.[99]

Conclusion

Public health was a pervasive and city-structuring element in the nineteenth-century Mediterranean world. The late Ottoman empire functioned as an effective bulwark against the spread of epidemics to Europe. Where the plague had involved theological debates, cholera brought scientific discourse, analytics of sexuality, and technologies of race to urban politics.[100] The struggle against cholera united European, Ottoman, Egyptian and local hygienists and integrated the Eastern Mediterranean and Ottoman provinces through a medical network that spanned from Istanbul to Cairo and from Lyons to Beirut.

In terms of city–hinterland relations we have almost come full circle and reached a double contradiction. On the one hand, while Beirut was considered a healthy place when first civil war and then periodic outbreaks of cholera threatened it from without, the city became considered as pathological precisely at a time when the municipality had actually stemmed the threat of disease visitation. On the other hand, while the Mountain had been identified by Beirut's municipal language as the locus of social disease in the immediate aftermath of the civil war of 1860, in the 1890s the pristine nature of Mount Lebanon came to be associated with cleanliness and even therapeutic qualities. The mental asylum was established precisely on the lofty plains above Beirut in order to cleanse the city of its outcasts. In other words, while *fin de siècle* Beirut became measurably better equipped to maintain public health, the processes of capitalist urbanization and an increasingly colonial discourse on health rendered the condition of the new provincial capital ever more 'prone' and 'at risk'.

Health and hygiene measures in their various manifestations (practical, metaphorical, and discursive) played foundational roles in the new urban culture of the *tanẓīmāt* in general, and in the establishment of the Beirut municipality in particular. The creation of the province of Beirut favoured the health conditions of its capital where foreign and local medical experts collaborated to improve the health conditions of this 'teasingly' modern city.

99 Ziegler (1999: 105).

100 For an application of Michel Foucault's notion of bio-politics to colonial situations, see Stoler (2000).

Hamidian institutions, too, helped root out cholera. Thus Beirut's dynamic developments in public health that this chapter has traced shatter the colonial certainty that 'hygiene wasn't practiced at all under the Turks'.[101] However, after the typhoid outbreak of 1895 and into the new century, the discourses and practices of colonial medicine took public health to a new level. The French Medical Faculty, in particular the work of Benoît Boyer, and the Lebanese Hospital for the Insane provided medical knowledge which informed the gendered nature of French colonial discourse during the mandate period that Elizabeth Thompson so painstakingly dissects.

[101] Thompson (1999: 77).

5

The Intermediary Bourgeoisie and Municipal Politics

'Le réglement organique du nouveau cercle municipal de Beyrouth . . . a été presque entièrement copié sur celui de Pera.'[1] Thus begins the first assessment of the newly created municipal council in Beirut in 1868. Its two authors, George Laurella and Edmond de Perthuis,[2] were to occupy municipal posts until the 1877 law on provincial municipalities restricted membership of the council to Ottoman subjects. The report of these two European businessmen—the former Austrian, the latter French—was full of praise for their local colleagues on the council, which was 'composed of enlightened and highly spirited men. They capture all that is good for this city and country in this new institution that represents a new step on the road to reform and progress. They expend time and efforts to ensure its success.'[3]

Institutional exceptionalisms of Istanbul's or Alexandria's municipality have dominated and shaped our understanding of the origins of modern urban management in the Middle East.[4] Traditionally, Orientalists and modernization theorists have viewed early Ottoman municipalities as attempts to Westernize, and the dithering of these urban institutions as a symptom for larger cultural ineptitudes. This is simplistic and misleading.

In the newspapers of the day, the municipality was represented and identified as the most important institution in Beirut. Ibrāhīm J. Thābit, who pub-

1 MAE, Nantes, CB 1868–1913, carton 332, Beirut, 26 May 1868.

2 We have encountered de Perthuis in previous chapters. George Laurella was from an Italian-Austrian family in Trieste. It is likely that he was the son of Pietro Laurella, who had been a medical doctor in Beirut for forty years, representing all nations as consul in Beirut since 1808, before he mysteriously disappeared in 1841. George Laurella's daughter married Mūsā de Frayj in the 1880s. For more prosopographical details on George Laurella and other municipal actors in this chapter, see Hanssen (D.Phil. thesis, 2001: Annex).

3 MAE, Nantes, CB 1868–1913, carton 332, Beirut, 26 May 1868.

4 For decades, Gabriel Baer's comparative article (1969) was treated as the yardstick for debates on urban government in the modern Middle East.

lished an article on the state of Beirut in 1909, linked the condition of the city to incipient nationalism: 'One of the most interesting laws of sociology is certainly that of good administration of one's place of residence, or the milieu where one lives, that is to say one's city and one's homeland.'[5] While local newspapers often contested the municipal council's efficacy to enforce and implement its imperatives—urban planning, market control, health, public morality, and public welfare—this kind of coverage identified the municipality as the medium of the urban idea.

This chapter addresses a number of interconnected issues of Ottoman historiography, urban institutions, and provincial paths to modernity. First, the municipality of Beirut was modelled on Ottoman urban reforms in Istanbul. To the extent that the eclectic municipal code of 1856 can be essentialized down to Western roots, the transfer of municipal knowledge to provincial Beirut erased all traces of singular and alien origins.

Second, while Beirut's municipal origins were not directly linked to the city's growing encounter with the West, Beirut's municipality was not solely an imperial imposition from Istanbul either. Rather, the development of the Beirut municipality was primarily born out of local contingency necessitated by the refugee crisis and urban health concerns in the wake of civil war in Mount Lebanon.

Third, despite its baptism of fire, Beirut's heterogeneous population, and port-city location, in the long run municipal council conformed much more to the institutional ideal-type constructed by Ottoman law and its subsequent scholars than the imperial capital and British-administered Alexandria themselves.[6] Last but not least, this chapter explores the local merchants and urban notables as an intermediary bourgeoisie whose socioeconomic status, involvement in—and utilization of—the novel structures of the municipal council as well as the electoral ways in which they came to represent the city, impacted both the everyday life and the vision of Beirut.

Local Foreigners

The role of foreigners in late Ottoman cities has elicited an overwhelming portion of academic attention either for their contribution to urban development or for their culpability in stifling it.[7] Steve Rosenthal convincingly argued that

[5] MAE, Nantes, CB 1868–1913, carton 332, enclosure: *La Lumière* (17 July 1909).

[6] Compare Yerasimos (1992).

[7] Rosenthal (1980*b*); Cleveland (1978: 33–61); Reimer (1997); Kark (1980: 117–41).

domestic politics determined the course and outcome of urban reform in Istanbul but that tragically improvements in urban planning paved the way for financial dependency on European debtors and a colonial bifurcation of the city. In contrast to the imperial capital, Beirut managed to avoid foreign domination of urban institutions. Provincial municipalities like Beirut's were legitimate institutions and popularly accepted because they were integral to the Ottoman state. Municipalities in the Ottoman empire generated, in the words of urban anthropologist Anthony Leeds, 'locality power in relation to supra-local institutions'.[8] In the case of Beirut, the municipality was central to the production of space and the crystallization of a sense of locality. This sense of locality was not determined by colonial dependency—despite chronic budget deficits—but rather by an active network of local urban notables.

In Beirut, de Perthuis himself reserved staunch criticism for his fellow foreign residents who refused to pay their share of municipal taxes:

> [The foreigners are] the first to complain about the ill-administration and the resulting insalubrity, the traffic jams, the deficient regulations and policing—in one word the insufficiency of the public services of the municipality. They forget that the services benefit everybody regardless of their origins [and] can only function, if they are well distributed and equitable, and if everyone in Turkey contributes as they do in other countries . . . We cannot maintain [our] mandate for long if [foreigners] put us into a dishonest and unacceptable situation *vis à vis* our indigenous colleagues [in the council].[9]

As long-term residents of Beirut, de Perthuis and Laurella had a vested interest (and, in the case of de Perthuis, a financial stake) in urban improvement. As council members they took their new job seriously and accused their resident fellow expatriates of myopia and lack of public spirit. The powerful plea from de Perthuis quoted above hints at the fact that, at least for the duration of foreign membership, the municipality incorporated or absorbed the interests of what were arguably Beirut's most influential foreign residents in the second half of the nineteenth century. Reading between de Perthuis's lines, his anti-foreign accusations also impart an acute sense—indeed a fear—of the changes and challenges that this new local institution might bring about in relation to Beirut's foreign community. What was looming for the European communities through the introduction of regular municipal institutions was an eclipse of the extraordinary consular powers gained in the wake of the Crimean War.[10]

[8] Leeds (1973: 15–42). [9] MAE, Nantes, CB 1868–1913, carton 332, Beirut, 26 May 1868.
[10] Iseminger (1968: 297–316).

To de Perthuis, the success of this municipal institution, integrated into a modern bureaucratic hierarchy, meant a loss of political leverage by consuls and, by extension, rendered foreign intervention in urban matters more illegitimate. Echoing de Perthuis, who acknowledged that the municipality was an Ottoman institution, the British consul in Beirut concurred in 1871 that 'the days when Governor Generals trembled before Consular Dragomans had passed—never it is hoped, to return . . . no Governor General would submit to the subserviency of a Consul which was common twenty years ago'.[11]

One of the unknown legacies of Fu'ād Pasha, the special imperial envoy to war-torn Bilad al-Sham, was his contribution to the creation of the Beirut municipality and the application of the Ottoman Land Code as a means to manage the challenges to the city's fiscal capacities. Before arriving in Beirut, Fu'ād Pasha had been an instrumental figure in the struggle for the first Ottoman municipality in Istanbul. Indeed, many of his duties as foreign minister in the late 1850s had consisted of negotiating with recalcitrant European embassies the outlines of a municipal government for Istanbul. As a staunch supporter of the municipal idea, he fought hard for the survival of the first Ottoman municipal council of Galata and Pera against the machinations of the foreign powers.[12]

While Fu'ād Pasha's experience in Istanbul may explain his proclivity towards implementing municipal government, the human misery he witnessed in Beirut made swift action mandatory. The population of Beirut had swollen between 1858 and 1863 from an estimated 50,000 to an estimated 70,000 inhabitants.[13] The gargantuan task of emergency relief for the thousands of refugees flooding into the safe haven of Beirut from Damascus and the embattled regions of Mount Lebanon was provided by an over-stretched body of international aid operations, benevolent societies, and congregations that set up makeshift shelters across the city.[14] Beirut itself was on the verge of sectarian violence in late June 1860 with vendetta squads roaming the streets that were barely contained by a miniature Ottoman military presence and a disempowered notable leadership.[15] Having restored Ottoman law and order in Damascus by deterrence executions, Fu'ād Pasha returned to Beirut where the residence of the European general consulates required setting up his own headquarters for the duration of his eight months' stay in Syria.

[11] PRO, 78/2259, 9 Sept. 1871. Quoted in Gross (Ph.D. thesis, 1979: 161).

[12] See Rosenthal (1980*b*).

[13] For a compilation of the diverse contemporary population estimates, see Davie (1996: 141).

[14] Fawaz (1983: 54–6).

[15] Ibid. 193.

The Municipality and the Application of the Land Code

The restoration of Ottoman order in Syria after the civil wars—skilfully manœuvred by Fu'ād Pasha—had come at a huge fiscal price. In order to finance the sum of indemnities to Christian victims, Fu'ād Pasha was forced to raise special taxes from the province of Damascus and the port of Beirut in the range of 6.5 million piastres.[16] The desperate need for revenue in post-war Beirut encouraged Fu'ād Pasha to apply vigorously the imperial Land Law of 1858 to the city where the annual tax income of merely 150,000 to 160,000 piastres 'ha[d] become incompatible with modern progress'.[17] In the context of Ottoman imperialism, 'closing the gap with modernity' meant first devising a fiscal structure that would establish better knowledge and tighter control over Beirut's property relations for the benefit of effective surplus extraction and distribution of resources. Second, it meant more reliable planning of urban revitalization (*inʿāsh al-madīna*[18]).

Prior to the *tanẓīmāt*, the governor general of the province of Sidon decided over public work initiatives. Towns generally lacked budgetary autonomy.[19] At the same time, 'particularly in port towns urban dwellers . . . were spared many types of taxes, paying instead the traditional market dues (*iḥtisāb resmi*) and customs duties imposed on goods imported and exported from the Empire'.[20] While the Gülhane Rescript of 1839 introduced individual taxation through *virgu* (or *per capita* tax), the 1858 Land Law's novelty was that urban property and buildings—owned or rented—became subject to taxation in their own right (as opposed to earlier modes that merely taxed the goods produced on or in them). The legal stipulations affected the relationships of the urban-propertied inhabitants not only with their government, but also with their city as they reinforced the sense of locality and urban consciousness that came with holding a stake in the city or with paying taxes for property and public services.

A central concern of the imperial government was to maximize efficient land use. To this effect, it needed to improve its knowledge of the actual size and quality of Ottoman lands around the empire.[21] In particular the fast-changing geography and demography around expanding cities and towns required imperial coordination, regulation, and planning. Indeed, the application of the

[16] Fawaz (1994: 169) and Gross (Ph.D. thesis, 1979: 49).

[17] MAE, Nantes, CB 1887–1914, carton 340, 2 Feb. 1868.

[18] 'Urban rehabilitation' became a central theme on the pages of *Ḥadīqat al-Akhbār* after 1860.

[19] Abdel Nour (1982: 188).

[20] Shaw (1975: 421).

[21] Rogan (1999: 83). The Ottoman Land Law was tr. by F. Ongley as *The Ottoman Land Code* (London, 1892).

Ottoman Land Law in Beirut not only provided the legal framework for security and transferability of title but also formalized—and arguably accelerated—the process of extramural urbanization.

The urgency of property administration was second only to the issue of war indemnities.[22] On the basis of Fu'ād Pasha's imperial property survey, which according to a notice in *Ḥadīqat al-Akhbār*[23] was 'nearly completed' by October 1861, Beirut's annual municipal revenue for subsequent years more than quadrupled to 750,000 piastres.[24] Taxes on state land were raised in early 1861.[25] Fu'ād Pasha had negotiated a 7 per cent tax on property possessions with the municipality (which rose to around 8.5 per cent by the end of the decade) on the condition that 150,000 piastres were reinvested into Beirut's urban rehabilitation each year.

Municipal directives facilitated the development of a property market outside the city centre which for centuries had been sparsely populated. Around a few strongly fortified outposts (e.g. Burj al-Kashshaf, Burj al-Barajna, Burj Abu Haydar), most of the extramural land was legally considered *arażi emīriye*, or state land, often held as hereditary tax farms by Druze and Maronite *muqāṭaʿjis* of the adjacent mountain districts of Gharb al-Shuf and Kisrawan, such as the Arslāns, Talḥūqs, and the Khāzins. Construction on these fields, groves, and wild orchards had been largely tolerated by local Ottoman governors prior to the new Land Law but extramural insecurity was a constant menace.

For the aspiring merchant notables of Beirut, the summer heat and winter floods in the city centre were an inconvenience and a health hazard they could well afford to do without. With time, the legal protection of extramural residence turned the large plots of land around Beirut into smaller parcels as more wealthy families purchased and populated land in the outskirts.

After Beirut was subordinated to the jurisdiction of Damascus in 1865, urban authorities faced the problem that the promised revenues were no longer redistributed directly to Beirut as previously agreed.[26] The landowners and merchants of Beirut felt the economic repercussions of the abolition of the old province of Sidon immediately. Moreover, the outbreak of cholera in 1865 reduced Beirut's trade to tatters. In *Ḥadīqat al-Akhbār*, editor-in-chief Khalīl al-Khūrī summed up the city's plight as follows:

> Last year Beirut was afflicted by severe financial setbacks leading to a suspension of its trade. This is clearly a consequence of the abolition of the *Eyalet* of Sayda and the

22 *Ḥadīqat al-Akhbār* (15 Oct. 1860).
23 *Ḥadīqat al-Akhbār* (17 Oct. 1861).
24 MAE, Nantes, CB 1887–1914, carton 340, Beirut, 10 Feb. 1868.
25 *Ḥadīqat al-Akhbār* (7 Mar. 1861).
26 MAE, Nantes, CB 1887–1914, carton 340, Beirut, 10 Feb. 1868.

transfer of the centre of the province to Damascus. Foreigners cease to make station [and] it did not take long before houses and shops had no tenants, income was reduced and the prices for land plots dropped. There had been hope that the losses of the Beirutis in land revenue could be made up by profits in trade this year, but the economic depression and adverse conditions in the hinterland have tied up capital . . . Beirut shivers at the dangers for its future.[27]

The governorship of Meḥmed Rashīd Pasha led Beirut out of this financial crisis. Municipal governance was transformed into a locally elected rather than appointed body of personalities and, in order to address pressing financial issues more effectively, it was raised to the administrative status of the Sixth District of Istanbul Pera/Galata.[28] In fact, the first elections to the municipal council of Beirut were held only a few months after the Ottoman government decided to apply the municipal model of Pera and Galata to the rest of Istanbul.[29] Whereas, as Ussama Makdisi has argued, Fu'ād Pasha's pacification policies for the mountain were driven by a 'temporal distancing' and denied Mount Lebanon its coevalness with the imperial centre, the city of Beirut had in a way entered the same 'time zone of reform' as Istanbul.[30] Or, in the medicalized vocabulary of modernization, the incubation period of imperial reform in Beirut was significantly shortened in the early 1860s.

The councillors were elected by an assembly of local notables presided over by Rashīd Pasha. Judging by the euphoric reception by the French consulate, it proved a success. Six Sunni Muslims, one Greek Orthodox (Ḥabīb Busṭrus), one Greek Catholic (Nakhla Mudawwar), one Maronite (Yūsuf Thābit), one Armenian Catholic (Naṣrallah Khayyāṭ), and two foreign entrepreneurs, Edmund de Perthuis and George Laurella, were elected. Aḥmad Pasha Abāẓa was appointed president of the first municipal council. Before his council was sworn in by Rashīd Pasha, its members made their mandate conditional on being granted a larger degree of fiscal independence from the central authorities in Damascus which, they argued, 'has interfered negatively in affairs regarding the city of Beirut'.[31] After tough imperial–local negotiations, the municipality was guaranteed a budget of no less than 300,000 piastres, of which 150,000 piastres annually were promised as imperial redistribution in return for local property revenue.[32]

[27] *Ḥadīqat al-Akhbār* (28 May 1867).
[28] MAE, Nantes, CB 1887–1914, carton 340, Beirut, 10 Feb. 1868.
[29] Rosenthal (1980*b*: 167).
[30] Makdisi (2002*b*: 601–17). Here Makdisi takes his cue from Fabian (1983).
[31] MAE, Nantes, CB 1887–1914, carton 340, 10 Feb. 1868, report by the French consul.
[32] Ibid.

The Composition of the Municipal Council, 1868–1908

Figure 3 is a tabulation of the terms of office of all one hundred municipal councillors between 1868 and 1908 that I could find in the Ottoman provincial almanacs (or *salnames*) and in local election coverage in *Thamarāt al-Funūn* and *Lisān al-Ḥāl.*

One of the most striking features of the municipal councillors was the conspicuous absence of scions of Druze and Maronite *muqāṭaʿjis*—or rural landlords—who had dominated Beirut from the surrounding mountain districts of Kisrawan, Matn, and Gharb al-Shuf since the seventeenth century. Strict legal residence requirements may account for the lack of their involvement in municipal politics. Those Maronites who were active in the municipal council were young professionals, lawyers, merchants, and journalists of non-feudal genealogy whose parents or grandparents had settled in Beirut as scribes and merchants.[33] Many had championed the Franco-Maronite alliance for a Maronite Mountain in the 1850s and 1860s and were collectively known as the 'Young Maronite League', which was formed by the bishop of Beirut during the civil war. Catalysed by the defeat of Yūsuf Karam Bey in 1866, this group dissolved and its members acquiesced to Ottoman rule. They began to identify with and actively promote what Albert Hourani considered 'the ideology of the city'.[34]

The complete absence of any Druze member in forty years of municipal history is significant. As I argued at the beginning of this book, Druze landowners were systematically expropriated in the first half of the nineteenth century. The Druze who remained or who arrived anew may not have fulfilled the tax requirement or if, indeed, they ever stood for office—only records of the successful candidates exist—they may simply not have been able to rally sufficient votes. In the second half of the nineteenth century, the Druze constituted the most underrepresented and politically marginalized religious community in Beirut.

To the extent that municipal members functioned as patrons to the confessional and residential constituencies that voted for them, promoting clientelist agendas had to be squared with the general Ottoman reform discourse as well as the letter and spirit of the municipal law in particular. Sporadic communal violence was commonplace in Beirut. Nevertheless such outbreaks should not be treated as a rule. In the future-oriented municipal discourse of the age, they

[33] See Ch. 1. [34] Hourani (1981). See also Ch. 7.

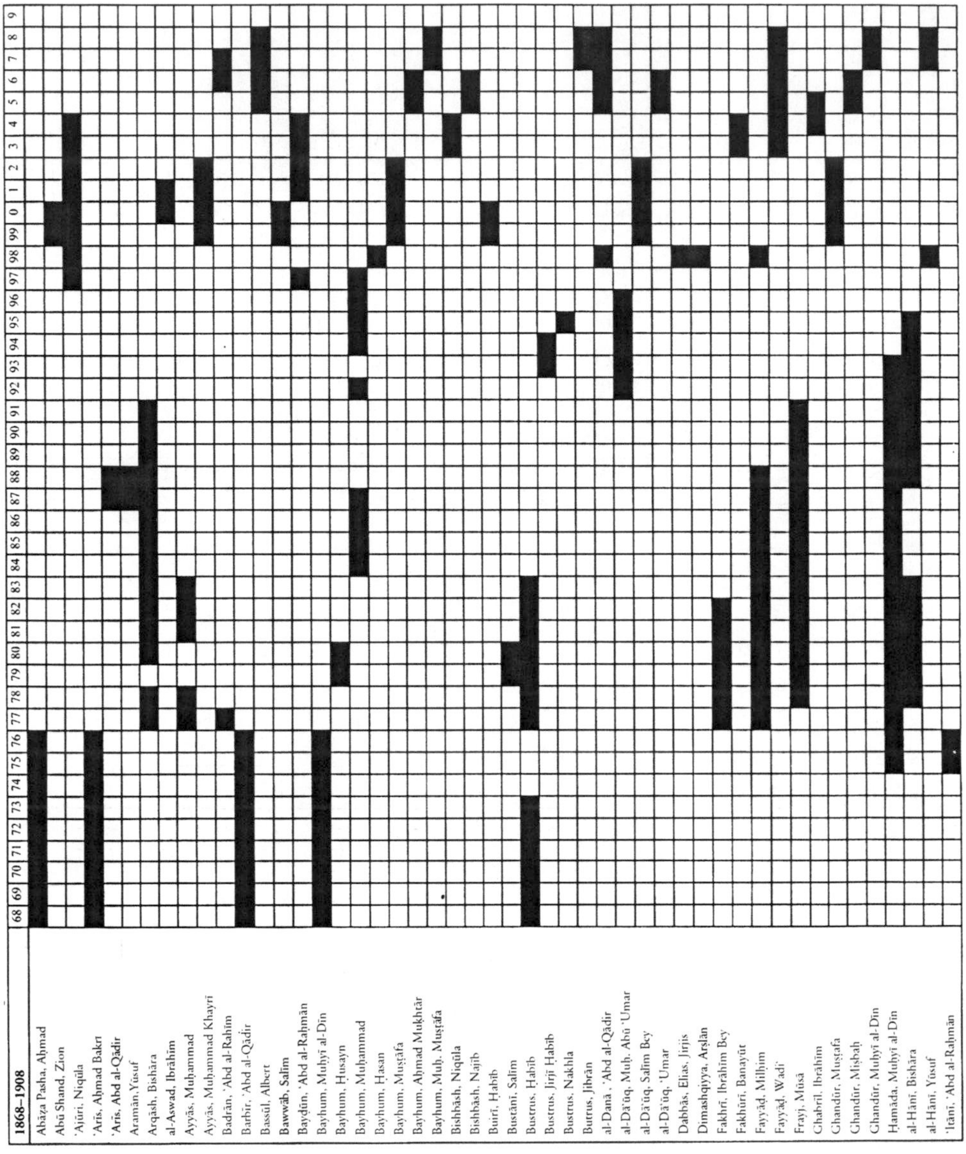

FIG. 3. Beirut's municipal members

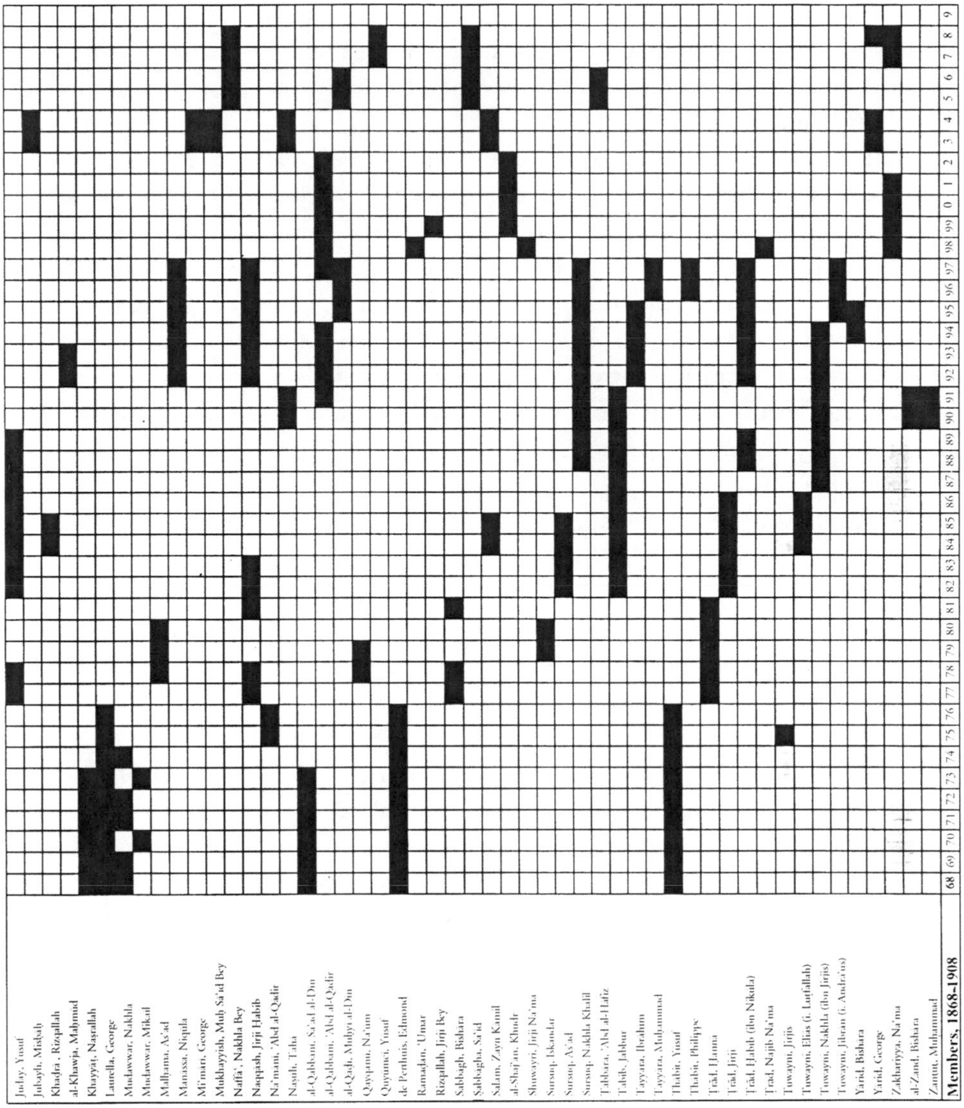
Members, 1868–1908
Juday, Yusuf
Jubayli, Misbah
Khadra, Rizqallah
al-Khawja, Mahmud
Khayyat, Nasrallah
Laurella, George
Mudawwar, Nakhla
Mudawwar, Mikail
Malhama, As'ad
Manassa, Niqula
Mi'mari, George
Mukhayyish, Muh Sa'id Bey
Naffa', Nakhla Bey
Naqqash, Jirji Habib
Na'mani, 'Abd al-Qadir
Nasuli, Taha
al-Qabbani, Sa'ad al-Din
al-Qabbani, 'Abd al-Qadir
al-Qadi, Muhyi al-Din
Qayqanu, Na'um
Quyumci, Yusuf
de Perthuis, Edmond
Ramadan, 'Umar
Rizqallah, Jirji Bey
Sabbagh, Bishara
Sabbagha, Sa'id
Salam, Zayn Kamil
al-Shaj'an, Khudr
Shuwayri, Jirji Na'ma
Sursuq, Iskandar
Sursuq, As'ad
Sursuq, Nakhla Khalil
Tabbara, 'Abd al-Hafiz
Tabib, Jabbur
Tayyara, Ibrahim
Tayyara, Muhammad
Thabit, Yusuf
Thabit, Philippe
Trad, Hanna
Trad, Jirji
Trad, Habib (ibn Nikula)
Trad, Najib Na'ma
Tuwayni, Jirjis
Tuwayni, Elias (i. Lutfallah)
Tuwayni, Nakhla (ibn Jirjis)
Tuwayni, Jibran (i. Andra'us)
Yarid, Bishara
Yarid, George
Zakhariyya, Na'ma
al-Zand, Bishara
Zantut, Muhammad
68 (69) 70 71 72 73 74 75 76 77 78 79 80 81 82 83 84 85 86 87 88 89 90 91 92 93 94 95 96 97 98 99 0 1 2 3 4 5 6 7 8 9

were viewed by Ottoman governors, local journalists, and municipal members alike as dangerous instances of deviance and as obstinate remnants of a backward past which undermined the 'enlightened' municipal project of modernization and urban reform.

It is in this sense that the institution of the municipality transcended the communal politics of Beirut's various confessional groups. Although *millet*s were organized as political communities and although their leaders often tended to agree on candidates for the municipal council before the election, the municipal council was more than the sum of its composite confessions. Confessional block voting for the municipal council was checked—if not explicitly by law—by an in-built mixture of confessional and residency requirement in the electoral procedures and geography. This led to a surprising degree of fluctuation of the confessional quotas on the council (Figure 4).

Moral indignation by municipal members and local journalists as well as *ad hoc* intervention by Ottoman governors worked to prevent rare cases in Beirut of slanting municipal law. When the first full municipal elections during Sultan Abdülhamid's rule were held in the spring of 1878, ʿAbd al-Qādir al-Qabbānī emerged as the moral guardian of the civic nature of the municipality. In his newspaper, *Thamarāt al-Funūn*, he published a number of lengthy, pedagogical articles on the virtues of municipal government and printed the Arabic translation of the Ottoman Municipal Law of 1877.[35] Qabbānī accused the *muftī* of Beirut, ʿAbd al-Bāsiṭ Fākhūrī, of using his religious network to encourage Sunni block voting. Qabbānī's accusations against this most senior of *ʿulamāʾ* in Beirut were presented in no uncertain binary terms between his adversary's 'age of tyranny' and his own age of 'free choice'.[36]

This conflict between two powerful representatives of the conservative and reformist camps in Beirut politics confirms another conspicuous absence from the list of municipal members: the urban Sunni group of *ʿulamāʾ*. After 1888, *muftī*s, *faqīh*s, and *naqīb*s *al-ashrāf* were guaranteed permanent positions on the provincial council, and some of them played an important role in the electoral college for the municipal council. But families from Beirut's religious estate, like Fākhūrī, al-Kastī, al-Naḥḥās, al-Khālid, al-Nabḥānī, Najjā, ʿAbbās, al-Unsī, al-Aḥdāb, and al-Ḥūt did not enter the municipal council. Those members in the early decades of the municipality who hailed from important

[35] *Thamarāt al-Funūn* (14 Jan. 1878). [36] Shareef (MA thesis, 1998: 52).

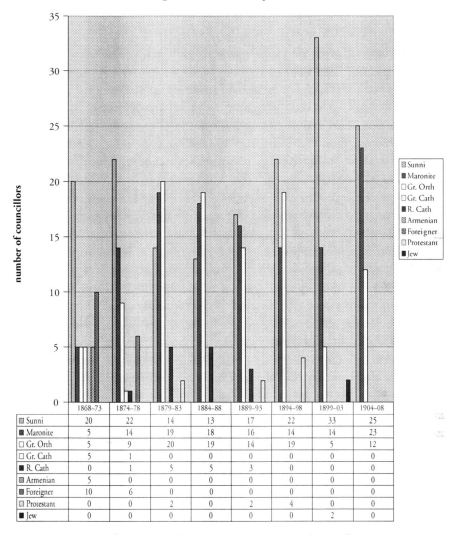

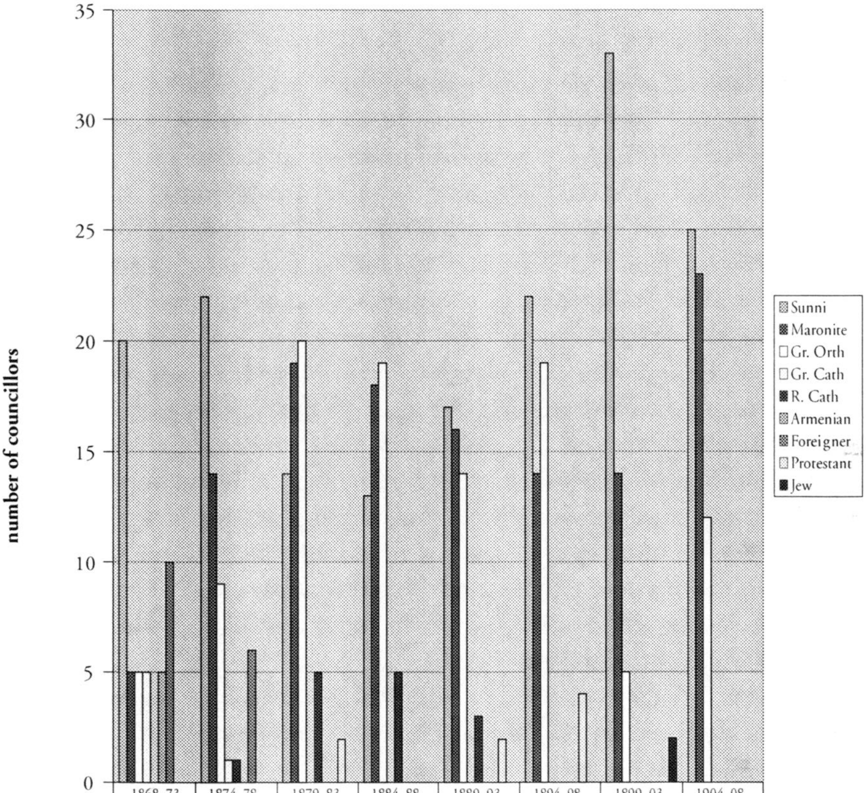

	1868–73	1874–78	1879–83	1884–88	1889–93	1894–98	1899–03	1904–08
Sunni	20	22	14	13	17	22	33	25
Maronite	5	14	19	18	16	14	14	23
Gr. Orth	5	9	20	19	14	19	5	12
Gr. Cath	5	1	0	0	0	0	0	0
R. Cath	0	1	5	5	3	0	0	0
Armenian	5	0	0	0	0	0	0	0
Foreigner	10	6	0	0	0	0	0	0
Protestant	0	0	2	0	2	4	0	0
Jew	0	0	0	0	0	0	2	0

FIG. 4. Confessional distribution in Beirut's municipal council, 1868–1908

ʿ*ulamāʾ* families of the eighteenth and early nineteenth centuries, like Aḥmad Bakrī ʿArīs and ʿAbd al-Qādir Barbīr, were eligible for their own credentials but owed their status to that of their forefathers. Christian religious dignitaries—patriarchs, priests, and clergymen—were equally absent from the municipal council.

Municipal Elections

Arguably the most important specification in the municipal law of 1877 was the election process.[37] The municipal members were chosen in a long, highly public, and, indeed, publicized process that merits a detailed analysis. Voting was restricted to male Beirut residents above 25 years of age who paid a minimum of one hundred Ottoman piastres of (unspecified) tax annually and held no criminal record. Candidates for municipal office had to be 30 years of age, Ottoman residents in Beirut of at least ten years' standing, fluent in Ottoman, and hold no criminal record or parallel employment in foreign institutions.

Although the phrase 'notable of the city' was dropped from the 1867 law, by the time the 1913 Administrative Law was passed eligibility hinged on payment of an annual property tax of £150 sterling.[38] Clearly, the number of eligible candidates was limited as this was not a system of universal suffrage. The policy was to incorporate extant local elites into a tighter imperial power structure. In 1880, for example, Henry Jessup estimated that 461 Christians of varied denominations and 263 (Sunni) Muslims were eligible to stand for municipal elections.[39] In a city nearing the 100,000 mark this was less than 1 per cent of the total population.

Before the residents voted for the candidates, an elaborate vetting process took place, which usually lasted from December to February. The municipal president asked *imāms*, priests, and quarter officials (*mukhtārs*) to nominate two candidates from their neighbourhood towards an Electoral College. This assembly then proceeded to draw up two lists of residents, one for the eligible voters and one for candidates. Within fifteen days these lists were required to be posted at public places where they remained for eight days. During this time, the public was entitled to challenge the list for names omitted or ineligible candidates. Usually by 1 February, the candidates of the respective quarters were required to present themselves to the electorate. The voting took place over the following ten days by district, and was cast by 'secret ballot into one urn, the keys to which were kept by the municipal president and the most senior member of the Electoral College'. After the election, the votes were counted and recorded by the members of the Electoral College. The results were handed over to the local authorities in a report. Upon official verification, the results were announced in an official notification.[40]

[37] BBA, YEE, 37, 302/47/112, 5 Oct. 1877, ch. 4, artis. 40–1.

[38] See George Antonius, 'Interim Report, Final Version [June 2, 1924]', art. 18. Quoted in Boyle (2001: 309). To compare the Ottoman to the French mandate municipal laws, see Ritsher (1934).

[39] Jessup (1910: ii. 466).

[40] Young (1906–7: i. 73).

No systematic data exist on election results and those results that were published in the local press normally only contained the votes for the winners. In the 1893 elections, for example, *Thamarāt al-Funūn* reported that 8,892 votes were cast for the candidates.[41] Two years later, the newspaper announced that a total of 10,473 votes were cast for six municipal posts.[42] As a rule, half the council was up for election annually, but some members managed to get re-elected up to five times (see Fig. 3). On at least three occasions, in 1878/9, 1892/3, and 1898, the governor dissolved the municipal council. In the 1878/9 election, of the twelve successful candidates, Bishāra Efendi Hānī received most votes (672) and Hannā Efendi Ṭrād fewest (318). Despite Hānī's victory, Ibrāhīm Bey Fakhrī was appointed president with the second highest score as the president had to be a Sunni Muslim.[43]

In the 1892/3 general election, Muḥammad Efendi al-Khawja received 1,113 votes, closely followed by Nakhla Jirjis Efendi Tuwaynī with 1,033. This time round, Bishāra Efendi Hānī only just scraped through with 612, the lowest score of all elected members. Although Muḥyī al-Dīn Efendi Ḥamāda achieved a meagre 675 votes, the council members re-elected him as president in an internal vote.[44] Elections were clearly very competitive and a matter of a few votes could decide the success or failure of a candidacy.

Despite their frequent change of location the municipal offices always remained in the triangle between old city, Sahat al-Burj, and the port. At the centre of political and economic power in Beirut it dominated the outlying fifteen districts as it delegated the control over the electoral geography to local *mukhtārs* (Christian or Muslim 'majors' depending on the quarter) and Sunni *imāms* in the city (Table 3).

These *mukhtārs* and *imāms* played a pivotal role in the municipal affairs of *fin de siècle* Beirut.[45] They not only staffed the Electoral College once every two years, but were also people's representatives in dealing with state authorities and arbitrators in quarter affairs. At the same time, they were considered the executive arm of the municipality. The *mukhtārs* held a tacit policing and mobilizing role in their respective quarters. Most quarters had a Sunni and a Christian *mukhtār*, evidence of the general prevalence of confessionally mixed quarters in the late Ottoman period (see Map 6).

Only two eastern districts, Ashrafiyya (Maronite) and Rumayl/Jumayza (Greek Orthodox), had one *mukhtār*. The Protestants—fewest in number and

41 *Thamarāt al-Funūn* (2 Jan. 1893). 42 *Thamarāt al-Funūn* (25 Feb. 1895).

43 *Lisān al-Ḥāl* (18 July 1878). 44 *Thamarāt al-Funūn* (21 Jan. 1893).

45 The *mukhtār* in late Ottoman Beirut evolved out of—and held similar functions to—the *shaykh al-hāra* in pre-*Tanẓīmāt* times. See Abdel Nour (1982: 163).

TABLE 3. Geographical and confessional distribution of Beirut's *mukhtārs* and *imāms* in 1909

Mukhtārs* and *Imāms	**Quarter**
A (Sunni) *Imām*: Shaykh Aḥmad al-Naḥḥās *Mukhtār*: Ḥājj ʿAbdallah al-Jayzī	(*intramuros*) (1) Mahallat al-Sharqiyya, (2) Rijal al-Arbaʿin, (3) al-Darka, (4) al-Tuba, (5) al-Khadra
B (Sunni) *Imām*: Shaykh Ibrāhīm al-Majdhūb *Mukhtār*: Muḥammad al-Rayyis *Mukhtār*: Salīm Ṭabbāra	(*intramuros*) (6) Mahallat al-Gharbiyya, (7) Hamam al-Saghir, (8) al-Shaykh Raslan, (9) al-Fakhuri, (10) al-Dabbagha
C (Christian mukhtars) *Mukhtār*: Ḥabīb al-Shāmī *Mukhtār*: Majīd Maʿrabas	(*intramuros*) (1) and (2) Da'ira (central) and their dependencies, al-Balda (city centre) and (11) al-Sayfi
D (Sunni) *Imām*: Shaykh Munīr Jamāl al-Dīn *Mukhtārs*: Salīm Jawhar, Rajab al-ʿUmarī	(south-western districts) (12) al-Bashura, (13) Maydan al-Mazra'a, (14) Mazraʿat al-ʿArab [(25) Museitbeh?]
E (Maronite and Greek Orthodox) *Mukhtārs*: Khalīl Qalawz, Mitrī al-Jamīl	(south-eastern, south central districts) (12) al-Bashura, (15) al-Qirat, (16) al-Ashrafiyya
F (Sunni) *Imām*: Shaykh ʿAbdallah Khālid, *Mukhtārs*: Ḥājj ʿAbd al-Qādir Al-Shiʿār, Yūsuf Qrunful	(south-central district) (17) Ras al-Nabaʿ (west)
G (Sunni) *Imām*: Shaykh Khuḍr Khālid *Mukhtār*: Muḥyī al-Dīn Bayḍūn	(south central, south-eastern districts) (18) Ras al-Nabaʿ (east), (16) al-Ashrafiyya
H (Maronite) *Mukhtār*: Filip al-Brins	(south central districts) (17 and 18) Ras al-Nabaʿ, and dependencies
I (Maronite and Greek Orthodox) *Mukhtārs*: Faḍūl Ṣabbāgh, Eliās Kurm	(south-eastern districts) (16) Ashrafiyya and dependencies
J (Sunni) *Imām*: Shaykh ʿAbd al-Ghānī al-Bundāq, *Mukhtārs*: Rashīd Saʿāda, ʿUmar al-Dibs	(south-western districts) (19) Zuqaq al-Blat, (20) Jumayze al-Yamin
K (Sunni) *Imām*: Shaykh ʿAbd al-Ghanī al-Bundāq *Mukhtār*: Ḥājj ʿAbd al-Qādir al-ʿĪtānī	(far western district) (21) Ras Bayrut, (not listed as district) Jubb al-Nakhl
K (Sunni) *Imām*: Shaykh Tawfīq al-Hibrī, *Mukhtārs*: Yūsuf Iskandarānī, Ḥājj Muḥammad Fākhūrī	(western coastal districts) (22) Minet al-Husn, (23) ʿAin al-Mreisse
L (Maronite and Greek Orthodox) *Mukhtars*: Jibrān al-Ḥaddād, Jirjī Qashūʿ	(western coastal districts) (22) Minet al-Husn, (23) ʿAin al-Mreisse
M (Greek Orthodox) *Mukhtār*: Elias Rubays	(far eastern coastal districts) (24) Hayy al-Rumayl and dependencies [(26) Rumayl?]
O (Protestant community for all Beirut) *Mukhtār*: Salīm Darwīsh	

Source: al-Unsī (1910/11: 117–18).
Note: Of the officially listed quarters of Beirut, Museitbeh and al Raml have no independent mayor. Common area names like Qantari, Ghalghul, Wadi Abu Jamil, Sanaya, Manara, Zaytuneh, Santiyya, and Hawdh Saʿatiyya did not constitute electoral entities *c.*1909.

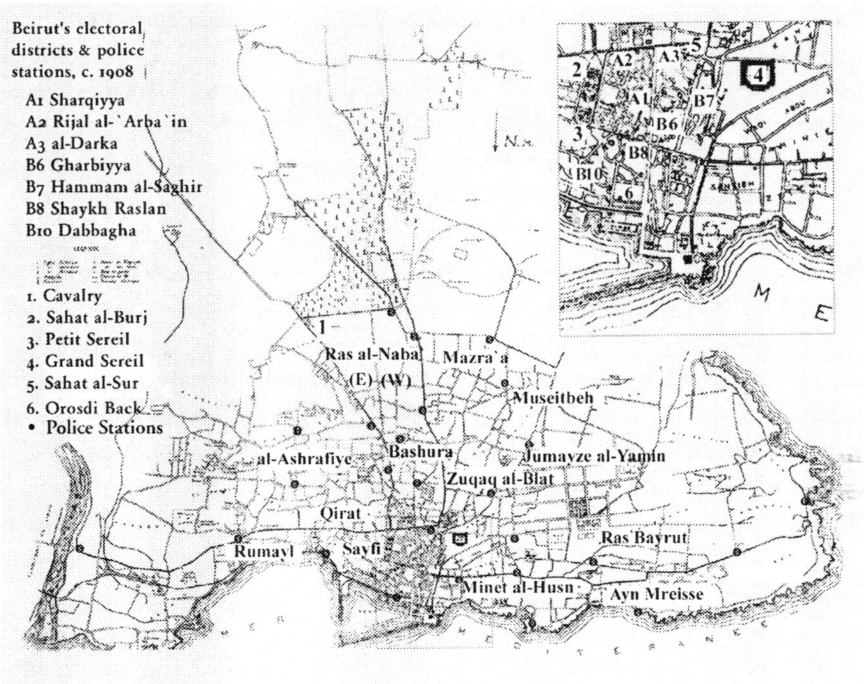

MAP. 6. Beirut map containing names of electoral districts and police stations (Hanssen 2004 based on Beirut Water Company Map, 1908)

probably most scattered geographically—formed the only community that had a confessional *mukhtār* for the entire city. Fourteen electoral quarters and thirty-one confessional representatives are a reflection of mixed quarters. The in-built, joined residency-confession requirement in the Electoral College conventions may explain the varying confessional ratios in the council over the forty years examined (Figure 4). Moreover, this structure of street-level politics became a vital asset to *zuʿāma* leadership after the Young Turk revolution of 1908 and into the French mandate period. In fact, when the Lebanese civil war broke out in 1975 and Beirut came to be divided into a patchwork of neighbourhoods, the *mukhtār* system continued to provide a modicum of services even as the *zaʿīms* lost control of the streets.[46]

Continuity and Change in the Municipal Presidency

Egyptian rule over Beirut may have ended officially in 1840 but the legacy of the urban administration put in place by Ibrāhīm Pasha in the early 1830s

[46] See Beyhum (Ph.D. thesis, 1991).

continued for much of the nineteenth century. A long lineage of municipal presidents with Egyptian origins was finally interrupted in 1893 when Muḥammad Bayhum successfully challenged Muḥyī al-Dīn Ḥamāda. Moreover, the members of Ibrāhīm Pasha's advisory council in the 1830s were distinguished local merchants whose families were to dominate Beirut's municipal affairs until the early twentieth century.

Until the 1880s, the Ottoman governors appointed municipal presidents from the ranks of Egyptian families who had stayed on. The first municipal president, Aḥmad Pasha Abāẓa, was himself a junior officer in the Egyptian army and a member of Ibrāhīm Pasha's advisory council before his appointment as the president of the first elected municipal council in 1868. His successor Ibrāhīm Fakhrī Bey was the son of Maḥmūd Nāmī Bey, the governor of Beirut during the 1830s whose given name may well have been a homage to the commander of the Egyptian army, Ibrāhīm Pasha. Like his father, Ibrāhīm Fakhrī was a much respected and very active lieutenant of the provincial authority. During the time of Midḥat Pasha's provincial reforms, he became the first president with an identifiable urban vision for Beirut.

The last municipal president of Egyptian background was also the longest-serving member on the council. From 1875 to 1893, Muḥyī al-Dīn Ḥamāda shaped municipal affairs, the last eleven years as president. He was a son of the military officer ʿAbd al-Fattāḥ *agha*, who was a member of the original advisory council and who managed Beirut's affairs from the Egyptian withdrawal to his death in 1858.[47]

The successful challenge of Ḥamāda by Muḥammad Bayhum in the early 1890s marked a sea change in Beirut's administration.[48] Bayhum's appointment meant a switch from presidents with an Egyptian military or engineering background to a leading civilian merchant notable. The next municipal president, the reformist ʿAbd al-Qādir al-Qabbānī, was noted for his journalistic and educational work and reappears as a central urban figure in this book.

After a brief presidential interlude by ʿAbd al-Raḥmān Bayḍūn—about whom little is known—ʿAbd al-Qādir al-Danā was appointed to the municipal presidency. A successful merchant and an ardent Ottomanist, he translated Aḥmed Cevdet's *Tārīh Devlet-i Osmānī* into Arabic. He was a personal friend of the grand vizier Kāmil Pasha with whom he joined the Syrian Scientific Society in 1867. Two decades later he launched the official provincial gazette *Bayrūt* and in 1907 he was instrumental in reviving the *maqāṣid khayriyya* society together with ʿAbd al-Qādir al-Qabbānī.

[47] See Ch. 1.

[48] See Shareef (1998). On the rivalry between the two families, see Yazbak (1955: 173–4).

The municipal presidency sharply reflected the larger social and intellectual trends of Beirut's urban elites during Abdülhamid's rule: urban rehabilitation, commerce, journalism, and education. Unfortunately, much less systematic information exists on the Young Turk period. However, one landmark event requires closer examination: the temporary partition of the municipality into an eastern and a western sector in 1909.

Beirut: East–West

Although the Ottoman municipal law of 1877 stipulated that cities with a population of over 40,000 should be granted two municipalities, in practice few large cities made use of this article. The authorities in Damascus experimented on a number of occasions with multiple municipal authorities as a way to improve urban services. Between 1884 and 1886, 1895 and 1897, and between 1905 and 1909, up to four municipal councils existed in Damascus.[49] In Beirut, too, there were suggestions, notably from the Maronite weekly newspaper, *al-Bashīr*, of dividing the municipality into two. Reporting on a previous article in *al-Bashīr*, *Thamarāt al-Funūn* informed its readership that

> the municipal department has refrained from dividing the municipality in two parts and to charge the department as a whole. This is a subject that needs investigation because the municipal law permits stipulations for a city's size and Beirut has started to grow, increase its constructions and expand its roads. The precedent had been an attempt to divide Damascus municipality into four sectors, then two but now it is going to stay as it was before.[50]

When the Beirut municipality did get divided into an eastern and western sector, it did not happen as the consequence of *al-Bashīr*'s Maronite disaffection with a Sunni-dominated municipal council. Rather it was rooted in an intra-Sunni power struggle between the municipal inspector, Munīḥ Ramaḍān, and the president of the municipal council, ʿAbd al-Qādir al-Danā. The latter had been elected to the presidency in 1906 'owing to his popularity with Muslims and Christians'.[51] But when 'the sultan allocated funds from the imperial municipal departments in Istanbul to be spent on construction and improvement', Munīḥ Ramaḍān submitted a report to the Ottoman government in Istanbul alleging 'that a large part of the money procured for public construction and decoration was actually used by ʿAbd al-Qādir al-Danā for personal gain and stolen from the municipal treasury'.[52]

49 S. Weber (Ph.D. thesis, 2001).
50 *Thamarāt al-Funūn* (30 Mar. 1896).
51 PRO, FO, 195/2217, 2 Apr. 1906.
52 BBA, Giden 274, vesika 250447, 5 June 1906.

This was a serious accusation against one of the local favourites of the Ottoman authorities. Although it was never confirmed that al-Danā embezzled municipal funds, his reputation was tarred. Al-Danā died soon afterwards, but Ramaḍān's career took a step up the Ottoman ladder. When the governor general saw no other way out of the general malaise of the municipality of Beirut than to divide it into two sectors, he appointed Munīḥ Ramaḍān as the president of the western sector. For a brief period, West Beirut was administered by a Sunni president and the eastern part by the Greek Orthodox merchant Buṭrus al-Dāghir.[53] The experiment did not work as 'the two municipalities rivalled against each other in the worst fashion'.[54] When a new governor general arrived, he immediately reverted to the old scheme. Despite 'vehement protest led by those who lost their municipal seat as a consequence, the Council of State [in Istanbul] approved of the decision' and Beirut's municipality was reunified.[55]

Some Observations on Beirut's Municipal Councillors

The councillors of the Beirut municipality shared a measure of Mediterranean cosmopolitanism with wealthy inhabitants of other trading centres in the Levant and Bilad al-Sham, often through marriage, business ties, and exchange of ideas.[56] But the municipal members' public and intellectual involvement in everyday activities—political, but also social and, above all, cultural—is a measure of their rootedness in—and identification with—the city of Beirut. Although many of the merchant council members spent much of their time abroad, in Istanbul, Egypt, or Europe, they needed to be registered as Beirutis during their absence to be eligible, and naturally had to be 'in residence' during their term of office.

Membership of the municipal council may not have yielded much in the way of pecuniary reward, but additional income was hardly an incentive to stand for election. The council members enjoyed autonomous sources of income. Definitionally closer to Weber's notion of *Honoratioren* ('local dignitaries') than Hourani's use of Weber's 'patriciate',[57] Beirut's municipal members were 'individuals whose economic situation allowed them to be publicly active . . . and whose social esteem and respect among the people they are to represent, evoked sufficient integrity to be trusted with authority . . . They have the means to live *for* politics without living *from* it.'[58]

53 al-Ḥakīm (1966: 28). 54 MAE, Nantes, CEB 1894–1911, Beirut, 28 Jan. 1911. 55 Ibid.
56 Ilbert (1992: 171–85). 57 Hourani (1968: 45). 58 M. Weber (1980: 170).

Who was related to whom, who socialized with whom, who supported whose policies in the municipal council? Biographical origins and common career patterns may serve as keys to understand underlying group identities, structures, and political relations of Beirut's elite society, but they need to be treated with caution.[59] Geographical, confessional, or occupational similarity cannot be treated as automatic indicators of common social identities or political agendas on the municipal council. Alliances, even within given families from one generation to the next, were always likely to change over time.[60]

Nevertheless, the high degree of genealogical continuity (grandfather, father, brother, son) on the municipal council was matched by an equally high degree of the councillors' memberships in the highly influential political lobby groups and literary organizations. These observations allow us to infer that over generations certain Beiruti families held a lasting group identification with the city and that they valued the municipality as the place to act out their identification. Generally, socio-political allegiances appeared to be organized around clusters of families linked by marriage and inheritance, residence and professional ties.

Although there were exceptions, the council normally consisted of twelve members. In forty years of municipal councils, 40 Sunnis (26 families), 28 Greek Orthodox (15 families), 23 Maronites (19 families), three Roman Catholics (two foreigners before the 1877 law abolished foreign membership), two Greek Catholics (one family), two Protestants, one Armenian Catholic, and one Jew shaped Beirut's municipal affairs—a ratio that largely represents the confessional distribution of Beirut's population, with a slight overrepresentation of Sunnis and a gross underrepresentation of the Druzes.

Of the one hundred municipal biographies studied, 41 per cent had either petitioned personally for the creation of Beirut as a provincial capital in 1865, or their immediate, paternal relatives—brothers, fathers, or grandfathers—had and at least seventeen members (or first degree relatives: brother or son) were involved in the Beirut Reform Committee of 1913.[61] The municipality formed the nucleus in the struggle for the political capitalization of Beirut. Identification with Beirut and promotion of the city's interest *vis-à-vis* Damascus and other coastal cities were two sides of the same coin. Both positions promised to launch and/or perpetuate their prominence in the city and the empire.

The majority of the members were merchants, entrepreneurs, bankers, or real estate owners. The Bayhums were easily the most active family force on the

[59] The inferences of this section are based on biographical data presented in Hanssen (D.Phil. thesis, 2001: Annex). [60] On prosopography as a historical method, see Stone (1971).

[61] For the lists of petitioners, members of the reform movement, and literary societies, see Hanssen (D.Phil. thesis, 2001: Annex).

municipal council. Out of eight municipal presidents between 1860 and 1908, two were Bayhums: Muḥyī al-Dīn and Muḥammad. The Egyptian traveller Shaykh Muḥammad ʿAbd al-Jawwād al-Qāyātī's description of the Bayhums' wealth as consisting of 'lofty villas (*quṣūr*) and houses (*buyūt*), vast properties and plots of land, caravansarays (*khānāt*) and shops (*khānawāt*)' is an extreme example of the general affluence of other member families.[62] The leading families on the council possessed regional—in the case of the Bayhums, the Dāʿūqs, and the Ghandūrs—and international trading networks, such as the Sursuqs or the Ṭrāds.

Others owned banking houses, like Jabbūr Ṭabīb or Albert Bassūl. Significantly, a few members even were concessionaires and executive members of international investment companies themselves, like Bishāra Ṣabbāgh. The vast majority of council members were big merchants in and of Beirut and several members were also active in Beirut's chamber of commerce.[63] Often merchant members benefited privately after their terms in public office expired. Al-Qāyātī noticed on his visit to Beirut in 1882 that 'Muḥyī al-Dīn Bayhum, formerly a municipal president, has now expanded his textile business basking in great wealth and affluence.'[64]

A small but significant number of councillors were what I would consider career bureaucrats in the Ottoman administration. These bureaucrats did not necessarily depend financially on the Ottoman administration—Ottoman salaries were a fraction of what a successful merchant would earn. Nevertheless, working for the Ottoman state endowed individuals with social status, participatory and transformative urban power. ʿUmar Ramaḍān's father, ʿAbd al-Ghanī Efendi, reportedly had ten sons, most of whom rose to eminent positions in the Ottoman civil service.[65] Amīn *agha* Ramaḍān had been in the Egyptian urban council for Beirut under Ibrahim Pasha in the 1830s, while his son became a member of the advisory council in the province of Syria a generation later. ʿĀrif Bey Ramaḍān was a clerk in the grand vizier's office and Munīḥ Bey we have already encountered as a long-serving municipal inspector in Beirut. As the only municipal member with a direct family background in the military estate, ʿUmar Ramaḍān constituted a noteworthy exception to the general civilian profile of the municipal council.

[62] al-Qāyātī (1981: 12–20).

[63] For a list of members of Beirut's chamber of commerce, see Hanssen (D.Phil. thesis, 2001: Annex).

[64] al-Qāyātī (1981: 14).

[65] Ibid. 15. Sunnis of Anatolian descent, the Ramaḍāns first appear in Beirut's annals in the mid-18th cent. when they lived in Suq Bazarkan. In 1843 the family registered a *waqf* endowment in the name of ʿUmar's father, Amīn *agha* Ramaḍān.

Generally, the transition from big merchants to literary elites came via employment with the Ottoman state. For example, over four generations, the Yārids 'metamorphosed' from advisory positions in al-Jazzār's Acre, to merchants in Beirut, to service in the Ottoman bureaucracy, and finally—in the fourth generation—to journalistic activity in Çairo's press. Municipal president in the 1900s, ʿAbd al-Qādir al-Qabbānī combined all these metamorphoses in his own lifetime.[66] Educated at al-Bustānī's National School (*al-madrasa al-waṭaniyya*), Qabbānī was a popular official in various departments of the provincial administration, the first president of the charitable Muslim organization *al-maqāṣid al-khayriyya*, and the editor-in-chief of *Thamarāt al-Funūn*, before his Hamidian proclivities caused a temporary demise during the Young Turk era.

The families of the council members generally held considerable urban *waqf* properties and/or were owners of large *wikālas*, streets, and entire *sūqs*. They also started to invest their fortunes in land outside the city of Beirut. It appears that the boundaries between different modes of wealth accumulation were too blurred to be significant in the politics of Beirut's municipal council, particularly since land could be bought freely on the market after the application of the Land Law to Beirut. More significant was the tendency amongst municipal members to cultivate the new quarters by founding schools, hospitals, mosques, churches, printing houses, and benevolent organizations.

Thus, one unexpected discovery accrued from the profiles of municipal members is the significant overlap of Beirut's literary elites and council members. Three municipal members had been personally involved in Beirut's first Oriental Society between 1847 and 1852 (and seven close relatives). Fourteen municipal councillors were also members of *al-jamʿiyya al-ʿilmiyya al-sūriyya*, 1867–8. Finally, eight original members of the *jamʿiyya al-maqāṣid al-khayriyya* were—or after its dissolution in 1880/1 became—municipal councillors.[67]

Likewise, the link between Beirut journalists and the council members is striking.[68] There were over a dozen families of owners, editors, publishers, and correspondents of local newspapers such as *Ḥadīqat al-Akhbār*, *Thamarāt al-Funūn*, *Lisān al-Ḥāl*, *al-Jinān*, *al-Taqaddum*, and *al-Maḥabba*. Moreover, brothers and paternal relatives of Beirut's municipal members were influential

[66] ʿAbd al-Qādir al-Qabbānī was born in Beirut in 1847 and died there in 1935.

[67] For a list of members of Beirut's literary societies, see Hanssen (D.Phil. thesis, 2001: Annex).

[68] Intellectuals and literati were not comparable to their counterparts in Europe who, to make a living, 'held minor posts in public offices'. See Zweig (1998: 160). In 19th-century Beirut, journalism was rarely a means of subsistence. Most journalists had other means of income, either through family endowments (Qabbānī), or involvement in fathers', brothers', or cousins' businesses (the Ṭrāds or Thābits, for example).

in Istanbul's and Egypt's press. Their articles in *al-Ittiḥād al-ʿUthmānī* and in Fāris al-Shidyāq's *al-Jawāʾib* in Istanbul, *al-Nakhla*, *al-Iṣlāḥ*, *al-Manār*, and *al-Aḥrām* in Cairo, or *al-Baṣīra* in Tunis suggest an incipient network of intellectuals around the Eastern Mediterranean.

In Beirut and connected cities, articles on the duties of modern municipal government reflected subtle campaign tactics by journalists with political ambitions. Compared to the largely foreign-run municipalities of Alexandria and Istanbul, it was Beirut's second generation of indigenous literary elites, born into the Ottoman age of reforms, who used the municipality to translate their social ideas and urban concepts into practical application: through the municipality's implementation of urban planning and regulations, through the construction of public utilities, or through personal funding of parks and local schools.

Like many municipal members, Ibrāhīm Bey al Aswad (1851–1940) learnt Ottoman at Bustānī's National School. He started his career in the Ottoman administration of Mount Lebanon before he opened the Lubnān printing press in 1891. Later he became the editor of the journal *Lubnān*, the author of the directories *Dalīl Lubnān*, and published the influential history book *Tanwīr al-Adhhān fi Tārīkh Lubnān* in 1925.

Some municipal members had been celebrated poets in the Arab world prior to their election and became members of the Ottoman parliament, such as Ḥusayn Bayhum (1833–81).[69] Others went on to become notable authors and educational activists after their term of office, such as his son and Arab nationalist Aḥmad Mukhtār Bayhum (1878–1922). In 1886, w*aṭaniyya* graduate ʿAbd al-Qādir al-Danā (1844–1910) established the *Bayrūt* printing press in Suq Sursuq where he and his brothers published the official Ottoman *Bayrūt Gazetesi*. The Mudawwars—among many other cultural activities—funded and co-edited the newspaper *Ḥadīqat al-Akhbār*, while Rizqallah Khaḍrā was the owner of Beirut's *al-Maṭbaʿa al-ʿumūmiyya* and composed a noted hagiography on Marun, the patron saint of the Maronite community.

By far the most influential intellectual who was also a member of the Beirut municipality was Salīm al-Bustānī. A polymath like his father Buṭrus, the younger Bustānī wrote a host of serialized historical novels—the first of the Arab world—in which he further developed his father's thoughts on Syria as a homeland embedded in Ottoman Arab history.[70] Moreover, as editor of the

[69] Ḥusayn was ʿUmar Bayhum's son. His father was an influential council member under Egyptian occupation and later sat on Beirut's post-civil war welfare council (*majlis al-iʿāna*). Huṣayn was a journalist, poet, and leading figure of the Arabic *nahḍa* and early Islamic reform movement.

[70] Moosa (1993: 157–83).

influential monthly journal *al-Jinān*, Salīm was the first Arab intellectual whose editorials and political commentaries—the most enduring form of engaged Arabic literature to this day[71]—became powerful public opinion shapers. He was arguably the most important socio-political thinker in Beirut in the 1870s and the 1880s, treating such topics as human rights, the ʿUrabi Revolt in Egypt, the Franco-Prussian War, religion, education, and the spirit of the age.

Conclusion

In Beirut as in Damascus, the most attractive channels of urban power and participation were the municipal and the provincial councils whose members wielded a high degree of decision-making power over the allocation of taxes, public construction, and planning procedures. The same individuals, and often family clusters, who struggled in petitions or in editorials for the creation of a provincial capital in Beirut reappear on the municipal council.

From the perspective of the Ottoman government, the municipality and other local and provincial forms of participation incorporated a socio-economic elite in the making into the political and cultural orbits of the state. From the point of view of the local and provincial notables, participation in Ottoman institutions and the reform project solidified their informal social ascendancy in a new formalized political realm.

I have argued that in provincial Beirut, this arrangement developed not merely in imitation of some Western ideal of modern governance. Rather, the Ottoman municipal council in Beirut emerged out of the application of the Istanbul model of Ottoman municipal reform on the one hand, and the humanitarian crisis and the urgency of health concerns in the wake of the civil war in Mount Lebanon on the other.

In the long run, participatory institutions brought along important modifications of existing patterns in the politics of notables, in terms of power-sharing, compromise, and cooperative decision-making for the sake of public welfare. The collective urban strategies of Beiruti notables reacted to changing conditions in the political economy of the Ottoman–Mediterranean world. Ultimately, however, local merchants and urban notables also produced specific perceptions of modern urbanity and discourses of progress and prosperity around the municipality that sustained Beirut as a provincial capital. It was

[71] Laroui (1984).

around these discourses that urban spaces in *fin de siècle* Beirut were contested and class distinctions produced.

The municipal council of Beirut formalized and perpetuated the dominance of a stratum of society that emerged co-terminously with—and crucially maintained—the regional ascendancy of Beirut in the nineteenth century. This middle-class politics was not driven by the interests of merchants or landowners alone but, significantly, by intellectuals on the municipal council who inscribed their ideas of urban culture, space, and time specific to Beirut. As such, the production of urban space and material culture was shaped in large measure by Beirut's emerging political field.

6

Provincial Classrooms: Intellectuals, Missionaries, and the State

> [I]t was the unspoken assumption of the great middle class in the nineteenth century that the city was the productive centre of man's most valued activities: industry and higher education.[1]

In the second half of the nineteenth century, Beirut's extramural quarter of Zuqaq al-Blat became home to intellectuals, converts, mavericks, exiles, and reformers—as well as the place where thousands of children went to school.[2] As in no other quarter in Beirut, and arguably in any Ottoman provincial capital, urban development was linked to its mushrooming educational institutions.[3] This chapter examines the schools, teachers, and literary societies that interacted to produce a vibrant intellectual atmosphere in *fin de siècle* Beirut not because of but aside from the presence of the much-studied missionary schools. Whether local or foreign, Muslim or Christian, the cultural activists of the late Ottoman period shared a sense of optimism that hard work and education would bring salvation from the traumas of the recent past. There were, however, differences in cultural diagnosis and remedy. This chapter traces some of the major educational projects and debates in Beirut. In particular, questions of civilization and public morality affected urban discourses of modernity that the next and final part will examine.

Thirty years ago ʿAbd al-Latif Tibawi criticized the scholarly tendency to reduce modern education and cultural innovation to a singularly 'Western' point of origin and has therefore called for an intellectual shift away from Beirut to Aleppo, Damascus, and Cairo.[4] I argue that, in late Ottoman Beirut

[1] Schorske (1998: 38).

[2] Elsewhere I estimate that over 2,000 pupils studied in the schools of Zuqaq al-Blat at the time. See Bodenstein *et al.* (2005).

[3] According to Shahīn Makārius, 12,452 boys and girls studied under 517 teachers in Beirut in the early 1880s. See his 'al-Maʿārif fī Sūriyya', *al-Muqtaṭaf*, 7 (1883/4), 385–92.

[4] Tibawi (1976: 304–14).

itself, the presence of foreign missionary schools was important but ostensibly hostile to the development of a critical political field. In close geographical proximity, missionary, imperial, and local educational initiatives vied with as well as complemented each other in their attempts to inculcate young minds and future generations with particular and universal qualities. I argue further that, although Protestant, Ottoman state, and Beiruti reform projects shared a number of pedagogical assumptions, education became one of the most contested fields of cultural production in *fin de siècle* Beirut.

Access to missionary education has long been viewed as the origin of Westernization, the Arab enlightenment, and—more generally—modernization in the Middle East.[5] More recently, modern schooling systems have been deconstructed as implicated in the colonial process of the formation of the modern nation state.[6] However, little attention has been paid to local schools and individual teacher/student experience in the late Ottoman world. Only very recently have the East–West, traditional–modern dichotomies been constructively challenged and has the educational role of Europe been put into perspective.[7] This chapter follows these efforts at provincializing the European impact on education and culture in the late Ottoman empire. I focus on Ottoman and local schools in Beirut and situate the city's emergence as the proverbial 'school of the Arabs' in the larger context of social reconstruction after the civil war of 1860 and emergent national consciousness.

Education after 1860: Bustānī's *al-madrasa al-waṭaniyya*

In the summer of 1860, Mount Lebanon witnessed the culmination of a spiral of sectarian violence between Druze and Maronite inhabitants that had lasted with various degrees of intensity for almost two decades. Massacres led to counter-massacres, killing a cautiously estimated 20,000 inhabitants. Thousands more were uprooted and forced to migrate, most of them to Beirut. Houses, shops, and monasteries were looted and countless villages destroyed. Buṭrus al-Bustānī estimated that 'if we calculate the value of the 30,000 houses (*bayt aw manzil*) and what burnt inside them and add to it the harvests and the cattle lost, the damage amounts to 367 million piastres, that is 367 million

5 See e.g. Antonius (1939: 35–60); Hourani (1984); Kedourie (1974*a*, 1974*b*). The Palestinian scholar ʿAbd al-Latif Tibawi has spent a lifetime refuting such Euro-centric views. See e.g. Tibawi (1966, 1969).

6 Mitchell (1988: 69–74).

7 Fortna (2001).

francs which corresponds to the income of three and a half silk harvests in Syria.' Moreover, he estimated that

> 50,000 active men were rendered unemployed, work has been suspended for six months. . . . The Syria we have seen six months ago, in a way so distinct from the rest of the [Ottoman] Empire—proudly flourishing in comfort of living, progressing so marvellously in architecture and wealth—has fallen. Yes, it has fallen, indeed! A devastating demise for which there is only hope of revival after long years unless by miracle or extraordinary feat.[8]

The settlement of the conflict was indeed a formidable undertaking which was not made any easier by the fact that it placed Mount Lebanon at the centre of international politics. High-level British, French, Austrian, Russian, and Prussian officials struggled with each other as much as with Fuad Pasha to find a resolution that would satisfy the Christian victims and their own governments back in European capitals. Under these circumstances the question of identifying the guilty parties and individuals followed more the logic of the 'Eastern Question' than the equitable distribution of justice. The local Ottoman and Druze leadership bore the brunt of the showcase tribunals, summary executions, imprisonment, conscription, and expulsion.[9]

European missionaries and diplomats (as well as most historians until very recently for that matter) shared with Ottoman inspectors the conviction that the violence that occurred in Mount Lebanon between 1840 and 1860 was an atavistic remnant of an inherently sectarian social order.[10] However, it was Fu'ād Pasha, the Ottoman foreign minister and special envoy dispatched in order to re-establish Ottoman imperial order, who translated these racist convictions into action by meting out severe punishment in order to restore imperial order and prevent European military intervention. Fu'ād Pasha viewed his pacifying mission as one 'of a supposedly rational modern Ottoman rule on a supposedly tribal and uncivilized periphery'.[11] A new imperial politics of difference aimed at containing the worst excesses of Mount Lebanon's allegedly intrinsic violent nature while pressing subaltern 'ignorant classes' into the 'traditional' place modern society assigned to them.[12]

Buṭrus al-Bustānī, Beirut's leading intellectual at the time, shared some of Fu'ād Pasha's views and vocabulary, as well as his urbane perspective. In general, however, Bustānī's view of the past was far more ambivalent, while his vision for the country's future was less authoritarian, more optimistic, and more

[8] Buṭrus al-Bustānī, *Nafīr Sūriyya*, sixth issue, Beirut, (8 Nov. 1860), 29–32. The page numbers refer to the version edited by Y. Khūrī (1990).

[9] For in-depth reconstruction of events leading up to the civil war and the war itself, see Fawaz (1994), and Farah (2000).

[10] Makdisi (2000).

[11] Makdisi (2002*a*: 605).

[12] Makdisi (2000: 157).

inclusive. Bustānī's analysis of Mount Lebanon's past was based on personal experience.[13] He was in Beirut when the civil war started in early May 1860, and 'observed from this town a chain of terrifying blazes rising from the Matn as if we saw the fires of bigotry go up with the fires of the houses'.[14] Buṭrus Bustānī was not only deeply shocked at what he witnessed, but also faced a test of conflicting loyalties between his adopted urbane social circles in Beirut and his ancestral Maronite community in the mountain.

The enormous scale of the refugees' displacement forced him and most people in Beirut to help with relief efforts. By September 1860—at the height of the international post-war negotiations—Bustānī decided to voice his personal anxieties and post-war disorientation publicly. Under the pseudonym of *muḥibb li al-waṭan* ('a patriot') he began to publish the pamphlet *Nafīr Sūriyya* 'Clarion of Syria'. The paper marks a culmination of Bustānī's political consciousness. Love for the fatherland, he argued, must supersede all other allegiances, and support for legitimate Ottoman rule and the dissemination of literary enlightenment was the duty of every citizen.[15] As he challenged every individual in society to undergo soul-searching and personal reforms, Bustānī advocated a notion of citizenship that was based on rights and taking responsibilities. The ignorant as much as the knowledgeable needed to transform themselves if Syria was to meet the requirements of the modern age.[16]

Bustānī's addresses to the Syrian nation ended with the eleventh issue of 22 April 1861 for unknown reasons, and he returned to educational work—putting into practice what he had preached on the pages of *Nafīr Sūriyya*. By 1862 he had severed his ties with the American consulate and the Protestant mission. On his own, he lobbied for Ottoman permissions and local funding for the establishment of a school that would help educate a new generation of young students who could be imbued with the auto-emancipatory and self-reflective virtues he espoused in his writings.[17]

In September 1863, 115 boarders were admitted to his *al-madrasa al-waṭaniyya*—the 'native Academy' as suspicious American missionaries called

[13] Buṭrus al-Bustānī was born into a family of Maronite clerics and clerks in 1819 and his education at the Maronite seminary in ʿAyn Warqa prepared him for a brilliant career in theology, philosophy, and biblical languages. In 1840 he came down to Beirut to teach Arabic at the Protestant Seminary. Through his friendship with Eli Smith, Bustānī quickly learnt English, trained to become a translator, and eventually converted to the Protestant faith. His well-known penchant 'to be preaching to the people' notwithstanding, he resisted the pressures of the American missionaries to become a minister. Instead he encouraged the establishment of local schools in the mountains around Beirut, and in 1846 assisted Cornelius van Dyck to move the Male Seminary from Beirut to ʿAbayh, 'away from the corruptive influence of a city'. Tibawi (1963: 158–160). See Y. Khūrī (1995) for the most extensive biography on Busṭrus al-Bustānī to date.

[14] *Nafīr Sūriyya*, Beirut, fifth issue. (1 Nov. 1860), 11.

[15] Tibawi (1963: 170).

[16] Sheehi (2000: 7–24).

[17] Cp Adorno (1998) on German education after the Holocaust.

it.[18] Although some missionaries complained that the school deprived the mission of its local teaching staff, and that it was not linked to their Protestant work, William Thomson and Cornelius van Dyck quickly realized the potential of Bustānī's institution:

> The teachers are not allowed to impart religious instruction, but still it is an interesting fact that in a little over three years after the dreadful scenes of massacres and blood[shed] in 1860, there should be gathered in Beirut a school of 115 boarders composed of almost all the various sects in the land and that children of Moslem sheikhs and papal priests, and Druze *okkals* should study side by side. . . . It is a promising fact, too, as bearing upon the future success of the college proposed to be opened in Beirut that the youth of Syria are willing to pay for education, and it is plain that the movement for a college started not a moment too soon.[19]

The school's opening caused huge distress among the Maronite clergy. A conflict erupted between the bishop of Sidon and Tyre, Yūsuf al-Bustānī—a distant relative of Buṭrus—who allowed Maronite children to enter the school on the one hand, and the bishop of Beirut, Tūbiyya ʿAwn, who found this mixture intolerable and attempted to physically remove Maronite boys from the school on the other.[20] Likewise Daniel Bliss, the president of the Syrian Protestant College from 1866 to 1902, continued to question the benefit and efficacy of a school that functioned as a preparatory school for his college but displayed so little missionary zeal and taught more students French than English. Efforts by the Syrian Protestant mission's board of directors to interfere with the curriculum of the National School and impose conditions on Buṭrus al-Bustānī ended in acrimony, and the financial and institutional ties between the two schools were severed once and for all.[21] Daniel Bliss concluded that '[w]e shall not consent to pay for anything we have not absolute control over'.[22]

In the few student recollections that exist, the school was remembered for its tolerance and the quality of its teachers. Buṭrus al-Bustānī recruited a dozen established literati and experienced educators for his school who shared the principal tenet that pupils should be accepted 'from all sects, *millet*s and races without discriminating against their personal beliefs or any attempt at proselytizing and [should be given] full licence to carry out their religious duties'.[23] In the early 1870s, Bustānī was able to enlist as member of staff Aḥmad ʿAbbās who had just returned from al-Azhar to teach Islamic religion and

18 ABCFM, 16.8.1, *Syrian Mission*, vol. 5, 'Annual Report of the Beirut Station for 1863', (Microfilm Reel 545). 19 Ibid. 20 Y. Khūrī (1995: 58). 21 Ibid. 58–65.

22 Daniel Bliss to his wife Abby, 6 Jan. 1874, in his (1993: 185).

23 Buṭrus al-Bustānī, 'al-Madrasa al-waṭaniyya', *al-Jinān*, 4 (1873), 627.

philosophy.[24] Most teachers were neighbours in Zuqaq al-Blat while the students came from Syria, Palestine, Egypt, Iraq, Istanbul, and Greece.[25] From the local student population, Ibrāhīm Bey al-Aswad, ʿAbd al-Qādir al-Dānā, and ʿAbd al-Qādir al-Qabbānī later became themselves Beirut's leading intellectuals as educators, publishers, lawyers, journalists, and municipal members in Beirut. The Beiruti *ʿulamāʾ* family Barbīr sent one of their boys to the *waṭaniye*.[26] The Sidon notable Aḥmad Pasha al-Ṣulḥ, too, entrusted Bustānī with the upbringing of his son when his Ottoman career brought him to settle in Beirut. Maḥmūd Minaḥ al-Ṣulḥ (1856–1925) later became judge and member of Beirut's provincial council under the Young Turks.[27]

Loanza and William Benton, two missionaries who had arrived in Beirut in 1847, lived in Bhamdoun, and were dismissed from the Syrian Mission in 1859 for 'going native', decided to send their two sons, Charles and Henry, to the new-style school. Despite the considerable costs and 'although there were not but Arab boys there', they entrusted their education to Buṭrus al-Bustānī, 'one of our best and brightest men of Beirut'.[28] Shākir al-Khūrī (1847–1911), who became a noted doctor and an important autobiographer of the Levant, was a schoolmate of the Benton boys and Maḥmūd al-Ṣulḥ between 1863 and 1865.

They were taught Arabic literature by Shaykh Naṣīf al-Yāzijī, French language by Shaykh Khaṭṭār al-Daḥdaḥ, and maths by Shahīn Sarkīs. The Bustānīs—Buṭrus, his sons Salīm and Saʿdallah and his daughter Sārā—directed the school and taught different levels of English. Strict discipline and authoritarianism was not what the National School—or colloquially the *waṭaniye*—was remembered for. In the admittedly overly jolly memoirs of Dr Khūrī, his teacher Naṣīf al-Yāzijī was credited with encouraging artistic expression, conducting student theatre, and remembered for his 'drinking coffee and tobacco during class'.[29] Overall, the school exuded a level of self-confidence that could afford to resist the disciplinarian practices so common in missionary schools.

[24] Y. Khūrī (1995: 59). Aḥmad ʿAbbās (1852/3–1926/7) was of modest Egyptian background. His father came to Beirut with Ibrāhīm Pasha's troops and, like so many, stayed behind after the occupation ended in 1840. The modern Ottoman and Islamic school system offered him access to social and religious status which he later used to establish new schools in Beirut. He went to study at al-Azhar aged 13 and became a follower of Muḥammad ʿAbduh. He spent six years in Cairo before returning to Beirut. See al-Ṣulḥ (1966: 17–18). For more biographical details on Aḥmad ʿAbbās and other Beiruti educators in this chapter, see Hanssen (D.Phil. thesis, 2001: Annex).

[25] Tibawi (1963: 137–82). See also al-Bustānī, 'al-wadrasa al-waṭaniyya', *al-Jinān*, 4 (1873), 626–9.

[26] Jessup (1910: i. 400). [27] Steppat (1969).

[28] Benton (n.d.: 116). For more details on the National School, see Bodenstein *et al.* (2005). For another sympathetic assessment of the Bentons, see Makdisi (1997: 706–7). [29] S. al-Khūrī (1992: 104).

The Literary Associations of Zuqaq al-Blat

In 1867, the teachers at Bustānī's National School were at the centre of a new literary club for young thinkers, the Syrian Scientific Society, which constituted itself 'for the spread of knowledge, science and arts'.[30] With its well over one hundred members, the society was decidedly inter-confessional and had a far greater outreach than its predecessors.[31] Most of the members were Beirutis in their early twenties, but its network spanned from Istanbul to Damascus and Cairo. The club convened thirteen times in its first two years before the minutes stopped and it may have been discontinued for financial reasons. Until then, in regularly held meetings, the topics varied from Syrian archaeology and Greek philosophy to translations of the works of François Guizot, author of *Histoire des origines du gouvernement représentatif en Europe*, and the historiography of civilization (*kalām ʿalā al-tamaddun*).[32] Doctors Sucquet, Wortabet, and Fāris discussed modern medical methods to contain cholera, while Ibrāhīm al-Yāzijī gave a presentation on the classical medicine of the Arabs. In sum, the Syrian Scientific Society engaged in an antiquity-referential discourse of their society and a Western-referential discourse of progress, modernity, and civilization.

The Islamic Benevolent Society: Charity and Patronage

A few years after the closure of the Syrian Scientific Society, preparations for the formation of a new association for the arts were afoot in Zuqaq al-Blat. The Society of the Arts—*jamʿiyyat al-funūn*—was founded in 1875 by the city's established *ʿulamāʾ* led by Hājj Saʿd Ḥamāda, Shaykh Ibrāhīm al-Aḥdab, and Shaykh Yūsuf al-Asīr who had returned from studies in Egypt and taught Arabic grammar at Bustānī's National School. They were joined by a younger generation of educational activists: ʿAbd al-Raḥmān al-Barbīr and ʿAbd al-Qādir al-Qabbānī who had been a pupil in Bustānī's school. The new society was a reaction to the short-lived Syrian Scientific Society and an intellectual continuation of Buṭrus al-Bustānī's educational ideas. It implemented an effective form of funding by subscription by tapping the resources of wealthy Muslim merchants and notables committed to reform. The first major investment

[30] In Arabic: *al-Jamʿiyya al-ʿilmiyya al-Sūriyya*. Y. Khūrī (1990: 1). Amīr Muḥammad Amīn Arslān was elected president, Ḥusayn Bayhum, Buṭrus al-Bustānī, and Ḥunayn al-Khūrī were elected club officers, and Rizqallah Khaḍrā was voted treasurer.

[31] For a list of members, see Hanssen (D.Phil. thesis, 2001: Annex).

[32] See table of content in Y. Khūrī (1990).

was a printing press for 2,500 piastres, and in April 1875 the first issue of the society's *Thamarāt al-Funūn* was sold on the streets of Beirut.[33]

By launching this bi-weekly newspaper, its reform-minded 28-year-old editor, ʿAbd al-Qādir al-Qabbānī reached far beyond the memberships of particular literary salons. The second major newspaper of Beirut after *Ḥadīqat al-Akhbār*, it appeared more frequently and covered more substantive news than Khalīl Khūrī's paper. Qabbānī's *Thamarāt al-Funūn* received company on 18 October 1878 when another resident of Zuqaq al-Blat, Khalīl Sarkīs, launched *Lisān al-Ḥāl* and a new printing press, *al-Maṭbaʿa al-adabiyya*.[34] Together *Thamarāt al-Funūn* and *Lisān al-Ḥāl* dominated Beirut's news world throughout the late Ottoman period.[35]

The activists of the Muslim Society of the Arts formed the nucleus of the *jamʿiyyat al-maqāṣid al-khayriyya al-islāmiyya* which was founded in ʿAbd al-Qādir al-Qabbānī's house in Zuqaq al-Blat on 31 July 1878.[36] The new society appealed to the then governor Midḥat Pasha as it promised to promote modern state education, uphold Islamic morality, and embrace the principles of the Ottoman Public Education Law of 1869. At the same time, the society consciously developed an alternative curriculum both to the traditional *madrasa*s and *kuttāb*, based as they were on memorizing religious scriptures, and to the monopoly of missionary education.

As the first president of the Benevolent Society, Qabbānī's main priority was to launch schools for Muslim girls. To this effect he rented a house in Basta Tahta, a south-western neighbourhood overlapping with Zuqaq al-Blat, and four months later 230 female pupils were admitted. The following year, other *maqāṣid* girls' schools were established in downtown Beirut and in Sidon for over two hundred pupils.[37] Despite Qabbānī's efforts, female education was an uphill task in an urban society which was uneasy about the side effects of urban growth and the expansion of the political field on gender hierarchies. As Kalthūm Barbīr—the wife of Beirut's leading *zaʿīm* during the Young Turk period, Salīm Salām—remembered: 'My friends and I were the first girls in the [*maqāṣid*] school and we faced some stiff resistance from most of our fathers who loathed sending their daughters to school'.[38]

In the aftermath of the scandals around Midḥat Pasha and rumours about a Syrian independence movement in 1880, the *maqāṣid* society was forcibly

33 Nashabi (1981) and Cioeta (1982).

34 For a brief biography, see Ch 3.

35 On the influence of newspapers on Beirut's urban design, see Chs. 8 and 9.

36 Shubaru (2000: 30).

37 Ibid. 35. Moreover, the society's first bulletin, *al-Fajr al-Ṣādiq* (1879), 8–9 (reprinted in Shubaru, 2000) announced the opening of its charity for the poor and scholarships to study medicine in Cairo.

38 Interview with ʿAnbara al-Khālidī published in Yazbak (1955: i. 137).

absorbed into Ottoman provincial structures. Many able administrators left for Egypt soon afterwards, but not before they had registered *maqāṣid* property as *waqf* endowments. Having secured title deeds in the name of the Society, most schools continued to function and provide education for thousands of students.

When the Young Turks swept aside the Hamidian regime in Istanbul, the *maqāṣid* Society reconstituted itself under the leadership of *waṭaniye* graduate ʿAbd al-Qādir al-Danā. When Salīm Salām took this charitable institution over in 1918, he turned it into a powerful source of Muslim patronage based on real estate investment, donations, free medical service, and generous grants for students to study abroad. Since Lebanese independence in 1943, the *maqāṣid* emerged as a key instrument for the Salām family to forge alliances in urban and national politics.[39]

An Islamic Liberal Arts Education: Muḥammad ʿAbduh and *al-madrasa al-sulṭāniyya*

The literary circles of Zuqaq al-Blat crystallized as a local force between the Protestant missionaries in West Beirut and the Catholic missionaries in East Beirut. By the 1880s they had intellectually emancipated themselves from the parochial agendas of these foreign institutions out of which they had originally emerged.[40] However, after the excitement of the early 1880s, there followed a hiatus. Buṭrus al-Bustānī died in 1883 and his son Salīm a year later. The same year, the most controversial and provocative figure of this group, Adīb Isḥāq, renounced God on his deathbed.[41]

Other rebellious spirits went into exile. When Edwin Lewis, a popular professor of geology and chemistry at the Syrian Protestant College, was forced to resign for mentioning the works of Charles Darwin in an annual address in Arabic, his local colleagues Ṣarrūf, Makārius, and Fāris Nimr left not only the college but ultimately also the city.[42] In spite of support from influential teachers and *ʿulamāʾ*, such as Huṣayn al-Jisr, Ibrāhīm al-Aḥdāb, and Yūsuf al-Asīr, they took their influential journal *al-Muqtaṭaf* to Cairo in 1884.

Their move set in motion a certain 'brain drain' in Beirut for the next three decades. Yet, Beirut's post-war educational experiments continued, and they were reignited by another external impetus: the unexpected arrival—from

[39] Johnson (1986: 51–3).
[40] See Bodenstein *et al.* (2004).
[41] Kedourie (1974*b*: 86).
[42] Jūḥa (1991).

Egypt—of one of the foremost Islamic scholars and anti-colonial activists of the Arab world at the time, *al-imām al-shaykh* Muḥammad ʿAbduh. As an Egyptian in exile in Zuqaq al-Blat ʿAbduh was to push hard both the Ottoman government to take seriously its educational reform project in Beirut and conservative local clerics to accept it.

The expansion of public education in the Ottoman empire did not stop under Abdülhamid II. On the contrary, imperial educational reforms had a profound impact on the empire. Between 1876 and 1908 the education policies of the *tanẓīmāt* were continued and systematized into a tighter hierarchy of age levels and school types.[43] The Hamidian policy of mass education was designed to inculcate both loyalty to the state and a modern morality based on Islamic cultural referents.[44] In the Muslim schools of Zuqaq al-Blat, too, Islamic reformist teaching methods were applied to produce—in the best Lockean liberal arts tradition—virtuous, and able men in their distinct calling' to operate the institutions of the modern Ottoman state.[45] As Durkheim reminds us, 'education perpetuates and reinforces this homogeneity by fixing in the mind of the child, from the beginning, the essential similarities that social life demands'.[46]

In Beirut, neither was Istanbul the sole referent for educational reform in Beirut, nor were reformers the only Islamic thinkers in town. Muslim reformers despised missionaries and Muslim conservatives in equal measure, if for different reasons. Missionaries, as we shall see presently, were seen as rivals with a head start, conservatives as obstacles to Muslim enlightenment. Young Muslim reformers around *jamʿiyya al-funūn* dominated the press, older conservatives the mosques. Reformers sought to adapt Islamic scriptures and practices to the requirements of the state, while conservatives called for the state to adopt—'imitate'—the conventional tenets of Islamic government. Beirut's reformers who read and discussed Guizot's *History of Civilization in Europe* in Arabic translation, shifted their attention from Islam as a religion to the theme of Islam as a civilization. Albert Hourani has summed up this shift concisely and argued that, with the Muslim reformers Jamāl al-Dīn al-Afghānī and Muḥammad ʿAbduh, the 'aim of man's act is not the service of God; it is the creation of human civilization flourishing in all its parts'.[47]

One conservative thinker in Beirut published extensive anti-missionary and anti-reformist treatises. Yūsuf al-Nabḥānī (1849/50–1932) was appointed the head of the civil courts during the bureaucratic reshuffling in 1888 and subsequently became one of the most prolific and polemic Arabic writers of the

[43] Somel (2001) and Fortna (2001). [44] Rogan (1996: 83–107) and Fortna (2000: 369–93).
[45] Locke (1880: 56). [46] Durkheim (1995: 203). [47] Hourani (1984: 114).

Hamidian generation of conservatives.[48] His loyalty was to the Ottoman dynasty and having greatly benefited from sultanic patronage, al-Nabhānī was purged after Abdülhamid was ousted in the Young Turk revolution of 1908/9.[49]

He considered sending Muslim students to missionary schools 'worse than committing adultery during the day in front of people' and was no less uncompromising on teaching natural sciences or foreign languages.[50] Echoing the foreign missionaries self-view, al-Nabhānī held such subjects to be essentially Christian and Western. Therefore, his logic went, foreign schools corrupted the noble pursuit of an ideal Islamic society, and the identity of Muslims.

Even worse than the missionaries were the Muslim reformers who had come to dominate Beirut's public opinion over the past decade and who were evidently willing to pay the price of mass cultural alienation of an entire generation of Muslim youths for the benefit of scientific knowledge and foreign languages. He identified Sayyid Jamāl al-Dīn al-Afghānī (1838/9–1897) as the source of this evil development for attempting to 'reopen the gates of *ijtihād*'—the interpretative approach to Islamic scriptures that ended with canonization of four legal schools of Quranic interpretation in the tenth century.[51]

Al-Afghānī's 'co-evil' colleague, the Egyptian Imām, Shaykh Muḥammad ʿAbduh, was subjected to severe *ad hominem* attacks for arrogating for himself the right to base his opinions and judgements on subjective criteria. Al-Nabhānī intimated that by mixing and matching the Holy Quran, legal doctrines, and the Prophet's sayings with the exigencies of contemporary social and political concerns, ʿAbduh and his colleagues lent themselves to the pressures of the 'Europeanized' state.

The British occupation of Egypt in 1882 had a profound effect on the intellectual and educational life in Beirut. Among the hundreds of Egyptian refugees who were stranded outside the *cordon sanitaire* around Beirut during the cholera pandemic that year were a number of Muslim reformers, the most prominent of which was the Egyptian Shaykh Muḥammad ʿAbduh (1849–1905). ʿAbduh was warmly welcomed by ʿAbd al-Qādir al-Qabbānī, the lexicographer Saʿīd al-Shartūnī, and the poet Ibrāhīm al-Yāzijī.[52] He was offered the hospitality of the municipal president Muḥyī al-Dīn al-Ḥamāda before he found his own accommodation, first in Burj Abi Haydar and then in Zuqaq al-Blat.[53]

[48] Seikaly (2002: 176). An Azhar student, al-Nabhānī penned at least nine long treatises (out of an estimated total of over sixty publications) on the dangers of the influences of 'the West, Christian missionaries and "modernity"'. [49] Ghazal (2001: 241–46). [50] Nabhānī quoted ibid. 248.

[51] For a scathing critique of al-Nabhānī, see the Baghdadi intellectual Shukrī al-Alūsī's *Ghāyat al-āmānī fī al-radd ʿalā al-Nabhānī* (Cairo, 1907). [52] Amīn (1953: 71). [53] Ibid.

In Ḥamāda's house, ʿAbduh started translating Jamāl-al-Dīn al-Afghānī's treatise 'Refutation of the Materialists'[54] and received a constant flow of guests from Beiruti intellectual circles and the incipient Salafi movement around Ṭāhir al-Jazāʾirī in Damascus.[55] The friendships went beyond the intellectual and the political conventions when ʿAbduh's first wife died and he decided to marry the daughter of Muḥyī al-Dīn Ḥamāda's late brother Sa'd, a founding member of the *jamʿiyyat al-funūn*.[56]

In 1883, Aḥmad ʿAbbās al-Azhari and members of the local educational authority founded an Ottoman high school—*al-madrasa al-sulṭāniyya*—to teach six grades.[57] The rank and file of the provincial bureaucracy, clergy, merchants, and notables donated funds towards the project. *Thamarāt al-Funūn* meticulously recorded the governor general Aḥmad Ḥamdī Pasha's contribution of sixty-two mosquito nets; the 513 silver *mecidiye* (or 11,286 piastres) from the religious dignitaries of Hama, the 1,170 piastres from the inhabitants of Rashaya.[58]

The 1869 Law of Public Education had stipulated that an imperial lycée (Ottoman and colloquial: *sulṭāniye*) be built in every provincial capital, but the Beirut school was a local initiative and one of only three of its kind in the Ottoman Empire at the time.[59] 'Modelled on the example of other foreign schools in organization and instruction', the *sulṭāniye*'s design was praised as a masterpiece of aesthetic and effective school architecture.[60] A red-tiled roof towered over this two-storey building whose vast courtyard looked into every classroom. The rectangular building spanned the length of over a dozen glass windows and the width of eight (see Figure 5).[61]

With the recruitment of the eminent Tripoli-based scholar Shaykh Huṣayn al-Jisr as the school's director, Aḥmad ʿAbbās managed to present a formidable ensemble of teachers in the first year of the school's existence.[62] Muḥammad ʿAbduh who lived a stone's throw away was approached to teach Islamic philosophy. After a brief stint in Paris in 1884 where he published the influential

[54] Keddie (1972: 187).

[55] al-Qāyātī (1981: 28). On ʿAbduh's connection with Ṭāhir al-Jazāʾirī, see Albert Hourani (1984: 222). On the *salafiyya* movement in general, see Commins (1990).

[56] Amīn (1953: 71).

[57] *Thamarāt al-Funūn* (16 Apri 1883). See also *al-Muqtaṭaf*, 'al-madrasa al-sulṭāniyya fī Bayrūt', (1883), 570.

[58] *Thamarāt al-Funūn* (Apr.–June 1883).

[59] Kodaman (1991: 133–44). The other two were in the capital and in Crete. On the seven-year curriculum of *sulṭāniye* schools, ibid. 143–4. On *iʿdādiyes*, see Somel (2001: 117–22).

[60] *al-Muqtaṭaf*, 'al-madrasa al-sulṭāniyya fī Bayrūt', 7 (1883), 570.

[61] Shubārū (2000: 60).

[62] Like Aḥmad ʿAbbās a former Azhar student, Shaykh Ḥusayn al-Jisr (1845–1909) had studied under al-Marṣafī in Cairo before returning to found Tripoli's *al-madrasa al-waṭaniyya* in 1879. After his year in Beirut al-Jisr was invited by Sultan Abdülhamid to stay at his Yıldız Palace and do research on Islamic theology. In 1887 al-Jisr published the acclaimed *al-Risāla al-ḥamīdiyya*. See Ebert (1991: 79–83).

FIG. 5. Postcard of Beirut's *sulṭāniye* school

anti-imperialist journal 'The Firmest Bond' (*al-ʿUrwa al-wuthqa*) with Jamāl al-Dīn al-Afghānī, ʿAbduh returned to Beirut and elaborated on the journal's themes of Islamic unity. ʿAbduh's theological lecture series at the Sultanic School on Abū Ṭālib and al-Hamaḍānī became the basis of what is considered his most important work of scholarship, 'Essays on the Theology of Unity', *Risālat al-tawḥīd*. Muḥammad ʿAbduh and Ḥusayn al-Jisr shared the view that modern Islamic education was the way out of the current cultural and political dilemma of the Arab world, but during their time together in Zuqaq al-Blat ʿAbduh was unable to convince a more conservative al-Jisr of his reformist teaching methods or of joining the *salafiyya* movement.

The school and its teachers attracted a variety of ambitious students from around the Arab provinces of the Ottoman empire. In its first year, around fifty-five students were registered, seven from the Ḥusaynī family in Jerusalem, six from al-Balqa, and others from Beirut's notable families, such as Ghandūr, Sursuq, and Tuwaynī.[63] Many *sulṭāniye* students were on scholarships from Ottoman provincial governors or Beirut's municipal elites—for example, Ibrāhīm Fakhrī Bey, al-Khawja, al-Khūrī, al-Tayyāra, al-Qāḍī, and al-Ghazzāwī who scouted the best students from the Syrian provinces.[64] The

[63] *Thamarāt al-Funūn*, (4–16 Apr. 1883). [64] *Thamarāt al-Funūn*, (April–May 1883).

school quickly attracted the sons and grandsons of Ottoman officials who were either on assignments in Damascus, Jerusalem, and Lattakia or stationed in Istanbul. In both cases, the children were sent away from home and stayed in the *sulṭāniye*'s dormitories.[65]

The nationalist writer and Muslim politician Shakīb Arslān (1869–1946) was one of the most famous graduates of the *sulṭāniye* school in Beirut. The scion of a minor branch of this family of mountain emirs, he switched from the Maronite *al-ḥikma* college to add fluent Ottoman Turkish to his immaculate French. Shakīb was drawn to the circle of Muḥammad ʿAbduh whom he followed to Cairo in 1892. He recalls in his memoirs the intellectual excitement that discussions with ʿAbduh aroused in him and his fellow students. At night, the residence of the municipal president, Muḥyī al-Dīn Ḥamāda, was 'always submerged with visitors' who debated politics and religion.[66] Shakīb and his classmates 'became infatuated during that time with news of writers, poets, and men of letters; it was our sole concern and we viewed the entire world as poetry and prose'.[67]

Muḥammad ʿAbduh revised the school's curriculum and teaching methods, which he still found too locked up in the mechanical disciplining of students and forced memorizing in class. The school, he argued, should be a place of 'industrial sciences', intellectual discussion, and moral character-building, not a 'prison in which they spend their year waiting for their release'.[68] For 8 Ottoman lira per year the school taught Turkish, French, and English, accounting and algebra, geometrics, natural philosophy, geography and history, chemistry, painting, legal sciences, engineering, and calligraphy in a curriculum that spanned six years.[69] For Muslim students sharīʿa law, theology, and Hanafi jurisprudence were compulsory, while Christian students were taught the Ottoman civil code and allowed to attend church on Sundays under the supervision of a priest appointed by the school.[70]

65 *Salnāme—Sūriyya Vilāyeti* (1303/1885), 123. Two years after its inauguration, *c.*150 students attended classes. They were taught by seventeen Turkish and Arab teachers.

66 Shakīb Arslān in Riḍā (1931: 400–1); quoted from Cleveland (1985: 9).

67 Arslān in Riḍa (1931) 399; quoted in Cleveland (1985: 7). Note the near-identical phrase used by Zweig in his memoirs on *fin de siècle* Vienna: 'We were beardless undeveloped lads who had to swot on school benches during the day and formed the ideal audience a young poet could dream of, curious, critical and enthusiastic about enthusiasm. Because our ability for enthusiasm was boundless; during class, on the way to and from school, in the coffeehouse, in the theatre, on promenades, we half-grown-ups did nothing but discussed books, paintings, music and philosophy.' Zweig (1998: 57).

68 ʿAbduh quoted in Amīn (1953: 67).

69 *al-Muqtaṭaf*, 'al-Madrasa al-sulṭāniyya fī Bayrūt,' 7 (1883), 570. Boarders paid 15 lira for board (three meals a day) and lodging in the school's dormitories.

70 *Thamarāt al-Funūn* (18 July 1887). Quoted in Kassab and Tadmori (2002: 61).

Notwithstanding the beauty of the school, his new Beiruti wife, the nocturnal socials, and the loyalty of his Beiruti students, Muḥammad ʿAbduh never lost his sense of exile: 'At last, here I am in Beirut, by the Grace of God, Whom I thank . . . My station remains intact among them and my rank is respected, but they are not like my own people, and a day spent here is not like a day spent at home.'[71] Before he was pardoned by Lord Cromer and could return home, he launched two scathing critiques against the alarming state of Ottoman education and called for a radical reform of the school system. In late 1887, he sent a long memorandum to the *shaykh al-islām* in Istanbul warning him that

> Muslims do not shrink from sending their children to [American, Jesuit, Lazarist or Frères] schools in expectation of learning sciences or European languages . . . By the end of their schooling their hearts become void of every Islamic bond and pass out as infidels under the cover of the name of Islam. Love of the foreigner becomes rooted in their hearts, and they become more inclined to follow the foreigners and execute their wishes.[72]

ʿAbduh proposed practical reforms combining an Islamic 'liberal arts' tradition with Muslim orthodoxy in an attempt to put Islam at the service of the state.[73] He demanded a curriculum that included classes on Quran exegesis, Islamic theology, the sciences of the Arabic language, grammar, rhetoric, and textbooks on Islamic and Ottoman history and morals. However, no answer was forthcoming from Istanbul, so ʿAbduh sent another letter in March 1888 to the first governor general of the new province who had just arrived in Beirut.[74] By having absorbed the *maqāṣid* society into state structures back in 1880, he argued, the Ottoman government shot itself in the foot. Expansion rather than discouragement of educational activity was needed to revive the East. Boarding schools had to be founded for the townspeople and the bedouins of Syria, in order to imbue the youth with a sense of 'the revival of religion and the love of the [Ottoman] state'.[75]

Muḥammad ʿAbduh left Zuqaq al-Blat for Cairo in 1888 where he soon became the grand mufti of Egypt. But his recommendation for another boarding high school for Beirut was implemented soon after Beirut became a provincial capital. Indeed, the creation of an Ottoman provincial capital in Beirut and the arrival of its first governor general were landmark events in the field of

[71] Tibawi (1976: 124–8). [72] Quoted ibid. 124–5.

[73] Starrett (1998: 9–10) calls this process the 'functionalization of religion—putting it consciously to work for various types of social and political projects'. As such, ʿAbduh's functionalization of Islam would 'stand opposed to the modernization paradigm in which religion is viewed as benignly irrational and actively obstructionist'.

[74] Muḥammad ʿAbduh, *al-Lāʾiḥa al-thāniyya fī al-iṣlāḥ al-quṭr al-Sūrī* (Beirut, 1888), reprinted together with the first letter in Riḍā (1931: 329–45 and 356–63). [75] Tibawi (1976: 126–7).

Ottoman education efforts in this province.[76] But before we turn to these events, let us share some of the childhood experiences of a student at the *sulṭāniye* in Zuqaq al-Blat.

Dodging Discipline: A Student's Experience of the Sultan's School

In the summer of 1907, the 14-year-old Palestinian boy ʿUmar Ṣāliḥ al-Barghūtī was sent by his father from his village Dayr Ghassaneh north of Jerusalem to study at the *sulṭāniye* school in Beirut with the following words of farewell:

> We have agreed to send you to Beirut to enrol in the *sulṭāniye* School. This is a letter for ʿAbd al-Majīd Abū Naṣr, the director of the newspaper *Bayrūt*. Here are twelve Ottoman gold liras, the school fee for one year of full boarding. And here are ten more liras for the boat trip, and whatever is left should cover your expenses. This is a letter to Ṭabbara if you need extra money go to him and take it from him. If you need anything else, send a telegramme and I will send it to you. May god vouch for you, I want you to let me hold my head up high among the people [of Beirut].[77]

ʿUmar Ṣāliḥ was to become a professor of law in the 1930s, a Palestinian politician in the 1940s, and a Jordanian minister in the 1950s, but his one-year stay in Beirut as a teenager was a journey he did not forget. He had already studied at a number of foreign schools in Jerusalem, the francophone Alliance Israélite and the Frères schools as well as the anglophone St George. However, his father's ambition was to send the boy to Istanbul to study at the Faculty of Law—the pinnacle of thousands of ambitious fathers across the Ottoman Empire—and he figured that Beirut's *sulṭāniye* was the nearest place and the best way to provide ʿUmar with the language skills and high school diploma necessary for this formidable undertaking.[78]

ʿUmar Ṣāliḥ arrived in Beirut by boat and was stunned by the skyline of the city which shimmered in the morning sun as far as his eyes could see. He was also impressed by the size, the beauty, and the electric lighting of his new school, 'whose two floors were very similar to the Alliance school'. When ʿUmar Ṣāliḥ presented himself to the headmaster he explained that 'he had fled the foreign schools to come and attend a government school'.[79] Although the headmaster was clearly pleased to hear such flattery, Ṣāliḥ's Ottoman Turkish

[76] The yearbook of the Ottoman Ministry of Education recorded the opening of a string of secondary schools (*iʿdādiyes*) in Tripoli (1890), Lattakia (1890), Nablus (1893), Acre (1894), and the opening of a boarding *iʿdādiye* in Beirut in 1887—possibly a conversion of the existing *sulṭāniye* school. See Kodaman (1991: 86, 89, 125–6).

[77] al-Barghūtī (2001: 118). I am very grateful to Salim Tamari for pointing me to this source and for providing me with a manuscript copy of his article on the life of ʿUmar Ṣāliḥ al-Barghūtī.

[78] See Tamari (2002). [79] al-Barghūtī (2001: 119).

was less impressive so that he was placed in fourth grade—two below the level of his 'scientific knowledge'. Students were given identification numbers, which were stitched on the collars of their indigo-coloured uniforms. A yellow sultanic crest indicated their school and red stripes their class affiliation. On the whole, he felt that the boarding school was obsessively structured around the five daily prayers while classes commenced and ended with drumbeats. In the mornings,

> the supervisor made the rounds and woke everybody up. Then they got dressed, washed their hands, face and limbs, and performed the ablutions and morning prayers. After that they went to the dining room, had breakfast and tea, then they went out onto the yard where they lined up in rows at the drumbeat. Then they attended class until noon, ate, prayed and returned to class. Then came the time for afternoon prayers and the day's work ended. . . . The students relaxed playing games until the evening prayer, and then they ate dinner and prayed again. Then they studied in the reading room before going to the dormitories.[80]

Thursday was the boarders' washday when 'the students went in droves and droves to the public bath (which was reserved for the occasion) where they washed and changed their clothes and then returned to the school'.[81] Regular outings took the students to picnics in Dibbayya and Junieh. ʿUmar Ṣāliḥ regretted that the school did not encourage sports like back in Palestine or, for that matter, in the rival Greek Catholic school nearby. The new student from Palestine was struck by the detailed system of incentive and punishment that maintained the regimented daily routine. The best students received academic distinctions and prizes at ceremonies while delinquents who repeatedly dodged prayer, curfews, or homework were denied meals, given house arrest, or were beaten in front of the rank and file of teachers and fellow students in the school yard.[82]

ʿUmar Ṣāliḥ felt caged inside the school which operated a system of collective denunciation. Outside school students were also marked because, as he explains, even when they did find a pretext to go out, the uniforms and their identification numbers they were forced to wear exposed them to the watchful eyes of the police and potentially to every apprehensive inhabitant of Beirut. For the students, the school's painful system of denunciation and surveillance was effectively expanded over the entire city.

However, the students had developed a number of ploys to be able to leave the school and avoid getting caught once outside the precinct. They took it in turn to jump the school walls after dark and were let back in by their peers before dawn. The runaways made it a sport to 'slip into civilian clothes hidden

[80] Ibid. 121. [81] Ibid. [82] Ibid. 125.

somewhere outside school' and to immerse themselves in Beirut's nightlife.[83] Although ʿUmar Ṣāliḥ was occasionally teased for his rural background, his Palestinian accent, and his feeble Turkish—all of which led him to be considered as less sophisticated than his peers from Beirut—he presents himself in his memoirs very much as a ringleader in protest against inequalities in the school's daily life, whether mediocre food or special culinary treatment for teachers. He was also determined to partake of the nocturnal pleasures on offer in Beirut 'because the city was roaring with places of seduction, brothels and nightclubs for adolescents.' ʿUmar Ṣāliḥ and his classmates spent 'these stealthy nights revelling, watching films or popular dances . . . or for sexual pleasures with a young girl or other matters (*mutʿa maʿ ghāda aw ghayr dhalika*)'.[84]

ʿUmar Ṣāliḥ's year in Beirut was a world of extremes: on the one hand the tight discipline and religious fastidiousness at school, on the other hand the positive licentiousness of Beirut's forbidden places, the gramophones in cafés and nightclubs 'where popular songs sounded over loudspeakers'.[85] He witnessed 'cars that moved without horses' for the first time in his life, and he mused that none of the abundance of fine hotels, clean restaurants, and the variety of culinary delights existed in Palestine. He noticed in mock surprise that even the cemeteries were meticulously designed, the graves lined with flowers and the tombstones made of marble. To ʿUmar Ṣāliḥ, the fact that most people were elegant in their dress and carriage was evidence that Beirutis were a 'wealthy and a noble people': 'The city is among the most spacious cities known and the mark of civilization is eminent within it. The aristocratic appearances and authority is all the more sublime and magnificent because it is a provincial capital'.[86]

Comparing Notes: The Ottoman College and The Syrian Protestant College

In 1884, the Meḥmed Kāmil Pasha's government in Istanbul established the Education Fund based on increased taxation on agricultural production. This initiative marked the sultan's renewed commitment to secondary schools in the provinces.[87] Four years later, Beirut's first governor general, ʿAlī Pasha, dispatched a memorandum to the Yıldız Palace in Istanbul in which he gave his own assessment of the state of Ottoman and Islamic education in his new

[83] al-Barghūtī. [84] Ibid. 124–5. [85] Ibid. 126. [86] Ibid.
[87] Fortna (2001: 120–2).

province. He echoed Shaykh Muḥammad ʿAbduh's opinion that the only way to prevent a wholesale surrender to the competition of missionary schools was to provide 'indigenous' alternatives for Ottoman Muslims who were suffering from the inferior quality of their education.[88] In 1889, Beirut's private, charity-based *sulṭāniye* was incorporated into the wider *iʿdādiye* system of advanced secondary education. From then on, the Ministry of Education in Istanbul assumed control and financial responsibility for the school.

Six years later the 'Ottoman College', as local and foreign commentators referred to it, was inaugurated in Zuqaq al-Blat.[89] Founded in 1895—again by Aḥmad ʿAbbās al-Azharī—'in a magnificent building on an airy plateau overlooking Beirut and the Mountain', *al-madrasa al-ʿuthmāniyya* started as

> a small scientific institute accommodating a small number of pupils of different origins. Two years later, the school secured a larger number of teachers and pupils. Now almost thirty teachers offer education to 150 pupils, boarding to half of them, most of whom come from all corners of Syria, some from the Hijaz, [Basra, Kuwait,] Yemen, Tunis and Anatolia, and the capital, Istanbul.[90]

Since the Education Tax Act of 1884, a combination of curricular and extracurricular activities provided Hamidian schools with modes to inculcate students with 'loyalty, moral character and right conduct'.[91] The school, which offered eight grades of education, was divided into an 'elementary' and a 'scientific' section, a day and a boarding section. The curriculum was similar in form to but more diverse in content than previous Islamic liberal arts institutions in Zuqaq al-Blat. 'In the scientific section the students learn religious sciences and are taught affection for the observance of orthodox Islam'.[92] Turkish and French were obligatory, English and even German were optional.[93]

Seven wide-ranging subjects were offered: religious studies, general history 'from the ancients and the middle ages to the modern, the prophet's life and Arab history'; economic geography, map drawing (*rasm al-jughrāfiya*); maths, algebra, geometry, accounting and 'introductions' to astronomy; natural sciences—biology, botany, physics, chemistry, and 'hygienic maintenance'; drawing, calligraphy, and (marching) music; oratory arts, debating, logic,

88 BBA, YMTV 32/45/1, 1 May 1888. Quoted in Fortna (2001: 52).

89 Muḥammad Jamīl Bayhum, 'al-Kulliyya al-ʿuthmāniyya al-islāmiyya', *al-Mufīd*, 3 (15 April 1911), 1–2. *Al-Mufīd* emerged as the leading Arab nationalist newspaper after the Young Turk revolution. Its co-owner/co-editor ʿAbd al-Ghanī al-ʿUraysī was a dean of the Ottoman College and a political activist who helped organize the First Arab Congress in Paris in 1913 that brought together the clandestine nationalist *al-Fatāt* group, the Cairo-based Decentralists, and the Beirut Reform Committee. See above, Ch. 2.

90 Anon., *al-Madrasa al-ʿuthmāniyya* (1914), 5.

91 Fortna (2000: 375).

92 *al-Madrasa al-ʿuthmāniyya*, 5.

93 In 1913, forty students were enrolled in German-language classes. See Hartmann (1913: 32).

political economy, moral sciences (*ʿilm-i aḫlāḳ*), and 'matters in the spirit of society and civilisation'.[94] Early morning swimming in the Mediterranean and weekly physical education in the school's new sports facilities were part of the curriculum. A school orchestra and cultural club were offered after class and seemed to have enjoyed considerable popularity.[95]

The school's prospectus—published in 1914—emphasized, in a notably emphatic tone, that

> Arabic is the principal language of the school taught in all elementary and scientific classes. The school has allocated compulsory lessons to perfect grammar and inflection and rhetorical sciences (interpretation, eloquence and style), language and poetic rendering, creativity of expression so that a boy graduates who is in full command of the Arabic language in its classical diction, in writing and free speech. The school encourages its teachers to translate modern sciences into Arabic to teach them because this serves the student and the Arab nation (*umma*).[96]

This passage ends with the only mention of the Arab nation in the school's prospectus. It does so less in an affirmation of an ethnic identity than in the utilitarian cultural sense of knowledge production. In contrast to the *maktab ʿanbār* in Damascus, where most classes seemed to have been conducted in Turkish,[97] the *ʿuthmāniye* offered Turkish merely as an option—another qualification to widen job prospects on account of being 'the official language of the state'.[98]

Moreover, in this particular school, the Arabic language was identified as serving the cultural refinement of the imagined community of Arabs. On the occasion of its twentieth anniversary, the school was presented in a distinctly corporate, elite spirit. Whether this was actually the case or merely aimed at an audience of alumni, parents, and sponsors, cannot be said with certainty. ʿUmar Ṣāliḥ's childhood memoirs suggest that the atmosphere in Muslim Ottoman schools was stifling and uninspiring. However, as the largest Muslim boarding school in Beirut with 150 boarders by 1913, it generated a sense of *ésprit de corps*. Moreover, the way the deans Aḥmad ʿAbbās, ʿAbd al-Ghanī al-ʿUraysī, and Aḥmad Ṭabbara promoted the pedagogical strengths of his school is significant, in particular—as I shall argue presently—in comparison with the way the Syrian Protestant College treated its student population at around the same time:

> a diploma of the school . . . qualifies them to specialize in any of the advanced arts or to go out into the wide world of work. [The student] is a man in every sense of the

[94] *al-Madrasa al-ʿuthmāniyya*, 8.
[95] Hartmann (1913: 32).
[96] *al-Madrasa al-ʿuthmāniyya*, 7.
[97] Rogan (2004).
[98] *al-Madrasa al-ʿuthmāniyya*, 8.

word—full of scientific competence (*istiʿdād ʿilmī*) and self-belief (*iʿtimād ʿalā al-nafs*) with eloquence and rhetoric of the tongue. [The school] instructs the students and imbues them with morals and noble affection with the complete dedication to implant love of self-belief in their hearts.[99]

Entitlement, masculinity, pride, and independence of mind were the attributes which the school administration aspired to impart to its students. The prospectus saw the school's purpose to mould and gender their talents, develop their interpersonal skills, command respect and self-assertion. Like the Anglo-Saxon liberal arts tradition, these children were brought up to be useful to society and to be equipped with applicable knowledge. They were trained as an intelligentsia of well-educated professionals who were meant to serve in Ottoman institutions and private businesses.[100] But Beirut's *ʿuthmāniye* school also planted the seeds of Arab nationalist sentiment for an entire generation of Muslim youths.[101] Here, arguably more so than in other elite schools of the empire, students were imbued with the necessity of Arab moral regeneration, civilizational pressure, and self-governing subjectivity.

The most important missionary institution founded in Zuqaq al-Blat was the Syrian Protestant College (SPC). Its first classes were held in ʿAbd al-Fattāḥ Ḥamāda's house, the same place where his son Muḥyī al-Dīn accommodated Muḥammad ʿAbduh's literary salon in the 1880s, and in a Bustānī property adjacent to the National School.[102] The SPC bought its new premises in distant Ras Beirut in the late 1860s. The inauguration of the College Hall clocktower in 1871 marked the beginning of a series of constructions—faculty buildings, a chapel, student dormitories, and a park—which constituted the college's vast new campus.[103] At a public lecture in London in 1888, Revd George Post, one of the founding fathers of the SPC, commented on the significance and symbolism of College Hall in no uncertain terms: 'Would you blot out this lighthouse, would you take down that landmark from the East? Rather tear down the classic halls of Oxford and Cambridge and leave this standing to enlighten the Mohammedan world and bring it to the cross'.[104]

After 1860, Ussama Makdisi argues, most American missionaries embraced the idea of colonial transformation over spiritual liberation of the Holy Land.[105] The move out of Zuqaq al-Blat signalled their new commitment to a

99 Ibid. 6. 100 Ibid. for a list of *ʿuthmāniye* graduates. 101 Khalidi (1981: 41).

102 On the early years of the Syrian Mission in Zuqaq al-Blat, see Bodenstein *et al.* (2005).

103 The SPC's student numbers also rose steadily to reach 900 by the First World War.

104 Quoted in Khalaf (1995: 68).

105 Makdisi (1997: 768–96). Makdisi quotes one missionary as saying 'may be that a war is needed to purify the land and prepare the way for the gospel'. Another, Jessup, wrote that the war 'may prove to be the very discipline which is needed to bring these people to take refuge in Christ'.

more full-heartedly secular, scientific discourse of the 'pilgrims' progress'. Laying the cornerstone of College Hall in 1871, President Daniel Bliss declared that '[t]his College is for all conditions and classes of men without regard to colour, nationality, race, or religion'. Bliss continued—making sure that he did not get carried away by the significance of the moment—that, nevertheless, 'it will be impossible for any one to continue with us long without knowing what we believe to be the truth and our reasons for that belief'.[106] In other words, everyone is welcome but must adapt to Presbyterian practice in order to be treated equally.

From 1866 to 1903, the SPC remained a bastion of social conservatism and Protestant sectarianism.[107] During Daniel Bliss's presidency, the SPC turned the Protestants' 'gentle crusade' of the pre-civil war period into a religious apparatus of institutional coercion.[108] Violence was a universal trait in schools and would have featured in the *waṭaniye* and the *sulṭāniye*, too, although ʿAbduh himself opposed the traditional *falaq* beatings.[109] The mental strain of the SPC was somewhat more insidious. By forcing daily prayers and non-*halāl* food on Jewish and Muslim students, or by forbidding Greek Orthodox time off for their religious holidays, the college systematically attempted to uproot non-Protestant students from their previous socialization in community schools and family.

Bustānī, ʿAbduh, and Bliss were driven by an urge to extricate society from what they all considered was evident backwardness. They shared the belief that modernity and progress had to be compatible with morality as part of the same project of modernity. For Buṭrus al-Bustānī the cathartic experience was the civil war, for ʿAbduh Muslim alienation in colonial and pre-colonial Egypt. The pedagogical philosophy in Bustānī's *waṭaniye* and to a certain extent in ʿAbduh's *sulṭāniye* was based on tolerance of other religions, the universal origins of—and access to—modern science.

To President Bliss, however, scientific thought and rational method were generally Western attributes while backwardness and fanaticism were innately Oriental qualities. In their uniquely American synthesis with Puritan values both science and reason would gradually erode the irrationality and 'supersti-

106 F. J. Bliss, *Reminiscences of Daniel Bliss* (New York, 1920), 198; quoted in Makdisi (1997: 708).

107 Scholz (Ph.D. thesis, 1997).

108 See Makdisi (2000): 'The Gentle Crusade', especially p. 25: 'Perhaps the foreign missionaries best exemplify the spirit of the gentle crusade and reflect the intrusive power of nineteenth-century Western imagination. They provide the clearest example of the will of Europeans and Americans to shape the land according to their expectations, regardless of and indeed despite the realities they found on the ground'.

109 For a description of this form of corporal punishment, see Zaydān, (1979: 137).

tion so prevalent in the East'.[110] The difference from local schools was that the SPC did not intend to foster students' talents as the *'uthmāniye* had pledged, but to crush existing personalities before recalibrating them from scratch. Thus, looking back over the first decade of his *œuvre*, Bliss gave a positive assessment of the work of the college: 'The graduates . . . are now utterly unable to accept or tolerate the superstitions so prevalent in the East. They have no longer any faith in their own religions, and have at least a full understanding of what we hold to be the only salvation'.[111]

The irony—as has been noted recently—that it was early Western missionaries who brought sectarianism to Bilad al-Sham in the 1830s, persisted into the early twentieth century.[112] This was manifest in the fallout after the so-called Darwin lecture in 1882, when President Bliss forced his staff to sign a declaration of principles committing them to rejecting 'the erroneous teachings and practices of the Romish and Eastern Churches'.[113] The contrast to al-Bustānī's work could not be starker: the SPC sectarianized the landscape of Beirut while the *waṭaniye* was set up to overcome sectarianism. The whole affair also signalled the ambivalence within the Syrian Mission over a secular SPC's relation to the evangelical project that persisted since its establishment in 1866.

The schools of Zuqaq al-Blat eschewed the Manichean dichotomy between 'traditional Muslim' and 'modern secular' schools. Muḥammad ʿAbduh had designed a curriculum in Beirut that would make Islamic morality and industrial science compatible and mutually inclusive. His was a mixture of sharp criticism against Muslims in foreign schools (far less harsh against Ottoman Christians, it should be noted) and an espousal of exchange between the people of the book. Historically, this syncretism may have turned out to be utopian, not because of ʿAbduh's naivety but because of the increasingly confrontational imperial world around him. Daniel Bliss, for one, was opposed to tolerating other confessions. Other missionaries involved with the SPC were even more outspoken. Henry Jessup reminded his president as late as 1893 that:

> Education is only a means to an end in Christian missions, and we do not hesitate to say that such a mission has stepped out of the Christian and missionary sphere [that] aim[s] to have the best astronomers, geologists, botanists, surgeons and physicians in the realm for the sake of the scientific prestige and world-wide reputation.[114]

110 Scholz (Ph.D. thesis, 1997: 127).

111 Quoted ibid. 127 n. 9. It should be added that Bliss's assessment did not change much over the years and in 1904 he reaffirmed that 'we do aim to make perfect men, ideal men, God-like men, after the model of Jesus Christ'. Quoted in Khalaf (1995: 73).

112 Makdisi (2000: 90).

113 Kedourie (1974*a*: 68).

114 Jessup (1910: ii. 592).

Over the years, students and staff at the SPC managed to undermine its parochial foundations and co-opt their education for universal ends. In the nineteenth century as in the twentieth century, SPC students took collective action against the college authorities.[115] This led to a polarization between 'liberal' and 'conservative' factions within the administration towards the end of the nineteenth century. The liberals around Cornelius van Dyck gradually retreated from the college out of protest against the authoritarian measures imposed on the student body.

The prayer crisis of 1909 exposed the sectarian nature of the SPC even more starkly.[116] Two hundred Muslim and Jewish students publicly demonstrated against mandatory prayer attendance and almost caused the first of a number of international crises in the history of the SPC (and later AUB). A missionary's speech to the habitually mixed audience at the SPC did little to quell the resistance. The following excerpt of the address was published in *al-Ittiḥād al-ʿUthmānī* by Aḥmad Ṭabbāra, a dean of the rival Ottoman College:

> We, Christians, are surrounded with great walls of enemies, the Moslems and others. They prevent us from spreading the true call and await the opportunity to devour us. It is our business, then, our sacred duty to break down these walls and tread upon them. . . . These obstacles to our faith and to our religion are doomed if we will only fight them as we should.[117]

After a prolonged struggle with the students and the Young Turk governor general, the SPC administration was forced to distance itself officially from proselytizing zeal once and for all. The renaming of the college as the American University of Beirut in 1920 finally signalled the 'abandonment of compulsory religion for students and of religious tests for the teachers'.[118] From the mandate period onwards, student protest at American University of Beirut became a distinct political force in the Arab world, even though during the cold war another president could still argue in deeply prejudiced terms that 'In the Near East . . . the necessity for rather stricter supervision over student life is greater than in America. Not only are serious temptations more numerous and more accessible, but the early training of young men does not produce in them as much facility for moral judgment as is found in the average American student'.[119]

[115] Scholz (Ph.D. thesis, 1997: 160 ff). [116] Ibid. 175 ff.

[117] James Nicol on 18 Jan. 1909, quoted in Scholz (Ph.D. thesis, 1997: 177). The Ottoman College's deans Aḥmad Ṭabbāra and ʿAbd al-Ghanī al-ʿUraysī were among the Beirutis hanged for treason by Cemal Pasha during the First World War.

[118] Kedourie (1974*a*: 66). [119] Penrose (1941: 90).

Parents who continued to send their children to the American school made sure the risk of conversion was minimal. Most student memoirs insisted that the SPC provided the highest quality education in Beirut but they also articulated a sense that the parental calculation to expose their teenagers to Western missionaries further tightened family and kinship controls.[120]

Ironically, youth alienation not religious conversion severed the last generation of Ottomanists from the first generation of Arab nationalists, as the AUB became—in spite of itself—the most fertile ground in the region for all varieties of radical nationalisms, Marxism and socialism, Palestinian liberation movements, and Pan-Arabism. At the same time as staff and student population gradually turned the AUB into an anti-colonial bastion, it continued to provide personnel for the Anglo-Egyptian economy and colonial administration in Sudan, where graduates constituted a vital bureaucratic layer of colonial occupation into the 1950s.[121]

Conclusion

This chapter has excavated not only an unexpected network of intellectuals but also a hitherto unknown Ottoman and local educational 'beehive' in Zuqaq al-Blat where considerable synergy between Muslims and Christians occurred. Buṭrus al-Bustānī's *madrasa al-waṭaniyya* may have stopped teaching during its founder's lifetime—the exact date of the school's closure is uncertain—but it was the intellectual well for most cultural activities between the civil war of 1860 and the dissolution of the Ottoman empire in 1918. Its teachers and students went on to form cultural societies, establish newspapers, found other schools, and become leading municipal politicians.

The discussion of Zuqaq al-Blat's many colleges complicates the existing historiography on educational history in the Middle East, historicizes the role of the imperial Ottoman government, and compares the colonial pedagogy of the Syrian Protestant College with interconfessional and Muslim colleges. While the first president developed a modern teaching philosophy that aimed at erasing his students' existing beliefs and personalities, the official utterances

[120] For a study on students' family background, AUB education, and nationalist socialization from the 1930s to the 1950s, see Schumann (2001).

[121] See the student entries in AUB Alumni Association (1953). In the 1920s and 1930s, AUB also trained the very Sudanese officials who would replace Egyptian, Lebanese, and later British administrators of independence. Conversation with Tayyib Salih, Toronto, 16 Oct. 2004. See also Leila Fawaz's memoirs (2002).

of local and Ottoman educators showed a greater measure of appreciation of existing student talents which they vowed to enhance.

However, even as we criticize missionary education, we must not be drawn into either granting excessive charity to local schools or reproducing the self-centred worldview of colonialism. I insist that, while the Jesuit and Protestant universities were the most prestigious institutions in *fin de siècle* Beirut, foreign schools were neither the only ones nor the natural choice for concerned parents, as we see in the case of ʿUmar Ṣāliḥ al-Barghūtī, a Palestinian boy sent to Beirut to receive the education necessary to enter law school in Istanbul. The rare account of ʿUmar Ṣāliḥ's negative experiences in an Ottoman high school also calls for scepticism regarding official school literature.

It is significant for this book's historical framework that the *sulṭāniye* school started as a local private initiative but was absorbed into the evolving imperial structure of governance almost immediately after Beirut became a provincial capital. Like other Ottoman schools during of the reign of Abdülhamid II, the *sulṭāniye* was a reaction against both foreign and recitalist schools. This did not mean that Muslim reformers and the Ottoman government advocated a secularist education system. On the contrary, Benjamin Fortna's general observations that 'the moral element in the late Ottoman approach was overtly Islamic' held true also for Beirut.[122] But the initiative for elite schools such as the *sulṭāniye* came from local Muslim intellectuals before the state absorbed the existing structure into the imperial education system.

Whereas conservatives like Yūsuf al-Nabḥānī argued that the state and state education should exist to serve the proper enactment of conventional codes of Islamic religion, Beirut's reformists shared Muḥammad ʿAbduh's project of—as Jakob Skovgaard-Petersen aptly put it—'defining Islam for the state'.[123] State officials and Muslim reformers alike desired the alignment of a new concept of Islamic orthodoxy with the project of state-building.[124] In this process, the role of education in the *sulṭāniye* and *ʿuthmāniye* schools was to infuse young minds with a sound judgement of public morality and state loyalty. Courses on moral sciences and Islamic civilization taught students to understand the lessons drawn from the scriptures and apply them to Ottoman realities.[125] Although we know few details about the education of the majority of the thousands of students who had passed through Beirut's extensive education

122 Fortna (2000: 370).
123 Skovgaard-Petersen (1997).
124 Asad (2003: 218–29).
125 Fortna (2000: 379).

system by the end of the nineteenth century,[126] we may assume that the newspaper debates and editorials attracted a wide enough literate audience to shape public opinion. It is to the intertwining physical and discursive realities of Beirut's emerging political field that the following and final part of this book now turns.

126 The 1310/1892 *Salnāme* for Beirut (pp. 234, 242–4) lists a total of twenty-one Islamic primary schools for boys with a student population of 2,320 and four Islamic schools for a total of 247 girls for Beirut. Seventeen boys' schools were marked as 'special Islamic elementary schools' (*ḫuṣūṣ makātip iptidāʾiye islāmiye*).

III

Urban Words—Urban Worlds

Within us genies rebel,
And we are tempted by sins
And crime:
'In Beirut there is a life other than the life of
Hard work and monotonous death,
There are magic Taverns,
Wine, perfumed beds
For the perplexed
Lost in the deserts.'

(Hawi 1993: 52, tr. Khairallah)

7

Public Morality and Social Marginality

This final part of the book examines physical places and mental spaces of the city: on the one hand the central places of commerce, literature, and bourgeois sociability such as theatres, coffeehouses, cabarets, early cinemas, and public squares, and on the other the marginal places of perceived lower class vice and bourgeois fear. A host of texts—newspaper editorials and medical publications, diaries and consular reports—invested all these spaces real-and-imagined with meaning.

In the process, I argue, an elite discourse of morality and deviance emerged in post-1860 Beirut which attempted a geographical alignment of evolving class and gender notions. In other words, social activities were labelled as deviant precisely because they occurred in central places that were envisaged to represent more enlightened urban images for Beirut. Alcohol consumption, gambling, prostitution, or lewd shadow plays were dangerous nocturnal activities that took place too close for comfort to respectable citizens.

As a consequence, elite notions of civility generated gender and class tensions that were fought over urban space. Generally, Arabic journalists felt a sense of panic or trauma that their society might be possessed by a civilization deficit. The discrepancy in *fin de siècle* Beirut between actual security and relative peacefulness and perceived lawlessness could not be greater.

The police system was under intense scrutiny by the foreign community, which regarded occurrences of criminal activity, whether assault, theft, or smuggling, as irrefutable signs of state weakness and moral laxness, in particular when they led to sectarian violence. Although Beirut was spared the sectarian violence of 1860, the maintenance of peace and stability in the city, and its intellectuals' quest for social harmony and economic prosperity, evolved around—and was defined against—the memory of the devastating experience of the war in the Mountain.

The atrocities of 1860 continued to feed uneasiness and mutual suspicion between immigrants and inhabitants, social classes and religious confessions until well into the twentieth century. Generations later, families still dated events in their lives with reference to the civil war.[1] In this vein, Lebanon's foremost national historian, Kamal Salibi, has argued that, to many combatants, the most recent Lebanese civil war between 1975 and 1990 'was in a fundamental way, a war to determine the correct history of the country'.[2] The persistent urban *angst* about a return to the conditions of civil war is a common theme in the historical sources on Beirut. Crime and murder may have tended to be isolated and instantaneous night-time occurrences but local and foreign commentators at the time expressed unease that the 'slightest incident' would trigger 'the eruption of this dreadful volcano'. Such statements suggest that Beirut's social relations and physical layout may have been affected by the inhabitants' fears of disorder, instability, and, indeed, a 'relapse' into 'destructive primordialism'.[3] Not dissimilar from British public moralists at the time who identified London's poor as a root problem in society, Beirut's intellectuals were 'one in the belief that there were "savage tribes lurking at the bottom of our civilization", which if not tamed and disciplined would ultimately overthrow it'.[4]

The fragility of this order made public morality a recurrent theme as normative social gel and panacea in the writings of Buṭrus and Salīm al-Bustānī, Jirjī Zaydān, and others. In their writings they embraced the forces of modernity not merely as an adaptation of Western values but as an auto-emancipatory discourse from what was considered as a bleak past which needed to be overcome through progress in material advancement, efficient use of time, education, and social moral norms. Society was deemed dangerous unto itself and the ignorant individual was viewed as the microbe of anticipated social decay. It is in this sense that society in post-war Beirut was a moral creation.

Faced with such threats, the Ottoman provincial government and local notables, merchants, and intellectuals worked together to establish norms and forms of social containment. Legal stipulations and their physical enforcement did not necessarily lead to the disciplined society envisaged by discursive control mechanisms and their contestations. Nevertheless, they shaped the urban development of modern Beirut. It is in this sense that—to paraphrase Raymond Williams—much of the anxiety and instability that local intellectu-

[1] Fawaz (1983: 115). [2] Salibi (1988: 200–15).

[3] Buṭrus al-Bustānī, *Nafīr Sūriyya*, fourth issue, 25 Oct. 1860, 22. The page numbers refer to the version edited by Y. Khūrī (1990).

[4] Harris (1993: 242). The term 'public moralist' is borrowed from Collini (1991).

als and the authorities tried to overcome, as well as much of the physical squalor and perceived disorderliness, were also 'a consequence not simply of rapid expansion but of attempts to control that expansion'.[5] With this in mind, this chapter explores the uses and regulations of social spaces and public places and ties them to the discourses of morality and urban control that unfolded in Beirut before and after 1860.

As I argued in the previous chapter, Buṭrus al-Bustānī emerged as Beirut's guardian of moral consciousness after the civil war. His pamphlets *Nafīr Sūriyya* contained passionate appeals to his fellow countrymen to overcome their sectarian differences, individual and communal self-interest, and work together for a better and more dignified common future. With an acute sense of the judgement of history, he warns that the traumatic experience of civil war is 'like an ugly black spot that will remain a black spot in the history of Syria as long as the sky is a sky and the earth is earth . . . an ugly spot running through the pages of our history, replete with shame and desperation instead of love for the nation'.[6]

However, his compatriots must and could overcome social fragmentation, factionalism, fanaticism, ignorance, selfishness, and their basic instincts of revenge by diverting the struggle towards altruism, knowledge, tolerance, and love of the nation.[7] Such ideals would provide, Bustānī argued, strong foundations to restore popular confidence in state and society. Beiruti public moralists after Bustānī continued to display a sense of urgency in prescribing the desirable interaction between state and society. As public and secular moralists they increasingly turned the social life of Beirut into a new object of analysis and intervention and thus came to shape the physical structure of the city.

Stages of Everyday Life

When the French geographer Vital Cuinet arrived in Beirut in the early 1890s, he was impressed by what he saw: 'Today's city of Beirut is built as an amphitheatre. Seen from the sea, its sight is very beautiful. One notices first of all the imperial barracks', then the mosques and the churches, and the universities and the schools on the hillsides which educated a total of over 23,000 pupils and students.[8] Cuinet proceeded to count five public baths, ten public fountains, six hospitals, fifty medical practices, thirty pharmacies, twenty-four

[5] Williams (1973: 145).

[6] *Nafīr Sūriyya*, Beirut, fourth issue, 25 Oct. 1860, 22; and fifth issue, 1 Nov. 1860, 26.

[7] *Nafīr Sūriyya*, fifth issue, 1 Nov. 1860, 22.

[8] Cuinet (1896: 55).

cemeteries, thirty bazaars, and thirty caravanserails, twenty-five hotels, three casinos, two circuses, fifty-five cafés, ten public beaches, two public gardens, twenty-three police stations, ten carriage companies, thirty clockmakers, forty-five jewellers, twelve photographers, twelve printing presses, and twelve libraries.[9]

Cuinet further estimated that there were around 20,000 private houses in Beirut. The vast majority of these houses were rented by more than one family, either in collective occupancy (*ḥawsh*) or by wage-earning bachelors in modest second- or third-floor rooms in one of the *qayṣariyya*s for less than a *mecidiye* per month (equivalent to four francs or three shillings and about a sixth of their monthly salary).[10] In his youth, the Arab historian Jirjī Zaydān moved house six times and criss-crossed the entire city of Beirut:

> The tenant carries his house on his back. . . . Some houses had three rooms. There was no urgent need for many rooms since people did not use any beds. In the same room one could receive guests in the daytime and sleep at night. When getting up one would fold the bed rolls and pile them one on top of the other on a chest on the ground.[11]

Given the constantly rising rents, it is likely that the majority of Beirutis shared young Zaydān's experience of unsettled housing conditions. This was a world apart from the grand villas on the hilltops around the city centre. The growing prosperity and security in and around Beirut also affected aesthetic sensibilities and domestic architecture. Vast two- to three-storey mansions were built, whose high towers and multi-arched galleries commanded a magnificent view over the city centre and the port. At the beginning of the nineteenth century Beirutis had taken great risks by moving out of the sanctuary of the walled city and built fortress-like palaces. At the end of the century the terraces became so densely populated that fences and walls were erected around the properties to ensure privacy and security from the streets.

In contrast to Beirut's closed world of burgeoning private villas, public places—such as coffeehouses, theatres, squares, or streets—offered an extra-familial meeting place where people came together by chance as much as by personal choice. If, as we have seen in the previous chapter, Ottoman state schools educated conformity in Beirut, then—like in *fin de siècle* Vienna—the coffeehouse was 'the best educational institution for everything new' for the growing numbers of educated adolescents.[12] Coffeehouses and theatres on Beirut's main square, Sahat al-Burj, like the Café Qazzāz (Figure 6), moreover

[9] Cuinet (1896: 56).

[10] A *qayṣariyya* usually had a ground-floor shop front and private lodgings on the floors above.

[11] Philipp (1979: 133). [12] Zweig (1998: 57).

FIG. 6. Flâneurs on Sahat al-Burj in front of Café Qazzaz, *c.*1900. (Collection of W. D. Lemke)

became spaces where not only Ottoman *flâneurs* with their red fezzes and black frocks were ridiculed, but where stinging social criticism avoided punishment:

> Just before the Young Turk revolution, one Samʿān Būlus from Zgharta caused scandal in the café of Najīb al-Khūrī on Sahat al-Burj, when he dressed in the attire of a *mushīr* [general] smoking a *nargīla* and mocking the social hierarchy under Muzaffer Pasha [then governor of Mount Lebanon]. When reprimanded by an onlooker of the spectacle how he dares to wear the uniform of the highest rank in the Ottoman army, our hero of the day replied: 'Why should it matter to you, if I dress so smart?'[13]

Themes of the Night: Access, Security, and Danger

Throughout the year, Beirutis got up very early in the morning. Yet, daily routine in the summer differed greatly from winter months. In the heat of the summer business was conducted in the early hours of the day and late in the afternoon, with a long siesta in between either at home or in the coffeehouses near the workplaces. The limited daylight in the winter forced merchants and shopkeepers to conduct all their business before the afternoon sunset. With the

[13] B. al-Khūrī (1960: 50).

sudden nightfall, night-watchmen took to the street while workers, merchants, and schoolchildren rushed home before darkness closed in on the city. Then, the night ended as quickly as it began, as *mu'azzins* called for morning prayers well before the crack of dawn. Coffeehouses near the mosques and the port opened their doors in anticipation of their first customers and night-watchmen extinguished the sparse oil lamps—the day had just begun.

But the night was far from 'empty time'. Night and day were marked by a multitude of urban practices that varied from community to community. Saints' days, Mar Maroun, St George, and Imām Uzāʿī, as well as the annual 'Day of the Forty Men' (*yawm rijāl al-arbaʿīn*) on the wide, sandy beach south of Ras Beirut, were the city's very own festivals. And much anticipated by the Muslim population, the festive periods in the month of Shaʿban and Ramadan habitually defied the darkness of the night. During Ramadan, the day only really began in earnest with the setting of the sun. After the breaking of the day's fasting, the streets came to life late into the night, when relatives were visited, and people were drawn to the markets and coffeehouses nearby. All too soon, the drummers would make their rounds to wake up the city's Muslim population for early-morning prayers and *iftār* breakfast. Once a year, social activity lit up the dark hours of the night, while the days were reduced to a time of anticipation.

During the nineteenth century, another kind of night gradually emerged in Beirut. As the night was systematically conquered in the wake of physical and technological changes in the urban fabric, a different rhythm of everyday life and new dimension of urban thought began to dominate Beirut.[14] Technical advances such as street lighting brought about a new relationship between nature and culture. In Albert Hourani's words, the ideology of the city came to be distinguished from the ideology of the mountain in that 'for the villager, rural society is created by God, urban by man'.[15] As elsewhere, urban culture in *fin de siècle* Beirut relied on the idea that the city was the centre of commercial, aesthetic, and civilized life.[16]

The elite's urbanity coincided with the development of public places for leisure—shops, cafés, squares, and night-time places of entertainment—in the wake of rising levels of material consumption.[17] To Buṭrus al-Bustānī's son, Salīm, who worked closely with his father, as a coastal people (*al-sāḥiliyyūn*), the Beirutis were exposed to both the benefits and dangers of contact with

[14] Schlör's themes of the night—security, morality, accessibility, and danger—are as relevant to Beirut as to other cities of the turn of the 19th cent. Schlör (1998).

[15] Hourani (1981: 175).

[16] Salīm al-Bustānī, 'Markazuna', *al-Jinān*, 3 (1872), 135–47. See also next chapter.

[17] Bouman (1987: 10).

Europe. 'While the people of the interior covet their customs more than the coastal people, the latter were used to mixing with foreign nations and adopting both beneficial and offensive customs.'[18]

The city walls had been a marker of inside and outside as well as night and day for centuries. Beirut was a well-fortified, if frequently attacked, port town. The gates were closed at sunset (save one, which stayed open some hours later). 'Everybody dines at seven P.M.; and shortly after sunset, the promenade is deserted . . . the gates of the town are closed, and the busy hum of life subsides into calm and stillness, as night closes on the scene.'[19] However, what appeared as an absolute barrier of nocturnal access to the city was in fact negotiable through inside knowledge of the informal urban administration. For the Europeans, according to Blondel, the curfew was not much of an inconvenience, for when they acquired the password, they could enter and exit the city as they desired. Moreover, if the sudden nightfall took a reveller by surprise, he could enter the city by boat for a small fee.[20]

More severe was the enforcement of personal lighting at night. Once inside the city, it was strictly forbidden to walk without carrying a lantern after dark.[21] In an official address to the inhabitants of Beirut in early 1860, the governor of Sidon offered a strong warning 'to bear lanterns on every walk in the *sūqs* and the streets at night in order to ensure the maintenance of law and order in the city'. As if naturally connected, the press notification also made specific reference to the prohibition of night-time gambling.[22]

With the growth and prosperity of the city of Beirut and the changing habits and opportunities of its inhabitants, the night became a new problem zone for issues of law, order, and public morality that were particular to the urban environment. The night opened up for work and leisure through two watershed events whose transformation crucially determined Beirut's cultural history: the gradual erosion of the ancient city walls after 1840 and the introduction of gas lighting after 1887.

New coffeehouses mushroomed in the Zaytuneh quarter and further along the western seashore from the 1860s onwards. They started to attract people from all walks of life and soon metamorphosed into respectable institutions. The intramural coffeehouses stayed open for up to an hour and a half after sunset and became more crowded in the evenings. In contrast to the fashionable café culture on Beirut's promenades, some of the places of leisure inside the old city were generally seen as disreputable, not least by the foreign community,

18 Salīm al-Bustānī, 'Asbāb taqaddum Bayrūt wa numuwuha al-sarīʿ', *al-Jinān*, 15 (1884).

19 Neale (1851: 222). 20 Blondel (1840: 51, 72). 21 Ibid. 52.

22 *Ḥadīqat al-Akhbār* (17 Jan. 1860).

who held them to be a den of the 'Maltese, a dangerous people infesting the Levant and provoking riots, stealing and all too often murder'.[23] Most locals tended to look down upon the insalubrious conditions of the port quarter and avoided the area altogether. 'Two cafés labelled European have been opened there, but they are only frequented by sailors of all nations who belong to ships mooring in the port.'[24]

One of the main concerns in the first municipal budget of 1868 was how to finance 'the salaries of the night-watchmen and street lighting which had been incomplete and whose improvement had been postponed because it required resources'. At the same time, the projected 'increased revenue could put the services on a better footing, most notably the improvement of street lighting and the increasing of the number of night-watchmen'.[25] Their efficiency was noted in the memoirs of Lewis Farley, the first clerk of the newly opened Ottoman Bank whom we encountered in Chapter 3. In late 1857, one of his servants was arrested for not bearing a lantern after dark. He was brought to a police station and released only the next morning, well after an Ottoman man-of-war fired the cannon shots that customarily marked the dawn of a new day.[26]

Much changed for Beirut when the technological innovation of artificial lighting pushed the limits of the day deep into the night along the main traffic arteries. By 1906 over 1,300 gas lamps lit up the main arteries at fifty-metre intervals. An incident related by an Austrian tourist in 1909 captures the stark contrast of dealing with the night before and after the gradual introduction of gas lighting in Beirut:

> We leave the theatre and go home through the streets of Beirut which are gas lit only on every other corner. There is a throng of men under each of these gas lamps and as we pass them they are whistling a signal which is returned from the other end of the streets where the same groups of men in their dark coats are expecting us. This scenario accompanies us from street to street until we reach the hotel. 'They are police signals,' explained the consular agent.[27]

Far from being prevented and restricted as had been the mandate previously, the nocturnal activities of the foreign visitor came to be facilitated by the night-watchmen who effectively provided a safe cordon of passage. Individual responsibility for one's safety at night had passed into the hands of the state, here embodied by the night-watchmen. In the process, the Ottoman state had

23 Blondel (1840: 39). On the Maltese 'menace' in Tunis, see Clancy-Smith (2002: 149–82).
24 Blondel (1840: 42).
25 MAE, Nantes, CB 1868–1913, carton 332, Beirut, 26 May 1868.
26 Farley (1859: 114). On the cannon shots, see Rodier (1889: 244).
27 Strobel (1911: 42).

come to assume control of time and space in a routine, facilitating manner rather than through restrictive mechanisms. Moreover, lighting had become a factor of order while, conversely, nocturnal insecurity was increasingly associated with the absence of light. As certain parts of the city were brightly illuminated, in other parts the night's darkness grew more fearsome. Indeed, the arrival of artificial lighting brought out the contradictions within the city; the more brightly it shone in the centre, the more starkly did the outlines of the darker regions stand out.

A prominent Russian resident in Beirut between 1896 and 1898 expressed the ambivalent perception of the night when he confirmed in his memoirs that there was ample nightlife even if late nights were dangerous, with frequent gunshots being heard in the distance.[28] The 'underworld' may have been pushed out of sight by modern policing practices but not out of earshot. Consular reports from Beirut likewise identified the night as the temporal location of danger to the stability and security of the city. When an American consular official was ambushed in the city late one night, the 'individual . . . had posted himself near a street lamp the better to ensure the correctness of his aim. [The chase proved futile as] the latter however disappeared into the dark of the night.'[29] As the street lamp facilitated and exposed night revelry, so this episode highlights the ambivalent effects of artificial street lighting both as a spur of access and a source of danger for nocturnal leisure.

Coffeehouses, taverns, theatres, and later cinemas became locations of political and cultural threats to public order that seriously challenged Ottoman claims to urban control in Beirut. When a group of French actors was invited by Beirut's thespian community to perform an anticlerical play by the fashionable French author Eugéne Sue, students and staff of the French Medical Faculty in Beirut demolished the theatre in anti-masonic protest before being rounded up and evicted from Beirut.[30] Like theatres, cinemas posed a political threat to Ottoman authority. A little after the incident at the theatre, Beirut's first cinema on Sahat al-Burj showed a film on Moroccan resistance to French occupation. French consular reports warned of 'gallophobe' sentiments in the city and of a cross-Mediterranean conspiracy against the French mission. As a remedy, they suggested setting up pro-French cinemas in Beirut and the Levant to counter the bad influence of the Cinema Pathé which—despite its

[28] Ḍāhir (1986: 118).

[29] PRO, FO, 195/2140, 27 Aug. 1903. Indeed a little earlier, the British consul had complained, 'robbery with violence and murder are fast becoming matters of every day occurrence and . . . native Christians . . . dare not to go about in many parts of the city after dark'. PRO, FO 195/2140, 16 July 1903.

[30] Ismail and Chehab (1979: xviii. 362–5). See also *Lisān al-Ḥāl* (29 Mar. 1911).

French origin[31]—was operated by an Italian, a certain Crisofalli who, in turn, rented his films from Kramer's, a German distributor in Izmir.[32] Before the First World War, French theatre and cinema was well-established.[33] Under the French mandate, cinema continued to flourish on central public squares, especially on Sahat al-Burj, becoming the trendy entertainment for the male elites. They were also, however, the sites of an emerging gender conflict over female access to public space.[34]

An increasingly frequent theme of the night was the danger associated with the burgeoning industrial workforce that operated the city. With the emergence of small- and medium-scale industries, as well as international infrastructural investment sites such as rail and tramway work and factories, professions appeared that typically involved night labour: transport industries, water, gas, and electricity companies, newspaper printing presses, hotels and restaurants, street cleaning, and cellulose factories. In addition, casual construction workers migrated from the surrounding villages in Mount Lebanon to the contractors' collection points on Sahat al-Sur well before the crack of dawn and loitered throughout the day until picked.[35] Together with the traditional maritime industry—the pearl-divers and Druze fishermen along the shoreline of the Zaytuneh quarter—these night-time workers constituted 'the professional strangers of the floating worlds of the periphery'.[36]

The Invisible Cage: Locating Social Evil and Urban Vice

> We don't see in the world a city whose population aspires to work hard like Beirut's.[37]

In the first half of the nineteenth century, European visitors to Beirut had felt secure, particularly as the city was perceived as a sanctuary against the allegedly inherently violent nature of the 'tribes of the Mountain'. To Henri Guys, the Beirutis were a peaceful if simple people, 'their moral qualities have preserved something of their simplicity and their primitive purity'.[38] Missionaries pointed to the vices that tempted the inhabitants at every corner. Whereas before the 'Pasha of Beirut [had] closed the only grogshop', the Protestant missionary Henry Jessup complained that by the turn of the century there were

31 Weber (1986: 173).

32 MAE, Nantes, CEB 1894–1911, Beirut, 19 May 1911. Indeed, the following year a new French cinema of the Société Etablissement Gaumont opened its doors in Beirut. MAE, Nantes, CB 1907–1914, carton 363, Beirut, 16 Nov. 1912.

33 Buhairy (1981: 67).

34 Thompson (2000: 89–111).

35 For a Bonfils photograph of the Sur area entitled 'Labourers waiting for work', see Debbas (1994: 81).

36 Merriman (1991: 208).

37 *Lisān al-Ḥāl* (6 Feb. 1888).

38 Guys (1985: i. 156).

'120 licensed saloons, and Moslems of the two extremes of society, the Turkish civil and military officers and the lowest class of boatmen and artisans, drink as much as the foreign Ionian Greeks, and the native so-called Christian sects'.[39]

Jirjī Zaydān was a public moralist whose autobiography—written for his son in 1909—represents another kind of commentary on the perceived social dangers in Beirut. Born in downtown Beirut in 1861 and educated in the Syrian Protestant College, he left Beirut for Egypt in 1883 to pursue a distinguished career as a journalist. Fear of local knaves was a recurrent theme in his memoirs. His criticism was all the more severe as he was born into a modest family (*mutawassiṭ al-ḥāl*) and came in close contact with the roughs and toughs of Beirut while working in his father's restaurant off Sahat al-Burj. Subsequently he raised himself from his social background through 'hard work', 'perseverance', 'awareness of time', and discipline.[40] Reminiscing about his youth as a restaurant boy, Zaydān complained:

> There remained for company only the idle people who had no work that they enjoyed. These people would gather in my place; some would spend their leisure time during work between morning and evening here. Their talk differed from the talk of crooks only in form and expression: one would boast how he committed adultery taking possession of so-and-so, the wife of the honourable such-and-such . . . Another would show off with his abilities in fornication. Amongst them was a young hunchback whom I heard saying that his hunch was the result of immoderation. . . . Such were the *mores* of the masses of Beirut.[41]

The roughs and toughs of Beirut—or *al-qabadāy*—elicited the young Zaydān's fear and admiration. They were infamous in Beirut for their drinking bouts which 'would be attended by the wise man and the ignorant, because the Beirutis have for a long time believed Araq to be of benefit before the meal and wine with the meal'. Decent people would turn boisterous in the taverns:

> When the wine went to their heads, one would start singing a Baghdadi *mawwal*. They would listen well to his song and would interpret from it something that he wanted from them, be it by way of praise and laudation or criticism and negative comments. It would then behove him or one of his friends or his companions to answer to the *mawwāl*. Provided the singing was done with good humour, the party would take a turn for the better. But if it consisted of criticism and insinuations, it would lead to quarrelling and eventually to the drawing of knives and unsheathing of sticks.[42]

As outspoken public moralists, Buṭrus al-Bustānī and Jirjī Zaydān urged citizens to embrace new opportunities of learning, productivity, and the public good. Bustānī admonished those who wasted their time 'in coffeehouses which

[39] Jessup (1910: ii. 730–1). [40] Philipp (1979: 11). [41] Ibid. 145. [42] Ibid. 146–7.

are filled with youths and grown-ups who frequently visit them in order to kill time during the day and during the night they kill time at home playing dominoes and cards'.[43] Jirjī Zaydān was even more explicit in an answer to a letter to the editor (he probably also penned) which complained that 'in some of your articles on leisure time you consider sitting in a café an ugly habit. We don't understand what is so bad about this activity and those places. What breaches manners and culture?' Zaydān answered:

We are not saying that coffeehouses and their surroundings in public places are a breach of manners. What we have said and are saying is that staying in cafés for days on end is idleness and that this is particularly bad for the young given how difficult is has become to find work these days. After 35 you won't find a job. The chances for the youth are already diminishing after 15. Between 20 and 25 is the best time of life, so why waste it sitting in coffeehouses drinking beer and playing backgammon? It is then that we determine our future and the rest of our life depends on it. You lose time and money if you gamble.[44]

For local merchants, more than for the European travellers and Ottoman bureaucrats, it would appear, 'time is now currency: it is not passed but spent'.[45] City-time and local, merchant work ethic were becoming an invisible cage, fundamentally structuring Beirut's everyday life and measuring productivity and laziness, success and failure.[46]

Fin de siècle Beirut did indeed begin to acquire the reputation of a hard-working city where merchants and literary elites determined that leisure and laziness had no place. Observing the rhythm of the city, the perceptive Egyptian visitor to Beirut, Shaykh Muḥammad ʿAbd al-Jawwād al-Qāyātī, noticed when he resided in Zuqaq al-Blat in 1882 that

the people in this city work from day to night, rushing from their shops to the port, buying and selling . . . Indeed, they have no time for leisure, pleasure and personal passions. They did not revel in nocturnal activities. They are more devoted to socializing with friends and relatives than to get intimate with travelers and foreigners unless official functions like banquets or weddings make it necessary.[47]

The Neighbourhood Riots of 1903

Beirutis' constant fear of subaltern threats to public order and confessional harmony was confirmed tragically in September 1903 when a sectarian vendetta

[43] Buṭrus al-Bustānī [1869], '*al-Hayʾa al-ijtimāʿiyya fī Bayrūt*', in Y. Khūrī (1990: 207). For a more sympathetic and more analytical article on the problem of unemployment, see Aḥmad Fāris al-Shidyāq, 'Fī al-ʿamal wa al-baṭāla', *Kanz al-Gharāʾib fī muntakhabāt al-jawāʾib*, i (Istanbul, 1878), 151–3.

[44] *al-Hilāl* (15 Oct. 1897), 137–8.

[45] E. P. Thompson (1991: 358). See also Julkunen (1977: 5–23).

[46] *The Myth of the Lazy Native* by S. H. Alatas springs to mind. See Said's discussion (2000: 79–101).

[47] al-Qāyātī (1981: 28–9).

nearly caused a small-scale civil war between the lower class residents of the suburban quarters Museitbeh, Basta, and Mazraʿat al-ʿArab. Throughout that summer, 'robbery with violence and murder were fast becoming matters of every day occurrence'.[48] The authorities could do little to bring the situation under control. The municipality was close to insolvent after years of extravagant spending on public construction and the provincial government overwhelmed with combating tobacco and arms smugglers.[49]

At the same time, Christian and Muslim notables grew increasingly alienated from the governor general, Rashīd Bey, whom they accused of bribing palace officials in Istanbul and suspected of being implicated in the ongoing smuggling business south of Beirut.[50] In this atmosphere of mutual resentment and alienation between Ottoman officials and local notables, public security remained extremely fragile in Beirut. While notables joined forces to have Rashīd Bey removed from office, subaltern animosity erupted into open conflict on Beirut's first bloody Sunday of the twentieth century: 6 September 1903.

The spiral of violence had been triggered the previous day when a Muslim inhabitant was shot outside his place in the suburb of Mazraʿa. The next morning, a Muslim group belonging 'mostly to the lower classes, blacksmiths, boatmen, porters, smugglers [and] port loafers' laid an ambush for a group of Greek Orthodox Christians coming out of the parish church in the prosperous mixed quarter of Museitbeh. Allegedly connected to the elusive smuggler barons Khiḍr and Abido Inkidar, they were well-armed, young strongmen who had the audacity—reported the acting British consul in Beirut—to 'look their betters in the face with an insolent provocative stare'.[51]

To the surprise of the assailants and the investigating consular officials, the Greek Orthodox youngsters appeared to expect the attack and returned fire.[52] In what followed, a total of four Greek Orthodox Christians, four Sunni Muslims, and an Ottoman soldier were killed in gun battles across the southern suburbs—'the highest number of deaths in one incident'.[53] Scores of innocent bystanders 'regardless of age or sex' were wounded, houses of 'well-to-do people' were looted and destroyed.[54] By the time the governor general of Syria, Nāẓim Pasha, arrived on 9 September 'to an enthusiastic welcome by a large crowd', the police had the situation under control. However, fear of more violence was less easily quelled than actual violence. Between 15,000 and 20,000

48 PRO, FO, 195/2140, 16 July 1903. 49 Ibid. 5 Aug. 1903.
50 Ibid. 27 Aug. 1903. 51 Ibid. 16 Sept. 1903. 52 Ibid.
53 *al-Hilāl*, 'Bayrūt', 1 Oct. 1903, 9–12; *al-Muqtaṭaf*, 'Bayrut wa ḥawādithuha', 28 Nov. 1903, 902–4.
54 PRO, FO, 195/2140, 16 Sept. 1903.

Christians fled to the mountains in fear of Muslim reprisals and, as a consequence, Rashīd Bey was removed from office by the Porte.[55]

Rare though episodes like this one were in late Ottoman Beirut, it allows a glimpse into the volatile nature of sectarian relations between neighbouring quarters in moments of government crisis. In the case of Mazraʿat al-ʿArab, communal violence dated back—we will recall—to at least the political and territorial ambiguities of the creation of the province of Beirut in early 1888.[56] Revenge was taken collectively against both the members of the suspected community *and* their quarters. In other words, the Sunni vendetta for the Greek Orthodox attack in Mazraʿat al-ʿArab was directed not at the Greek Orthodox confession *per se*—the group could have ransacked wealthy Hayy Sursuq, the Greek Orthodox quarter *par excellence*.

The sectarian clashes of 1903 were likely driven by residential rivalry and professional animosity between Greek Orthodox stone masons from Ras al-Nabaʿ who worked in quarries behind Mazraʿa and Muslim port-workers and stevedores residing in the lower class district of Basta through which the masons passed on their way to and from work.[57] The simmering tensions between lower class Muslims and Greek Orthodox on the southern fringes of the city had previously been contained by effective police presence and by cooperation between the community's elites. In the summer of 1903, however, notables withdrew their support for a discredited provincial government and thereby no doubt precipitated the crisis.

The *post hoc* analysis in *al-Hilāl* of the September violence went as far as to suggest that 'a group of Beiruti notables from the two communities encouraged the criminals'.[58] Ultimately, the crisis was dissolved by cross-confessional negotiations between Sunni and Orthodox notables from the Bayhum and Sursuq families.[59] Their mediation was assisted by Beirut's consular corps and buttressed by the daunting presence of the USS *Brooklyn* in Beirut's harbour. Its commander let it be known—in a statement that eerily prefigured US foreign policy towards the Middle East since—that while the US would not intervene in 'civilized countries, . . . what happened was a cause for military intervention [through] the landing of the blue jackets'.[60]

What is curious about post-conflict moments like these is the ways in which they were worked out in the public domain. In Beirut whose municipality aspired so hard to make it a central and modern place, conflict management

[55] MAE, Nantes, CEB 1912, 11 and 28 Sept. 1903.

[56] Leila Fawaz dates the origins of the Mazraʿa conflict to 1881 when a Christian was stabbed trying to separate feuding Christian and Muslim boys. Fawaz (1983: 114).

[57] Johnson (1986: 19–22).

[58] *al-Hilāl* (1 Oct. 1903), 9–12.

[59] Johnson (1986: 19).

[60] PRO, FO, 195/2140, 7 Sept. 1903.

invariably ushered in a period of soul-searching and a resurfacing of what could be called the intellectual elite's trauma of perceived civilization deficit. Newspapers like *al-Hilāl* in particular led the way. While 'most local journals agreed that fanaticism and Muslim and Christian riff raff conspiring against each other in vendettas were to blame', Jirjī Zaydān's Egypt-based journal held that it was general lack of education and particularly irresponsible behaviour of some unnamed notables who 'set on fire their brains [of the lower classes] with the sciences [*sic*]'. Whether the vague reference to 'the sciences' was meant as an indictment of their revolutionary potential or of scientific racism that swept across the Mediterranean from Europe at the time, the author was acutely aware of the manipulative nature of scientific knowledge.[61]

This furious attack against Beirut's urban leadership was mitigated somewhat by the fact that *al-Hilāl* singled out Hājj Abū Salīm al-Mugharabil as an example of 'genuine nobility'. Mugharabil was credited by residents of Museitbeh for having 'protected Christians during this event as did Amīr ʿAbd al-Qādir in Damascus in 1860'.[62] Significantly, *al-Hilāl* argued that 'the distinction of this man lay not in the products of science, but in the fruits of his instinctive understanding and his good upbringing'.[63] In other words, scientific advancement is worth little—and potentially dangerous—unless it is accompanied by a sense of morality and tolerance—two virtues 'naturally' linked, it was felt, to 'good upbringing'.

But the article contained another layer of cultural criticism. *Al-Hilāl* continued: 'How, then, is the lower class to be blamed?' In fact, the journal argued, 'the rich who is ignorant is much more dangerous for humanity than the ignorant poor'. Zaydān's *al-Hilāl* blamed elite complacency and irresponsibility for Lebanese relapses into violence and insurgence. The only way to overcome harmful ignorance and indeed the perceived civilization deficit was through education and learning.

Policing the City

In his foundational speech *al-hay'a al-ijtimāʿiyya* of 1869, Buṭrus al-Bustānī declared that the highest goal for the city authorities was to provide for safety and happiness.[64] He both cherished and feared the melting pot of different 'races' that was Beirut, as there were constant challenges to the potentially

[61] On the emergence of a scientific discourse of race in the Eastern Mediterranean, see Bayly (2002: 285–309). [62] *al-Hilāl* (1 Oct. 1903), 9–12. [63] Ibid.

[64] Buṭrus al-Bustānī, 'Khitāb fī al-hay'a al-ijtimāʿiyya', excerpted in Y. Khūrī (1990: 206–7).

bright future of the city. As the discourse of security took centre stage in public opinion, imperial legitimacy and municipal accountability came to be strongly equated with the ability of the authorities to maintain law and order. The events of the summer of 1903 led many international observers and local inhabitants to blame the Ottoman authorities. There was a general perception that '[a]ll the violence was encouraged by the lack of an efficient police force'.[65] Public security was, however, a top priority of the Ottoman government which could ill afford such accusations.

By the end of Abdülhamid's reign, twenty-eight *corps de garde* posts—or police stations—were built in the burgeoning neighbourhoods and quarters around the city centre (Map 6). The distribution of these police stations had a profound impact on the location and opening hours of cinemas, cabarets, casinos, taverns, and alcohol shops. Policemen patrolled the streets to ensure that all the taverns and alcohol vending shops which mushroomed in the pericentral quarters of Minet al-Husn, Zaytuneh, and Sahat al-Burj between 1901 and the First World War were closed at sunset.[66] The task of the police was not just to secure public order and collect taxes from these establishments, but also to watch over public morality and check on a myriad of regulations: appropriate dress code, proper parking, storage weights and measures, or alcohol consumption.[67]

The new spatial regularizations were reinforced by police laws and watched over by Ottoman officers and local police units. It is striking that in the old city itself there were no *corps de garde* posts—the nearest ones being on Sahat al-Sur and the port. As for the *corps de garde* post marked on Zuqaq al-Blat (later, Rue Maurice Barrés), close to the Grand Serail, it consisted of two two-storeyed wings with an extensive annex for stables, arranged so as to frame a rectangular courtyard with a well in its centre.[68] Two more *corps de garde* posts were placed on the main arteries east and west along the tramway lines to Nahr Beirut and the lighthouse respectively. But the highest density of Ottoman *corps de garde* were found in the southern, low-class quarters of Sunni Basta, and Bashura, as well as the confessionally mixed quarters of Ras al-Nabaʿ, Museitbeh, and Mazraʿat al-ʿArab near the two southern tramway lines. These quarters were well-known trouble spots where a strong police presence was deemed necessary in order to prevent the recurrence of the 1903 riots.

In terms of maintaining public order and security, the *corps de garde* system was often strained. Sometimes only manned with one guard, the posts tended to be ineffectual in quelling large-scale unrest. The 1903 riots had been sup-

65 Fawaz (1983: 115).
66 MAE, Nantes, CB 1907–1914, carton 363.
67 Young (1906–7: i. 156).
68 Mollenhauer (2002: 275–96).

pressed by only fourteen Ottoman regulars. Occasional prison riots took days to subdue, even if they occurred inside the domineering imperial Grand Serail itself.[69] When three months later 1,400 Ottoman soldiers returning from a military campaign in Yemen passed through Beirut and were kept in the barracks for a medical check up, they staged a mutiny for arrears in their pay in front of the Grand Serail. The police were unable to disperse them and the governor general was forced to give in to their financial demands.[70]

Yet, overall, the period between 1903 and 1908 was one of relative calm and social cohesion. After occasional small-scale eruptions of violence in the bazaars, order was quickly restored by the speedy arrival of patrols. On 9 June 1909 a consular dispatch reported on the first public execution in Beirut in twenty-five years.[71] The French author considered the absence of state violence a sign of inefficiency and corruption on the part of the Ottoman government, but one could, in fact, also read the infrequent use of capital punishment as an indication of Beirut's informal patron–client system and effective elite control over society.[72]

Prostitution: Social Marginality in the Centre

Early in the nineteenth century the promiscuous European traveller had great difficulty in realizing his Orientalist fantasies in Beirut. 'Who would dare to penetrate these fortresses of maternal and paternal power, or rather who would not be tempted to dare? But alas! The adventures here are rarer than in Cairo.'[73] The Parisian literary scene had discovered Beirut in the 1840s and 1850s. The correspondence between Gérard de Nerval, Gustave Flaubert, Maxime du Camp, and Théophile Gautier are replete with lewd references to promiscuity in Cairo, Beirut, and other cities in the Ottoman empire.[74] Camille Rogier (1810–96), an Orientalist painter and director at the French post office in Beirut, was this group's trusted anchor in Beirut. Flaubert, who visited Beirut in 1850, wrote home that 'we have discovered that him and us are of the same band of artists'.[75] After visiting Rogier, de Nerval admitted to the high price of his conquests: 'In Beirut I contracted VII shancres [syphilitic sores].'[76]

Such debauchery was the pinnacle of the bad habits and European vices against which Beirut's public moralists repeatedly warned their fellow citizens. At around the same time that the hotly contested 1884 Victorian Contagious

69 MAE, Paris, NSTSL, vols. 104–5, Beirut, 28 Sept. 1901.

70 MAE, Nantes, CEB 1912, Beirut, 12 Jan. 1904.

71 MAE: Paris, NSSTSL 1908–1914, vol. 428, Beirut, 9 June 1909.

72 See Johnson (1986).

73 Nerval (1884: 82).

74 Pouillon (1990).

75 Gustave Flaubert, quoted in Debbas (2001: 34).

76 Pouillon (1990: 79).

Diseases Act introduced state regulation of sexual vice to London, prostitution came to be viewed as a nocturnal vice and as such a rallying point for urban discourses on morality, hygiene, and state control in Beirut. The frequent displacement of Beirut's brothels from one central quarter to another in the second half of the nineteenth century was very much a reflection of the dynamic growth of this city.

Before the urban expansion of the nineteenth century, the quarters of 'public women', the *sūq al-ʿummūmiyya*, were located around the Khan al-Arwam inside the city walls. Gradually the *sūq* settled in Sayfi on the south-eastern side of Sahat al-Burj. The soldiers of the French expeditionary force in 1860 were such rampant customers that apparently both Beirutis and foreign residents were shocked.[77] After the enlargement of the port of Beirut in 1895, some of the *maisons de tolérance*, the officially licensed brothels, moved to the vicinity of the city's growing administrative and commercial centre. According to a one-time head of the guild of porterage, 'the *sūq*, as it was called since then, established itself in *sūq al-khammāmīr* [the wine sellers' market], between the Petit Serail and the port east of the Muslim cemetery, before it was moved to the quarter of Sayfi in 1913'.[78]

With the return of the French army in 1920 the *maisons de tolérance* moved to an area then popularly known as *warāʾ al-bank* ('behind the bank') or *al-Manshiyya* behind the former Ottoman Bank building just east of Sahat al-Burj. According to the accounts of an old Beiruti, at that time 'the number of prostitutes (*al-mumsāt*) was around 850 Arab women from Syria, Palestine and Lebanon and no less than 400 foreign girls—Greek, Turkish and French'. According to al-Sayyid Sha'bān, the most famous prostitutes were considered great stars who offered their services in public houses that were the property of respected local families such as the Shartūnī, Saʿd, Wakīm, Salīm, Mirʿī, Sinnu, Faḍḥallah, Faraḥ, Ṣaʿb, and—no less—the Greek Orthodox *waqf*.[79]

The majority of prostitutes, however, were social outcasts who had arrived from the outskirts of Beirut where, according to Neale, 'hundreds of boys and girls earned in the silk factories a ready livelihood by working as reelers'.[80] These workplaces were 'manned' in the main by unmarried women, the *ʿamilāt* or *banāt al-karḥāne* ('female workers' or 'girls of the silk spinning mills'). According to Akram Khater's research, by 1890 thousands of unmarried village

[77] I am grateful to Beirut historian May Davie who has shared this information in a private correspondence.

[78] Barūd (1971: 5). At around the same time, the cemetery was destroyed to make way for the development of the expanding port facilities. See also Jabr (2000).

[79] Ibid. French medical journals in the early 1920s put the number of registered prostitutes for all Lebanon at an unconvincingly low 242. See Thompson (1999: 87).

[80] Neale (1851: 209).

women and girls worked in factories away from home on the mountain slopes above Beirut. They were initially sent to earn money in the factories to sustain their families' honour by subsidizing their agricultural revenue in adverse economic conditions. Yet, as the Maronite clergy and the patriarchal system considered female labour immoral in a factory where they would come into contact with men, these women suffered intense social stigmatization.[81] Some of the female workers who—through their occupation—had achieved economic self-sufficiency at the expense of having become unmarriageable left the mountain for the promises of the nearby city.

In Lebanon, the term *karḫāne* survived long after the demise of the silk industry. A *karḫāne* in Beirut became synonymous with 'brothel' while *bint al-karḫāne* was an appellation for a woman of ill-repute.[82] Whether the link between the *banāt al-karḫāne* in the rural silk factories and the urban brothels was actual or metaphorical, it appears that their image in the respective rural and urban societies marginalized them on the grounds of their assumed threat to the moral order. Both types of women were—to borrow the term for working women in nineteenth-century France—*femmes isolées*. The term suggested 'that all such working women were potential prostitutes, inhabiting a marginal and unregulated world in which good order—social, economic, moral, political—was subverted. . . . [T]he ambivalent causality (poverty or bad morals?) was less important than the association itself because there was only one cure for sexual license and that was control.'[83]

In mandate Lebanon and Syria the devastating and traumatic experiences during the First World War severely affected the role and the image of Lebanese women. Hundreds of female orphans and widows were incarcerated in workhouses so as to protect them 'from debauchery, to which poverty "inevitably" led them'.[84] By the time French mandate brought about what Elizabeth Thompson defined as a paternalist welfare state, the causal link between poverty and immorality, once drawn by Bustānī and Zaydān, had entered the repertoire of gendered colonial intervention.

Conclusion

This chapter has connected physical, temporal, and social transformations—the hidden rhythms of urban life and the effects of the conquest of the night. It

[81] Khater (1996: 325–48).

[82] Barūd (1971: 28). I am grateful to Samir Khalaf for pointing out this transposition of meaning. According to the Redhouse Ottoman–English dictionary, in Ottoman Turkish *karḫāne* had already this double meaning of workshop and brothel.

[83] Scott-Wallach (1988: 143).

[84] Thompson (1999: 86).

has examined the production of marginality in Beirut in the context of a city constantly growing and changing. Set in the dynamic conditions of everyday life, a social phenomenon like marginality was produced against its notional opposites—morality and order—through its multiple signifiers, Arabic newspapers and Ottoman institutions. More, the city as a whole became at one and the same time the place and the milieu, the stage and the stake of complex social interactions.

As in other Mediterranean cities, neither local intellectuals nor the Ottoman authorities objected to the vices they so painstakingly identified on 'conservative' grounds. In Zaydān's memoirs, for example, it is noticeable that his objections underlie a sense that deviance was an obstacle to social change rather than change being judged as a cause of that deviance. The mental concepts and the material aspects of morality and marginality were constantly engaging in reciprocal signification in Beirut's expanding urban space where central and marginal places—teeming trade and lewd leisure—refused to be separated and shared the same geography.

Fear and demonization lay at the heart of Beirut's bourgeois project of modernity. The attempts by Europeans, Ottomans, and public moralists to locate the internal enemies of society led to a constant drawing and redrawing of social and cultural boundaries. They were constitutive elements of concept of civility and the multiple civilizing missions in *fin de siècle* Beirut. As Freud reminds us, '[l]iberty of the individual is no gift of civilization'.[85]

[85] Freud (1989: 49).

8

Urban Narratives of Modernity

'The concept of civilization is derived from the city.'[1]

In the modern Arab world '[t]he newspaper is a "second articulation" of the city'.[2] This articulation is not restricted to providing information or establishing an urban mode of communication. Rather

> the press act[s] on the city: at certain times it becomes the city itself. . . . If the paper seeks to be the artful image of the city, it invites the city to incarnate the paper. Tirelessly, it exhorts the city to repeat these ready-made phrases, to resemble these many pictures on each page, to conform to these models of behavior, to remake its universe to these specifications. The exhortation re-echoes in successive readings and group discussions in coffee shops. The junior official begins his day going through the whole bundle, before even tasting his horse bean sandwich. On finishing his day he would not think of going back to his home neighborhood without a periodical, or preferably several, under his arm. Until quite late at night porters, artisans, the people of modest station will solemnly spell out these communications laden with modern power. The city has become information; information rebuilds the city.[3]

Beirut-as-text came into existence with the advent of a vibrant Arabic press in the 1850s and 1860s. Beirut's first regular newspaper, *Ḥadīqat al-Akhbār*, was published in 1858 and dedicated a prominent part of its news coverage to local affairs. As I have argued above, this biweekly paper was instrumental in lobbying for the establishment of a municipal council in the early years. Other newspapers expanded literary activity in Beirut in the following decades. In the course of this book we have encountered a number of them as they intervened in provincial politics, infrastructural development, health issues and municipal affairs. *Al-Jinān*, *Thamarāt al-Funūn*, *al-Muqtaṭaf*, and *Lisān al-Ḥāl* celebrated

[1] Buṭrus al-Bustānī, *Nafīr Sūriyya*, eleventh issue, 22 Apr. 1861, 64; and Aḥmad Fāris al-Shidyāq, 'Fī al-tamaddun', *al-Jawā'ib*, 6 (5 July 1861), 4. Quoted in Shidyāq (2001: 91).

[2] Berque (1978: 14). [3] Ibid. 17, 19.

Beirut's domestic architecture while vociferously continuing the cleansing crusade of their journalistic predecessor *Ḥadīqat al-Akhbār* towards a healthy, open city.

As a medium of mass communication through mass circulation they contributed to raising political awareness of local as well as international events. By way of public readings and discussions of daily issues, this awareness reached anybody who frequented places of banter and gossip, be it while chatting at the barber's shop, in coffeehouses, or, later, on the tramway. In particular, the *baladiyyāt* sections in the local newspapers provided vehicles for the expression of a sense of urban participation in the formation of public opinions and policies. Through their daily recurrence these news sections generated an unpremeditated contagion of urban identity in a shifting environment that reached far beyond the limits of the political and literary elites. Newspapers created a political field which theoretically was accessible to all, although in practice it was selective and discriminative. This discrepancy was most acute in the different intellectual attitudes towards Beirut's old and the new city.

The Old City and the Logic of the Straight Line

> I have never seen anything as bizarre, irregular, and extraordinary as the construction of the Arab city of Beirut; the houses—built in stone—are higher than in any other city of Syria; the vaults, the secret dead-ends, the dark passages, the narrow and winding alleys initially inspire a kind of terror in the traveler who wishes to cross the city [where] every house is shaped like an incaccessible dungeon.[4]

In the 1830s, Beirut's Egyptian planners had limited their urban design initiative to commercial, fiscal, and cosmetic measures. The harbour front was developed, new administrative divisions were created, and a number of extramural streets were paved.[5] The promulgation of new standardized construction laws and urban management directives in the wake of the Ottoman *tanẓīmāt* reforms orchestrated a fundamental restructuring, expansion, and diversification of Beirut's urban space.[6] These laws which applied to Istanbul and the provinces alike were revised and amended throughout the 1860s and 1870s, and it was not until 1883 that they constituted an enforced, reliable, and binding source of reference.

[4] Michaud and Poujoulat (1833: vi. 124). [5] See Ch. 1.

[6] On the urban 'bias' of the early *tanẓīmāt* reforms in general see Yerasimos (1992).

The building code was subsequently translated into Arabic and serialized by Naʿmatallah Nawfal and Niqūla Naqqāsh who made it available to the general public on the pages of *al-Jinān* and other newspapers.[7]

In 1896, the Beiruti municipal engineer Amīn ʿAbd al-Nūr edited the 1883 Ottoman building code. In his introduction, he laid out the benefits of modern urban design:

When cities began to develop and progress and in them rose the sun of science and knowledge, every inhabitant worked to improve and embellish his dwelling place and give freely everything he can in decor and architecture (*handasa*). The improvements of houses developed to the highest degree, but the streets and alleys remained in their natural state of narrowness, twistedness and filthiness that bothered the passers-by and jeopardized urban health. Thus all growth and expansion in the cities stopped completely. It is manifest that civilization and construction are a result of careful planning of roads, squares and buildings for the benefit of the *public*.[8]

ʿAbd al-Nūr expressed the hope that his publication would 'promote public works, enable the municipal departments to carry out their business and make the property owners aware of their rights and duties'.[9] Based on the latest scientific insights, voids between buildings were considered essential 'for the purification of the air, the dispersal of bad smells and the penetration of the light and heat of the sun into the cells in order to prevent them from rotting, especially in streets where high buildings are already constructed on both sides'.[10] This scientific discourse was set in a politicized framework in which public health, social hygiene, and urban pathology were elusive measures of modernity in the eyes of authorities and foreign experts alike. The text anticipated by a year—and thus proved wrong—Dr Benoît Boyer's damning report of the authorities' lack of concern for urban hygiene and geometry.[11]

In the name of 'the common good', the construction law gave the state an unprecedented legal framework for urban intervention and—ultimately—for large-scale expropriation. Such a codification of state power over private ownership by way of naturally ill-defined public interest not only augmented the purview of the state in the city's economic affairs. The text also expounded the virtues of the urban planner's 'logic of the straight line'—a logic which began to transform the city centre physically. The law regulated the width of streets, dividing them into five categories. At the beginning of each street a plate on a wall was to specify its width. Article 5 stipulated that 'private construction is

[7] *al-Jinān*, 14 (1883), 49–53.
[8] ʿAbd al-Nūr (1896: 3; italics added).
[9] ʿAbd al-Nūr (1896: 5).
[10] Ibid. 8.
[11] Boyer (1897). For a discussion of the impact of this text, see Ch. 4.

not allowed near places of worship, the port area, on the coast, in public places and parks. Similarly it was not permitted to transform these places in any way into private property except if the municipal departments deemed it necessary to replace the old constructed locations.' Any renovation or restoration had to be made in the 'original, customary form'. Part 2 of the construction law specified the procedures for street alignment. Before construction work was to begin a profile map and a bird's eye map were to be drawn of the street in question. The file with the maps was then kept at the municipality's registry for general access for fifteen days. The governor had to approve the plans before the municipality could put them into practice. The latter articles of the law were concerned with fire regulations and prevention, unifying the façades of houses facing the street, the norms for raising buildings, permits, fees, and prohibitions on restoration, registration fees, and penal codes.

In ʿAbd al-Nūr's edition, this already very detailed code was further explicated through footnotes in which the engineer made cross-references, applied the legal-normative text to particular situations, gave explanations for a meaning of particular terminology or reasons for seemingly arbitrary rulings. Time and again during the 1890s, the municipality found itself anxiously poised between its task of modernizing the city's infrastructure, applying the rule of municipal law, and its role as protector of the well-being of its population as a whole.

On Suq al-Fashkha

The old city of Beirut became publicly identified as a problem zone as soon as the biweekly newspapers *Lisān al-Ḥāl* and *Thamarāt al-Funūn* appeared in the mid- to late 1870s. In particular Suq al-Fashkha, once one of the centres of Beirut's local economy with its workshops and coffeehouses, came to embody a menace to 'the triad of civilization'[12]—beauty, hygiene, and order—during the Hamidian period of urban reform:

> Our city does not have the benefit of offering sight to beautiful, welcoming markets like the ones in European cities. Its commercial centre evokes [anxiety], and current plans to hasten the matter and to reform Sūq al-Fashkha are laudable. For the space (*aqdām*) suffers from overcrowding and delays in passage. If renovations were to appear between Bab Serail and Bab Idriss it would be more hygienic and aesthetic. For in the city the carriages and ambulant vendors continue [to block the way] from both sides.[13]

[12] Freud (1989: 33, 47).

[13] *Lisān al-Ḥāl* (5 May 1879).

Ten years later and just a few months after the general euphoria over the establishment of the provincial capital of Beirut had subsided, the newspapers took stock of the sobering state of affairs of Beirut's urban fabric. 'Beirut has become the garden of wealth [and] is truly the bride of the East (*ʿarūs al-sharq*). But there are persistent forces that belittle its role and that frustrate its order.' In particular, the lack of order and geometry led to 'crowding and aggression'. Straight streets were advocated because they would generate 'charm, peaceful perambulation and health of the country'.[14] The message was that something needed to be done to Beirut for it to merit its capital status.

Khalīl Sarkīs's publishing house decided to commission ʿAbd al-Nūr's edition of the Ottoman construction law at a time when unambiguous legal definitions had become necessary. Beirut's first major inner-city demolition scheme had just generated protest amongst the affected residents and governor general Ismail Kemal Bey began to tackle the problem of downtown traffic circulation. Much praised for his forceful hands-on approach to the old city, the governor general finally turned Suq al-Fashkha into a traffic 'artery' by widening and aligning the busy east–west connection between Bab Idriss and the Petit Serail.[15]

Backed by imperial rules and procedures, he ordered the alignment of the two parallel luxury market streets perpendicular to Suq al-Fashkha—Suq al-Tawila and Suq al-Jamil—thereby hoping to improve the connection between port, city centre, and Sahat al-Sur. Not only were these 'plots in the middle of the old city probably the most valuable ones in the entire city', Beirut's chamber of commerce had also recently moved to the corner of Suq al-Fashkha and Suq al-Tawila.[16] Nearby, on the fringes of the old city centre, the great khans of Beirut—Anṭūn Bey and Fakhrī Bey, Barbīr, Ḥamzī and Hānī & Raʿad—had emerged between the 1850s and the 1870s. Then, in the 1870s, 1880s, and 1890s, the *wikālas* of the great merchant-cum-notable families, Bustrus, Thābit, Sursuq, Ayyās, Shaqqāl, Aḥdāb, Dimashqiyya, and Zalʿūm, mushroomed around the khans.

Until 1888, the municipality of Beirut and Ottoman authorities had struggled to optimize the port facilities *for* the city centre. With capitalist urbanization, commerce, transport, and communication were conducted around and even *against* the original centre. The part to the south of Suq al-Fashkha continued to exist as a vibrant place of small- and medium-scale commerce and

[14] *Lisān al-Ḥāl* (27 Sep. 1888). [15] *Lisan al-Ḥāl* (9 Dec. 1894).

[16] *Thamarāt al-Funūn* (17 Dec. 1894). According to the British consul, the new Chamber of Commerce opened on 23 June 1887. In PRO, FO, 226/209, 1887, 'Details and History of the Chamber of Commerce.'

FIG. 7. Beirut from the air, 1917

dwelling, but it became perceived as an obstacle to the exigencies of traffic and the logic of the straight line.

The issue of compensation caused the implementation of the street alignment project to be stalled temporarily. This led the British consul general to speculate, 'maybe the ill-feelings on the part of some Muslims caused the removal of the *vālī*'.[17] But after Ismail Kemal Bey's premature recall to Istanbul, his successor, Khālid Bey Bābān, resumed and delegated construction works to the municipality. In 1894, the municipality decided that the streets would be widened from an average of seven to twenty *dhirāʿ* (5.25 to 15 m.) 'beginning at the coast (*sahl al-baḥr*) and finishing on Sahat al-Sur and running past the new municipality building, and from the *wikāla* Tuwayni and Sursuq in the north to Bab Idriss' in the west.[18] In the process, a number of markets were to be pierced and flattened, most notably the 'lower vegetable market' and parts of the blacksmiths' market. To this effect 'the municipality commissioned

[17] PRO, FO, 195/1761, Beirut, 2 Aug. 1892.

[18] *Thamarāt al-Funūn* (5 Mar. 1894).

the drawing of a map of the two large streets . . . decided to inform the inhabitants and to set up a committee to assess the appropriation of property' in accordance with article 12 of the building code.[19]

Such measures failed to appease the affected residents. Instead, they staged desperate protests against the governor general, claiming the compensation scheme in no way made up for the expulsion from their livelihood. When it transpired shortly afterwards that 'governor general Khālid Bey had made mistakes in the assessment of the widening of the streets' he was duly recalled to Istanbul.[20] Like his predecessor, he was unable to reach an equitable agreement with the residents. Khālid Bey's successor, Naṣṣūḥī Bey, appointed a committee of local notables to look into the dispute between the residents and the municipality.[21] They agreed that the only way to come to a solution in this conflict was to increase taxation on certain goods, and to hold the foreign community accountable, in particular the investment companies which benefited most from the effects of these urban renewal measures.

Although the new streets were officially opened amid public celebration in Bab Idriss in May 1894, the financial aspects of the construction remained unclear, and they were to haunt municipal politics throughout the mid-1890s.[22] In 1893, rumours circulated in Beirut's press that the project would be co-sponsored by a foreign 'financial company' which would share the expenses with the adjacent house owners whose property value rose.[23] No names were mentioned but during further demolition work in 1896, open confrontation erupted between de Perthuis and his port company on the one hand and the municipality and the local press on the other.

When de Perthuis issued a company statement pleading his company's exemption from the costs of the demolition, construction, and paving, on the grounds that it had already contributed enough to the city's welfare,[24] *al-Bashīr* and *Thamarāt al-Funūn* joined forces and ran articles that demanded that the port company shoulder its share of the costs: 'We had hoped that the port company was there for public benefit' and that 'the port company had promised assistance worth 100,000 francs or more'.[25] It is unclear whether the company yielded to these popular press demands but it appears that the municipality was forced to raise taxes in order to meet the legal and financial obligations *vis-à-vis* its constituency claiming reimbursement.

[19] *Thamarāt al-Funūn* (4 Apr. 1894). [20] *Thamarāt al-Funūn* (17 Dec. 1894).

[21] *Thamarāt al-Funūn* (13 May 1895). The committee included the mufti, the *naqīb al-ashrāf*, the municipal president Muḥammad Bayhum and the members Muḥyī al-Dīn al-Qāḍī, Nakhla Bustrus, Jibrān Tuwaynī, Ḥabīb Ṭrād, the secretary Yūsuf Aramān, and the engineer Yūsuf Aftimos.

[22] *Thamarāt al-Funūn* (21 May 1894). [23] *Thamarāt al-Funūn* (4 Oct. 1893).

[24] Quoted in *Thamarāt al-Funūn* (30 Mar. 1896). [25] *Thamarāt al-Funūn* (22 Apr. 1896).

Capitalist pressures notwithstanding, the old city of Beirut was not transformed into a colonial bridgehead, a fate that beset many other Mediterranean port-cities at the time. This episode signalled to the de Perthuis family that they had outstayed their welcome. Three years later, they packed their bags. After having dominated entrepreneurship in Beirut for forty years they put their three residences in the consuls' quarter and in Mount Lebanon up for sale.[26]

Beirut avoided the urban colonialism that so virulently partitioned North African cities in part because of the provincial scale of the economy and in part because municipal resistance was based on popular legitimacy. Devolution of power to the provincial and urban levels in Ottoman cities allowed local notables a significant measure of agency that colonial cities lacked. Although the old centre was spared complete hollowing out and deliberate erosion, more subtle shifts did take place. The modern markets and office buildings built from the 1880s onwards migrated to the fringes of the old city where the ramparts had fallen into disuse and left a relatively wide strip of undeveloped real estate. Often integrating old columns and stonework into the new structures, the Suq Sursuq off Sahat al-Burj or the elegant market streets on the western edge of the old town were marked by a high degree of symmetric urban design.[27]

Significantly, this relatively 'organic' gravitational shift in downtown development gave way to wartime expedience when local decision-making was severely restricted during the First World War. With the collusion of some of the city's speculating businessmen, the governor general ʿAzmī Bey ordered the destruction of the large sections of the old city in 1915 (see Figure 7). In what was part of a wider street-piercing campaign in the old towns of Aleppo, Damascus, Beirut, Jerusalem, and Jaffa, residents were forced to cede as much of their land as was deemed necessary to achieve the standard-size width of the street.[28] In cases where houses had to be partly or fully demolished, their value was estimated and the proprietor received a promissory note, or municipal bond.

This scheme was designed so that the municipality had an option on buying out the displaced without much cash flow being incurred. However, it also had the effect of creating a demand for the shares by the property speculators who, Ruppin implied, found it financially attractive to buy 'those plots the municipality acquired in this way . . . at municipal auctions', or to buy out the shares of the pressured owners directly. Thus, when the French took over Beirut in

[26] *Lisān al-Ḥāl* (30 Mar. 1903). The paper gives a detailed description of one of the properties on Hamidiye Street (later Rue Clemenceau).

[27] Ruppert (1969: 362–78).

[28] Ruppin (1917: 517–21).

1920, they found a half-destroyed old city and a speculative real estate market before them—ideal conditions to put into practice the latest fashions of urban design. Indeed, much of the colonial confection around Place d'Étoile that today marks Solidere's showcase for urban preservation is mandate architecture on land razed under the Ottomans.

Arthur Ruppin, the 'real estate agent' on a mission for the Zionist Fund, considered this method 'very successful because it enabled the cities—despite the cash shortage—to execute major and expensive urban development schemes, without damaging private interests unnecessarily'.[29] When adopted by the Zionists themselves, such a scheme was even more successful because during the mandate they could largely dispense with the bonds when Palestine was sold plot by plot by absentee landowners and intimidated peasants.

New City: Inscribing the *naḥḍa* into the Urban Fabric

While the old city was a constant source of anxiety and physical intervention, the new quarters of Beirut epitomized everything the city centre was not. 'Spacious', 'breezy', and 'lofty', Ashrafiyya in the east—where 'nothing was left but to soap the soap'[30]—Zuqaq al-Blat in the south, and Ras Beirut in the west, were the antitheses of the old city and imagined as beacons of enlightened urbanity. In Chapter 6 I argued that the quarter of Zuqaq al-Blat became the birthplace of Beirut's educational revolution after the civil war of 1860. Just south of the Grand Serail on Qantari hill, this new quarter also became the home of a host of municipal protagonists and public moralists who we have already encountered in the course of this study. The atmosphere of the quarter also attracted wealthy merchants to move out of the old city and who, by way of their lavishly designed mansions, came to be identified regionally as Beirut's 'aristocratic class'.[31]

The literary elites of Beirut were aware of their surroundings and regularly commented on the beauty of the houses at nightly socials. Architectural eulogies—both tongue in cheek and honestly exuberant—were rendered in honour of a guest or spontaneously made up as teasing allegories for the political power of the house owners in question. Few such poems have been passed on, let alone published. Some literary examples of poetry on the city's domestic architecture insinuate the intimate connection between the intellectual and

[29] Ruppin (1917: 518). [30] Philipp (1979: 133). [31] al-Qāyātī (1981: 13).

the physical levels of the production of space in *fin de siècle* Beirut. They also illustrate the aesthetic consciousness as much as the sense of humour that ruled the hedonists among the intellectual elites. One of the most magnificent houses in suburban Beirut belonged to Muḥammad Bayhum, municipal president between 1892 and 1894. It inspired a poem by Shākir al-Khūrī in the popular *qaṣīda* metre:

You possess a house the hearts desire	you have a heart that knows no vice
Never sets the sun upon your house	for your noble character knows no price
Emerging from your place in Ras Beirut	you are the literary head of all Beirut.[32]

If Muḥammad Bayhum's was the supreme house in all of Ras Beirut at the time, Ibrāhīm al-Yāzijī proclaimed—with neighbourhood pride reverberating—the mansion of Yūsuf Judāy, the wealthy Zuqaq al-Blat merchant and municipal member, as 'the most beautiful house in the Syrian lands' (see Figure 8).[33] This particular house had already entered the annals of the popular neo-*adāb* poetry shortly after it was built, when Ibrāhīm's father Naṣīf al-Yāzijī dedicated these verses to his new neighbour in 1862:

For Yūsuf al-Judāy was built today	a blessed house in which happiness roams
Nightingales of revelry sing nearby	and stars of fortune proudly rise in its heights
Uniquely built in the regions of the East	a unique soul who enjoys its merry nights
For me writing its history I pray for him	May God protect the house and its builder.[34]

Yaziji's affiliation with this mansion, where consecutive governors of Mount Lebanon resided, did not stop at the descriptive level. Yūsuf Judāy commissioned him to physically inscribe his poetry into the house as part of the luxurious interior decoration. Yāzijī's nineteen-verse *qaṣīda* was etched in golden ink as a frieze decoration around the high walls of the central hall. Nowhere was the semiotic nexus between the representation of space and the space of representation more intimate than in this incident.

[32] S. al-Khūrī (1992: 492). The play on the Arabic word *ra's*, head, and Ras Beirut is lost in translation.

[33] Yazbak, 'Yawm buniyat al-jāmi'a al-amrīkiyya bayna al-wawāya' (1955: i. 119). The Judāy family had Greek Orthodox and Catholic branches, and descended from a small but long-established family in Beirut. Some members of the family emigrated to Egypt at the end of the 19th century. For more biographical details on Yūsuf Judāy and the Beiruti intellectuals discussed in this chapter, see Hanssen (D.Phil. thesis, 2001: Annex).

[34] al-Yāzijī (1983: 290–1).

FIG. 8. The mansion of Yūsuf Judāy in Zuqaq al-Blat

Other 'aristocratic' central-hall mansions in Zuqaq al-Blat also used—to great effect—the architecture of their mansions to display and, indeed, stage their social status.[35] Multi-arched galleries like the al-Khūrī mansion in upper Zuqaq al-Blat had a commanding view over Beirut, the blue Mediterranean, and the snow-capped Mount Sanin in the background. While elaborate turrets distinguished the Sursuq quarter east of Sahat al-Burj, the quest for verticality also defined the domestic architecture in Zuqaq al-Blat and Museitbeh. The medieval-style Farʿūn palace and the villa of Mukhayyish were both completed around 1898.

The residence of Amīn Pasha Mukhayyish is the only physical reminder of Zuqaq al-Blat's late nineteenth-century history as a hotbed of freemasonry. An international textile merchant who was also a prominent Muslim member of the provincial council, he crowned his mansion's entrance with a collage of the symbol of a freemasons' lodge (a shining triangle with a star in its centre) and the Ottoman emblem of half-moon and star.[36] Likewise, neither the

[35] On the urban and architectural development of Zuqaq al-Blat, see Bodenstein *et al.* (2005).
[36] Mollenhauer (2002: 275–96).

impressive residence of Salīm Salām, nor the double-winged *qaṣr* of Marquis Mūsā de Frayj had merely aesthetic value. These urban villas and bourgeois palaces self-consciously expressed political purpose and elite perceptions. Large sections of these houses were designated as servants and staff quarters, which suggests either large families in residence or frequent and large social functions—or both.

On the occasion of the birth of his son in November 1889, the Marquis de Frayj put the latest gas-lighting techniques to great effect. In a spectacle of light and fireworks, he illuminated the ornate architecture of his residence. For those excluded from this 'luxuriant party [for some] 250 guests from amongst the elites (*zawāt*, *aʿyān* and *kubār*) of our city [where] leisurely play was performed, reforms of our customs and morals and the revival of the city's monuments was talked about', Khalīl Sarkīs, de Frayj's neighbour, gave a guided tour in his *Lisān al-Ḥāl*: 'akin to a celestial tower, beaming gas lights and torches were glowing. The courtyard, gardens, staircases and the rooms were decorated with a variety of lights surrounded by aromatics and flowers'.[37]

In Zuqaq al-Blat, the municipal members Ḥusayn Bayhum, Mūsā de Frayj, and Muḥammad Saʿīd Bey Mukhayyish also enjoyed the company of similarly successful journalists like *Lisān al-Ḥāl*'s Khalīl Sarkīs or French doctors at the Jesuit Medical Faculty, such as de Brun and Calmette. Municipal presidents like *Thamarāt al-Funūn*'s editor in chief ʿAbd al-Qādir al-Qabbānī, and Muḥyī al-Dīn Ḥamāda kept Zuqaq al-Blat at the heart of urban politics for decades. In terms of wealth per quarter, Zuqaq al-Blat was probably second only to the predominantly Greek Orthodox quarter of Jummayza/Mar Niqula where the mansions of the inter-married families of the Sursuqs, Bustrus, Ṭrāds, Tuwaynīs, Fayyāḍs and Dāghirs formed an exclusive network of merchants and rentiers around which other well-to-do Christian families grouped themselves.[38]

Jummayza/Mar Niqula's confessional homogeneity and exclusivity was exceptional for *fin de siècle* Beirut. On the whole, urban quarters and neighbourhoods were socially and confessionally mixed. To be sure, the wealthy houses of Jummayza and Zuqaq al-Blat were a world apart from insurgent Mazraʿa, Ras al-Nabaʿ, or Basta, although physically they were within walking distance. By the end of the Hamidian era, the city of Beirut became differentiated discursively and spatially between the old and the new city, wealth and poverty, morality and marginality, health and disease.

[37] *Lisān al-Ḥāl* (2 Dec. 1889).

[38] Kamel-Salameh (1998), Davie (1994: 99–111).

Markazuna: The Transformation of Beirut in the Eyes of the *nahḍa*

The most preferred and the highest form of accomplishment can only be achieved in a city—not in the smaller units of community. The truly good can only be achieved through choice and free will. However, as the same also counts for evil, it is possible that the city, too, supports itself in the attainment of evil. A city where happiness can be attained is one in which mutual support is directed towards that through which one reaches the common good of integrity. This is called a virtuous city.[39]

In Bilad al-Sham the image of the modern city was central to the two broad strands of the Arab cultural revival (*al-nahḍa al-ʿarabiyya*) of the late nineteenth century: secular renewal and religious reformism.[40] The Tripoli-born journalist and essayist Faraḥ Anṭūn (1874–1922) whose intellectual dispute with Muḥammad ʿAbdūh over the interpretation of the philosophy of Averroes (Ibn Rushd) polarized the newspapers of the day,[41] incorporated both these strands into his utopian works of fiction. Both *al-Dīn wa al-ʿilm wa al-māl; aw al-mudun al-thalāth* (Alexandria, 1903) and *Urushālim al-jadīda aw fataḥa al-ʿarab Bayt al-Maqaddis* (Alexandria, 1904) were critical commentaries on modern Arab society.[42] The enigmatic title *New Jerusalem; or the Conquest of the Arab Holy City* [*Jerusalem*], conjures up images of both celestial 'New Jerusalem' and the modern Jerusalem of historical renewal, *al-tajdīd*, 'the former being the archetype of the latter'.[43] *Religion, Science and Money; or the Three Cities* is set in an imaginary *fin de siècle* world split into three rival cities—Religion, Science, and Money—which had completely destroyed each other in war. The protagonist struggles to reconstruct them into a united organism superior in organization and harmony even to the city out of which they had emerged originally.[44]

In the context of the Ottoman empire, Faraḥ Anṭūn's urban perception differed fundamentally from previous urban biographies, such as Mikha'īl Burayk and Aḥmad Buḍayrī on eighteenth-century Damascus, or Faḍlallah Ḥalabī on early nineteenth-century Baghdad and Aleppo. Whereas their accounts had been chronicles of proud, urban pasts, Faraḥ Anṭūn's work projects his ideal city into the future. Much like Giambattista Vico's *The New Science*, Anṭūn's ideal society was not created by God, but it was built on secular

[39] Abū Naṣr al-Farābī (*c*.950), *Der Musterstaat von Alfarabi*, tr. and ed. Dieterici (1900: 85–6).
[40] See Sharabi (1970). [41] Hourani (1984: 255–9). [42] Anṭūn (1979: 43–88, 149–308).
[43] Ben Lagha (1999: 556). [44] Deheuvels (1999: 402–33).

'self-making'—as Edward Said has called Vico's project—the desire and ability to perfect the human condition.[45]

In Anṭūn's literary discourse the absolute space of the sacred city, the historical space of the secular, political city, and the abstract space of capitalism are engaged in a constant struggle.[46] Similar to Thomas More's *Utopia*, Vico's *The New Science*, Francis Bacon's *New Atlantis*, and—if read through a nineteenth-century bourgeois lens—al-Farābī's much earlier *City Virtuous*, Anṭūn's urban utopias were no mere fantasy but meant as proscriptive commentaries on pressing social issues such as the civil strife in Mount Lebanon and human struggle in general.

The urban writings of Beirut's literati were neither merely a reflection of the banality of lived reality nor of the colonial contempt in which imperial bureaucrats and Ottoman literary elites would hold distant provincial capitals like Baghdad or Sanʿa.[47] Rather, in their poems, essays, and editorials, literary imagination actively intervened in the process of the multiple production of urban space. They posited modern Beirut as the attainable utopia—the city hopeful—that would unify a war-torn country. In the three decades after the civil war in Mount Lebanon, Beirut became both the physical embodiment and the vision of modernity upon which the city authorities based the physical transformation of provincial capital urbanism in the 1890s and 1900s. Thus the urban development of Beirut emerged not only as the effect of Ottoman rule, but also fundamentally as the concerted effect of local, cultural production.

In the course of the nineteenth century the burgeoning city of Beirut inspired poets in Beirut, Istanbul, and Cairo. *Ḥadīqat al-Akhbār*, *al-Jawāʾib*, and *al-Muqtaṭaf* intermittently published homages to Beirut.[48] Internationally, Beirut's most famous urban epithet is probably Emperor William II's expression: 'The jewel in the crown of the Padisha'.[49] Local *qaṣīda*s endowed Beirut with ornamental epithets, like 'the cherished' (*al-maḥrūsa*), the 'bride of the sea' (*ʿarūs al-baḥr*), or 'the flower' (*al-zahra*). They suggest not only an emotional identification with the city—a particular pride of place—but also that it was very much present in the 'writerly' imagination.[50] Such 'urban *madīḥ*s' that extol Beirut's 'blessed geography', 'the splendid views', and 'the rich history',

[45] Said (2001: 78). [46] Lefebvre (2003).

[47] Herzog (2002: 311–28) and Kühn (2002: 329–48).

[48] e.g. Ḥusayn Bayhum, *Ḥadīqat al-Akhbār* (8 Nov. 1860), ʿAbd al-Raḥmān al-Naḥḥās, Beirut's *naqīb al-ashrāf*, in *Kanz al-raghāʾib fī muntaḥabbāt al-jawāʾib 3* (1878), and Rizqallah Ḥaddād's 'Bayrūt wa manāẓiruha', *al-Muqtaṭaf* (June 1896), 424–6. [49] Sarkīs (1997).

[50] The fact that other cities in the 19th-cent. Middle East were also given such epithets by their inhabitants does not detract from the argument. On the contrary, *maḥrūsa* was also the adjective used for the Ottoman Empire, *memālīk-i maḥrūse*.

constitute, in the terms of Raymond Williams, an essential ingredient of the production of difference between city and countryside whereby the city was viewed as the product of enlightened spatial practices and the countryside as unrefined pre-modernity.[51]

In al-Bustānī's *al-hay'a al-ijtimāʿiyya* essay, which literally translates into 'on social structure', the author laid out what he called the needs of Beirut society as follows: 'Beirut is the place of our residence and our homeland (*waṭan*). It is one of the links in that great chain [of harmony among the human race] and as the centre of this chain it is vital for us—for Syria, our country—because it is the connecting element between our country's soul, between itself and foreign countries.' In contrast to the urgent and emotional appeals to his compatriots in *Nafīr Sūriyya* just after the civil war, this speech was far more optimistic. Beirut has emerged once again as a place where people of different origins, Easterners and Westerners, mix and mingle. 'They may differ in race and taste but they share the same values, especially commercial, urban and cultural.' He conceded that 'riff raff' continued to 'contaminate the cleanliness of their country or the streets of their city' but, on the whole, 'healthy ties and harmony between the rest of the fellow countrymen and the foreigners' ensure that the situation could be improved. After all, he concluded, 'the majority of Beirut's population are civilized and their affection is entirely directed and inclined towards civilization'.[52]

Bustānī had a premonition that the city could once again become the site of 'barbarity' but he draws his optimism for the future of Beirut from the progress already made in the general project of 'establishing a civilized people'. In his world, the subaltern was illegitimate, poorer inhabitants were 'riff-raff' and had no place in a civilized city. Bustānī's 1870 Arabic dictionary *Muḥīṭ al-Muḥīṭ* extends the idea of Beirut's society as bearing a normative, civilizing mission to cities in general. The entry of the verbal noun *tamaddun* from the root *m-d-n* (inhabit, settle, dwell), is defined as the process whereby 'man is molded into people of cities (*ahl al-mudun*) by morals (*akhlāq*) and [the cities] move them [the people] from a state of barbarity and ignorance to a state of human sociality and refined learning'.[53]

Such bourgeois self-perception was to set the tone for thinking about *fin de siècle* Beirut. In the 1870s the Bustānīs introduced a new style of writing about Beirut in particular through their bi-monthly *al-Jinān* (1870–85). Unlike previous historical writings on the city, such as Buṭrus al-Bustānī's 'On the city of

[51] Williams (1973: 142–214).

[52] Buṭrus al-Bustānī, 'Khiṭṭāb fī al-hay'a al-ijtimāʿiyya', excerpted in Y. Khūrī (1990: 206–7).

[53] Buṭrus al-Bustānī, *Muḥīṭ al-Muḥīṭ*, i (Beirut, 1870), 843.

Beirut' (*c.*1850) which presented knowledge of Beirut's Ottoman past in dynamic cycles of prosperity and deterioration, *al-Jinān* began to ascribe to Beirut a particular geographical role and systematically mapped out the city's future.[54] In *al-Jinān*, three editorials by Salīm al-Bustānī stand out: 'Markazuna' ('Our Centre', 1872), 'Asbāb taqaddum Bayrūt wa numūwuha al-sarī'' ('The Reasons for Beirut's Rapid Progress and Growth', 1884), and shortly afterwards 'Madīnat Bayrūt wa iḥtiyājātuha' ('The City of Beirut and its Needs', 1884).

In 'Markazuna', Beirut's geographical centrality emerges through its natural and cultural position between Egypt and Istanbul and between Europe and India. Using expressive metaphors, Bustānī outlines Beirut's multiple future roles. As *al-bāb* ('the gate'), Beirut's 'natural strength' lay in the ways in which it centripetally absorbed the qualities of the worlds around it: trade and agriculture.[55] Mount Lebanon and the agricultural hinterland are ascribed the role of *al-batn* ('the interior'). Bustānī realized that in this geo-economic division of labour, the mountain and its ravines suffered most from the recent recession, but they are also the places where 'bedouins' and 'thieves' carry out attacks against the achievements of the centre and its lines of communication and transport. In contrast, the city is the place of 'steam and the telegraph'. He asserted that 'our centre commands two strengths, the agricultural and the commercial. The first rests on hard work and cultivation while the second thrives on connecting the East with the West in a way that corresponds to this age.'

In this division of labour the Ottoman state was seen as the regulator and arbitrator between the function of the gate and the hinterland—*al-bāb* and *al-baṭn*. 'Our Centre', Bustānī argued, requires

> moral security which is established through laws and regulations [by the Ottoman state]. . . . For the spirit of the [imperial] nation [*al-umma*] and the strength of its enterprise are responsible for the establishment of moral security inside and outside because the strength to implement laws and regulations prevents dangers . . . and facilitates unity between knowledge and wealth.

In 'Reasons for Beirut's Rapid Progress and Growth', Salīm Bustānī returns to the theme of Beirut's centrality as a product of economic practices in a world that had moved ever closer together through scientific discoveries and technological inventions. His style became more prescriptive as he urged his compatriots to embrace the present and 'open up' to the opportunities of modernity. It would be unwise to 'preserve the old' and pray that 'if only [change] would

[54] Buṭrus al-Bustānī, 'Fī madīnat Bayrūt', in Y. Khūrī (1990: 71–2).

[55] Salīm al-Bustānī, 'Markazuna', *al-Jinān*, 3 (1872) 145, in S. al-Bustānī (1990: i. 207–8).

remain alien to us', much as it would be loathsome for truly intelligent people (*ahl al-madārik*) to imitate superficially (i.e. materialistically) the habits and fads from the West.[56] He stresses that a blessed geographical position and good fortune in trade are not enough for sustained growth. The population of Beirut, he admitted, had obtained a bad reputation in the region for their profiteering and conspicuous consumption. However, these 'arrows of blame' were unjustified. Beirut's 'immense growth—if it was based on trade [alone]—would scare us for its consequences. Over time, the profits would decrease if not run into serious losses:'

A multitude and abundance of ways in which cotton is produced and around one thousand workers in its factories who process silk, 500 shops which manufacture [goods], not to speak of the carpenters, the blacksmiths, the tailors, the goldsmiths and the tanners . . . make sure that the city's industry achieves an annual [trade surplus] between 160,000 and 180,000 lira.

Clearly Beirut's men of letters were working hard to disarm the city's critics. Long-term prosperity lay in things profounder than material wealth, however. Beirut did have the right to be proud of its achievements in the field of industry and learning:

The situation and the courage of its people and their addiction to literary and material gains enable them to turn a place that only forty years ago was a sizeable village into a city in its own right (*madīnat dhāt sha'niha*). It became the school for a vast part of the Asian regions instructing knowledge (*ma'ārif*) and industry thanks to being the treasury of Syria and Palestine. The reason for the growth of this city lies with the acquisition of knowledge (*ma'ārif*) and industry that changed its people. If we considered what more than 1,000 foreign (*ghurabā'*) students spend in it, school fees, recreational expenditures, clothes, transport, the expenses of their parents or guardians together with the expenses of the religious host establishments by means of instructing the youngsters and dressing them and what they spend for spreading education (*ma'ārif*) and religious learning (*'ilm*) due to the seven or eight printing presses, the newspapers, books, hospitals etc. In one year we have an income from education between 100,000 and 120,000 lira.[57]

Salīm Bustānī's economic model put cultural capital at the centre: as 'a city in its own right' Beirut's accumulation of wealth allowed investment in cultural capital (education, newspapers, medicine) which in turn generated and diversified new sources of urban wealth. The acquisition of knowledge thus provided a sense of urban self and a 'solid foundation' in order to deal with

[56] Salīm al-Bustānī, 'Asbāb taqaddum Bayrūt wa numuwuha al-sarī',' *al-Jinān*, 15 (1884), 449–51, in S. al-Bustānī (1990: ii. 725–7). [57] Ibid.

'what continuous construction and consumption Beirut has witnessed'.[58] A few months later in 'The City of Beirut and its Needs', Salīm Bustānī expanded his urban scenario and tackled the dangers which urban health hazards posed for a prosperous future.[59] Stagnant water and open sewage 'running down the slopes of Beirut' attract mosquitoes and germs, and spread diseases and infections, especially in the hot months of summer. Taking Alexandria as an example where 'the summers are six to ten degrees hotter', he argued that climatic conditions can be overcome by modern planning measures—street paving, air circulation, water canalization and street cleaning. He called for 'temporary taxes on land, meat and [fruit]' and appealed to the wealthy merchants 'who are used to giving freely to improve urban order' to raise the necessary '15,000 lira to restore health and security'. Projecting into the future, Bustānī listed Beirut's four basic 'needs': affordable food prices, tighter food controls and selling regulations to avoid disease, improvement of the means of transport and movement on and off-shore, and the support of its inhabitants, especially the notables and intellectuals, in order to enrich the place with means of leisure and pleasure.[60]

The Beirut of the *nahḍa* relished metaphorical spaces such as the commercial 'Gate of the East that opened the agri- and sericultural interior to the West. Economically, Salīm Bustānī saw Beirut's future very much as a commercial bridgehead.[61] But his Beirut *al-maḥrūsa* emerged as more than just a regional economic powerhouse facilitating export trade. In order to fully understand the signs of the times, Beirut needed economic diversification, education, industry, and construction activity. In the eyes of its literary elite, Beirut stood for progress, for culture in the sense of cultivation and social refinement. The city's cultural and intellectual capital matched the annual revenues of its exported manufactures. Also, as the 'strategic' place of teaching and publishing, knowledge and medicine, Beirut appears to have attracted great journalistic attention precisely because it was constantly perceived as being under threat either from negligence or mismanagement by the authorities, negative foreign influence, rivalry from other towns, like Haifa and Damascus, and by the alleged ignorance of its own population.

[58] Salīm al-Bustānī, 'Asbāb taqaddum Bayrūt wa numuwuha al-sarī'', *al-Jinān*.

[59] Salīm al-Bustanī, 'Madīnat Bayrūt wa iḥtiyājātuha', *al-Jinān*, 15 (1884), 381–3, republished in S. al-Bustānī (1990: ii. 727–9). [60] Ibid. 728.

[61] For a critical assessment of the 'commercial bridgehead' interpretation of this article, see Fawaz Trabulsi, 'Salīm al-Bustānī fī nass ta'sīsī: "al-bāb" wa "al-batn" suratānī li-dawr Lubnān al-iqtiṣādī,' *Mulḥaq al-nahār*, (11 Jan. 1997).

Rebellious Spirits

This patent 'urban bias' espoused by the leading personalities of Beirut's literary movement fed the dominant discourse of modernity and progress for much of the second half of the nineteenth century. However, in 1908, a young poet shook Beirut's literary world from his exile in New York. Jibrān Khalīl Jibrān (1883–1931) was born in Bisharreh, a Maronite town in the northern mountains of Lebanon. He emigrated to the United States aged 11 and was to become a celebrated romantic poet and symbolist artist in Boston and New York. Before he was to make his literary mark on Arab-American culture, however, he returned to Beirut in 1898 where he spent three years in the renowned Collège La Sagesse—*madrasa al-ḥikma*. More a visiting student from abroad than a full-time student, he was given free rein to study Arabic literature and French language.

In his 1908 collection of short stories entitled *al-Arwāḥ al-mutamarrida* ('Spirits Rebellious') Khalīl Jibrān reflected on these formative yeas. He reiterated the programmatic opposition to arranged marriage that so defined his earlier collection, *al-Ajniḥa al-mutakassira* ('Broken Wings', written in 1906).[62] *Spirits Rebellious* is set more concretely in Beirut as he exposed the double standards of its *al-khāṣṣa* class. In the first story of *Spirits Rebellious*, the protagonist Warda al-Hānī, a Tolstoyan adulteress who had left the pretensions of Beirut's well-born families and found comfort in the simplicity and honesty of the countryside, takes the narrator to the edge of the city:

> Look towards those fine dwellings and noble mansions, that is where the rich and the powerful of human kind are living. . . . Between the walls hung with woven silk lives treachery with hypocrisy . . . and beneath ceilings of beaten gold stay lies and falseness. They are plaster tombs where a weak woman's deceit takes refuge behind the mascara of her eyes and the reddening of her lips; in whose corners are hidden the selfishness and brutality of a man behind the glitter of gold and silver. These are the places that raise high their walls in pride and splendor; yet could they feel the breath of trickery and deceit breathing over them, they would crack and fall to the ground. These are the houses to which the poor villager looks with tear-filled eyes, yet did he but know that in the hearts of their dwellers was not one grain of love and sweetness that filled the heart of his companion, he would smile in scorn and go back to his field with pity. . . .
>
> Come, I show you the secrets of these people whom I did not wish to be like. Look at that palace with the marble columns. In it lives a rich man who inherited the wealth of his avaricious father and learnt his way in corruption-infested streets. Two years ago he wed a woman of whom he knew little save that her father was of noble line and high

[62] Ostle (1992: 82–131).

> standing among the aristocracy of the town. Their honeymoon was hardly ended before he tired of her and went back to the companionship of women of pleasure and left her in that palace as a drunkard leaves an empty jar. At first she wept in her agony; then she took patience and consoled herself as one who admits an error. She learned that her tears were too precious to shed upon a man such as her husband. Now she busies herself with the passion of a young man with a handsome face and a sweet tongue into whose hands she pours her heart's love and whose pockets she fills with her husband's gold. . . .
>
> Those are the places wherein I do not wish to live. Those are the graves in which I do not want to be buried alive. Those people from whose ways I freed myself and whose yoke I cast away from me, they are those who mate and come together in their bodies, but in spirit contend one with the other.[63]

Like the Bustānīs one and two generations earlier, Khalīl Jibrān juxtaposed city and countryside. However, unlike the former's optimistic perception of the edifying powers of Beirut's urban economy and culture, Jibrān conjured images of the spiritual harmony of nature and the idyllic countryside of Mount Lebanon. He saw himself as writing in 'protest against a [specifically urban] society that persecutes the rebel against its edicts before knowing the cause of his rebellion'.[64]

Jibrān expressed the stifling effect of social conformity imposed by a corrupt elite in which the honest have-nots had no place. Critiques of the urban way of life as false and hypocritical such as his were not uncommon among the urban literati in cities of the Ottoman empire.[65] Moreover, in many ways Jibrān's short stories were shot through with manifestations of *Kulturpessimismus* that marked the finde siècle in Europe and the United States, places where he may have felt more at home than the country he left as a young boy. Nevertheless, Jibrān's development as an angry romantic was clearly nurtured by his prolonged stay in Beirut as a visiting student and his extended trips to the Lebanese mountains.

To Jibrān's (autobiographical) narrator, who took voluntary leave of society, 'auto-marginalization' was the only remedy against the vices of those professing and defining morality—the corrupt urban elites. As such, his powerful prose not only reversed the urban–rural dichotomy, but his anti-urban romanticism also stepped out of the seemingly naturalized nexus between modernity and urbanity that evolved in Beirut during the latter part of the nineteenth century. Significantly, it was his Mountain romanticism—arguably fostered by his residence in New York—which formed the basis of a new Lebanese national

[63] Jibrān (1908: 14–16). Translation adapted from H. Nahmad's 1949 translation.

[64] Ibid. 16.

[65] See, e.g. Şerif Mardin's explorations of Istanbul's literary elites (1974: 403–45).

idea formulated more systematically by the self-proclaimed 'New Phoenicians' after the First World War.[66]

Poetic Fantasy: the Syrian Opera of Beirut

In July 1908, Khalīl Jibrān went to Paris to study drawing, painting, and sculpture. His Paris experience was also shaped by Syro-Lebanese dissident activism in the French capital. Jibrān's friendship with Shukrī Ghānim and Amīn al-Rīḥānī in particular directed his youthful romantic anger about human injustice and oppressive family conventions towards a more concrete desire to contribute to his homeland's future. His close association with the critical thinker Amīn al-Rīḥānī came to constitute a lifelong influence on him. It was during their visit to London in the summer of 1910 that he drew the sketch of an imaginary opera house for Beirut shown in Figure 9.[67]

The sketch evokes a temple and depicts a two-storey front set on a row of steps leading up to the central portico. The entrance and rows of windows are shaped in vaguely Moorish style under a frieze of illegible Arabic inscriptions. The second floor of Jibrān and Rīḥānī's temple for the performing arts stood slightly recessed on the first floor and was flanked by two small domes on either side. On the top of the building a large central dome carries a semi-naked Athena figure. She stretches out her arms holding a hint of the scales of justice. At the rear of the building a minaret towers high.

The drawing bears some resemblance to the Ottoman revivalism that emerged in *fin de siècle* Beirut under the influence of Yūsuf Aftimos.[68] Yet, with its East–West eclecticism, the building's style is time- and placeless. Khalīl Jibrān's fantasy opera was dotted with Islamic and Christian evocations that were common in American, European, and Ottoman architectural Orientalism at the time and shared the then popular eclecticism of the Great Exhibition architecture in Antwerp, Chicago, Paris, and London.[69]

The drawing is heavily charged with symbolism. The composition of religious, secular, and arabesque elements also addressed the city in which the

[66] For a recent critique of Lebanese nationalism, see Hakim-Dowek (D.Phil. thesis, 1997). It would be interesting to trace not only how literature gave reality to the city, but also how urban changes contributed to the transformation of the literary text. While 'Mediterraneanism' pervaded Michel Chiha's writings as the essential component of Lebanese culture, Charles Corm's literary works e.g. expressed his nostalgia for 'atavistic forms of national sensitivities' embodied by the mountain culture in a series of publications: *La Montagne Inspirée* (1934), and *L'Humanisme de la Montagne* (1938). See Hourani (1984: 320). After the First World War, ancient Mount Lebanon, not the modern provincial capital of Beirut, became the idealized historical template for a future as a Lebanese nation state.

[67] Rīḥanī (1960: 154–9). Jibrān's drawing is on p. 160.

[68] See next chapter.

[69] Çelik (1992).

FIG. 9. Khalil Gibran's sketch for an opera house in Beirut

opera house was to be built. The Greek deity Athena was a fashionable neo-classical symbol of urban autonomy and democracy. While she had few connotative links with music and theatre, the figure wielding the scales of justice appears to arbitrate between the Muslim and Christian elements of the composition. Jibrān's and Rīḥānī's vision for Beirut was a sentimental one which celebrated religious diversity, worshipped freedom of expression, where confessions coexist in Mediterranean harmony, and Muslims and Christians enjoy the pinnacle of a capital city's cultural and artistic edification: 'the Syrian Opera'.[70]

Conclusion

Idealistic renditions such as Jibrān's of what Beirut should be and what it should stand for, emerged at a time of technological, scientific, and artistic

[70] Beirut became the national capital of the state of Lebanon before the city's leading architect, Yūsuf Aftimos, built the Grand Theatre in downtown Beirut.

transformations, changing worldviews, and new social categories. Riḥānī's and Jibrān's opera project never materialized and there is no evidence to suggest that they tried very hard to implement it. Even so, diverse renderings of urban symbolism—whether textual or pictorial—radiated abstract visions, human creativity, and future-oriented (even futuristic) discourses of the city.

As I have argued throughout this book, Beirut-as-text not only reflected urban reality but also continuously transformed the urban fabric itself. It is in this sense that the Arabic literary revival of the nineteenth century initiated, sustained, and directed the urban transformation of Beirut. At the same time, the modern urban fabric, architectural novelties, and monumental remnants of the past nurtured and shaped the very genres, motifs, and styles of literature that constituted the narratives of Beirut's modernity. This book, therefore, concludes with a closer look at public architecture in Beirut and the ways in which it structured perceptions of urbanity, modernity, and 'Ottomanness'.

9

Provincial Architecture and Imperial Commemoration

Monumental imperishability bears the stamp of the will to power.[1]

The last chapter ended with a discussion of Khalīl Jibrān's unusual sketch for a 'Syrian Opera of Beirut'. It may never have wielded any influence on Beirut's urban fabric but the American experience of another Lebanese public figure was to provide a more lasting effect on Beirut's architectural culture. Yūsuf Aftimos (1866–1952), the leading Lebanese architect and urban planner in the first half of the twentieth century brought Ottoman architectural revivalism from Istanbul and the world exhibitions to Beirut at the end of the nineteenth century.[2] This revival movement had multiple roots and took circuitous routes before it came to dominate Beirut's public constructions in the last two decades of Ottoman rule.

Fin de siècle Istanbul was a Mecca of Art Noveau.[3] In Istanbul the search for an Ottoman style had been ongoing since the appearance of Ibrāhīm Eldem Pasha's celebrated *Usul-i mimariyi osmani* ('Principles of Ottoman Architecture'), published for Vienna's world exposition of 1873.[4] Ottoman architectural revivalism itself was very much an amalgam of different styles, vernac-

[1] Lefebvre (1991*b*: 221).

[2] Aftimos graduated from the Syrian Protestant College with a BA in 1885. He taught Arabic at his university for a couple of years and co-authored a textbook in Arabic grammar before he left for New York to study civil engineering at the renowned Union College in 1887 or 1888. After graduating in 1891, he briefly worked for the Pennsylvania Railway Company and the Chicago Electricity Board. Alumni Association Beirut (1953: 16).

[3] See Godoli and Barillari (1996).

[4] The massive tome was based on 'the realization that the progress [of Ottomans] in the exalted realm of Fine Arts is possible only by recourse to the resplendent works of their past'. Bozdoğan (2002: 23–4). Bozdoğan argues that at the same time as Ottoman Revivalism sought to restore the historicity of Ottoman architecture and claimed its theoretical equality to European styles, it confirmed the superiority of European constructs of knowledge from which they borrowed their analytical frameworks, methods, and techniques.

ular Beaux Arts, neo-classical, Ottoman baroque, Islamic modern. Throngs of European architects came to Istanbul. Some, like a young Le Corbusier who visited Istanbul in 1911, were appalled by the modernizing experiments of Ottoman revivalism.[5] Others before him were lured by the prospects of lucrative business and stylistic freedom.

World exhibitions were Oriental phantasmagoria. When Chicago hosted the Columbia World Exposition in 1893, Aftimos—who at the time was working under a pioneer in 'Neo-Mauresque' architecture—was chosen to design the Ottoman and Persian pavilions and the 'Cairo Street' which had been so popular and controversial at the previous Paris exhibition in 1889.[6] Situated in a row of 'national pavilions', the Ottoman 'national' building was reconstructed 'with a particular "sense of elegance and luxury . . . quite as Oriental as if it was not the distance of half the globe from its origins"'.[7]

For Yūsuf Aftimos Chicago was his break as an Ottoman revivalist architect. He went on to work for the Egyptian pavilion at the Antwerp Exposition and conducted an extensive research trip in construction engineering to Berlin before returning home in late 1896.[8] In Beirut he was immediately offered the post of municipal engineer and directed the committee for the construction of the clocktower. Although he had little, if any, first-hand knowledge of Istanbul's architectural culture, his expatriate work for the Ottoman government familiarized him sufficiently with particular trends in the Ottoman capital to apply them to provincial Beirut.

State architecture in Beirut differed both from Istanbul's, and from the European architectural laboratories in the colonial cities of North Africa whose grandeur and eclecticism the Ottoman provincial capitals lacked. In Arab provincial capitals imperial government buildings and military installations were generally cast in imposing neo-classical varieties. I argue in this final chapter that the plain monumentality of Ottoman buildings in *fin de siècle* Beirut was a reflection of an imperial desire to present the state as a place of order, sobriety, and rationality. Chronically hamstrung by fiscal constraints, these buildings nevertheless effectively presented the empire to its provincial populations as a homogeneous and unified political entity.

There were other more experimental paths to modern architecture in late Ottoman Beirut, however. In particular Aftimos's civic and commercial landmark constructions blended ornamental styles of Ottoman revivalism with local materials, vernacular styles, and his personal tastes. Whether they were

[5] Bozdoğan (2002: 3–4). [6] See Mitchell (1988: 1–33).

[7] Captions to 'The Ottoman Pavilion' and 'Interior of Turkish Building', quoted in Çelik (2000: 77).

[8] To'meh (2000).

commissioned by the imperial government or a local initiative in honour of the sultan, these construction projects were often highly experimental and the precursors to Beirut's distinct modernism of the 1930–1960s.[9] Through the interplay of imperial and domestic architecture, provincial capitals like Beirut developed their own plurality of styles and building culture.

Representations of Power in Ottoman Provincial Capitals

During Sultan Abdülhamid's long reign, public architecture in the provinces inscribed Ottomanism onto the urban fabric of provincial capitals. Two dates punctuated the construction calendar in the 'well-protected domains' with quasi-religious regularity: 9 January, the sultan's birthday, and 1 September, the anniversary of his accession to the Ottoman throne. In the 1890s and 1900s, all of Beirut's important public buildings were inaugurated on these two occasions.

Architecture was used as a potent symbol of Ottoman modernity and a recurrent stage upon which to convey imperial permanence to the provinces. The material culture of the expanding provincial cities was a very suitable platform on which the imperial government staged what Selim Deringil called the 'new public image' of the Ottoman modernity.[10] Throughout the Ottoman Empire, commemorative rituals were rehearsed at opening ceremonies of public constructions. However, these rituals emerged not only at the whim of Abdülhamid II in distant Istanbul. They served as familiar spectacle in an ever accelerating urban life for officials and civilians alike.

The Ottoman government was acutely aware that staging a public ceremony needed careful timing and choreographing. Public events, such as the proclamation of a *firmān* by the incumbent governor, had been important markers of imperial authority since the beginning of the *tanẓīmāt*. But sometimes a dissatisfied populace would use this ceremony to send an unpopular governor packing.[11] After crushing the Beirut Reform Movement in 1913, for example, the new governor general of Beirut waited for weeks to read out the imperial *firmān* because the hostile atmosphere in the city promised a humiliating fiasco.[12]

Imperial ceremonies were volatile scenarios for the governor general precisely because they relied on the participation of local elites and the crowd. When Hāzim Bey finally felt confident that his inaugural speech would meet no popular opposition, the entire rank and file of local dignitaries refused to

[9] Arbid (Ph.D. thesis, 2002).
[10] Deringil (1993).
[11] See Inalcik (1973: 97–127).
[12] Hartmann (1913: 25).

attend the ceremony in protest against the dissolution of the Beirut Reform Movement. Without an audience, the governor general's speech lost its meaning and he his mandate. Four days later, he was recalled to Istanbul.[13]

While episodes like these were rare occurrences, they do hint at the subtle power of symbolic protest. As James Gelvin has recently argued, mass mobilization of the street emerged in the political struggle between competing nationalisms to fill the Ottoman vacuum *after* the First World War.[14] I argue that there also existed a comparative awareness of the symbolic importance of mass ceremonies in the pre-nationalist context. The imperial stage setting at public proclamations and opening ceremonies in the provinces followed a standardized pattern, captured for the sultan and for eternity by the snapshot camera of the military photographer. The participating cast of bureaucrats and notables was arranged around the central character, the governor general, by order of official rank.

Photography of Ottoman architecture in provincial capitals emerged as a popular mode of urban representation. In particular, during the rule of Sultan Abdülhamid II, photos from the provinces constituted instruments of imperial control, power, and legitimacy. The sultan taught himself photography and amassed a vast collection of pictures in his palace, mainly of public construction and modern infrastructure. Under Abdülhamid, who rarely ventured outside his palace himself, 'cities and provinces were registered in a sort of photographic survey, the peoples of the empire catalogued, and even portraits of higher civil and military officials could be collected and centrally kept'.[15] The documentary focus was on progress and industry, on railways and bridges, barracks and hospitals, sites where provincial governors and engineers staged themselves under Ottoman flags as the harbingers of the modern era in the name of the sultan.

As mass-produced commodities, postcards, too, were important tools of reality-shaping urban (self-)representations. The recurrent bird's eye perspectives and panoramic vistas of Beirut across the old city, either onto the sea or the mountains, reproduced aesthetic and total images of sanitized urban landscapes. Postcards were to the tourist what Ottoman photography was to Abdülhamid: a template of what an ideal, modern Ottoman city should look like. As Beirut became an increasingly attractive destination of Orient tourism, local photography flourished. The reproduction of selected images to be sent to Europe by mail produced expectations of city, sun, and the sea, and the site

[13] Ibid. 114. [14] Gelvin (1998: 226). [15] Lemke (1998: 82).

geography of public buildings and gardens, schools and hotels that reified the *fin de siècle* image of Beirut's beauty, contemporaneity, and progress.

The Political Economy of Beirut's Urban Landscape

Beirut's urban fabric was shaped by an imperial sensitivity to the city's topography as a potent staging ground for the Ottoman will to power. Despite dominating Beirut's site geography, Ottoman monumental architecture competed with the concurrent mushrooming of ostentatious palaces of the urban elites on the slopes above the old town.[16] Moreover, the development of Beirut's public places and town squares firmly remained in municipal hands. The numerous Ottoman buildings, the barracks, the fountains, the hospitals, the schools, and the serails were eye-catching. Not all of them responded to practical necessity. The emphasis was on their strategic locations and, through the magnificence of the buildings' dimensions, the amplitude of their lines, the uniformity of their design, the effect of their decorative elements, they confirmed the power of the state and provided visual and physical evidence of Ottoman claims to modernity.

In Beirut and other provincial capitals, Ottomanization of urban space engendered not just physical changes of the built environment but also filled that urban space (and time) with new social and political meaning. Ottoman attempts to inscribe the state's presence onto the urban fabric were historically nothing new. Prior to the *tanẓīmāt*, a recurring transmitter of Ottoman rule had been the construction of mosques with characteristic pencil minarets. Often, as in the case of the 'Ottomanization of Crete', accessible though mosques were to the public, their functional aspect as places for prayer was secondary to the aspect of representation of Ottoman power.[17]

In Aleppo, Damascus, and Baghdad, but also in the port towns like Izmir and Beirut, numerous public buildings and government palaces (or serails) were constructed as the architectural embodiment of the centralizing and regularizing, urban project of *tanẓīmāt* and Hamidian rule.[18] The repetition and uniformity of state architecture provided visual and physical representations of progress and modernity with which the Ottoman imperial government strove to enlighten, modernize, and homogenize these cities and their provincial hinterlands. From the beginning of the *tanẓīmāt*, public buildings

[16] See Saliba (1998).

[17] See e.g. Irene Bierman's work on Crete in the 16th and 17th centuries, in Bierman (1991).

[18] For Ottoman postcard images of these constructions, see Lemke (2002).

were purposefully erected on large, extramural squares (like Sahat al-Marja in Damascus), creating new urban centres in the process.[19] Just as Damascus was targeted by the Ottoman government for extramural urban development after it became the capital of the 'super-province' of Syria in 1865, two decades later Beirut became a platform of concerted architectural inscription after Abdülhamid II made it a provincial capital.

The construction of public buildings and squares in central urban locations, on hilltops, or river banks outside the old cities, signified the presence of Ottoman central authority in provincial capitals. Yet, at the same time, this presence made imperial authority more tangible, accessible, and accountable. Moreover, the buildings acquired a highly local meaning through the choice of local architects—particularly Bishāra Dīb and his son-in-law Yūsuf Aftimos—and building material, and because the buildings were largely financed locally, that is, by municipal funds or private donors.

Grand Serail—Petit Serail: Changing Architectures of Imperial Power

Ever since its construction during the Crimean War, Beirut's imperial barracks (*qishlat al-humāyūn*) on the Qantari hilltop had seen the most conspicuous reminder of Ottoman state power in this flourishing port-city. The construction stood as the architectural expression of the new Ottoman military organization, the *niẓām-ı cedīd*, or 'New Order', at the time. Both in terms of its lofty location and austere façade, it resembled a smaller version of the Selimiye Barracks on Istanbul's Asian side which was completed in 1853—the year construction in Beirut begun.[20] Like the Istanbul barracks, the completion of the Beirut construction took over a decade.[21] Two tall floors spread well over 80 metres on the elongated side, easily making it the largest building in Ottoman Beirut. Its arcaded portico, protruding on the eastern façade, was flanked by two symmetrical wings which were structured by three rows of sixteen small, identical windows.

The building dominated—seemingly incorruptible—the bustle on Sahat al-Sur and the old city, and afar, the port and Mediterranean Sea. The emphasis was on its imposing order whose monumentality was duplicated and amplified when, in 1861, a similar but smaller structure of the military hospital

[19] S. Weber (1998). [20] Goodwin (1991: 420).

[21] In a photograph dated 1867, the imperial barracks in Beirut still consisted of only one floor. The second floor must have been added in the 1870s since it is depicted in pictures of the 1880s. For the rare reproduction of the 1867 photo, see Debbas (2001: 108).

Fig. 10. Ottoman skyline on Qantari Hill, Grand Serail, clocktower, and military hospital

emerged alongside it. Within two generations the urban profile of Beirut was to change dramatically from what it had been in 1840. An impressive skyline appeared on the Qantari hilltop which erased all traces of Burj Umm Dabbus and Burj al-Jadid, two early modern urban watchtowers (Figure 10).

With time, the barracks' military purpose of accommodating regular and mobile units was supplanted by civic uses. Fu'ād Pasha, the sultan's special envoy to Mount Lebanon and Damascus after the civil wars of 1860, made the building his headquarters. It was in the barracks that the plans for a new Ottoman order in Mount Lebanon and Bilad al-Sham took shape. It housed the city's main prison and—with the addition of a second floor in the 1870s—Ottoman medical units. After the creation of the province of Beirut, the governor general used the barracks for official ceremonies, such as imperial commemorations, military parades, and awarding of state insignia. Although the area around the imperial barracks continued to be used for military exercises and parades, by the late nineteenth century the imperial barracks underwent a semantic switch from 'Imperial Barracks' to 'Grand Serail'—from *qishlat al-humāyūn* to *al-sarāy al-kabīr*—to match the building's accumulated public functions.

The monumentality of the Grand Serail stood in contrast to the Petit Serail on the other side of the old city. The difference in scale is all the more striking because it stood on the larger and—as I will argue below—more showy of Beirut's two main squares. The Petit Serail was commissioned by the municipal president, Ibrāhīm Fakhrī Bey, who had already constructed Khan Fakhrī Bey, Beirut's second largest merchant house, a decade earlier.[22]

Construction started in late 1881 and lasted for three years. The correspondence between the governor general of the province of Syria, Aḥmad Ḥamdī Pasha, and the Porte in Istanbul reveals considerable difficulties in financing the construction. Ḥamdī Pasha was forced to take up a loan from the Ottoman Bank to mortgage public buildings, and finally to impose new taxes on the population to buy office installations.[23] As the palace of local government, it was to accommodate municipal and subprovincial offices such as the city's legal court, the *maḥkamat al-sharīʿa*. Ten years later, when Beirut became a provincial capital, it housed the seat of Beirut's governor general.

Most probably, the building's historicist style—or eclectic 'Occidentalism'—was designed by Fakhrī Bey himself who was, after all, an engineer by training. The mixture of playful ornamentation and solid, geometric structure was very much a reversal of Orientalizing trends in European architecture and very much in fashion in Istanbul at the time.[24] More importantly for our discussion of examples of the Ottomanization of urban space in Beirut, there was neither a single agent nor a single style. And yet both government buildings were architectural manifestations of Ottoman modernity. The next example is an Ottoman landmark that became a common architectural feature across the cities and towns of the empire during the Hamidian period.

The Ottoman Clocktower—a Sign of the Times on Beirut's 'Capitol Hill'

To His Exalted Court Chamberlain

In the city of Beirut there are a number of foreign institutions that have established clocktowers with bells, all of them with a western clock. Because there is no public clock which shows the mandatory Muslim (prayer) times Muslims, even officials and (other) civil servants have regrettably had to adapt to the time of foreign clocks.

The urgent need for a general [public] clock which determines the religious times of the Muslims was acknowledged and the provincial council has put the construction of a clocktower on its agenda and has discussed [its funding] from the revenues of the municipality whose prosperity it owes to the Padishah.

22 Ibrāhīm Fakhrī Bey was the son of Maḥmūd Nāmī Bey, governor of Beirut between 1833 and 1840. See Chs. 1, 3, and 5.

23 BBA, YAHUS 180/77, 31 Dec. 1884.

24 For a picture and detailed description of this building, see Hanssen (1998b: 60).

> Because in the vicinity of the government building [the Petit Serail] no suitable location was found and because the imperial barracks here are built on a plateau which looks out over the city in all directions, it was considered—provided the Most Exalted approval—to build a tower dressed with a large bell clock either on top of the main gate of the said barracks or in a suitable place on the square in front of it. If His Majesty deigns to graciously grant permission for the proposed construction of the tower together with the suspension of the clock, it would be carried out immediately. An imperial order is for who is master of orders.
>
> signed: The Governor General[25]

This letter from Rashīd Bey to Sultan Abdülhamid's palace in Istanbul is significant for the production of space in an Ottoman provincial capital in many ways. First, it demonstrates an acute awareness that 'Islamic time' was particular—or should be so—in order to unify the space of the imperial state. Second, it suggests that the compression of time and space in the late Ottoman Empire was a formative aspect of imagining oneself as a modern Ottoman and that streamlining imperial time informed and enforced the Ottoman project of modernization. At least the governor general, Rashīd Bey, had quite a literal sense of a distinctly Ottoman *Zeitgeist* that was being undermined by the regrettable fact that Muslims had to resort to 'foreign clocks'. Third, this document ultimately relativizes our perception of the Hamidian regime's ability to impose an imperial rhythm of time on a city where at least five different calendars structured public life, two of which were Ottoman—the fiscal and the Islamic calendars, or *māliye* and *hijrī*. Beirut's plurality of temporal structures only accentuated Ottoman efforts to manipulate the city's daily rhythms.

Fourth, the letter captures the relations between provincial capital authorities and the imperial government. The tone—a mixture of flattery and pressure—speaks of a dedicated local population represented by an equitable governor general humbly assuring the sultan of their loyalty. Although this loyalty was unconditional, the particular discourse of the advancement of 'foreign rivals' implied that the imperial government had certain expectations to live up to. Reference to the particulars of the discussions already under way in the provincial council were included as an additional persuasive strategy to granting the necessary building permission.

Finally, in the case of Beirut the initiative and the design for the clocktower was entirely local and pre-dated the provincial construction frenzy in 1900–1 to mark the twenty-fifth anniversary of Abdülhamid's accession to the sultanate.

[25] BBA, YMTV 167/200, 25 Sept. 1897.

The decision to place the tower on an elevated (*mürtefī*) point evinces a keen sense of the visual effect of such a building structure on the city.[26]

Over 120, various-styled clocktowers dotted towns of the Ottoman empire. In the Arab provinces they were rarer than in Anatolia and the Balkans. Most of the thirty-five clocktowers in Anatolian towns were built or rebuilt during Abdülhamid's reign.[27] Amasya's minaret-style clocktower was built in 1865. The Campanile-style clocktower in Adana dates back to 1882 and Ankara's was built into a pre-existing structure in 1884. The Orientalist design of Izmir's clocktower of 1901 donned a clock presented by the German emperor, William II.[28] Most clocktowers in Bilad al-Sham mushroomed during the sultan's jubilee year of 1900–1.[29] The municipalities of Acre, Haifa, Safad, and Nazareth announced the erection of clocktowers in the sultan's honour.[30] Others were built in public squares of Tripoli, Aleppo, and Jaffa. Components of a concerted imperial policy, they were marked by greater stylistic similarity than those in Anatolia. Invariably, they were built on the central town square and were placed inside public gardens.

Beirut's clocktower project pre-dated such constructions by three years and was possibly triggered by the expectation of the German royal visit to Bilad al-Sham in November 1898. The clocktower's location between Grand Serail and imperial hospital reinforced the Ottoman skyline of Beirut. Coinciding with the demolition of Beirut's historic maritime citadel by the port company, the provincial council designated Qubbat al-Qantari as its unmistakable 'capitol hill'. Ottoman commemoration of the modern as well as capitalist exigencies were fast replacing and erasing previous landmarks of political power.

There had been a few towers with clocks and bells in Beirut as the governor general's letter suggested. There was the church tower of the Anglican parish on the Qantari hill, with 'a fine bell . . . and a $1,200 tower clock given by the Madison Square Church in New York'.[31] The clocktower of College Hall at the

[26] The letter's argument for shortage of space in other locations seems a spurious argument since the tower could have easily been integrated into the recently redesigned square in front of the Petit Serail.

[27] Özdemir (1993: 165–232). According to Klaus Kreiser's ongoing research on Ottoman monuments, there were up to 120 clocktowers in the empire. Forty-one of them were built during the Hamidian period, five of which were connected to the sultan's jubilee constructions in 1900–1. I am grateful for Klaus Kreiser's generous sharing of his research findings.

[28] Ibid. 208.

[29] The first municipal clocktower in the Arab provinces appears to have been the clocktower in Tarablus Gharb, the capital of Libya today. While the idea for its construction dates back to the 1830s, the project was realized to herald the beginnings of Ottoman municipal reform in the province of Tripoli in the late 1860s. See Lafi (2002: 219–22).

[30] PRO, FO, 195/2075, 'Quarterly Report', Beirut, 22 Nov. 1900. However, most plans were never put into effect.

[31] Jessup (1910: 331): '[T]he Mohammedans who abominate bells, and the Jews who dislike Christian churches, contributed to the erection of a Christian bell-tower.'

Syrian Protestant College was inaugurated in a grand ceremony.[32] Clocks stood atop the Jesuit College building and the French Hospital from the early 1880s. The two bell towers of the Maronite cathedral on Rue Emir Bashir were completed in 1888. In contrast to these icons of missionary rivalry in Beirut, this new, Ottoman 'conquest' of verticality addressed the rhythms of the city as a whole. Such 'towers were considered "civic art" . . . as they expressed the dissociation of time and religion', while the imperial chronometer signalled in state-time a distinct regularity, order, and consciousness on the city.[33]

The 25-metre-high clocktower became the highest building in Beirut and was duly celebrated as such in repetitive and highly ritualized ceremonies:

> The viewer on the roof can have a panoramic view of the whole city. Nothing would escape his eyes. Its view stretches to the outskirts, as far as the coastal plains and to the border with [Mount] Lebanon. The public laying of the first stone of the clocktower took place on January 9, 1897—the birthday of the Sultan. The celebration was carried out in the presence of the high officials of the province, military rank and file, and members of the municipality. A military orchestra played a most delightful melody, and later a speech was delivered in Arabic and Ottoman calling upon the Sultan's resplendent and eternal nature, and the assembled crowd believed in these emotional exclamations. After the celebrations the governor general symbolically laid the first two stones with a silver hammer. At the end of the party, several photographs were taken.[34]

The construction cost the municipality 126,000 gold piastres—around £1,000 at the time. It was built from a variety of local wood and marble, Jounieh limestone, Beiruti sandstone, Damascene basalt, and red stone from Dayr al-Qamar. The obligatory Hamidian *tughra* was installed above the entrance. Inside its 4 by 4 metre square shaft, 125 steps in pioneering cast iron led up to the top. On the third floor a 300 kilogram bell was suspended. This floor contained four miniature neo-orientalist balconies to which *mashrabiyya*-style doors led. Above the bell, four large clock faces imported from Paris by the Ottoman embassy, two clock faces with Arabic and two with Latin numerals, soberly heralded exact (but dual) city-time.

This symbiosis of the imperial and the local was also reflected in the planning procedures of Beirut's clocktower. In fact, they probably exemplified those of other Ottoman public works. First, the governor general, Rashīd Bey, had 'put together a construction cadre and asked for permission from the

[32] Khalaf (1995: 67). [33] Çelik (1986: 130).

[34] Louis Shaykhu, 'al-Sāʿa al-ʿarabiyya fī Bayrūt', *al-Mashriq*, 2 (1899), 769–74. The author, Father Louis Rizqallah Shaykhu (1859–1928), a Chaldean Catholic from Mardin, was educated at the Jesuit seminar at Ghazir and became librarian and teacher of languages and philosophy at St Joseph University. See Dakhli (MA thesis, 1995: 136).

authorities in Istanbul for the municipal agency to build, out of its own financial allocations, a grand tower in oriental style, and to install a huge clock and a bell to announce the time in Arabic'.[35] When the imperial decree was read out amidst great public celebration, a planning committee of ten was established consisting of two municipal engineers, two members of the municipal council, the president of the municipality, the provincial chief engineer, and four Ottoman military officers. Together, they decided on the location and charged Yūsuf Aftimos with designing the building.[36]

Beirut's clocktower exhibited public, distinctly 'Ottoman time' in a routinely, daily manner. The Hamidian clocktower began to shape city rhythms. Just like the Italian 'freestanding campanile . . . dominated space—[it] would soon, as clock-tower, come to dominate time, too'.[37] Simultaneous celebrations conjured up this 'Ottoman time' on a larger scale: on 1 September 1900, the twenty-fifth anniversary of Abdülhamid II, all Ottoman citizens performed—or were supposed to—the same collective ritual wherever they were in the empire. Simultaneity of symbolic action would thus bring about the imagining of a common community on a common geography in a common time frame.

The next section discusses the urbanist considerations behind—and the urban effect of—another landmark from the Hamidian period: the School for Arts and Crafts (*maktab al-ṣanāʾiʿ wa al-tijāra al-ḥamīdī*).

The Sanaya Complex—the Design of Modern Ottoman Education

The idea of building an industrial school complex emerged in Beirut's reformist circles at the turn of the nineteenth century. Sunni notables established a small private vocational school in 1892 where women learnt sewing and tailoring and men were trained in the skills of shoe-making, book-binding, goldsmithery, painting, engraving, printing, and other arts and crafts.[38] Ten years later, Beirut's notables began to raise the issue in Istanbul where, conveniently, Syrians had established a considerable presence near the sultan. The idea gained momentum when the provincial council of Beirut sent a proposal to Istanbul trying to convince the Ottoman government and the sultan to support plans for an industrial school in Beirut. The project was to be a day and boarding school for one hundred students who were to be taught 'in all

[35] Shaykhu, 'al-Sāʿa al-ʿarabiyya', 771. It is not clear from the Shaykhu text whether 'Arabic time' meant a different way of counting the hours of the day or whether he merely referred to the Arabic numerals on the clock face. [36] Ibid. [37] Lefebvre (1991*b*: 265). [38] Kassab and Tadmori (2002: 61).

disciplines'.[39] The indefatigable Aḥmad ʿAbbās al-Azharī—the school's founder and designated director—lobbied for the project in Istanbul. He proposed to concentrate on teaching practical skills in crafts, arts, and manufacture for underprivileged children who aspired to become industrialists and merchants.[40] At the same time, ʿAbbās, Aḥmad al-Dāʿūq, and Ḥasan Qrunful requested teachers from French authorities emphasizing the school's international nature.[41]

After imperial approval was granted for both a hospital and a school, the municipality set about finding a suitable location. Ramlat al-Zarif, the plateau south-west of the old city, was chosen as the ideal place for the project. As 'the most important spot of the city, on a wide stretch of land west of the city, [al-Ramla provided] a pleasant location with good climate as the wind passes over it from the sea before heading towards the city'.[42]

Throughout the early phases of Beirut's urbanization, the sand dunes had remained a deserted stretch of land. Too rocky for cultivation, Ramlat al-Zarif was a wasteland that occasionally served as a quarry,[43] while the glinting colour of the plateau's fine, red sand had helped navigate sailors into Beirut harbour prior to the construction of the Beirut lighthouse.[44] The French travelling poet-politician Lamartine called the area 'un morceau du désert d'Egypte, jeté au pied du Liban'.[45]

But to Beirut's inhabitants the sand dunes of al-Ramla had been a menace to health and trade for centuries. Twice a year, the city suffered sand storms as heavy spring and autumn winds carried the sand across the city. Henri Guys noticed over the course of his fourteen years of residence in Beirut that several properties near the sand dunes had disappeared under the shifting sands and 'judging from the annual encroachment, one can predict that it will take less than two centuries for this part of the cape to be covered in its entirety'.[46]

From the 1880s onwards, with the growing elimination of natural impediments that jeopardized routine commercial operations, scientific methods began to be applied to urban renewal in Beirut. The French natural scientist and resident of Beirut in 1882, Dr Louis Lortet, was alarmed that a British company's 'half-hearted bid' to stop the erosion yielded no results the previous year. He warned 'if the Turkish administration does not care to take an energetic measure to combat these dunes—pushed incessantly by the winds—they will rapidly engulf the whole city under their moving shroud'.[47]

[39] BBA, Giden 274, vesika 234938, 30 Dec. 1903. [40] BBA, YMTV 267/140–1, 9 Aug. 1904.
[41] MAE, Paris, NSTSL 1903–05, vol. 109, 2 Sept. 1905. [42] al-Unsī (1910/11: 110). [43] Ibid.
[44] Lamartine (1887: i. 131). [45] Ibid. ii. 336. [46] Guys (1985: 46). [47] Lortet (1884: 69).

In 1886, *al-Muqtaṭaf* published a thorough article on the problem of wind erosion. The author reported on French engineers who had recently invented new horticultural techniques to reinforce an area of 85,000 hectares in the Gascoigne and turned it into fertile land. The author encouraged Beirut's authorities to learn: 'It is no secret that the sand weighs heavily on the city of Beirut and oppresses it by burying its gardens. It now threatens a number of its proudest residences so that one cannot neglect the importance of preventing further encroachment'.[48]

In September 1905—again on the sultan's coronation anniversary—the governor general ceremonially laid the first stone of the school. But construction ran into financial difficulties that forced him into levying extra taxes of two silver *mecidiye* on travel permits. Ibrāhīm Khalīl Pasha, the governor general, expected these and other taxes on merchandise to generate additional and sufficient revenue of 1,000 Ottoman lira per year.[49] Moreover, he suggested raising special taxes on produce, such as grain exports, oranges, and tobacco.[50] The governor general also asked the imperial government for funding for a municipal hospital for some one hundred in-patients as a complement to the school of industry.[51]

However, even before the first stone had been laid, the head of the grain exporters' guild in Beirut, one Amīn Sinnu, cabled a petition to the Porte requesting that his guild not be expected to bear the brunt of the costs.[52] He considered the taxes 'another punishment' against them, too high and too one-sided as they affected their export rather than the already favoured foreign imports. While it is not clear how the Sanaya complex was ultimately financed, a levy of 20 para (equivalent to half a piastre) for each traded sack of flour valued at 130–50 piastres was agreed on between the provincial council and the grain merchants.[53] The provincial council had considered other sources of revenue, and a cross-reference in the Ottoman archives claimed that money generated from reclaimed coastal land was used—against the protest of the municipality.[54] Finally a special imperial inspector was charged with overseeing the implementation and sound financing of the project.[55]

The main two buildings spanned 60 by 30 and 44 by 30 metres and both had two floors. Both floors were fitted with large reception halls, offices and

[48] *al-Muqtaṭaf*, 'Rimāl Bayrūt wa hājiz al-rimāl', 10 (1886), 310.

[49] PRO, FO, 195/2217, 13 Nov. 1906.

[50] BBA, Giden 274, vesika no. 234938, 30 Dec. 1903.

[51] Ibid. 25 May 1905.

[52] Ibid.

[53] Ibid.

[54] BBA, Gelen 271, vesika no. 197149, 28 Feb. 1904.

[55] It consisted of ʿUmar Khulūṣī, ʿAbd al-Qādir al-Qabbānī, director of education at the time, Muḥammad al-Kastī, Rashīd Fākhūrī, Muḥammad Lababīdī, Amīn Ḥilmī, Muḥammad Ṭabbāra, Najīb Ṭrād, Najīb al-Hānī and Bishāra al-Dīb. Kassab and Tadmori (2002: 61).

FIG. 11. Inauguration of the School for Arts and Crafts, 1909

classrooms and several galleries decorated with marble columns. Beirut's municipal hospital was located across the newly planted park (Figure 12). All buildings were made of carved stone from Lattakia and the roofs were supported by iron beams.

Although the funding for this huge, 350,000 lira project remained uncertain, the school and the hospital were inaugurated with the annual ritual commemorating the sultan in August 1907. The Sanaya complex was the largest urban development project in Beirut during Abdülhamid's reign. The obligatory photograph with carefully choreographed rows of Ottoman and Beiruti civil and military dignitaries was sent back to Sultan Abdülhamid's palace as visual evidence of provincial enterprise and loyalty (Figure 11).

The example of the protracted struggle for construction of the *maktab al-ṣanāʾiʿ wa al-tijāra al-ḥamīdī* allows a number of important insights into the process of urban planning in Ottoman provincial capitals at the turn of the century. It involved the three levels of government, the local (the residents and the municipality), the regional (the provincial council and the governor general), and the imperial (the Palace and the Porte in Istanbul). Clearly not a profit-making enterprise, the project did succeed because, despite different views on how to finance it, all three levels were ultimately convinced of its benefits.

FIG. 12. The public park in front of the School for Arts and Crafts

When completed, the Sanaya complex 'resemble[d] a self-contained townlet with cultivated fields'.[56] Walkways through artificial patches of lawn and lines of young palm trees reclaimed destructive wasteland and turned it into prime urban property. Additionally, the new Sanaya garden, the hospital, the teacher training seminary, and the school itself were celebrated as a triumph of man, culture, and science over volatile climates and nature's hazards to health and trade. The impressive presence of educational and medical institutions promised to reproduce the same modern, scientific knowledge that made it possible to overcome the sand drifts. Such remarkable achievements boosted the Beirutis' optimism and belief in modernity. The city's future seemed to look bright.[57]

The next section traces the ways in which the city's bourgeoisie claimed the port of Beirut, which—we recall—had been associated with the 'dangerous classes', as a space for banking, leisure, and conspicuous consumption.

[56] al-Unsī (1910/11: 110).

[57] During the struggle of the Beirut Reform Committee in 1912/13, however, the Ottoman governor general temporarily closed the school as many of its teachers supported the Beirut reform movement.

The Orosdi Back Department Store—Gentrifying the Port

The Orosdi Back building accommodated the first large-scale department store in Beirut. It was part of a Franco-Egyptian chain of department stores founded by French businessmen of Hungarian origin in 1855.[58] In Beirut's watershed year of 1888, Léon and Philippe Orosdi and Joseph Back began to open branches in Paris, Istanbul, Salonika, Izmir, Adana, Aleppo, Beirut, Alexandria, Cairo, and Tunis.[59] The branch in Beirut was the first and the largest to open in the Eastern Mediterranean. By 1914, the Beirut branch generated a net profit of 117,699 francs annually.[60]

The Beirut port company had sold a plot of land to this department store as early as 1894 but it took until the magic date of 1 September 1900 to complete constructions and open it to the public as part of the citywide celebrations in honour of Sultan Abdülhamid II's silver jubilee. Situated on the quays next to the customs offices and warehouses at the port, it lay at the intersection between maritime trade—that is, the import of luxury goods from Europe—and the inland trade—that is, the export of regionally produced goods (see Map 5). The opening of a railway station on the port premises, which coincided with that of the department store, further enhanced the central location of the building whose customers consisted both of residents of Beirut and of regional and international visitors, especially since Beirut became a popular transit stop for Muslim pilgrims to Mecca.

The international character of its merchandise and customers was reflected in the building's architectural style. On the ground floor of the two seaside façades that looked onto a wide area, large glass windows offered an easy and attractive view onto the merchandise presented inside. The upper floors impressed through their rich variety of structuring and ornamenting elements—pilasters, differently shaped and sized windows, statues, shells, garlands, and small towers—with eye-catching effect (Figure 13).

This arcaded department store introduced modern consumerism and gadgetry to Beirut.[61] Inside the building an elevator facilitated consumers' access to the assorted commodities, and an in-house telephone service connected the

[58] BIO Archive, Istanbul, AD002A: 'Dossier de Messieurs Orosdi Back Co.'

[59] Saul (1997: 170–4).

[60] Ibid. 173. Beirut's revenues were inferior to those of Paris (854,651 Ff) and Istanbul (452,831 Ff), less than the branches in Izmir (168,992 Ff) and Salonika (124,610 Ff), but superior to Tunis (93,720 Ff), Alexandria (84,535 Ff), Cairo (65,960 Ff), Aleppo (44,336 Ff), and Adana (42,638 Ff).

[61] The particular form and function of the Orosdi Back building evokes Walter Benjamin's *Das Passagenwerk* and his analysis of the spatial organization of modern consumerism.

FIG. 13. Postcard of the Orosdi Back department store, *c.*1910

different shops.[62] In this instance, Orosdi Back spearheaded technological innovations in Beirut, as two years later a local concession holder started a rudimentary telephone system for the city.[63] On the whole the building was strongly ostentatious, even exhibitionist. The Orosdi Back building held every feature of an *en vogue* contemporary European consumers' temple. The *magasins des nouveautés* or the galleries in Paris were, in fact, originally based on the perception of an 'Oriental Bazaar' that tended to be reproduced in world exhibitions.[64] The only trace of Ottoman influence on the Orosdi Back building itself were the small token stars on top of the pilasters. Yet, through the simultaneous inauguration ceremonies of the department store, the railway station, and the fountain on Sahat al-Sur on 1 September 1900, the building became part of the stage setting, perhaps even an actor, for the self-projection of the modern Ottoman state as manifested in the provincial capital.

The port company's aim to attract property investors proved successful. It was able to sell a number of plots on the newly reclaimed landfill to companies like Orosdi Back whose 'radiant' presence on the port premises contributed to gentrify the area. Opposite the department store and inside the customs office,

62 BBA, YMTV 214/197, 5 Mar. 1902.
63 BBA, YMTV 249/18, 5 Aug. 1903.
64 Girouard (1985: 293).

a police station maintained law and order and safeguarded the properties. In the 1900s, merchant families like the Thābits and the Badawīs erected buildings on the quays and rented them out as office space to the Beirut–Damascus railway company and other businesses.[65] Beirut's port area was an urban space previously consigned to negative perceptions, where Greeks, Maltese, and riotous 'sailors of all nations' were seen to 'infest the people of the Levant'. Now, it was subjected to its first comprehensive gentrification—a bourgeois conquest of the commercial hub and the seascape of the city.[66] After the construction of Orosdi Back, respectable Beirutis began to claim the port area as a place of leisure. *Flâneurs*, photographers, and travellers discovered the quays and boardwalks for themselves, where formerly the nuisance of customs and health officials and the pushing and shoving of bustling porters had kept the port as a place of hasty transit and stubborn avoidance.

The decision of the Ottoman Imperial Bank in 1905 to open its new provincial headquarters on the first quay was both a reflection of the financial stakes it had in the port company and the process of gentrification in the port district. For 152,000 francs ('not comprising furniture, cloth awnings, ringing system and electric ventilation, heating, drainage and sewage, gas lighting and municipal taxes'[67]) the bank was designed in a style reminiscent of European modernist buildings of other, much grander, land reclamation schemes. Beirut had joined other Ottoman port-cities, like Istanbul and Izmir, in claiming land from the sea.[68]

One cannot help but notice that the gentrification of the port area by placing monumental representative buildings on the landfills was another late Ottoman precursor to today's planning strategies. At the end of both the nineteenth and twentieth centuries large construction companies—then the Compagnie Impériale Ottomane du Port, des Quays et Entrepots de Beyrouth, now Société Libanaise de Developpement et Reconstruction—were at liberty to farm out lucrative public space to private retail companies and banking houses in an effort to energize Beirut as a commercial hub.

Compared to Solidere's façade-fixated compression of historical styles, however, the Ottoman port area was a place of multiplicity of styles and harmonious contrast. Architecturally, the bank and the department store formed an ensemble which was to become a new landmark of Beirut and a popular seaside

[65] al-Unsī (1910/11: 110).

[66] Alain Corbin (1994) has traced the 19th-cent. transition from human anxiety to mastery over the Atlantic and Mediterranean seashores.

[67] BIO Archive, AD 002A; 'Litiges diverses;' Istanbul, 7 June 1905.

[68] Zandi-Sayek (2000: 55–78).

photo motif. Its building material, the colour of the two-storey façade, and the triple domed grey rooftop, effectively contrasted with the conventional sandstone structures and red-tiled roofs of nearby *khāns*, *qaysariyyas*, and *wikālas*. Despite their innovative building structures and their popularity, so far Solidere heritage strategists have considered neither the bank building, nor the Orosdi Back store, sufficiently 'authentic' period pieces to be restored.

'It is like Someone Selling His Eyes to Buy Glasses': Two Public Squares Compared

This section compares the struggle over the differential transformation of the two major squares of late Ottoman and French mandate Beirut located on either side of the old town. In the late nineteenth century, Sahat al-Burj[69] and Sahat al-Sur (later Riadh Solh square) were the objects of a series of major physical and functional transformations. Yet, comparing the development of both squares, there emerged sharp contrasts between levels of urban integration and spatial politics. While Sahat al-Sur maintained its local organization and function, Sahat al-Burj became a regional traffic hub and a place of imperial and bourgeois ostentation. In this capacity, it was constantly compared to other 'great squares' in Europe and the Azbakiyya gardens in Cairo.

Urban renewal on Beirut's main open area dates back to 1632, when Emir Fakhr al-Dīn al-Maʿnī, ruler over Mount Lebanon from 1599 to 1633, built Burj al-Kashshaf, a number of gardens and stables for pack animals.[70] The barren field between the tower Burj al-Kashshaf and Fakhr al-Dīn's palace had long been an area of strategic value.[71] The Russian military expedition of 1772 had placed its cannons here to destroy the city's fortifications.[72] When the French army entered Beirut after the civil war of 1860, Poujoulat relished the sight of this '300 by 150 metre square' and the multicoloured 'omnibuses' which took officers and leisurely strollers to the French military camp in the pine forest at fifteen-minute intervals. More so, he enjoyed the dominance 'of restaurants, cafés, shops or boutiques held by the French' who had arrived in the wake of the Crimean War.[73] Significantly, following this description of the 'Frenchness' of Sahat al-Burj, Poujoulat's *La Verité* appealed strongly for a French

[69] Or 'Place des Canons'; from 1876 it was 'Place Hamidiyya'; in 1908, it became 'Place de la Liberté' and after 1909 'Place de l'Union.' After the First World War it became 'Martyrs' Square' because of the hanging of dozens of nationalists by the Ottoman governor general on allegations of treason.

[70] Duwāyhī (1976:500).

[71] The near mythical marble palace and hanging gardens of Fakhr al-Dīn deteriorated after the late 17th century. The palace became a quarry for subsequent construction work on the city walls before the Cinema Opera was built on its site in 1923.

[72] al-Wālī (1993:85).

[73] Poujoulat (1986:229).

military intervention in Lebanon. Such colonial designs having been thwarted by Fu'ād Pasha, the square gradually came to embody the model of an Ottomanized Beirut, the 'jewel in the crown of the Padishah', as the German emperor William II called the city on his 1898 visit.[74]

When Ibrāhīm Fakhrī Bey became municipal president in 1878, he made Sahat al-Burj his top priority and even committed private funds to its development. Money was collected from the notables for the planting of young trees and pathways. In an article entitled 'Improvements on Sahat al-Burj' *Lisān al-Ḥāl* announced that

> The entire municipal council under the able leadership of Ibrāhīm Fakhrī Bey has begun the work for the ordering of the city, especially on Sahat al-Burj's park. For a while now, lamps have been promised to be put up around the park at a cost of at least 10,300 piastres. . . . As we see it at this moment, it is absolutely necessary to improve al-Burj. Already it was necessary to collect the sum of 41,000 piastres from [Fakhrī Bey's] private money to pay for this work [but] the municipality needs to decide that it is necessary to invest 30,000 piastres from its budget to develop the square according to the map which had been drawn [by Bishāra Dīb].[75]

Lisān al-Ḥāl appealed to its readers' taste and pride of place by urging them to contribute financially in order to make Sahat al-Burj 'as beautiful as the Azbakiyya Park in Cairo'.[76] At the same time, the newspaper resorted to customary name-dropping of 'local investors'.[77] Unlike the infrastructural projects discussed in Chapter 3, development plans for Sahat al-Burj were never taken over by foreign companies.

The construction of the Petit Serail was the main trigger of municipal development plans for Sahat al-Burj. Subsequent landscape design transformed the field (*al-saḥla*) into a modern space (*al-sāḥa*) replete with trees, fences, and fashionable architectural features in Ottoman urban design—the octagonal kiosk and the sumptuous fountain in the middle of the park. In 1903, 'the governor general paved al-Burj to make it the beauty spot it deserves to be.' It was the entrance to the governor's palace and to the Ottoman Bank and other administrative buildings as well as the garages of the railway company, the Tobacco Régie, the Beirut tramway, the gas company, and the Lebanese tramway company.[78]

At the same time as the government palace appropriated the square as an extension of its own structure and emanation of imperial power, Sahat al-Burj continued to function as an outlet for the pursuit of leisure and popular protest.

[74] PRO, FO, 195/2024, 10 Oct. 1898. [75] *Lisān al-Ḥāl* (1 May 1879). [76] Ibid.
[77] *Lisān al-Ḥāl* (26 May 1879). [78] *Lisān al-Ḥāl* (16 Mar. 1903).

Time and again, conflicts between what Henri Le Jebore distinguished as 'conceived' and 'lived spaces' ignited over the right to enter and define this as Beirut's most central place. Any threat to this order, however unpremeditated, was also seen as a challenge to the government's generalized project of modernity. A few months into the establishment of the provincial capital, *Lisān al-Ḥāl* took an attack on a bureaucrat strolling along Sahat al-Burj as a pretext to stage a verbal assault on the lower classes writ large while claiming to speak in their interest:

The *Burj* is surrounded by small, entangled shops which offer easy escape routes [for the criminal] despite the presence of the Serail and the barracks of the cavalry. We hope the new system of justice will sort out such threats to the peace and stability of the city. They are a menace to society and [their owners] need to be punished severely. . . . It is known that in a city like Beirut which thrives on trade, more security means more profit. Those most affected by such crises are the ones with medium income and the poor. Anybody who halts our progress with such acts [commits] theft.[79]

Here, *Lisān al-Ḥāl* blamed the tortuous bazaars for the impunity of criminals but fell short of advocating wholesale demolition. As it was, the regularization on Sahat al-Burj gave the square something external, severed from its immediate surroundings. It was generally felt that the square was being designated as elite space with restricted access. This view was expressed in a polemic article in *Lisān al-Ḥāl* which compared Beirut's two main squares' histories to strengthen his argument. In the 1880s, the author argued, the few scattered *Azdarahit* plants, the last reminders of the 'old' Sahat al-Burj, had been fenced in to produce a picturesque oval garden. The article complained about the fact that entry to this garden was forbidden, subject to an entrance fee and that it was turned into a commercial area:

The municipality had built some small huts on the edge of its fences and today [1913] large shops made of stone and lime are built for revenue, in the knowledge that in Beirut there are a number of very rich people who hope to buy them for no less than 150,000 piastres. But if the municipality sells this public garden, *it is like somebody selling his eyes to buy glasses*. . . . What is the need for a garden if it is inside a wall? It is upon us to remove these constructions [around the park] and open its gates to everyone who wishes to enter them. For we deserve better than an inaccessible park, as it represents for us the fabric of the previous century.[80]

Large public squares or parks like Sahat al-Burj were targeted by the Ottoman authorities for rituals of state power as they provided political order despite a high degree of popular, urban mobilization (see Figure 14). At the

[79] *Lisān al-Ḥāl* (25 June 1888). [80] *Lisān al-Ḥāl* (6 Nov. 1913; emphasis added).

FIG. 14. The new Burj square and Petit Serail

same time, the imperial state never quite mastered these public squares which also became the rallying points of popular anti-government protest. When a group of notables demanded that the governor general release political prisoners in the aftermath of the Ottoman clampdown on the Beirut Reform Committee, 'a large mass quietly gathered on Assour and the Place des Canons' to put pressure on the government. When the prisoners were finally set free from the Grand Serail late into the night, they were greeted with manifestations of solidarity across the city.[81]

The barracks of the imperial light cavalry next to the Petit Serail signalled the maintenance of political order as it was conveniently situated at the intersection between the square and the newly aligned Suq al-Fashkha that led west through the old city. Next to the barracks, a large office building accommodated the Hijaz railway company, the epitome of Hamidian development of the Arab provinces. On top of the red-tiled roof of its three-floor building, a central crest displayed local time to the leisurely *flâneurs* and to the newly arrived from the mountain as the Beirut–Damascus road led directly onto the square.

[81] Samneh (1920:85).

Rue Emir Bashir formed the axis between the two main squares in *fin de siècle* Beirut. From Sahat al-Burj wide pavements lined with trees led the way to the 'other' square, Sahat al-Sur. Compared to Sahat al-Burj, the organic development of Sahat al-Sur resisted the regulatory forces of the Ottoman and French colonial authorities and 'has guarded its curious triangular form which seems to have persistently disturbed urbanists'.[82] In many ways, Sahat al-Sur became the main local traffic junction in late nineteenth century Beirut where the main tramway lines crossed. Situated on the south-western side of the old city, it 'was a natural outlet for the district of Zuqaq al-Blat and for the more working-class area of Bashura and its prolongation, Basta'.[83] The square functioned as a meeting point of public processions and the venue for popular festivities where '[s]wings and merry-go-rounds [were] installed around the square's famous cafes'.[84] Here migrant workers arrived early in the morning to wait for work opportunities at one of the many construction sites of the city.

Designs to turn Sahat al-Sur into a public park, too, dated back to 1869 when the newly formed municipality requisitioned recently built, popular stores and tore them down. Lack of funding aborted all further development until 1892 when the governor general decided to construct a public building on the square and create a leisure park around it. With the dismissal of Ismail Kemal Bey, the incomplete building was torn down again and the idea of a public park was dropped 'due to pressure from some of the local inhabitants'.[85]

The celebrations commemorating Abdülhamid II's jubilee on 1 September 1900 brought Sahat al-Sur into the limelight of imperial, regional, and municipal affairs. To the sound of military music and under flying imperial banners, an 8 metre tall, white marble fountain was unveiled in the square's centre. The governor general turned on the gilded water tap and symbolically drank the first cup from the fountain's pipes. As with the Ottoman clocktower, Yūsuf Aftimos was the chief architect and Yūsuf al-ʿAnīd the sculptor.

The golden Arabic and Ottoman calligraphy, engraved by the local artist Shaykh Muḥammad ʿUmar al-Barbīr on commemorative plates in honour of the sultan, reflected the larger phenomenon of using architecture to promote the Hamidian personality cult. The commemorative plates on monuments were a constant reminder of the noble donor (although most public construction was actually paid for out of municipal funds). As a way to express the city's gratitude a delegation of Beiruti notables including Iskandar Tuwaynī, Amīn

[82] Tabet (1993:131). [83] Debbas (1994:90).
[84] Ibid. [85] *Lisān al-Ḥāl* (6 Nov. 1913).

Muṣṭafa Arslān, and Asʿad Laḥḥūd paid a personal visit to the sultan in Istanbul 'carrying valuable presents'.[86]

In sum, a comparison of the two main squares of Beirut reveals their differentiated historical trajectories and temporal rhythms that marked late Ottoman urban life. In the second half of the nineteenth century, Sahat al-Burj transcended the local character which Sahat al-Sur embodied. The latter's smaller size and odd shape resisted the imposition of larger, external rhythms. The former, on the other hand, became a catalyst of urbanist change, for example, as the French-dominated Place des Canons that Poujoulat had described after the civil war in Mount Lebanon as an elite space whose accessibility was deeply contested. Indeed, by the turn of the century, Sahat al-Burj had become the showpiece of Ottomanized Beirut, just as it was to become a symbol of French rule during the mandate period.

'The Jewel in the Crown of the Padishah'

In the course of this book, I have discussed the medical roots of French colonialism, the sectarian paths of Anglo-American missionary education, and the architectural manifestations of Ottoman imperialism. Imperial Germany, too, affected *fin de siècle* Beirut when the German emperor visited the city during his widely publicized tour of the Holy Land in November 1898. This particular encounter with European imperialism proved the ultimate ritual of commemoration for the population as much as for the provincial government of Beirut. The visit ushered in frantic preparations and offered the city an opportunity to stage itself in all its glamourous Ottoman modernity.

The Beirut press eagerly awaited the visit of Wilhelm II. *Thamarāt al-Funūn* and *Lisān al-Ḥāl*, ever the mouthpieces of public opinion in Bilad al-Sham, heralded the visit as a milestone of German–Ottoman friendship.[87] The Beiruti journalists argued that Wilhelm II's journey to the East marked a symbolic departure from German foreign policy in the Middle East from Bismarck's non-interventionism to a declared pro-Ottoman stance.[88] Under these conditions, the fact that Beirut was chosen as the point of Wilhelm's departure caused a frantic surge among the city authorities and urban notables to present Beirut in the best of lights. In preparation, the governors of Beirut, Damascus,

[86] Yazbak (1958:ii 132). It should be noted that in the shadow of much publicized commemorative construction, a number of neighbourhood building projects, too, were carried out for the occasion. For example, *Lisān al-Ḥāl* reports on 19 Nov. 1901 that 'a new mosque was officially opened in conjunction with His Majesty's birthday at Burj Abu Haydar in Museitbeh [and] founded by ʿAbd al-Ghanī Bayḍūn'.

[87] Sinno (1998:115–33).

[88] Scheffler (1998:25).

and Mount Lebanon set up planning committees for his final reception in Beirut.

Khalīl Sarkīs, the ubiquitous editor of *Lisān al-Ḥāl*, was one of the official local representatives who accompanied the emperor on his tour in Beirut and to Damascus. He published a detailed description of the preparations in both cities and the perambulations of the royal visitor.[89] Under the supervision of Yūsuf Aftimos the municipality erected special gas lanterns decorated with German and Ottoman flags and garlands along the imperial paths. The Ottoman infantry and cavalry were trained long in advance to line up and parade in their new uniforms on the quays and on the marching square in front of the Grand Serail.

> Along the entire path, the offices of the port company, the customs, the Khedival Lines and the adjacent mansions and all the official and unofficial Ottoman government offices were laid with cedar twigs, pine branches and splendid lighting. And especially Sahat al-Burj was decorated by [the *muftī*] ʿAbd al-Bāsiṭ [al-Fākhūrī] and the engineer Yūsuf Efendi Aftimos with three arcs of the highest order, one on top of the other with a German and an Ottoman flag above.[90]

When the emperor's yacht arrived at the port of Beirut, a crowd of some 50,000 people welcomed him.[91] The city's student population was given a day off to mark the occasion.[92] Before the emperor and his wife went ashore, the governor general and the municipal president of Beirut, Rashīd Bey and ʿAbd al-Qādir al-Qabbānī, were received aboard the ship for lunch, and they returned the favour by presenting a host of gifts and memorabilia from the city of Beirut.[93] The parade through the city along designated imperial buildings and municipal landmarks led the procession to German charitable organizations in Ras Beirut, to Sahat al-Burj, and the Grand Serail.[94] At the end of Emperor William II's guided tour, speeches were made and a sumptuous military parade was staged on Beirut's 'capitol hill'.

> While refreshments were served, His Majesty feasted his eyes on the beautiful view of the city, the harbour, and the deep blue sea. In the other direction, he looked across a densely wooded plain up to the heights of Mount Lebanon. . . . The return trip resembled a triumphal procession. The route was flanked by countless people, all cheering endlessly. Night had already set in as the procession continued through the brightly illuminated city, across the cannon square with its decorative public garden, and down

89 Sarkīs (1997). 90 Ibid. 84. 91 For images of the visit, see Lemke (1998).
92 Sarkīs (1997:86). 93 Sinno (1998:127).
94 Davie (1998:98–100). For their relief work, Fu'ād Pasha had granted them the land to erect the buildings Wilhelm visited in 1898.

to the harbour. Everywhere the streets, the windows, and balconies were lined with people, who were outdoing each other in expressing their joy.[95]

The emperor's entourage was uncomfortably hot in Beirut but very impressed at the apparent outpouring of so much pro-German sentiment. The sultan had made sure the city displayed itself at its most exuberant and 'most Ottoman' for the occasion. At the end of this book, written one hundred years and many standing ovations to foreigners later, however, I cannot help but suspect that the crowd was mocking the visitor, the ruler, and its chroniclers. I surmise that in the event, Beirut was probably celebrating itself more than the hapless emperor or the absent sultan. German flags and Ottoman ribbons notwithstanding, the real subject of commemoration was *fin de siècle* Beirut.

Conclusion

The Beiruti petitioners for a provincial capital speculated accurately. The final period of Ottoman rule in the Arab world, the Hamidian and Young Turk era, was an age of extraordinary urban revitalization and Beirut benefited enormously from being a provincial capital.

The third and final part of this book has explored the places and spaces of nineteenth-century Beirut. I have traced the production of multiple geographies of the city; the struggle over representations and meanings of urban space as well as the dreams and nightmares of growth; the structures and practices of everyday life as well as imperial impositions; the city's hidden rhythms as well as its landmark architecture. The previous chapter examined the effects of literary imaginations of Beirut's role and function of urban planning and regularization. By way of extending this argument to public architecture, this chapter has offered an imperial 'site geography' which—I have argued—punctuated the urban landscape and shaped the rhythm of the inhabitants' everyday itineraries.

Beirut's *fin de siècle* styles paved the way for Lebanon's architectural modernism of the mid-twentieth century.[96] Monumentality and visuality in architectural and urban planning marked the political power of provincial capitals, while the economic struggle between local merchants and municipal authorities and the imperial government over the funding of public buildings such as

[95] *Das deutsche Kaiserpaar im Heiligen Lande im Herbst 1898. Mit allerhöchster Ermächtigung Seiner Majestät des Kaisers und Kömigs bearbeitet nach authentischen Berichten und Akten* (Berlin, 1899). Assembled and designed by Wolf-Dieter Lemke (1998), and translation by Monika Guerino, as 'The official report' in Neuwirth *et al., Baalbek; Image and Monument*, 56.

[96] Arbid (Ph.D. thesis, 2002).

schools, palaces, and hospitals was matched by a symbolic struggle over access to, and interpretation of, public squares and gardens. Public construction in *fin de siècle* Beirut had many patrons and styles. The annual recurrence of Ottoman rituals of commemoration at opening ceremonies was a pervasive way in which the imperial government attempted to Ottomanize public space and provincial architecture that without its semiotic claims may have had (and in later periods did have) alternative significations.

These rituals ultimately inscribed into the urban fabric of provincial capitals the Ottoman will to power and the imperial project of reform. Yet, the urban fabric defied a clear separation of Ottoman domination and Beiruti subjection. The physical Ottomanization of the landscape did not lead to a superimposition of a 'modern Ottoman' on a 'traditional Arab' city. Rather, the process of planning and construction was carried out by an at times hotly contested political convergence of imperial elites and local notables.

Conclusion

> Beirut how you have changed—Beirut how we have changed
>
> (Nizar Kabbani)

This study has introduced the year 1888 as a landmark date in the modern history of Ottoman rule in the Arab provinces and in Beirut itself. In the first part of this book, the narrative of the build-up to, and the subsequent effect of, the creation of the province of Beirut demonstrated both the significance of this date and the emergence of an ever-growing urban elite which brought about this watershed event. In the early nineteenth century, when Acre ruled supreme in the Levant and Bilad al-Sham, provincial rulers were conducting military campaigns against each other. Neither property nor position was secure. Egyptian rule between 1830 and 1840 turned Beirut from a tax farm of the regional overlords to a port-city that served the expanding Mediterranean economy. Then, Ottoman reform and provincial centralization set in motion a process of strongly hierarchized, but also participatory rule in Bilad al-Sham.

Since its first urban expansions in the mid-nineteenth century, Beirut has developed in the shadow of civil war. After 1860, fear and promise structured the conception of time and space. The municipality of Beirut emerged as the institutional location for the vision of Beirut as a modern Ottoman port-city. In particular the members of its elected councils provided the red thread of civilian rule and urban governance that ran through this book. Beirut's literary middle class—journalists, poets, novelists, and editorialists, many of whom sat on the municipal council—was the hermeneutic force behind the making of the modern city.

Recurrent urban themes in newspapers and public speeches—security, hygiene, sustainable economic growth, educational expansion, and public construction—coalesced into a future-oriented discourse and urban identity. In this 'enlightened process', however, the luminaries of the Arab cultural revival were invested in the socially conservative Ottoman reform project. By generating a distinctly elitist shape of the city they arguably helped lay the foundations of social inequality for the Lebanese nation state.

Beirut was also a child of the 'benevolent reforms' of the *tanẓīmāt* period before it matured into a provincial capital during Abdülhamid II's rule. The imperial government and the sultan personally played a formative role in shaping Beirut as a modern city and a provincial capital. Administrative correspondence between Istanbul and Beirut, as well as detailed book-keeping, evince both a remarkable degree of interference in daily activities in the province and the systematic permeation of Ottoman power into everyday life in Beirut.

Imperial knowledge and proximity made the Ottoman state dominant but not hegemonic.[1] It dominated through the management of urban sites, architectural display of the will to power, and through the temporal narratives of its *mission civilisatrice* in the provincial peripheries. However central the Ottoman state and Istanbul were in the development of Beirut, alternative points of reference were also at work, such as Egyptian, German, British, and French influence in the fields of trade, municipal politics, health, and education. Moreover, the dominant Ottoman provincial order was both shaped and challenged locally.

During the protracted struggle for the creation of the province between 1864 and 1888, Beirut's representatives displayed an acute awareness of the political geography of their city and of the complex relationship between capital status and economic prosperity. Within the administrative framework of the provincial capital, and particularly through the provincial council, Beiruti notables were able to impose their will and vision on Beirut's administrative hinterland. Within Beirut, local merchants-cum-bureaucrats were able to manipulate Ottoman imperial and provincial authorities to invest funds and efforts into the transformation of the urban fabric. There existed a causal link between Beirut's creation as a provincial capital and the investment of international capital in the city's infrastructural development. The 1890s ushered in a fundamental transformation of urban space in Beirut. The port and railway construction secured Beirut's structural economic advantage over rival towns in the Eastern Mediterranean, while the tramway and the gas lighting companies revolutionized inner-urban mobility. Urban space, time, and distance became marketable commodities that significantly restructured the practices of everyday life.

[1] Guha (1997).

As a consequence, certain groups became alienated from their customary work and place in the city by the effects of Beirut's 'capitalization'. Strikes, demonstrations, and boycotts were physical attempts to claim the right to their city and their livelihood. Industrial action elicited political support from certain local lawyers and, during Hamidian rule, from the sultan personally. After a brief 'liberal' period of Young Turk government, the CUP abolished pro-labour regulations and Beirut's workforce lost its bargaining power against investment companies.

Although the productive and, indeed, constructive power of Ottoman rule was manifested through public works, urban planning, and architectural style, conception of these projects and their funding often originated in Beirut itself. Nevertheless, through recurrent rituals of commemorations that turned opening ceremonies of public buildings into great social spectacles, the urban fabric of capital Beirut served as a platform for inscription of imperial authority and the Ottoman will to power. Monumental Ottoman buildings, public squares, and streets named after sultans were not seen as an alien imposition as they contributed to the realization of local elites' ideas of Beirut as a 'City Beautiful'. On the contrary, public construction—literally as well as figuratively—cemented Ottomanism as a state ideology. Everyday life in *fin de siècle* Beirut was the space onto which Ottoman imperial rule and elite literary discourses projected modernizing norms and forms of social order. As such it emerged as a highly contested arena of the conflict between perceived, conceived, and lived spaces. Local literary elites and Ottoman authorities shared normative projections of law and order. Marginality was produced as the obstacle to temporal conceptions of linear progress, the creation of healthy and salubrious spaces as well as concerns over public security. The solution was not to tackle the roots of social inequality that led to marginalization in the first place, but rather spatial containment, physical suppression, and social stigmatization.

Shared values and norms, socio-economic status, and wealth united literary elites, Ottoman bureaucrats, and urban notables, into a self-contained bourgeois class with shared political and economic interests and a distinct class consciousness that was expressed in this elite's political and economic relations to the expanding space of the city. Class relations were intertwined with—and sustained by—interconfessional elite collusion. Through networks of patron–client dependencies, this collaboration contained urban conflict which often turned sectarian through the very act of crisis management as during the September 1903 riots.

One of the veiled aims of the book has been to tackle the important historiographical issue of the political transition from the Ottoman to the mandate periods. This touches on the core of today's historical sensibility in the successor states of the Ottoman empire Lebanon, Syria, Iraq, and Palestine. The First World War constituted the most important rupture in the history of modern Bilad al-Sham not only because it ushered in the end of a 400-year-long Ottoman rule but also because it prompted a frenzy of political and intellectual activity to fill the legitimacy vacuum left in its wake.

The question of the origins of Arab nationalisms and the formation of nation states in the Middle East has generated a rather selective interest in the late Ottoman period. Because this study has treated the Ottoman period in its own right, with the strategic choice of the framework of a vanished province, it holds valuable advantages. For one, it allows for a detailed analysis of the evolving social relations over time within the space of the late Ottoman empire with its own 'internal' ruptures, such as 1888 for Beirut and the Young Turk revolution of 1908/9 for the entire region.

It also frees this Middle East history from an inevitable teleological gaze of national emergence that tends to posit in opposing blocks 'the Ottoman era' against 'the mandate period'. Instead—as I have hinted to throughout—historical continuity is evident in urban culture. Comparisons between Ottoman and colonial Beirut has recently elicited charitable revisions of the Orientalist trope of Ottoman despotism. Compared to urban intervention by the French mandate regime and, indeed, the destruction wreaked by Solidere in the 1990s, the late Ottoman political system and its 'auto-regulatory mechanisms' of urban development have come to be seen as benign, organic, and harmonious—a veritable 'golden age'.[2]

After the demise of evolutionary histories there remain (at least) three ways to approach urban history in particular. Between a devil of deconstructionism, which shatters the all too familiar past, and a deep blue sea of a nostalgic search for authenticity, solace, and solution in the past, this third, critical history of Ottoman Beirut has attempted to restore historical subjectivity to the city and its inhabitants in all its contradictions. Beirut clearly defied a Cartesian colonial order. By extension, the urban elites—notables, merchants, and moralists—are fully accountable for the particular class–confession constellation that emerged during the post-1860 era of 'the long peace'. Yet, they were not the only history-making subjects in town. On the one hand, port and construction workers, students and prostitutes, pedestrians and city users generally, played crucial roles in the transformation of *fin de siècle* Beirut. On the other hand, the Ottoman and foreign communities, be they bureaucrats or

[2] Davie (1996:70).

businessmen, had an enormous impact on the development of Beirut as a modern city, too.

Late Ottoman Beirut, then, shared many of the cosmopolitan features of other Mediterranean port-cities with which its inhabitants communicated on a daily basis: a pluralist urban society in 'a place of compromises and alliances'—to paraphrase Henri Lefebvre—a hub of commercial networks and cultural production with family ties and trade links to Tunis, Alexandria, Izmir, Mersin, and Istanbul. By and large, however, late Ottoman cosmopolitanism—tolerant and open though it may appear in comparison to the identitarian closures brought about by European colonialism and the nation state system—was generally confined to elite spaces. It was also overwhelmingly a male-dominated world, although women slowly entered 'respectable' public positions through education and health work from the 1870s and 1880s onwards. For the most part, however, women in the public domain were suspect and stigmatized. During the mandate period women became better organized and began to enter male domains such as politics, journalism, leisure, and entertainment but, as Elizabeth Thompson has shown, new forms of gender proscription emerged even as old ones were overcome.[3]

To say that nineteenth-century Beirut was a Mediterranean city is either to state the obvious or to project a twentieth-century Lebanese political discourse into the past. A common geography, cultural affinities, trade links, and shared modes of social and gender exclusion notwithstanding, Lebanese intellectuals did not articulate a Mediterranean consciousness until after the First World War, and even then it was an intellectual subsidiary to a small Phoenicianist minority around Charles Corm's *La Révue Phénicienne*.

By far the most widespread mode of urban identification in late Ottoman Beirut was the provincial capital. Beirut was a late-comer to the family of provincial capitals but a broad spectrum of its inhabitants were willing to fight hard, particularly against their Damascene rivals, for a place at the top of the Ottoman urban hierarchy. Despite the rivalry between Beirut and Damascus, however, the nineteenth- and twentieth-century tales of the two cities were intimately connected, administratively, politically, and culturally.

I have introduced the provincial capital as an alternative to previous, ascriptive paradigms which tended to trace urban essences and track changes (or lack thereof) over time in a particular city or category of cities. Rather, what has emerged in my research is that the profound physical changes that Aleppo, Damascus, Jerusalem, Mosul, Baghdad, Basra, or Beirut share in the

[3] See Thompson (2000).

nineteenth century owed much to the transformative character of geography and space and the ways in which their inhabitants thought about this character.

Finally, the provincial capital as a relational unit of analysis also helps us to better understand the precise nature of continuity and rupture between Ottoman imperial and colonial national periods in Middle East social and intellectual history. The experience of the Ottoman provincial capital put in place political structures for Arab national capitals after the First World War long before colonial powers carved up nation states. With independence in the 1940s and 1950s revolutionary governments attempted to reverse the urban bias inherited from the late Ottoman period by launching land reforms. But urban immigration has risen sharply in the Arab world since the 1960s and severely strained the political systems in many post-Ottoman states. Most demoralizing of the phenomenon of land flight was the experience of Maronite and Shiite migrants who were lured to the promise of 1960s Beirut but found themselves economically and legally marginalized as well as politically underrepresented. Beirut was unable and unwilling to cope with the new arrivals whose urban presence subsequently unhinged the persistent city-centred, post-Ottoman order of the Lebanese nation state and this was a crucial factor that led to the Lebanese civil war of 1975–90.

The Lebanese politician Elie Salem, speaking in front of the United Nations Assembly in 1976, declared that Lebanon was 'a lost star from the Ottoman galaxy'.[4] Any parallels between the current *fin de siècle* Beirut and that of the nineteenth century are neither coincidental nor intended, merely inevitable. As a laconic Nizar Kabbani commented in the 1960s—writing from his apartment in Qubbat al-Qantari, the new, old 'capitol hill' of independent Lebanon—Beirut changed its inhabitants and they in turn changed the city of Beirut. But the relation between city and citizens remains as close as it remains tense. After the long civil war, a deep-rooted middle class struggles to retain Beirut and its 'inherited space' against the capitalist projections of a new global city at the hands of the international investment company Solidere.[5] Communal conflict continues to be contained and managed by political patronage in the sectarian frame of crisis management. And the majority of Beirut's inhabitants, forced to dwell with utmost dignity in the squalor of the urban fringes, are denied the right to that city, 'inherited' or 'projected'; denied access to even the most basic urban services, such as running water, sewage, and electricity.

[4] Quoted in Barbir (1996:108).

[5] Hanssen and Genberg (2001:231–62).

Meanwhile, the rapid destruction and reconstruction of the downtown area is driven by the economic and political elite's sense of physically reclaiming Beirut against the 'threat' of the perennial social demons—the urban poor—whose access to the new Beirut has to be blocked at all costs: 'If we don't build the centre of the capital now, it will become like a wasteland with Dick, Tom and Harry turning it into a political and social time bomb'.[6]

The vocabulary and imagery of the two post-war scenarios are almost identical. While today's post-war, global city has changed physically beyond recognition from the days as a provincial capital, like in the late nineteenth century the panacea against sectarian violence remains class consolidation. In both *fin de siècles*, genuine social equality was sacrificed for a false sense of political stability.

[6] Interview with Fāḍil Shalaq, the head of the Council of Development and Reconstruction, in *al-Hayāt* (11 July 1991). Cited in Leenders (2001).

BIBLIOGRAPHY

UNPUBLISHED ARCHIVAL AND MANUSCRIPT SOURCES

Başbakanlık Devlet Arşivi, Istanbul

YEE: Yıldız Esās Evrāḳı.
YAHUS: Yıldız Tasnifi—Sadarat Hususi
YMTV: Yıldız Mütenevvi Tasnīfī.
AMTZ-CL: Cebel-i Lübnān Kataloğu
SD: Sadāret Defterleri, vol. 71.
ID: Irādeler Dāhiliye, 1888.
AD: ʿAyniyāt Defterleri, vols. 902, 905, 908.
Gelen: Gelen Defterleri Vilāyetler, vols. 268–71, 1890–1901.
Giden: Giden Defterleri Vilāyetler, vols. 272–5, 1890–1909.
Sicill-i Aḥvāl
Ḥarītalar Kataloğu

IRCICA, Yildiz Photographic Library

OBA: Ottoman Bank Archive, Istanbul

Litigations and account details

MAE, Paris: Archive du Ministère des Affaires Étrangères à Paris

CPT: Correspondance Politique, Turquié.
CCCTB: Correspondance Consulaire Commerciale, Turquié—Beyrouth.
CPCTB: Correspondance Politique Consulaire, Turquié—Beyrouth.
NSTSL: Nouvelle Série, Turquié, Syrie-Liban.
NSSTSL: Nouvelle Série, Supplement, Turquié, Syrie-Liban.

MAE, Nantes: Archive du Ministère des Affaires Étrangères à Nantes

CB: Consulat Beyrouth.
CEB: Constantinople–Beyrouth, Correspondances avec les Échelles.

PRO: Public Record Office, Kew, London.

FO: Series Foreign Office 195, 206.

Houghton Library, Harvard University

ABCFM: American Board of Commissioners Foreign Missions, Syrian Mission.

PRINTED CONTEMPORARY SOURCES

Arabic and Beirut Literature (years consulted)

Ḥadīqat al-Akhbār, Beirut (1858–68).
Al-Jinān, Beirut (1870–84).
Kanz al-Jawāʾib, Istanbul (1870–90).
Lisān al-Ḥāl, Beirut (1878–1913).
Al-Manār, Cairo (1903).
Al-Mufīd, Beirut (1911–13).
Al-Mashriq, Beirut (1900–20).
Al-Muqtaṭaf, Cairo (1881–1920).
Le Réveil, Beirut (1908–13).
Thamarāt al-Funūn, Beirut (1875–1909).

Salnāme—Sūriyya Vilāyeti 1864–1888.
Salnāme—Bayrūt Vilāyeti, 1888–1909.

UNPUBLISHED THESES

ARBID, GEORGE, 'Practicing Modernism in Beirut: Architecture in Lebanon, 1946–1970' (Harvard University, Ph.D. thesis, 2002).

BEYHUM, NABIL, 'Espaces éclatés, éspaces dominés: Étude de la recomposition des espaces publiques centraux de Beyrouth de 1975–1990' (Université de Lyons, Ph.D. thesis, 1991).

BLAKE, CORINE, 'Training Arab-Ottoman Bureaucrats: Syrian Graduates of the Mülkiyye Mektebi, 1890–1920' (Princeton University, Ph.D. thesis, 1991).

BLECHER, ROBERT, 'The Politics of Public Health in Syria and Lebanon, 1821–1958' (Stanford University, Ph.D. thesis, 2002).

BODENSTEIN, RALPH, *Qasr Heneiné; Memories and History of a Late Ottoman House in Beirut* (Universität Bonn, MA thesis, 1999).

DAKHLI, INÈS-LEYLA, 'Naissance de l'intellectuel arabe: L'Action des Jésuites au Liban de 1840 à la veille de la Première Guerre Mondiale' (Paris IV, Mémoire Maîtrise, 1995).

GROSS, MAX, 'Ottoman Rule in the Province of Damascus, 1860–1909' (Georgetown University, Ph.D. thesis, 1979).

HAKIM-DOWEK, CAROL, 'The Origins of the Lebanese National Idea, 1840–1914' (Oxford University, D.Phil. thesis, 1997).

HANSSEN, JENS, 'The Effect of Ottoman Rule on *Fin de Siècle* Beirut: The Province of Beirut, 1888–1914' (Oxford, D.Phil. thesis, 2001).

KALLA, MUHAMMAD, 'The Role of Foreign Trade in the Economic Development of Syria, 1831–1914' (Washington University, Ph.D. thesis, 1969).

KAUFMAN, ASHER, 'Reviving Phoenicia: The Search for an Identity in Lebanon' (New York, Brandeis University, Ph.D. thesis, 2000).
ÖZVEREN, EYÜP, 'The Making and Unmaking of an Ottoman Port-City: Beirut in the 19th Century' (SUNY University at Binghampton, Ph.D. thesis, 1990).
SAJDI, DANA, 'Peripheral Visions: The Worlds and Worldviews of Commoner Chroniclers in the 18th Century Levant' (New York, Columbia, Ph.D. thesis, 2002).
SCHOLZ, NORBERT, 'Foreign Education and Indigenous Reaction in Late Ottoman Lebanon: Students and Teachers at the Syrian Protestant College in Beirut' (Georgetown University, Ph.D. thesis, 1997).
SEHNAOUI-SALAM, NADA, 'L'Occidentalisation de la vie quoti-dienne à Beyrouth (1860–1914)' (Paris, Nanterre, Mémoire Maîtrise, 1981).
SHAREEF, MALEK, 'Urban Administration in the Late Ottoman Period: The Beirut Municipality as a Case Study, 1867–1908' (Beirut, AUB, MA thesis, 1998).
WEBER, STEFAN, *Zeugnisse Kulturellen Wandels: Baugeschichte von Damaskus zwischen 1808 und 1918* (Freie Universität Berlin, Ph.D. thesis 2001).

CITED BOOKS AND ARTICLES

CUP-Cambridge University Press; HUP-Harvard University Press; PUP-Princeton University Press; OUP-Oxford University Press.

ʿABD AL-NŪR, AMĪN (1896) *Qānūn al-abnāʾ wa qirar al-istimlāk li-ajl al-manāfiʿ al-ʿumūmiyya* (Beirut: al-Maṭbaʾa al-adabiyya).
ABDEL NOUR, ANTOINE (1982) *Introduction à l'histoire urbaine de la Syrie ottomane (XVIe–XVIIIe siècles)* (Beirut: Université Libanaise).
ʿABDUH, MUḤAMMAD (1966 [1897]) *The Theology of Unity*, tr. Ishaq Musa'ad and Kenneth Cragg (London: George Allen & Unwin).
ABOU-EL-HAJ, RIFʿAT (1991) *Formation of the Modern State: The Ottoman Empire, Sixteenth to Eighteenth Centuries* (Albany: SUNY Press).
ABŪ ḤALQA, FAḌLALLAH (1890) *Muḥtaṣir fī-al-jughrāfiya* (Beirut: Maṭbaʿa jarīdat Bayrūt).
ABU-HUSAYN, ʿABD AL-RAHMAN (1985) *Provincial Leadership in Syria, 1575–1650* (Beirut: AUB).
ABU MANNEH, BUTRUS (1980) 'The Christians between Ottomanism and Syrian Nationalism: The Ideas of Buṭrus al-Bustānī', *International Journal of Middle East Studies*, 11: 287–304.
—— (1992) 'The Establishment and Dismantling of the Province of Syria, 1865–1888', in J. Spagnolo (ed.), *Problems of the Middle East in Historical Perspective: Essays in Honour of Albert Hourani* (Oxford: OUP), 9–26.
ABU MANNEH, BUTRUS (1998) 'The Genesis of Midhat Pasha's Governorship in Syria 1878–1880', in T. Philipp and B. Schaebler (eds.), *The Syrian Land in the Eighteenth and Nineteenth Century: Integration and Fragmentation* (Stuttgart: Steiner Verlag), 251–67.

Abu Manneh, Butrus (1999) 'The Rise of the Sancak of Jerusalem in the Late Nineteenth Century', in Ilan Pappé (ed.), *The Israel/Palestine Question: Rewriting Histories* (London: Routledge).

Abū Sa'd, Aḥmad (1997) *Mu'jam asmā' al-usar wa-l-ashkhās wa-lamḥāt min tārīkh al-'ā'ilāt* (Beirut: Dār al-malāyin).

Administration Sanitaire de l'Empire Ottoman (1906) *Rapport de la Commission d'Inspection des Lazarets sur le Lazaret de Beyrouth; présenté au conseil supérieur de santé le 9 Octobre, 1906* (Constantinople: Imp. Lœffler).

Adonis (1993) *Ha anta, ayyūha al-waqt; Sīra shi'riyya thaqāfiyya* (Beirut: Dār al-ādāb).

Adorno, Theodor (1998 [1967]), 'Education after Auschwitz', in his *Critical Models; Interventions and Catchwords* (New York: Colombia University Press).

Akarli, Engin (1986) 'Abdulhamid II's Attempt to Integrate Arabs into the Ottoman System', in D. Kushner (ed.), *Palestine in the Late Ottoman Period* (Leiden: Brill), 74–89.

——(1993) *The Long Peace, Ottoman Lebanon, 1860–1920* (London: Centre for Lebanese Studies and I. B. Tauris).

——(forthcoming) 'Daughters and Fathers: A Druze Damsel's Experience (1894–1897)', in Karl Barbir and Baki Tezcan (eds.), *Identity and Identity Formation in the Middle East: Essays in Honour of Norman Itzkowitz.*

Amīn, Osman (1953 [1944]) *Muḥammad 'Abduh*, tr. from the Arabic by Charles Wendell, (Washington, DC: American Council of Learned Societies).

Anderson, Benedict (1992 [1983]) *Imagined Communities* (New York: Verso).

Antonius, George (1939) *The Arab Awakening* (London: Hamish Hamilton).

Anṭūn, Faraḥ (1979) *al-Dīn wa-l-'ilm wa-l-māl; al-waḥsh, al-waḥsh, al-waḥsh; Urushalim al-Jadīd aw: fataḥ al-'Arab bayt al-maqaddis* (Beirut: Dār al-ṭalī'a).

Appadurai, Arjun (1996) *Modernity at Large: Cultural Dimensions of Globalisation* (Minneapolis: University of Minnesota Press).

Arslān, Shakīb (1969) *Sīra dhātiyya* (Beirut: Dār al-ṭalī'a).

Asad, Talal (2003) *Formations of the Secular: Christianity, Islam, Modernity* (Stanford: Stanford University Press).

AUB Alumni Association (1953) *Who's Who: Alumni Association American University of Beirut, 1870–1952* (Beirut: AUB).

'Awwāḍ, 'Abd al-'Aziz M. (1969) *al-Idāra al-'uthmāniyya fī wilāya Sūriyya, 1864–1914* (Cairo: Dār al-ma'ārif).

Ayalon, Ami (1995) *The Press in the Arab Middle East: A History* (Oxford: OUP).

Badawi, Mustafa (1985) *Modern Arabic Literature and the West* (London: Ithaca Press).

Baer, Gabriel (1969) 'The Beginnings of Municipal Government', in his *Studies in the Social History of Modern Egypt* (Chicago: Chicago University Press), 190–209.

Bahjat, Muḥammad, and Muḥammad Rafīq Tamīmī (1987 [1915–16]) *Wilāyat Bayrūt*, 2 vols. (Beirut: Lahad Khater).

Barbir, Karl (1980) *Ottoman Rule in Damascus: 1708–1758* (Princeton: PUP).

——(1996) 'Memory, Heritage, and History: The Ottoman Legacy in the Arab World', in L. C. Brown (ed.), *Imperial Legacy: The Ottoman Imprint on the Balkans and the Middle East* (New York: Columbia University Press), 100–14.

AL-BARGHŪTĪ, ʿUMAR ṢĀLIḤ (2001) *al-Marāḥil* (Beirut: Mu'assasa al-ʿarabiyya li-al-dirāsāt wa al-nashr).

BARTH, FREDRIK (1979) *Scale and Social Organisation* (Oslo: Oslo University Press).

BARŪD, ANTOINE (1971) *Shāriʿ al-Mutanabbī, ḥikāyyat al-baghā' fī Lubnan* (Beirut: Ḥaqā'iq wa arqām).

BARŪDĪ, FAKHRĪ (1951) *Mudhakkirāt al-Barūdī* (Damascus: Maṭābiʿa dār al-hayah).

BASTÉA, ELENI (2000) *The Creation of Modern Athens: Planning the Myth* (Cambridge: CUP).

BAYHUM, NABIL (1992) 'The Crisis of Urban Culture: The Three Reconstruction Plans for Beirut', *Beirut Review*, 4: 43–62.

BAYKARA, TUNCER (1992) *Osmanlilarda medeniyet kavrami ve ondokuzuncu yüzyila dair araştirmalar* (Izmir: Akademi Kitabevi).

BAYLY, SUSAN (2002) 'Racial Readings of Empire: Britain, France and Colonial Modernity in the Mediterranean and Asia', in C. A. Bayly and L. Fawaz (eds.), *Modernity and Culture: From the Mediterranean to the Indian Ocean* (New York: Columbia University Press), 285–309.

Bayrūt Vilāyet-i meclis umūmisinin 1330 [m.] senesi ictimāʿındaitiḥāz eylediği mükarirat (Beirut, 1915).

Bayrut Vilāyet-i meclis umūmisinin; üçüncü devre-i ictimaʿında ceryan eden muzakeratin ẓābitdir, 1331 [m.] (Beirut, 1916).

BAYUR, KAMIL (1954) *Sadrazam Kamil Pasha—Siyasi Hayati* (Ankara: Sanat Basimevi).

BENJAMIN, WALTER (1988 [1968]) *Illuminations; Essays and Reflections*, ed. and with an introduction by Hannah Arendt (New York: Schocken Books).

——(2002) *The Arcades Project*, tr. Howard Eiland and Kevin McLaughlin (Cambridge, Mass.: Belknap).

BEN LAGHA, ZAINEB (1999) 'The New Jerusalem by Farah Antun: From the Mythical City to the Modern City—Social Project and Literary Project', in A. Neuwirth, B. Embalo, and S. Guenther (eds.), *Myths and Archetypes* (Beirut: Orient Institut), 553–71.

BENTON, LOANZA G. (n.d.) 'The Diaries, Preminiscenes and Letters of Loanza Goulding Benton (Mrs. William Austin Benton) and William Austin Benton, DD.; Missionaries to Syria, 1847–1869' (Beirut: AUB typescript).

BERQUE, JACQUES (1978) 'The City Speaks', in his *Cultural Expression in Arab Society Today*, tr. Robert Stookey (Austin: University of Texas Press).

BERMAN, MARSHALL (1988 [1983]) *All that is Solid Melts into Air: The Experience of Modernity* (London: Penguin Books).

BHABHA, HOMI (1997) 'Of Mimicry and Man', in F. Cooper and L. A. Stoler (eds.), *Tensions of Empire: Colonial Cultures in a Bourgeois World* (Berkeley and Los Angeles: University of California Press), 152–60.

BIERMAN, IRENE (1991) 'The Ottomanisation of Crete', in D. Preziosi, R. El-Haj, and I. Bierman (eds.), *The Ottoman City and its Parts: Urban Structure and Social Order* (New Rochelle: Aristide D. Caratzas), 53–76.

BIRKEN, ANDREAS (1976) *Die Provinzen des osmanischen Reiches* (Wiesbaden: Reichert).

BLISS, DANIEL (1993) *Letters from a New Campus*, ed. Alfred Howell (Beirut: AUB).

BLONDEL, EDOUARD (1840) *Deux ans en Syrie et en Palestine (1838–1839)* (Paris: P. Dufart).

BODENSTEIN, RALPH, H. GEBHARDT, J. HANSSEN, B. HILLENKAMP, O. KÖGLER, A. MOLLENHAUER, D. SACK, and F. STOLLEIS (2005) *History, Space, and Conflict in Beirut: The Quarter of Zokak el-Blat* (Beirut: Orient Institut).

BOOTH, MARILYN (2001) *May her Likes be Multiplied: Biography and Gender Politics in Egypt* (Los Angeles: California University Press).

BOUMAN, MARK (1987) 'Luxury and Control: The Urbanity of Street Lighting in Nineteenth-Century Cities', *Journal of Urban History*, 14/1: 7–37.

BOURDIEU, PIERRE (1998 [1985]) *Praktische Vernunft: Zur Theorie des Handelns* (Frankfurt: Suhrkamp).

——(1991) 'Social Space and the Genesis of "Classes"', in his *Language and Symbolic Power* (Cambridge: Polity), 229–51.

——(1996 [1979]) *Distinction: A Sociological Critique of the Judgment of Taste* (London: Routledge).

BOWRING, JOHN (1840) *Report on the Statistics of Syria* (London: William Clowes & Sons for HM Stationary Office).

BOYER, BENOÎT (1896) 'La Fièvre typhoide à Beyrouth', *Lyon Médical*.

——(1897) *Conditions hygiéniques actuelles de Beyrouth et de ses environs immédiats* (Lyons: Imprimerie Rey).

BOYLE, SUSAN SILSBY (2001) *Betrayal of Palestine: The Story of George Antonius* (Boulder, Colo.: Westview).

BOZDOĞAN, SIBEL (2002) *Modernism and Nation Building: Turkish Architectural Culture in the Early Republic* (Seattle: Washington University Press).

BRAUDE, BENJAMIN (1982) 'Foundation Myths of the Millet System', in *Christians and Jews in the Ottoman Empire: The Functioning of a Plural Society*, ii, ed. B. Braude and B. Lewis (New York: Holmes & Meier).

BRAUDEL, FERNAND (1992 [1949]) *The Mediterranean and the Mediterranean World in the Age of Philipp II*, i (London: Fontaine, 6th edn.).

——(1977) *Afterthoughts on Material Civilisation* (Baltimore: Johns Hopkins University Press).

BRENNER, ROBERT (1977) 'The Origins of Capitalist Development: A Critique of Neo-Smithian Marxism', *New Left Review*, 104: 25–91.

BRUMMETT, PALMIRA (1995) 'Gluttony, Cholera and High Fashion: Political and Cultural Imperialism in the Ottoman Cartoon Space', *Révue des Études du Monde Muselman et Meditérranéen*, 77–8: 145–64.

BUHAIRY, MARWAN (1981) 'Bulus Nujaym and the Grand Liban Ideal, 1908–1919', in Buhairy (ed.), *Intellectual Life in the Arab East, 1890–1939* (Beirut: AUB).

BURKE, EDMUND (1984) 'The First Crisis of Orientalism, 1890–1914', in J.-C. Vatin (ed.), *Conaissances du Maghreb: sciences sociales et colonialisation* (Paris: CNRS), 213–26.

AL-BUSTĀNĪ, BUṬRUS (1875–81) *Dā'irat al-ma'ārif: Encyclopédie arabe*, 6 vols. (Beirut: al-Maṭba'a al-adabiyya).

——(1990*a*) *al-Jam'iyya al-Sūriyya li al-'Ulūm wa al-Funūn, 1838–1852*, ed. Yūsuf Quzma Khūrī (Beirut: Dār al-Ḥamrā').

——(1990*b*) *Nafīr Sūriyya* (Beirut: Dār al-fikr li al-abḥāth wa-al-nashr).

AL-BUSTANĪ, SALĪM (1990) *Iftitāḥāt Majallat al-Jinān al-Bayrūtiyya, 1870–1884*, 2 vols., ed. Y. Khūrī (Beirut: Dār al-Ḥamrā').

CALVINO, ITALO (1974) *Invisible Cities* (New York: Harcourt).

CANKAYA, ALI (1968–9) *Mülkiyye Tarihi ve Mülkiyeliler*, 3 vols. (Ankara: Mars).

ÇELIK, ZEYNEP (1986) *The Remaking of Istanbul: Portrait of an Ottoman City in the Nineteenth Century* (Los Angeles: University of California Press).

——(1992) *Displaying the Orient Architecture of Islam at Nineteenth Century World's Fairs* (Los Angeles: University of California Press).

——(1997) *Urban Forms and Colonial Confrontations: Algiers under French Rule* (Los Angeles: University of California Press).

——(2000) 'Speaking Back to Orientalist Discourse at the World's Columbian Exposition', in Holly Edwards (ed.), *Noble Dreams—Wicked Pleasures: Orientalism in America, 1870–1930* (Princeton: PUP), 77–97.

CHAKRABARTY, DIPESH (2000) *Provincializing Europe: Postcolonial Thought and Historical Difference* (Princeton: PUP).

CHARMES, GEORGES (1891) *Voyage en Syrie: Impressions et souvenirs* (Paris: Calman-Levy).

CHEVALLIER, DOMINIQUE (1968) 'Western Development and Eastern Crisis in the Mid-Nineteenth Century: Syria Confronted with the European Economy', in W. Polk and R. Chambers (eds.), *Beginnings of Modernisation in the Middle East* (Chicago: Chicago University Press), 205–22.

——(1971) *La Société du Mont Liban à l'époche de la révolution industrielle en Europe* (Paris: Librairie Orientaliste Paul Geuthner).

——(1982) 'Signes de Beyrouth en 1834', *Villes et travail en Syrie du XIX au XX siècle* (Beirut: Cahiers du CERMOC), 9–28.

CIOETA, DONALD (1979) 'Ottoman Censorship in Lebanon and Syria, 1876–1908', *International Journal of Middle East Studies*, 10: 167–86.

——(1982) 'Islamic Benevolent Societies and Public Education in Syria, 1875–1882', *Islamic Quarterly*, 26: 40–55.

CLANCY-SMITH, JULIA (2002) 'Marginality and Migration: Europe's Social Outcasts in Pre-Colonial Tunisia', in Eugene Rogan (ed.), *Outside In: On the Margins of the Modern Middle East* (London: I. B. Tauris), 149–82.

CLEVELAND, WILLIAM (1978) 'The Municipal Council of Tunis, 1858–1870: A Study in Urban Institutional Change', *International Journal of Middle East Studies*, 9: 33–61.

CLEVELAND, WILLIAM (1985) *Islam against the West: Shakib Arslan and the Campaign for Islamic Nationalism* (Austin: Texas University Press).

CLICIAN, A. VASSIT (1909) *Son Altesse Midhat Pacha: Grand vizir* (Paris: Société Anonyme de l'Imprimerie Kugelmann).

COHEN, AMNON (1973) *Palestine in the Eighteenth Century: Patterns of Government and Administration* (Jerusalem: Magnes Press).

COHEN, WILLIAM (1998) *Urban Government and the Rise of the French City: Five Municipalities in the Nineteenth-Century* (New York: Macmillan).

COLLINI, STEFAN (1991) *Public Moralists, Political Thought and Intellectual Life in Britain, 1830–1930* (Oxford: Clarendon Press).

COLQUHOUN, ALAN (1994 [1989]) *Modernity and the Classical Tradition: Architectural Essays, 1980–1987* (Boston: MIT Press).

COMMINS, DAVID (1990) *Islamic Reform: Politics and Social Change in Late Ottoman Syria* (Oxford: OUP).

CONKLIN, ALICE (1997) *A Mission to Civilize: The Republican Idea of Empire and West Africa, 1895–1930* (Stanford: Stanford University Press).

COOPER, FRED, and LAURA ANN STOLER (eds.) (1997) 'Between Metropole and Colony', in *Tensions of Empire: Colonial Cultures in a Bourgeois World* (Los Angeles: University of California Press), 1–50.

CORBIN, ALAIN (1994) *The Lure of the Sea: The Discovery of the Seaside in the Western World* (Los Angeles: University of California Press).

CORM, CHARLES (ed.) (1996 [1919]) *La Révue Phénicienne 1919* (Beirut: Dar an-Nahar).

COZE, EDOUARD (1922) *La Syrie et le Liban* (Paris: Etampes).

CUINET, VITAL (1896) 'La Syrie, Liban et Palestine', *Turquié d'Asie*, ii (Paris: Ernest Leroux).

ḌĀHIR, MASʿŪD (1986) *Bayrūt wa Jabal Lubnān ʿalā mashārif al-qarn al-ʿashrīn; dirāsa fī al-tārīkh al-ijtimāʿī min khilāl mudhakkirāt al-ʿālim al-rūsī al-kabīr A. Kremski; rasāʾil min Lubnān, 1896–1898* (Beirut: Dār al-maḍā).

D'ARMAGNAC, BARON (1985 [1844]) *Nézib et Beyrouth: Souvenirs, 1833–1841*, introd., notes et index by Camille Boustany (Beirut: Lahad Khater).

DAVIE, MAY (1994) 'L'Espace communautaire orthodoxe dans la Ville de Beyrouth, 1775–1850', in D. Chevallier (ed.), *Du privé au public* (Beirut: Cahiers du CERMOC), 99–111.

—— (1996) *Beyrouth et ses faubourgs (1840–1940): Une intégration inachevée* (Beirut: CERMOC).

—— (1998) 'Beyrouth au temps de la visite de Guillaume II en 1898', in A. Neuwirth, H. Sader, and T. Scheffler (eds.), *Baalbelk: Image and Monument* (Beirut: Orient Institut), 97–114.

—— (2001) *Beyrouth, 1825–1975: Un siècle et demi d'urbanisme* (Beirut: Order of Engineers and Architects of Beirut).

DAVIE, MICHAEL (1984) 'Trois Cartes inédites de Beyrouth: Eléments cartographiques pour une histoire urbaine de la ville', *Annales de Géographie de l'Université Saint-Joseph*, 5: 37–82.

Davis, John (1977) *People of the Mediterranean* (London: RKP).

Davison, Roderic H. (1994) 'The Advent of the Electric Telegraph in the Ottoman Empire', in his *Studies on Turkish History* (Princeton: PUP), 133–65.

Dawn, Ernest (1973) *From Ottomanism to Arabism* (Chicago: Urbana Press).

Debbas, Fouad (1994 [1986]) *Beirut our Memory: A Guided Tour Illustrated with Picture Postcards* (London: Folios).

—— (2001) *Des photographes à Beyrouth, 1840–1918* (Paris: Marval).

Deheuvels, Luc-Willy (1999) 'Le Livre des trois cités de Farah Antun: Une utopie au cœur de la literature arabe moderne', *Arabica*, 46: 402–33.

Deringil, Selim (1993) 'Invention of Tradition as Public Image in the Late Ottoman Empire, 1808–1908', *Comparative Studies in Society and History*, 35/1: 3–29.

—— (1998) *The Well-Protected Domains: Ideology and the Legitimation of Power in the Ottoman Empire, 1876–1909* (London: I. B. Tauris).

Devereux, Robert (1963) *The First Ottoman Constitutional Period: A Study of the Midhat Constitution and Parliament* (Baltimore: Johns Hopkins University Press).

Dieterici, Friedrich (1900 [1895]) *Der Musterstaat von Alfarabi* (Leiden: Brill).

Doumani, Beshara (1996) *Rediscovering Palestine: Merchants and Peasants in Jabal Nablus* (Los Angeles: University of California Press).

Douwes, Dick (1993) 'Knowledge and Oppression: Nusairis in the Late Ottoman Period', in *La Shia nell impero ottomano* (Rome: Accademia Nationale dei Lincei), 149–69.

Dubar, Claude, and Selim Nasr (1976) *Les Classes sociales au Liban* (Paris: Presses de la Fondation Nationale des Sciences Politiques).

Ducousso, Réné (1913) *L'Industrie de la soie en Syrie et au Liban* (Beirut: Imp. Catholique).

Dumont, Paul, and François Géorgeon (1985) 'Un bourgeois d'Istanbul au début du XX siècle', *Turcica*, 17: 125–83.

Durkheim, Emile (1995) *Selected Writings*, ed. and tr. Anthony Giddens (Cambridge: CUP).

Dūwayhī, Isṭifān (1976 [1699]) *Tārīkh al-Azmana*, ed. and introd. by Buṭrus Fahd (Junieh: Maṭābiʿ al-karīm al-ḥadītha).

Ebert, Johannes (1991) *Religion und Reform in der arabischen Provinz: Ḥusayn al-Ǧisr at-Ṭarabūlusi (1845–1909): Ein islamischer Gelehrter zwischen Tradition und Reform* (Frankfurt and New York: Peter Lang).

Eldem, Edhem (1998) *A 135-year-old Treasure: Glimpses from the Past in the Ottoman Bank Archives* (Istanbul: Ottoman Bank).

—— Daniel Goffmann, and Bruce Masters (1999) *The Ottoman City between East and West: Aleppo, Izmir and Istanbul* (Cambridge: CUP).

Fabian, Johannes (1983) *Time and the Other: How Anthropology Makes its Object* (New York: Columbia University Press).

Fahmy, Khaled (1997) *All the Pasha's Peasants: Mehmed Ali, his Army and the Making of Modern Egypt* (Cambridge: CUP).

Fani, Michel (1996) *Atelier de Beyrouth*, 2 vols. (Beirut: Éditions de l'Escalier).

FANON, FRANTZ (1967 [1959]) *A Dying Colonialism* (New York: Grove Weidenfeld).

——(1990 [1961]) *The Wretched of the Earth* (London: Penguin).

FARAH, CAESAR (1977) 'Censorship and Freedom of Expression in Ottoman Syria and Egypt', in William Haddad and William Ochsenwald (eds.), *Nationalism in a non-Nation State; the dissolution of the Ottoman Empire* (Ohio: Ohio State University Press).

——(2000) *The Politics of Interventionism in Ottoman Lebanon, 1830–1861* (Oxford: Centre for Lebanese Studies and I. B. Tauris).

FARLEY, LEWIS (1859) *Two Years in Syria* (London: Saunders & Otley).

FAROQHI, SURAYA, BRUCE MCGOVERN, DONALD QUATAERT, and ŞEVKET PAMUK (1997) *An Economic and Social History of the Ottoman Empire*, ii. *1600–1914* (Cambridge: CUP).

FASSIN, DIDIER (1998) *Les Figures urbaines de la santé publique: Enquête sur des expériences locales* (Paris: La Découverte).

FATTAH, HALA (1997) *The Politics of Regional Trade in Iraq, Arabia, and the Gulf, 1745–1900* (New York: SUNY Press).

FAWAZ, LEILA (1983) *Merchants and Migrants in Nineteenth-Century Beirut* (Cambridge, Mass.: HUP).

——(1994) *An Occasion for War: Civil Conflict in Lebanon and Damascus in 1860* (London: I. B. Tauris and Centre for Lebanese Studies).

——(1998) 'The Beirut–Damascus Road: Connecting the Syrian Coast to the Interior in the Nineteenth Century', in T. Philipp and B. Schaebler (eds.), *The Syrian Land in the 18th and 19th Century: Integration and Fragmentation* (Stuttgart: Steiner Verlag), 19–28.

——(2002) 'From Sudan to Medford: A Teacher's Guide', lecture given at the Fares Center for Eastern Mediterranean Studies, 21 Apr. available online at: http://farescenter.tufts.edu/sudan/presentation.asp

FINDLEY, CARTER (1986) 'The Evolution of the System of Provincial Administration as Viewed from the Centre', in D. Kushner (ed.), *Palestine in the Late Ottoman Period* (Leiden: Brill), 3–29.

——(1989) *Ottoman Civil Officialdom* (Princeton: PUP).

FLEISCHMANN, ELLEN (2002) 'The Impact of American Protestant Missions in Lebanon on the Construction of Female Identity, c. 1860–1950', *Islam and Christian–Muslim Relations*, 13: 411–26.

FORTNA, BENJAMIN (2000) 'Islamic Morality in Late Ottoman "Secular" Schools', *International Journal of Middle East Studies*, 32: 369–93.

——(2001) *Imperial Classroom: Islam, the State, and Education in the Late Ottoman Empire* (Oxford: OUP).

FOUCAULT, MICHEL (1986 [1973]) *The Birth of the Clinic: An Archaeology of Medical Knowledge* (London: Tavistock).

——(1978 [1973]) *The History of Sexuality: An Introduction*, i (New York: Vintage).

——(1980) 'Questions of Geography', in *Power/Knowledge, Selected Interviews and Other Writings, 1972–1977*, ed. C. Gordon (Brighton: Harvester Press).

——(1984) 'Space, Knowledge and Power: Interview with Paul Rabinow', *The Foucault Reader*, ed. Paul Rabinow (New York: Pantheon Books).

FREUD, SIGMUND (1989 [1930]) *Civilization and its Discontents*, with a biographical introduction by Peter Gay (New York: Norton).

FREYHA, ANIS (1974) *A Dictionary of Modern Lebanese Proverbs* (Beirut: Librairie du Liban).

FRIETZSCHE, PETER (1998) *Reading Berlin* (Cambridge: HUP).

FUESS, ALBRECHT (2001) *Verbranntes Ufer, Auswirkungen mamlukischer Seepolitik auf Beirut und die syro-palästinensische Küste (1250–1517)* (Leiden: Brill).

GALLAGHER, NANCY (1994) *Approaches to the History of the Middle East: Interviews with Leading Middle East Historians* (Reading: Ithaca Press).

GÉDÉON, E. (1922) *L'Indicateur Libano-Syrien, annuaire de la Syrie et du Liban*, 1st year (Beirut: Gédéon Press).

GEERTZ, CLIFFORD (1973) *The Interpretation of Cultures* (New York: Basic Books).

GELVIN, JAMES (1998) *Divided Loyalties: Nationalism and Mass Politics in Syria at the Close of Empire* (Los Angeles: University of California Press).

GÉORGEON, FRANÇOIS (1994) 'La Formation des élites à la fin de l'Empire Ottoman, le cas de Galatasaray', *Révue des Études du Monde Muselman et Meditérranéen*, 72: 15–25.

GHAZAL, AMAL (2001) 'Sufism, *Ijtihād* and Modernity, Yūsuf al-Nabhānī in the Age of ʿAbd al-Ḥamīd II', *Archivum Ottomanicum*, 19: 239–72.

GHORAYEB, MARLEINE (1994) 'L'Urbanisme de la ville de Beyrouth sous le mandat français', *Révue des Études du Monde Muselman et Meditérranéen*, 73–4: 297–309.

——(1998) 'The Work and Influence of Michel Ecochard in Lebanon', in H. Sarkis and P. Rowe (eds.), *Projecting Beirut: Episodes of the Construction and Reconstruction of a Modern City* (Munich: Prestel), 106–21.

GILSENAN, MICHAEL (1996) *Lords of the Lebanese Marshes: Violence and Narrative in an Arab Society* (London: I. B. Tauris and the Centre for Lebanese Studies).

GIROUARD, MARK (1989) *Cities and People: A Social and Architectural History* (New Haven: Yale University Press).

GODOLI, EZIO, and DIANA BARILLARI (1996) *Istanbul 1900: Art Noveau Architecture and Interiors* (New York: Rizzoli).

GOODWIN, GEOFFREY (1997 [1971]) *A History of Ottoman Architecture* (London: Thames & Hudson).

GRAMSCI, ANTONIO (1977) *Selections from the Prison Notebooks of Antonio Gramsci*, ed. and tr. Q. Hoare and G. Smith (New York: International).

GRAN, PETER (1979) *Islamic Roots of Capitalism: Egypt, 1760–1840* (Austin: University of Texas Press).

GUHA, RANAJIT (1997) *Dominance without Hegemony: History and Power in Colonial India* (Cambridge, Mass.: HUP).

GUYS, HENRI (1985 [1847]) *Relation d'un séjour de plusieurs années à Beyrouth*, i (Beirut: Lahad Khater).

HABERMAS, JÜRGEN (1994 [1961]) *Strukturwandel der Öffentlichkeit* (Frankfurt: Suhrkamp, 4th edn.).

HADDAD, MAHMUD (1998) 'The City, the Coast, the Mountain and the Hinterland: Beirut's Commercial and Political Rivalries in the Nineteenth and Early Twentieth Century', in T. Philipp and B. Schaebler (eds.) *The Syrian Land in the 18th and 19th Century: Integration and Fragmentation* (Stuttgart: Steiner Verlag), 129–53.

AL-ḤAKĪM, YŪSUF (1966) *Suriyya wa al-ʿahd al-ʿuthmānī* (Beirut: Dār al-nahār li al-nashr).

HANÁK, PETER (1998) *The Garden and the Workshop Essays on the Cultural History of Vienna and Budapest* (Princeton: PUP).

HANIOĞLU, ŞÜKRÜ (1995) *The Young Turks in Opposition* (Oxford: OUP).

ḤANNA, ʿABDALLAH (1973) *al-Ḥaraka al-ʿummāliyya fi Sūriyya wa-Lubnān, 1900–1945* (Damascus: Dār Dimashq).

——(1983) *al-Ittijahāt al-fikriyya fī Sūriyya wa Lubnan, 1920–1945* (Damascus: Dār al-taqaddum al-ʿarabī).

HANSSEN, JENS (1998*a*) 'Imperial Discourse and an Ottoman Excavation in Lebanon', in A. Neuwirth, H. Sader, and T. Scheffler (eds.), *Image and Monument: Baalbek, 1898–1998* (Beirut: Orient Institut), 157–72.

——(1998*b*) '"Your Beirut is on my Desk": Ottomanizing Beirut under Sultan Abdülhamid II (1876–1909)', in H. Sarkis and P. Rowe (eds.), *Projecting Beirut: Episodes of the Construction and Reconstruction of a Modern City* (Munich: Prestel), 41–67.

——(2000) 'Bayrūt—madīna li al-tanẓīmāt', in J. Mouawad (ed.), *ʿAṣr al-nahḍa: muqaddimāt librāliyya li al-ḥadātha* (Beirut: Fondation René Mouawad), 99–110.

——and D. GENBERG (2001) 'Beirut in Memoriam: A Kaleidoscopic Space out of Focus', in A. Pflitsch and A. Neuwirth (eds.), *Crisis and Memory: Dimensions of their Relationship in Islam and Adjacent Cultures* (Beirut: Orient Institut), 231–62.

——(2002) 'Practices of Integration: Centre–Periphery Relations in the Ottoman Empire', in Thomas Philipp and Stefan Weber (eds.), *The Empire in the City: Arab Provincial Capitals in the late Ottoman Empire* (Beirut: Orient Institut), 49–74.

——THOMAS PHILIPP, and STEFAN WEBER (eds.) (2002) *The Empire in the City: Arab Provincial Capitals in the Late Ottoman Empire* (Beirut: Orient Institut).

ḤAQQĪ, ISMĀʿĪL (1970 [1918]) *Lubnān: Mabāḥith ʿilmiyya wa ijtimāʿiyya*, 2 vols. (Beirut: Université Libanaise).

HARIK, ILYA (1968) *Politics and Change in a Traditional Society, Lebanon, 1711–1845* (Princeton: PUP).

HARLEY, BRIAN J. (1989) 'Deconstrucing the Map', *Cartographica*, 26/2: 1–20.

HARRIS, JOSE (1993) *Private Lives, Public Spirit: Britain, 1870–1914* (London: Penguin).

HARTMANN, MARTIN (1891) 'Das Liwa el-Ladkije und die Nahije Urdu', *Zeitschrift des Deutschen Palestina Vereins*, 14: 166–78.

——(1895) 'Das Bahnnetz Mittelsyriens', *Zeitschrift des Deutschen Palestina Vereins*, 17: 56–64.

——(1913) *Unpolitische Reisebriefe aus Syrien* (Berlin: Dietrich Reimer).

HARVEY, DAVID (1985) *Consciousness and the Urban Experience: Studies in the History and Theory of Capitalist Urbanization*, 2 vols. (Oxford: Blackwell).

——(1999 [1982]) *The Limits to Capital*, new edn. (London: Verso).

HATTOX, RALPH S. (1985) *Coffee and Coffeehouse: The Origins of a Social Beverage in the Medieval Near East* (Seattle: University of Washington Press).

HAUSSMANN, GEORGES-EUGÉNE (1890) *Mémoires du Baron Haussman*, 3 vols. (Paris: Havard).

HAUT COMMISSARIAT DE LA REPUBLIQUE FRANÇAISE EN SYRIE (1922) *Récueil des lois et règlements: taxes* (Beirut: Imp. Zing Tabbara).

—— (1925) *Récueil des actes administratives, 1919–1924* (Beirut: Imp. Zing Tabbara).

HAVEMANN, AXEL (1983) *Rurale Bewegungen im Libanongebirge des 19. Jahrhunderts* (Berlin: Klaus Schwarz Verlag).

ḤĀWĪ, KHALĪL (1993) *Diwān Khalīl Ḥāwī* (Beirut: Dār al-ʿawda).

HERZOG, CHRISTOPH (2002) 'Nineteenth-Century Baghdad through Ottoman Eyes', in J. Hanssen, T. Philipp, and S. Weber (eds.), *The Empire in the City: Arab Provincial Capitals in the Late Ottoman Empire* (Beirut: Orient Institut), 311–28.

HILFERDING, RUDOLF (1968 [1910]) *Das Finanzkapital: Eine Studie über die jüngste Entwicklung des Kapitalismus* (Vienna: Europäisches Verlagshaus).

HISHSHĪ, SALĪM (ed.) (1973) *Yawmiyyāt Lubnān fī ayyām al-mutaṣarrifiyya* (Beirut: Publications of the General Directorate of Antiquities).

HOBSBAWM, ERIC (1995 [1987]) *The Age of Empire, 1875–1914* (London: Abacus).

HOTTINGER, ARNOLD (1966) 'Zu'ama in Historical Perspective', in L. Binder (ed.), *Politics in Lebanon* (New York: Willey), 85–105.

HOURANI, A. (1968) 'Ottoman Reform and the Politics of Notables', in William Polk and Richard Chambers (eds.), *The Beginnings of Modernization in the Middle East* (Chicago: Chicago University Press), 41–68.

—— (1981) 'Ideology of the Mountain and the City: Reflections on the Lebanese Civil War', in his *The Emergence of a Modern Middle East* (Los Angeles: University of California Press), 173–81.

—— (1984 [1962]) *Arabic Thought in the Liberal Age* (Cambridge, CUP).

ILBERT, ROBERT (1992) 'Alexandrie, Cosmopolite?', in P. Dumont and F. Géorgeon (eds.), *Villes Ottomanes à la fin de l'empire* (Paris: l'Harmattan), 171–85.

—— (1996) *Alexandrie, 1830–1930* (Cairo: IFEAO).

INALCIK, HALIL (1973) 'Application of the Tanzimat and its Social Effects', *Archivum Ottomanicum*, 5: 97–127.

ISEMINGER, G. L. (1968) 'The Old Turkish Hands: The British Levantine Consuls, 1856–1876', *Middle East Journal*, 22: 297–316.

ISLAMOĞLU-INAN, HURI, and IMMANUEL WALLERSTEIN (eds.) (1980) *The Ottoman Empire and the World-Economy* (Cambridge: CUP).

ISMAIL, ADEL, and MAURICE CHEHAB (1976) *Documents diplomatiques et consulaires relatifs à l'histoire du Liban*, vols. i–xx (Beirut: Éditions des Oeuvres Politiques et Historiques).

ISSAWI, CHARLES (1977) 'British Trade and the Rise of Beirut, 1830–1860', *International Journal of Middle East Studies*, 8: 91–101.

—— (1988) *The Fertile Crescent, 1800–1914: A Documentary Economic History* (Oxford: OUP).

al-Jābiri, Muḥammad ʿĀbid (1991) *al-Turāth wa-l-ḥadātha* (Beirut: Markaz dirasāt al-waḥda al-ʿarabiyya).

—— (1999) *Arab-Islamic Philosophy: A Contemporary Critique*, tr. from the French by Aziz Abbassi (Austin: University of Texas Press).

Jabr, Bahjat (2000) '1913 bidāyāt al-'aṣr al-dhahābī fī Lubnān li-aqdām minḥa', *al-nahār* (28 Mar.)

Jameson, Frederic (2002) *A Singular Modernity: Essays on the Ontology of the Present* (London: Verso).

Jenkins, Jennifer (2003) *Provincial Modernity: Local Culture and Liberal Politics in fin de siècle Hamburg* (Ithaca, London: Cornell University Press).

Jessup, Henry (1910) *Fifty-Three Years in Syria* (New York: Fleming Revell Co.).

Jibrān, Khalīl (1908) *al-Arwāḥ al-mutamarrida* (New York: Al-Mohajir).

—— (1912) *al-Ajniḥa al-mutakassira* (New York: Mir'at al-Gharb).

Jīḥa, Michel (ed.) (1989) *Silsilat al-Aʿmāl al-Majhūla: Salīm al-Bustānī* (London: Riyāḍ Rayyis).

Johnson, Michael (1986) *Class and Client in Beirut: The Sunni Muslim Community and the Lebanese State, 1840–1985* (London: Ithaca Press).

—— (2001) *All Honourable Men: The Social Origins of War in Lebanon* (London: I. B. Tauris).

Jordan, David P. (1995) *Transforming Paris: The Life and Labours of Baron Haussmann* (New York: Free Press).

Jouplain, M. [Būlus Nujaym] (1908) *La Question du Liban: Étude d'histoire diplomatique et de droit international* (Paris: n.p.).

Jūḥa, Shafīk (1991) *Darwin wa-azmat 1882 bi al-dā'irāt al-ṭibbiyya* (Beirut: AUB).

Julkunen, R. (1977) 'A Contribution to the Categories of Social Time and the Economy of Time', *Acta Sociologica*, 20/1: 5–23.

Kaidbey, Naila (2002) *Mukhtaṣarāt tārīkh al-asāqifa alladhīna raqū martabat ri'āsat al-Kahanūt al-jalīla fī madīnat Bayrūt* (Beirut: Dār al-nahār).

Kamel-Salameh, Leila (1998) *Un quartier de Beyrouth: Saint-Nicolas. Structures familiales et structure fonciers* (Beirut: Dar el-Mashreq).

Kāmil Pasha, Meḥmed (1329 [1913]) *Hatīrāt-i Ṣadr-i Esbak Kāmil Pāshā* (Istanbul no publisher).

Kark, Ruth (1980) 'The Jerusalem Municipality at the End of Ottoman Rule', *Asian and African Studies*, 14: 117–41.

Karpat, Kemal (1992) 'The Ottoman Adoption of Statistics from the West in the Nineteenth Century', in E. Ihsanoğlu (ed.), *Transfer of Modern Science and Technology to the Muslim World* (Istanbul: ISIS), 283–95.

Kasaba, Reşat (1988) *The Ottoman Empire and the World-Economy: The Nineteenth Century* (Albany: SUNY).

Kassab, Sawsan, and Khaled Tadmori (2002) *Beirut and the Sultan: 200 Photographs from the Albums of Abdul Hamid II (1876–1909)* (Beirut: Éditions Terre du Liban).

Kayali, Hasan (1992) 'Greater Syria under Ottoman Constitutional Rule, Ottomanism, Arabism, Regionalism', in T. Philipp (ed.), *The Syrian Land in the Eighteenth and Nineteenth Century: The Common and the Specific in the Historical Experience* (Stuttgart: Steiner Verlag), 27–41.

——(1997) *Arabs and Young Turks: Ottomanism, Arabism and Islamism in the Ottoman Empire, 1908–1918* (Los Angeles: University of California Press).

Keddie, Nikki (1972) *Sayyid Jamāl ad-Dīn al-Afghānī: A Political Biography* (Los Angeles: University of California Press).

Kedourie, Elie (1974*a*) 'The American University of Beirut', in his *Arab Political Memoirs and Other Studies* (London: William Clowes & Sons), 59–72.

——(1974*b*) 'The Death of Adib Ishaq', in his *Arabic Political Memoirs and Other Studies* (London: William Clowes & Sons), 81–100.

——(1974*c*) 'The Impact of the Young Turk Revolution on the Arabic-Speaking Provinces of the Ottoman Empire', in his *Arabic Political Memoirs and Other Studies* (London: William Clowes & Sons), 124–61.

Kekule, S. (1892) *Über Titel, Ämter, Rangstufen und Anreden in der offiziellen osmanischen Sprache* (Halle: Kaemmerer).

Kemal, Ismail (1920) *The Memoirs of Ismail Kemal Bey*, ed. Sommerville Story (London: Constable & Co.).

Kern, Steven (1983) *The Culture of Time and Space, 1870–1918* (Cambridge, Mass.: HUP).

Keyder, Çağlar (1988) 'Bureaucracy and Bourgeoisie: Reform and Revolution in the Age of Imperialism', *Review*, 11/2: 151–65.

Khairallah, As'ad (2002) 'Besieged Beirut', in A. Pflitsch and A. Neuwirth (eds.), *Crisis and Memory: Dimensions of their Relationship in Islam and Adjacent Cultures* (Berlin and Beirut: Orient Institut), 509–26.

Khairallah, Shereen (1991) *Railways in the Middle East, 1856–1948* (Beirut: Librairie du Liban).

Khalaf, Samir (1968) 'Primordial Ties and Politics in Lebanon', *Middle Eastern Studies* 4: 243–69.

——(1995) 'New England Puritanism and Liberal Education in the Middle East: The American University of Beirut as a Cultural Transplant', in Ş. Mardin (ed.), *Cultural Transformations in the Middle East* (Leiden: Brill), 50–85.

——(2000) 'On Doing Much with Little Noise: Early Encounters of Protestant Missionaries in Lebanon', working paper at the Belagio Conference on *Altruism and Imperialism: The Western Religious and Cultural Missionary Enterprise in the Middle East*, Aug.

al-Khālidī, ʿAnbara (1997 [1979]) *Jawla fī al-dhikrayāt bayna Lubnān wa Filasṭīn* (Beirut: Dār al-nahār, 2nd edn.).

Khalidi, Rashid (1981) 'Abd al-Ghani al-'Uraisi and *al-Mufid*: The Press and Arab Nationalism before 1914', in M. Buhairy (ed.), *Intellectual Life in the Arab East, 1890–1939* (Beirut: AUB), 38–61.

——(1984) 'The 1912 Election Campaign in the Cities of Bilad al-Sham', *International Journal of Middle East Studies*, 16: 461–74.

——(1992) 'Society and Ideology in Late Ottoman Syria: Class, Education, Profession and Confession', in J. Spagnolo (ed.), *Problems of the Middle East in Historical Perspective: Essays in Honour of Albert Hourani* (Oxford: OUP), 119–31.

KHALIDI, RASHID (1997) *Palestinian Identity: The Construction of Modern National Consciousness* (New York: Columbia University Press).

KHATER, AKRAM FUAD (1996) '"House" to "Goddess of the House": Gender, Class, and Silk in Nineteenth Century Mount Lebanon', *International Journal of Middle East Studies*, 28: 325–48.

——(2001) *Inventing Home: Emigration, Gender, and the Middle Class in Lebanon, 1870–1920* (Los Angeles: University of California Press).

KHOURY, PHILIP (1991) 'Urban Notables Paradigm Revisited', *Révue du Monde Musel-man et Meditérranéen*, 55–6: 215–28.

AL-KHŪRĪ, AMĪN and KHALĪL (1889) *Al-Jāmiʿa aw Dalīl Bayrūt* (Beirut: Maṭbaʿa al-wilāya).

AL-KHŪRĪ, BISHĀRA (1960) *Al-Haqāʾiq al-Lubnāniyya*, i (Beirut: Manshūrāt awrāq Lubāniyya).

AL-KHŪRĪ, SHĀKIR (1992 [1908]) *Mujma ʿal-masarrāt* (Beirut: Lahad Khater).

KHŪRĪ, YŪSUF QUZMA (ed.) (1990) *Aʿmāl al-jamʿiyyāt al-ʿilmiyya al-sūriyya, 1868–1869* (Beirut: Dār al-Ḥamrāʾ).

——(1995) *al-Muʿallim Buṭrus Bustānī, 1819–1883* (Beirut: Bisām).

KODAMAN, B. (1991) *Abdülhamid Devri Eğitim Sistemi* (Ankara: Türk Tarih Kurumu Basimevi).

KORNRUMPF, HANS-JÜRGEN (1998) *Fremde im Osmanischen Reich, 1826–1912/13: Bio-Bibliographisches Register* (Stutensee: Fischer Schnelldruck).

KREISER, KLAUS (1997) 'Public Monuments in Turkey and Egypt, 1840–1916', *Muqar-nas*, 14: 103–17.

KÜHN, THOMAS (2002) 'Ordering Urban Space in Ottoman Yemen, 1872–1914', in J. Hanssen, T. Philipp, and S. Weber (eds.), *The Empire in the City: Arab Provincial Capitals in the Late Ottoman Empire* (Beirut: Orient Institut), 329–48.

KUNERALP, S. (1989) 'Pilgrimage and Cholera in Ottoman Hedjaz, 1831–1911', *Studies in Turkish–Arab Relations*, 4: 69–81.

KUSHNER, DAVID (1987) 'The Ottoman Governors of Palestine, 1864–1914', *Middle Eastern Studies*, 23: 274–90.

LABAKI, BOUTROS (1984) *Introduction à l'histoire économique du Liban: soie et commerce et lérieur en fin de periode Ottomane (1840–1914).* (Beirut: Université Libanaise).

LAFI, NORA (2002) *Une ville du Maghreb entre ancient régime et réformes ottomans: Genése des institutions municipals à Tripoli de Barbarie (1795–1911)* (Paris: l'Harmattan).

LAMARTINE, ALPHONSE DE (1887 [1843]) *Voyage en Orient (1832–1833)* (Paris: Hachette).

LANDAU, JACOB (1958) *Studies in the Arab Theatre and Cinema* (Philadelphia: University of Pennsylvania Press).

LAROUI, ABDALLAH (1984) *The Crisis of the Arab Intellectual: Traditionalism or Histori-cism?* (Los Angeles: University of California Press).

LEACH, NEIL (ed.) (1997) *Rethinking Architecture: A Reader in Cultural Theory* (London: Routledge).

LEEDS, ANTHONY (1973) 'Locality Power in Relation to Supralocal Institutions', in Aiden Southall (ed.) *Urban Anthropology* (New York: OUP), 15–42.

LEENDERS, REINOUD (2001) 'Public Means to Private Ends: State Building and Power in Post-War Lebanon', draft paper presented at a conference on *A Critical Reassessment of the Lebanese System* at AUB, Beirut, 25–6 May.

LEFEBVRE, HENRI (1968) *Le Droit à la ville* (Paris: Anthopos).

——(1991*a* [1947]) *Critique of Everyday Life*, with a preface by Michel Treibitsch (London: Verso).

——(1991*b* [1974]) *The Production of Space*, tr. Donald Nicholson-Smith, with an afterword by David Harvey (Oxford: Blackwell).

——(1996) *Writings on Cities*, ed. E. Kofman and E. Lebas (Oxford: Blackwell).

——(2003 [1970]) *The Urban Revolution*, foreword by Neil Smith, tr. Robert Bononno (Minneapolis: University of Minnesota Press).

LEMKE, WOLF-DIETER (1998) 'Postscript: The Emperor's and the Sultan's Images', my translation from German, in A. Neuwirth, H. Sader, and T. Scheffler (eds.), *Baalbek: Image and Monument, 1898–1998* (Beirut: Orient Institut), 82–92.

——(2002) 'Ottoman Photography: Recording and Contributing to Modernity', in J. Hanssen, T. Philipp, and S. Weber (eds.), *The Empire in the City: Arab Provincial Capitals in the Late Ottoman Empire* (Beirut: Orient Institut), 237–49.

LEWIS, WARREN (1962) *Levantine Adventurer: The Travels and Missions of the Chevalier d'Arvieux, 1653–1697* (London: A. Deutsch).

LIPIETZ, ANDREAS (1980) 'The Structuration of Space, the Problem of Land and Spatial Policy', in J. Carney, R. Hudson, and J. Lewis (eds.), *Regions in Crisis: New Perspectives in European Regional Theory* (London: Croom Helm), 72–83.

LOCKE, JOHN (1880 [1695]) *Some Thoughts Concerning Education* (London: Spottiswoode).

LOCKMANN, ZACHARY, and JOEL BENIN (1988) *Workers on the Nile: Nationalism, Communism, Islam, and the Egyptian Working Class, 1882–1954* (London: I. B. Tauris).

LORTET, LOUIS (1884) *La Syrie d'aujourd'hui* (Paris: Librairie Hachette).

LOUET, ERNEST (1862) *Expédition de Syrie* (Paris: Amyot).

al-Madrasa al-ʿuthmāniyya (Beirut: al-Maṭbaʿa al-'uthmāniyya, 1914).

MAKDISI, USSAMA (1997) 'Reclaiming the Land of the Bible: Missionaries, Secularism, and Evangelical Modernity', *American Historical Review*, 102: 680–713.

——(2000) *The Culture of Sectarianism: Community, History and Violence in Nineteenth-Century Ottoman Lebanon* (Los Angeles: University of California Press).

——(2002*a*) 'After 1860: Debating Religion, Reform and Nationalism in the Ottoman Empire', *International Journal of Middle East Studies*, 34: 601–17.

——(2002*b*) 'Ottoman Orientalism', *American Historical Review*, 107: 768–96.

——(2002*c*) 'Rethinking Ottoman Imperialism: Modernity, Violence and the Cultural Logic of Ottoman Reform', in J. Hanssen, T. Philipp, and S. Weber (eds.), *The Empire in the City: Arab Provincial Capitals in the Late Ottoman Empire* (Beirut: Orient Institut), 29–48.

MARDIN, ŞERIF (1974) 'Super Westernisation in Urban Life in the Ottoman Empire in the Last Quarter of the Nineteenth Century', in Peter Benedict, Erol Tümertekin,

and Fatma Mansur (eds.), *Turkey, Geographic and Social Perspectives* (Leiden: Brill), 403–45.
MARSEILLE, JACQUES (1984) *Empire colonial et capitalisme français: Histoire d'un divorce* (Paris: Albin Michel).
MARX, KARL (1987 [1963]) *The Eighteenth Brumaire of Louis Bonaparte* (New York: International Publishers).
MATSUDA, MATT (1996) *The Memory of the Modern* (Oxford: OUP).
MERRIMAN, JOHN (1991) *The Margins of City Life: Explorations in the French Urban Frontier, 1815–1851* (Oxford: OUP).
MICHAUD, JOSEPH and BAPTISTIN POUJOULAT (1833–5) *Correspondance d'Orient, 1830–1831*, 7 vols. (Paris: Ducollet).
MITCHELL, TIMOTHY (1988) *Colonising Egypt* (Cambridge: CUP).
——(1990) 'The Invention and Reinvention of the Egyptian Peasant', *International Journal of Middle East Studies*, 22: 129–50.
——(1999) 'The Stage of Modernity', in Timothy Mitchell (ed.), *The Question of Modernity* (Minneapolis: University of Minnesota Press), 1–34.
MOLLENHAUER, ANNE (2002) 'The Central Hall House: Regional Communalities and Local Specificities', in J. Hanssen, T. Philipp, and S. Weber (eds.), *The Empire in the City: Arab Provincial Capitals in the Late Ottoman Empire* (Beirut: Orient Institut), 275–96.
MOOSA, MATTI (1993) *The Origins of Modern Arabic Fiction* (Boulder: Lynne Rienner).
MORRIS, ROBERT (1875) *Freemasonry in the Holy Land: Or Handmarks of Hiram's Builders* (New York: Masonic Publishing Co.).
Mukhtarāt min al-qawānīn al-ʿuthmāniyya (Beirut: Dār al-Ḥamrā', 1995).
MUNDY, MARTHA (1996), 'Qāḍā Ajlūn in the Late Nineteenth Century', *Levant*, 28: 77–94.
MUSLIH, MUHAMMAD (1988) *The Origins of Palestinian Nationalism* (New York: Columbia University Press).
NASHABI, HISHAM (1981) 'Shaykh ʿAbd al-Qader al-Qabbani and Thamarat al-Funun', in M. Buhairy (ed.), *Intellectual Life in the Arab East, 1890–1939* (Beirut: AUB), 84–91.
NAWFAL, NA'MATALLAH (1301h [1883–4]) *al-Dustūr* (Beirut).
NEALE, FRED ARTHUR (1851) *Eight Years in Syria, Palestine and Asia Minor from 1842–1850* (London: Colburn).
NERVAL, GÉRARD DE (1884) *Voyage en Orient*, i (Paris: Maison Michel Lévy Frères).
OCHSENWALD, WILLIAM (1968) 'The Vilayet of Syria', *Middle East Journal*, 22: 73–87.
ONGLEY, F. (1892) *The Ottoman Land Code* (London: William Clowes & Sons).
ORTAYLI, ILBER (1974) *Tanzimattan Sonra Mahalli Idareler 1840–1878* (Ankara: Sevinç Matbaasi).
——(1994) *Studies on Ottoman Transformation* (Istanbul: ISIS).
OSTLE ROBIN (1992) 'The Romantic Poets', in Mustafa Badawi (ed.), *Modern Arabic Literature* (Cambridge: CUP), 82–131.

OWEN, ROGER (1981) *The Middle East in the World-Economy, 1800–1914* (London: Methuen).

——and BOB SUTCLIFFE (1972) *Studies in the Theory of Imperialism* (Bristol: Arrowsmith).

ÖZDEMIR, KEMAL (1993) *Ottoman Clocks and Watches* (Istanbul: TYT Bank).

PAMUK, ŞEVKET (1988) 'The Ottoman Empire in Comparative Perspective', *Review*, 11/2: 127–49.

PANZAC, DANIEL (1985) *La Peste dans l'empire ottoman, 1700–1850* (Louvain: Édition Peters).

——(1986) *Quarantaines et lazarets: L'Europe et la peste d'Orient* (Aix-en-Provence: Edisud).

——(1991) *Les Villes dans l'empire ottoman: Activités et sociétés*, 2 vols. (Paris: CNRS).

PARKE-TAYLOR, MICHAEL (2002) 'The Myth of the Midi: Landscape as Earthly Paradise', in *Voyage into Myth: French Painting from Gauguin to Matisse from the Hermetage Museum, Russia* (Montreal: Montreal Museum of Fine Arts), 47–79.

PENROSE, STEPHEN (1941) *That they may have Light: The Story of the American University of Beirut, 1866–1941* (New York: Trustees of the American University of Beirut).

PHILIPP, THOMAS (ed. and tr.) *Ǧurǧi Zaidan: His Life and Thought*, (Beirut: Orient Institut).

——(1984) 'Class, Community and Arab Historiography in the Early Nineteenth Century: The Dawn of a New Era', *International Journal of Middle East Studies*, 16: 161–75.

——(2002) *Acre: The Rise and Fall of a Palestinian City—World-Economy and Local Politics* (New York: Columbia University Press).

POLK, WILLIAM (1963) *The Opening of South Lebanon, 1788–1840: A Study of the Impact of the West on the Middle East* (Cambridge, Mass.: HUP).

PORTER, HARVEY (1912) *History of Beirut* (Beirut: [n.publ.]).

POUILLON, FRANÇOIS (1990) 'Un ami de Théophile Gautier en Orient, Camille Rogier: Reflexions sur la condition de dragoman', *Bulletin de la Société Théophile Gautier*, 12: 55–87.

POUJOULAT, BAPTISTIN (1986 [1861]) *La Vérité sur la Syrie et l'expédition française*, introd, notes and index by Camille Boustany, 2 vols. (Beirut: Lahad Khater).

PRAETOR, SABINE (1993) *Der Arabische Faktor in der jungtürkischen Politik: Eine Studie zum Osmanischen Parlament der II. Konstitution 1909–1918* (Berlin: Klaus Schwarz).

AL-QĀYĀTĪ, MUḤAMMAD ʿABD AL-JAWWĀD (1981 [1884]) *Nafḥāt al-bashām fī riḥlat al-Shām* (Beirut: Dār al-rāʾid al-ʿarabī).

QUATAERT, DONALD (1983) *Social Disintegration and Popular Resistance in the Ottoman Empire, 1882–1908* (New York: SUNY Press).

——REŞAT KASABA, ELENA FRANGAKIS-SYRETT, BASIL GOUNARIS, ÇAĞLAR KEYDER, and EYÜP ÖZVEREN (1993) 'Port Cities in the Ottoman Empire', *Review*, 16: 387–557.

RABINOW, PAUL (1989) *French Modern: Norms and Forms of the Social Environment* (Cambridge, Mass.: MIT Press).

RAYMOND, ANDRÉ (1985) *Grand Villes arabes á l'époche ottomane* (Paris: Sindbad).

——(1994) 'Islamic City, Arab City: Orientalist Myths and Recent Views', *British Journal of Middle East Studies*, 21/1: 3–18.

REIMER, MICHAEL (1991) 'Ottoman-Arab Seaports in the Nineteenth Century: Social Change in Alexandria, Beirut and Tunis', in Rešat Kasaba (ed.), *Cities in the World System* (Westport, Conn.: Greenwood Press), 135–57.

——(1997) *Colonial Bridgehead: Government and Society in Alexandria, 1807–1882* (Boulder: Westview Press).

RIALL, LUCY (1998) *Sicily and the Unification of Italy: Liberal Policy and Local Power* (Oxford: OUP).

RIḌĀ, RASHĪD (1931) *Tārīkh al-Ustādh al-Imām al-Shaykh Muḥammad ʿAbduh* (Cairo: al-Manār).

RĪḤĀNĪ, ALBERT (1960) *Rasāʾil Amīn al-Rīhānī, 1896–1940* (Beirut: Dār al-Riḥānī).

RITSHER, W. (1934) *Municipal Government in the Lebanon* (Beirut: AUB).

RODIER, GEORGES (1889) *L'Orient: Journal d'un peintre* (Berlin: Dietrich Reimer).

ROGAN, EUGENE (1996) '*Aşiret mektebi*: Abdülhamid II's School for Tribes (1892–1907)', *International Journal of Middle East Studies*, 28: 83–107.

——(1998) 'Instant Communication: The Impact of the Telegraph in Ottoman Syria', in T. Philipp and B. Schäbler (eds.), *The Syrian Land* (Stuttgart: Franz Steiner) 113–28.

——(1999) *Frontiers of the State in the Late Ottoman Empire* (Cambridge: CUP).

——(2000) 'The Catafago Family and the Commerce of Acre, 1816–1825', *National Museum Bulletin*, 9: 42–9.

——(ed.) (2002) 'Madness and Marginality: The Advent of the Psychiatric Asylum in Egypt and Lebanon', *Outside in: Shifting Boundaries of Marginality in the Modern Middle East* (London: I. B. Tauris), 104–25.

——(2004) 'The Political Significance of an Ottoman Education: *Maktab ʿAnbar* revisited', in Christoph Schumann and Thomas Philipp (eds.), *From the Land of Syria to the States of Syria & Lebanon* (Beirut: Orient Institut), 77–94.

ROSENTHAL, STEVEN (1980*a*) 'Foreigners and Municipal Reform in Istanbul, 1855–65', *International Journal of Middle East Studies*, 11: 227–45.

——(1980*b*) *The Politics of Dependency: Urban Reform in Istanbul* (Westport, Conn.: Greenwood Press).

——(1980*c*) 'Urban Elites and the Foundation of Municipalities in Alexandria and Istanbul', in Elie Kedourie and Sylvia Haim (eds.), *Modern Egypt: Studies in Politics and Society* (London: F. Cass), 125–33.

ROSS, ROBERT, and GERARD, J. TELKAMP (1985) *Colonial Cities: Essays on Urbanism in a Colonial Context* (Leiden: Martinus Nijhoff Publishers).

RUPPERT, H. (1969) *Beirut: Eine Westlich Geprägte Stadt des Orients* (Erlangen: Palm & Enke).

RUPPIN, ARTHUR (1917) *Syrien als Wirtschaftsgebiet* (Berlin: Mittler in Komm.).

RUSTUM, ASʿAD (1967*a*) 'Bayrūt fī ʿahd Ibrāhīm Bāshā al-maṣrī', in his *Ārā' wa abḥāth* (Beirut: Université Libanaise), 55–62.

——(1967*b*) 'al-Shaykh Aḥmad al-[A]ghārr', in his *Ārā' wa abḥāth* (Beirut: Université Libanaise), 79–85.

SAʿADŪN, FAWWĀZ (1994) *Al-ḥaraka al-iṣlāhiyya fī Bayrūt fī awākhir al-ʿaṣr al-ʿuthmānī* (Beirut: Dār al-nahār).

AL-ṢAFĀ, MUḤAMMAD Jābir (1998 [1960]) *Tārīkh Jabal ʿĀmil* (Beirut: Dār al-nahār).

SAID, EDWARD (1994 [1979]) *Orientalism* (New York: Vintage).

——(2000) 'The Voyage in: Third World Intellectuals', in D. Hopwood (ed.), *Arab Nation, Arab Nationalism* (London: Macmillan), 79–101.

——(2001) *Power, Politics and Culture: Interviews with Edward Said*, ed. with an introduction by Gauri Viswanathan (New York: Vintage).

SALĀM, ʿALĪ SALĪM (1981) *Mudhakkirāt Salīm ʿAlī Salām, 1868–1938*, ed. Hasan Ḥallāq (Beirut: Dār al-jamiʿiyya).

SALIBA, ROBERT (1998) *Beirut 1920–1940; Domestic Architecture between Tradition and Modernity* (Beirut: Syndicate of Architects and Engineers).

SALIBI, KAMAL (1976) 'Beirut under the Young Turks as Depicted in the Memoirs of Salim Ali Salam', in J. Berque and D. Chevallier (eds.), *Les Arabes par leurs archives* (Paris: CNRS), 193–209.

——(1988) *A House of Many Mansions: The History of Lebanon Reconsidered* (Los Angeles: University of California Press).

——(1993 [1965]) *The History of Modern Lebanon* (Delmar: Caravan Books).

SALZMANN, ARIEL (1993) 'An Ancient Régime Revisited: Privatization and Political Economy in the Eighteenth Century Ottoman Empire', *Politics and Society*, 21: 393–423.

SĀMĪ BEY (1981 [1894]) *Al-qawl al-ḥaqq* (Beirut: Dār al-rā'id al-ʿarabī).

SAMNEH, GEORGES (1920) *La Syrie* (Paris: Bossard).

SARKĪS, KHALĪL (1997 [1898]) *al-Shām qabla mi'at ʿam; riḥla al-imparatur Guillaume II al-Almānī ilā Filasṭīn wa Sūriyya ʿām 1898* (Damascus: Dār al-qādrī).

SAUL, SAMIR (1997) *La France et l'Egypte de 1882 à 1914: Intérêts économiques et implications politiques* (Paris: Ministère de l'Économie, des Finances et de l'Industrie).

SCHEFFLER, THOMAS (1998) 'The Kaiser in Baalbek: Tourism, Archaeology, and the Politics of Imagination', in A. Neuwirth, H. Sader, and T. Scheffler (eds.), *Image and Monument: Baalbek, 1898–1998* (Beirut: Orient Institut), 13–49.

SCHILCHER, LINDA (1986) *Families in Politics* (Wiesbaden: Steiner).

SCHLÖR, JOACHIM (1998) *Nights in the Big City: Paris, London, Berlin* (London: Reaktion Books).

SCHMIDT-NOWARA, CHRISTOPHER (1999) *Empire and Anti-Slavery; Spain, Cuba, and Puerto Rico, 1833–1874* (Pittsburgh: Pittsburgh University Press).

SCHORSKE, CARL (1994 [1980]) *Wien, Geist und Gesellschaft in Fin de Siècle* (Munich: Piper).

——(1998) *Thinking with History: Explorations in the Passage to Modernism* (Princeton: PUP).

SCHUMANN, CHRISTOPH (2001) *Radikalnationalismus in Syrien und Libanon: Politische Sozialisierung und Elitenbildung* (Hamburg: Deutsches Orient Institut).

SCOTT, JAMES C. (1998) *Seeing like a State: How Certain Schemes to Improve the Human Condition have Failed* (New Haven: Yale University Press).

SCOTT-WALLACH, JOAN (1988) *Gender and the Politics of History* (New York: OUP).

SEEDEN, HELGA, and RUBEN THORPE (1997–8) 'Beirut from Ottoman Sea Walls and Landfill to a Twelfth-Century BC Burial', *Berytus*, 43: 221–54.

SEIKALY, SAMIR (2002) 'Shaykh Yūsuf al-Nabḥānī and the West', in Bernard Heyberger and Carsten Walbiner (eds.), *Les Européens vus par les Libanais à l'époche ottomane* (Beirut: Orient Institut), 175–81.

SENNETT, RICHARD (1993) *The Fall of the Public Man* (London: Faber & Faber).

SHAMIR, SHIMON (1974) 'Midḥat Pasha and the Anti-Turkish Agitation in Syria', *Middle Eastern Studies*, 10: 116–41.

SHARABI, HISHAM (1970) *Arab Intellectuals and the West: The Formative Years, 1875–1914* (Baltimore: Johns Hopkins University Press).

SHAW, STANFORD (1975) 'The Nineteenth Century Ottoman Tax Reforms and Revenue System', *International Journal of Middle East Studies*, 6: 421–59.

——(1978) 'The Ottoman Census System and Population, 1831–1914', *International Journal of Middle East Studies*, 10: 325–38.

——and EZEL SHAW (1977) *History of the Ottoman Empire and Modern Turkey*, ii (Cambridge: CUP).

SHEEHI, STEPHEN (2000) 'Inscribing the Arab Self: Butrus al-Bustani and the Paradigms of Subjective Reform', *British Journal of Middle East Studies*, 27: 7–24.

SHEHADI, NADIM (1987) 'The Idea of Lebanon', *Papers on Lebanon*, 5.

AL-SHIDYĀQ, AḤMAD FĀRIS (2001) *Mukhtārāt min āthār Aḥmad Fāris al-Shidyāq*, ed. Yūsuf Quzma Khūrī (Beirut: al-Mu'assasa al-sharqiyya li al-nashr wa al-ṭabāʿa).

SHORROCK, WILLIAM (1975) *French Imperialism in the Middle East: The Failure of Policy in Syria and Lebanon, 1900–1914* (Madison: University of Wisconsin Press).

SHUBĀRŪ, ʿISSĀM (1987) *Tārīkh Bayrūt* (Beirut [n. publ.]).

——(2000) *Jamʿiyyat al-maqāṣid al-khayriyya al-islāmiyya fī Bayrūt* (Beirut: Dār miṣbāh al-fikr).

SHUMAYYIL, SHIBLĪ (1991) *Kitābāt siyāsiyya wa iṣlāhiyya* (Beirut: Dār al-Ḥamra').

SINNO, ABDEL-RAOUF (1998) 'The Emperor's Journey to the East as Reflected in Contemporary Arabic Journalism', in A. Neuwirth, H. Sader, and T. Scheffler (eds.), *Image and Monument: Baalbek, 1898–1998* (Beirut: Orient Institut), 115–33.

SKOVGAARD-PETERSEN, JAKOB (1997) *Defining Islam for the Egyptian State* (Leiden: Brill).

SOJA, EDWARD (1993) 'History: Geography: Modernity', in S. During (ed.), *The Cultural Reader* (London: Routledge), 135–50.

——(1996) *Thirdspace: Journeys to Los Angeles and Other Real-and-Imagined Places* (Oxford: Blackwells).

SOMEL, SELÇUK AKŞIN (2001) *The Modernization of Public Education in the Ottoman Empire, 1839–1908: Islamization, Autocracy, and Disipline* (Leiden: Brill).

SPAGNOLO, JOHN (1969) 'French Influence in Syria Prior to World War I: The Functional Weaknesses of Imperialism', *Middle East Journal*, 23: 45–62.

——(1971) 'Constitutional Change in Mount Lebanon: 1861–1864', *Middle Eastern Studies*, 10: 25–48.

——(1973) 'The Definition of a Style of Imperialism: The Internal Politics of the French Educational Investment in Ottoman Beirut', *French Historical Studies*, 9: 563–84.

——(1977) *France and Ottoman Lebanon, 1861–1914* (London: Ithaca).

STALLYBRASS, PETER, and A. WHITE (1986) 'The City: The Sewer, the Gaze and the Contaminating Touch', in *The Politics and Poetics of Transgression* (London: Methuen), 125–48.

STARRETT, GREGORY (1998) *Putting Islam to Work: Education, Politics and Religious Transformation in Egypt* (Los Angeles: University of California Press).

STEPPAT, FRITZ (1972) 'Eine Bewegung unter den Notablen Syriens', in W. Voigt (ed.), *XVII Deutscher Orientalistentag vom 21.–27. Juli 1968 in Würzburg* (Tübingen: Deutsche Morgenländische Gesellschaft).

STERN, BERNHARD (1903) *Medizin, Aberglaube und Geschlechtsleben in der Türkei*, i (Berlin: Barsdorf).

STOLER, ANN LAURA (2000 [1995]) *Race and the Education of Desire: Foucault's History of Sexuality and the Colonial Order of Things* (Durham, NC, and London: Duke University Press).

STONE, LAWRENCE (1971) 'Prosopography,' *Daedalus*, 100/2: 46–79.

STROBEL, K. H. (1911) *Romantische Reise im Orient* (Berlin: Vita).

STROHMEIER, MARTIN (1993) 'Muslim Education in the Vilayet of Beirut, 1880–1918', in Cesar Farah, *Decision-Making in the Ottoman Empire* (Kirksville: University Press at Northeast Missouri State University), 215–41.

AL-ṢULḤ (1966) *Suṭūr min al-risāla: Tārīkh ḥarakat istiqlāliyya qāmat fī al-Mashriq al-ʿarabī sana 1877* (Beirut: Dār al-ʿilm wa al-malāyīn).

TABET, JADE (1993) 'Trois Plans pour une ville', *Mediterranées*, 5: 127–43.

TAMARI, SALIM (2002) 'The Last Feudal Lord in Palestine', *Jerusalem Quarterly File*, 16, available online: http://www.jqf-jerusalem.org/2002/jqf16/lord.html.

TARRAZI, PHILIPPE DE (1913–33), *Tārīkh al-ṣaḥāfa al-ʿarabiyya*, i–iv (Beirut: al-Maṭbaʿa al-adābiyya).

TAUBER, ELIZIER (1993) *The Emergence of the Arab Movements* (London: F. Cass).

THOBIE, JACQUES (1977) *Intérêts et imperialisme française dans l'empire ottoman, 1895–1914* (Paris: Publications de la Sorbonne).

——(1991) 'European Banks in the Middle East', in R. Cameron (ed.), *International Banking, 1870–1914* (Oxford: OUP).

——(1993) 'Mouvement d'affaires et mouvement ouvrier: La compagnie ottomane du gaz de Beyrouth, 1887–1914', in his *La France et l'est Méditerranéen depuis 1850* (Istanbul: ISIS), 139–61.

THOMPSON, E. P. (1991) 'Time, Work-Discipline and Industrial Capitalism', in his *Customs in Common: Studies in Traditional Popular Culture* (New York: New Press), 352–403.

THOMPSON, ELIZABETH (2000) *Colonial Citizens: Republican Rights, Paternal Privilege, and Gender in French Syria and Lebanon* (New York: Columbia University Press).

THOMSON, WILLIAM M. (1863) *The Land and the Book; or, Biblical Illustrations Drawn from the Manners and Customs, the Scenes and Scenery of the Holy Land* (London: Nelson).

THOUMIN, RICHARD (1936) *Géographie humaine de la Syrie centrale* (Paris and Tours: Arrault).

TIBAWI, ʿABD AL-LATIF (1963) 'The American Missionaries in Beirut and Buṭrus al-Bustānī, *St Antony's Papers*, 16:137–82.

——(1966) *American Interests in Syria, 1800–1901: A Study of Educational, Literary and Religious Work* (Oxford: Clarendon Press).

——(1969) *Islamic Education: Its Traditions and Modernization into the Arab National Systems* (London: Macmillan).

——(1976) *Arabic and Islamic Themes: Historical, Educational and Literary Studies* (London: Luzac).

TOLEDANO, EHUD (1997) 'Ottoman-Local Elites', in M. Maoz and I. Pappé (eds.), *Historical Ideas and Politics in the Middle East* (London: I. B. Tauris), 145–62.

TOʿMEH, CARMA (2000) 'Yūsuf Aftimos (1866–1952)', *al-Mouhandiss: Révue de l'ordre des ingénieurs et architectes de Beyrouth*, 11: 36–40.

TRESSE, RENÉ (1936) 'Histoire de la Route de Beyrouth à Damas', *La Géographie*, 56: 227–52.

TUÉNI, NADIA (2001) 'Beirut', tr. from the French by Samuel Hazo, in *The Poetry of Arab Women: A Contemporary Anthology*, ed. Nathalie Handal (New York: Interlink), 302–3.

UNIVERSITÉ SAINT JOSEPH (1908) *Bulletin de l'association des ancient élèves de la faculté* (Beirut).

AL-UNSĪ, ʿABD AL-BĀSIṬ (1910/11) *Dalīl Bayrūt wa taqwīm al-Iqbāl li-sanat* 1327h *1909–1910* (Beirut: al-Iqbāl).

URQUHART, DAVID (1860) *The Lebanon: A History and a Diary*, 2 vols. (London: Thomas Cautley Newby).

Us, Haqqi Tariq (ed.) *Meclis-i Mebusan Zabit Ceridesi*, 1293h [1877/8] (Istanbul, 1939–54). [Parliamentary minutes]

VERNEY, N., and G. DAMBMANN (1900) *Les Puissances étrangères dans le Levant en Syrie et en Palestine* (Paris).

VOGUË, EUGÈNE MELCHIOR DE (1875) 'Journée de voyage en Syrie', *Révue des Deux Mondes*, 1.

VOLNEY, C. F. (1798) *Travels through Syria and Egypt in the Years 1783, 1784 and 1785*, 2 vols. (New York: J. Tiebout).

AL-WĀLĪ, ṬĀHĀ (1993) *Bayrūt fī al-tārīkh wa al-ḥaḍāra wa al-ʿumrān* (Beirut: Dār al-malayin).

WEBER, EUGEN (1986) *France, Fin de Siècle* (Cambridge, Mass.: Belknap Press).

WEBER, MAX (1958) *The City* (New York: Free Press).

——(1980 [1921]) *Wirtschaft und Gesellschaft* (Tübingen: J. C. B. Mohr, 5th edn.).

WEBER, STEFAN (1998) 'Der Marja-Platz in Damascus: Die Entstehung eines Modernen Stadtzentrums unter den Osmanen als Ausdruck Strukturellen Wandels (1808–1918),' *Damaszener Mitteilungen*, 10 (Damascus: DAI), 292–343.

WILD, STEFAN (1981) 'Néguib Azoury and his Book *Le Réveil de la Nation Arabe*', in M. Buhairy (ed.), *Intellectual Life in the Arab East, 1890–1939* (Beirut: AUB), 92–104.

WILLIAMS, RAYMOND (1973) *The Country and the City* (Oxford: OUP).

WINTER, STEFAN (2004) 'The Nusayris before the Tanzimat in the Eyes of Ottoman Provincial Administrators, 1804–1834', in Christoph Schumann and Thomas Philipp (eds.), *From the Land of Syria to the States of Syria & Lebauou* (Beirut: Orient Institut), 97–112.

WIRTH, EUGEN (2000) *Die Orientalische Stadt im islamischen Vorderasien und Nordafrika* (Mainz: Philipp von Zabern).

WRIGHT, GWENDOLYN (1991) *The Politics of Design in French Colonial Urbanism* (Chicago: University of Chicago Press).

YAHYA, ṢĀLIḤ (1969) *Tārīkh Bayrūt: Récits des anciens de la famille de Buhtu B. ʿAli, Emir du Gharb de Beyrouth*, ed. Kamal Salibi and Francis Hours (Beirut: Dār al-Mashriq).

YAVUZ, YILDIRIM, and SUHA ÖZKAN (1984) 'The Final Years of the Ottoman Empire', in R. Holod and A. Evin (eds.), *Modern Turkish Architecture* (Philadelphia: University of Pennsylvannia Press), 34–57.

YAZBAK, IBRĀHĪM (1955–8) *al-Awrāq al-lubnāniyya*, 3 vols. (Beirut: Dār al-rā'id al-lubnānī).

AL-YĀZIJĪ, NAṢĪF (1983) *Diwān al-shaykh Nasīf al-Yāzijī*, with a foreword by Mārūn ʿAbbūd (Beirut: Maṭbaʿa ʿAbbūd), 290–1.

YERASIMOS, STÉPHANE (1992) 'A propos des reformes urbaines des *tanzimat*', in P. Dumont and F. Géorgeon (eds.), *Villes ottomanes à la fin de l'empire* (Paris: l'Harmattan) 17–32.

YOUNG, GEORGE (1906–7) *Corps de droit ottomane* (Oxford: Clarendon Press).

ZACHS, FRUMA (2000) '"Novice" or "Heaven-Born" Diplomat? Lord Dufferin and his Plan for a Province of Syria: Beirut, 1860–61', *Middle Eastern Studies*, 36/3: 160–76.

—— (2001) 'Toward a Proto-Nationalist Concept of Syria?', *Welt des Islams* 41: 145–73.

ZANDI-SAYEK, SIBEL (2000) 'Struggles over the Shore: Building the Quay of Izmir, 1867–1875', *City and Society*, 12: 55–78.

ZEINE, N. ZEINE (1973 [1958]) *The Emergence of Arab Nationalism* (Delmar: Caravan).

ZIEGLER, ANTJE (1999) 'al-Haraka Baraka; The Late Rediscovery of Mayy Ziyada's Works', *Welt des Islams* 39: 98–111.

ZUBAIDA, SAMI (1989) 'Class and Community in Urban Politics', in K. Brown, S. Zubaida, *et al.* (eds.) *État, Ville et Mouvements sociaux à Maghreb et au Moyen Orient* (Paris: Harmattan), 57–71.

ZWEIG, STEFAN (1998 [1944]) *Die Welt von Gestern: Erinnerungen eines Europäers* (Frankfurt: Fischer).

INDEX

Printed in the United States
57308LVS00001B/134